The King's Council in the Reign of
Edward VI

To Berry

The King's Council in the Reign of Edward VI

D. E. HOAK

Associate Professor of History
The College of William and Mary

CAMBRIDGE UNIVERSITY PRESS

CAMBRIDGE

LONDON · NEW YORK · MELBOURNE

Published by the Syndics of the Cambridge University Press
The Pitt Building, Trumpington Street, Cambridge CB2 1RP
Bentley House, 200 Euston Road, London NW1 2DB
32 East 57th Street, New York, NY 10022, USA
296 Beaconsfield Parade, Middle Park, Melbourne 3206, Australia

First published 1976

Printed in Great Britain by
Western Printing Services Ltd
Bristol

Library of Congress Cataloguing in Publication Data
Hoak, D E 1941–
The King's Council in the reign of Edward VI
Bibliography: p. 351
Includes index
1. Great Britain. Privy Council – History. 2. Great
Britain – Politics and government – 1547–1553. I. Title.
JN378.H6   354'.42'05   75–9286
ISBN 0 521 20866 1

Contents

List of Tables

Preface

My chief purpose in this book has been to describe the workings of the privy council and how, through that institution, the dukes of Somerset and Northumberland conducted the government of the realm. I am aware of the recent observation that 'we have passed beyond recall the stage where the machinery [of government] alone, however intimately understood, can answer the questions of the period' (Hurstfield, *E.H.R.* LXXVII, 1962, 730) but in the case of Edward VI's reign, one of those questions itself comprehended the personnel, business, and procedure of the central organ of government, and so I thought it of interest to discover first how that body really worked. I have attempted to state the significance of the council's function, not only in relation to the history of royal councils generally in the sixteenth century, but also in respect of the life of the nation subject to the Edwardian council's exceptional authority.

Personality and political action have found a natural place in this story, since the council's factious strife clearly influenced the manner in which the King's men acted upon their presumed institutional responsibilities, but on the subject of council politics I have confined myself to two questions only, why Somerset tore up the provisions of Henry's will with respect to the membership of Edward's council, and why Northumberland (then Earl of Warwick) moved so suddenly after the *coup d'état* (1549) to cast his lot with the left-wing reformers. Among the several topics that one could have chosen, I settled upon these for two reasons: new evidence warranted a reappraisal of both points, and both touched directly upon the arrangements for the subsequent appointment of new members. And, of course, each topic carries its own interest: the first considers the opposition to Somerset, the second the politics of the Reformation in England.

The endnotes record completely the extent to which I have availed myself of the labours of others; full references to these secondary sources will be found in the bibliography. The original sources cited are listed alphabetically in the bibliography according to place of deposit. Unless otherwise noted, all references are to manuscripts in the Public Record Office and these are cited by the call numbers there in use. The reader will notice that I have modernised the punctuation of quotations from the manuscript sources.

It is a pleasure to acknowledge the assistance which others have so generously afforded me. The fullness of my gratitude goes to Professor G. R. Elton, who supervised the production of an earlier version of this work; for his constant encouragement and patience I can only very inadequately record here my substantial debt to him. Early on in my research, the Master and Fellows of Clare College provided me with funds for travel to various archives; for that aid and much more I am deeply appreciative. For permission to consult the unpublished biographical materials at the History of Parliament Trust I owe particular thanks to Mr E. L. C. Mullins and Professor S. T. Bindoff, who have both shown me special favour in this matter. For permission to view and quote from the Paget Papers at Plas Newydd and Stafford I wish to thank the Most Hon. the Marquess of Anglesey, whose hospitality I remember especially. I should also like to recognise here His Grace the Duke of Northumberland, for permitting me access to the papers originally at Alnwick Castle; the Most Hon. the Marquess of Salisbury, for granting me permission to quote from the Cecil Papers at Hatfield House; the Right Hon. the Earl Fitzwilliam, of Milton, Peterborough, for generously allowing me to publish portions of the Paget letter-book; Lord Bagot, for his permission to cite Lord Stafford's letter-book; the Dean and Chapter of Westminster Abbey, for giving me leave to inspect and use material from the muniments that they hold; the Society of Antiquaries of London and the Mercers' Company, for agreeing to let me search the records in their keeping; the Corporation of London, for the courtesy of enabling me to publish extracts from the Corporation records; and the Trustees of the British Museum, for kindly consenting to my request to quote from the various documents cited herein, and especially to print in full Egerton MS. 2603, folios 33–4. Transcripts of Crown-copyright records in the Public Record Office appear by permission of the Controller of H.M. Stationery Office.

Finally, I wish to register my gratitude to all of the following: to Professor J. J. Scarisbrick and Mrs Margaret Bowker for their gentle questions and very kind support; to Mr Roy Davids for permission to read his unpublished sketch of Thomas Seymour; to Mr David Potter for his help in obtaining microfilmed copies of documents at the Bibliothèque Nationale, Paris; to Miss Clare Talbot for her assistance at Hatfield House; to Mr P. I. King for his kindness at Delapré Abbey; to Mr F. B. Stitt of the Staffordshire Record Office for locating several manuscripts; to Miss Imray at the Mercers' Hall; to Mr N. H. MacMichael, Keeper of the Muniments at Westminster

Abbey; to the personnel of the Students' Manuscript Room at the British Museum and the staff of the Public Record Office; to the Director and Staff of the Institute of Historical Research; to the President and Fellows of Clare Hall, Cambridge, for the honour that they bestowed upon me in 1972; to the American Council of Learned Societies and the Division of Sponsored Research within Florida Atlantic University for the research and travel grants they awarded me; to Marti Stiteler and Cecilia Bibby for typing the manuscript; to the staff of the Cambridge University Press for their assiduous reading of the final typescript; and to my wife, Berry, for having introduced me to Greece where I discovered so much in first setting down the words of this book.

D.E.H.

Boca Raton, Florida
April 1975

List of Abbreviations

A.H.R. *American Historical Review*

A.P.C. *Acts of the Privy Council of England.* J. R. Dasent (ed.)

B.I.H.R. *Bulletin of the Institute of Historical Research*

B.M. British Museum

Cal. Pat. Rolls, Edw. VI Calendar of Patent Rolls, Edward VI.

Cal. S.P., Dom. Calendar of State Papers, Domestic Series, of the reigns of Edward VI, Mary, Elizabeth 1547–1580. R. Lemon (ed.)

Cal. S.P., Foreign Calendar of State Papers, Foreign Series, of the reign of Edward VI, 1547–1553. W. B. Turnbull (ed.)

Chronicle The Chronicle and Political Papers of King Edward VI. W. K. Jordan (ed.)

D.N.B. *Dictionary of National Biography*

E.H.R. *English Historical Review*

G.E.C. G. E. Cokayne, *The Complete Peerage of England, Scotland, Ireland, Great Britain, and the United Kingdom.* New ed. by V. Gibbs

H.M.C. Historical Manuscripts Commission

H.P.T. History of Parliament Trust, Tavistock Square, London

Hughes & Larkin *Tudor Royal Proclamations*, vol. 1 (1485–1553). P. L. Hughes and J. F. Larkin (eds.)

N.R.O. Northamptonshire Record Office

P.R.O. Public Record Office

Span. Cal. Calendar of Letters, Despatches, and State Papers, relating to the negotiations between England and Spain. M. A. S. Hume and R. Tyler (eds.)

Introduction

The courtiers privy to the making of Henry VIII's last will and testament knew that the death of their sovereign lord would force the announcement of an extraordinary proposition, that under Edward VI the King's council should rule the King and all of England. Royal minorities had earlier introduced government by council, just as royal councils had occasionally assumed the government of the realm. But the sixteen regents who replaced Henry VIII on 28 January 1547 represented an unprecedented experiment in executive rule, for these executors were also privy councillors; by virtue of their appointment in the will they became at Henry's death the only members of an already existing, quite formal institution. In one sense, perhaps nothing was more logical than that Henry VIII should have willed the rule of his kingdom to his privy council; certainly nothing could more plainly have revealed the competence of the Tudor privy council than the accession of a minor to the throne. Henry's charge to his executors in fact merely reflected the all-pervasive character of the institution: his executors, he said, were to be Edward's privy councillors 'in all Maters concerning both his private Affaires and publicq Affaires of the Realm . . .'[1]

As all of the King's affairs became the council's concern under Edward VI, it is natural to describe what the council actually did then in terms of its tripartite function. Traditionally, the council advised the King; in Edward's reign it could be said that all policy orginated in council. Traditionally, the King relied upon his council to see to the enforcement of much of that policy; to the privy council in Edward's reign fell the responsibility for the administration of the whole realm. Through his privy council Henry VIII had exercised that reserve of judicial power which remained traditionally in the royal person;[2] in Edward's reign one may describe similarly what is best referred to as the council's quasi-judicial activity. So comprehensive were the council's actions in all three of these areas that from the state of the evidence it would appear that everything which happened in England fell potentially within the scope of the board's work[3] – except for a time during the Protectorate, when the Duke of Somerset understood himself to be able to conduct the King's affairs with or without the council's participation. In practice, the business of the council usually embraced the greatest of these affairs as well as the most trivial: the defence of the realm; proceedings in Parliament; the exercise of the royal supremacy; the regulation of England's trade; the management of foreign affairs; the supervision of the King's coins and finances and the Crown's courts and servants; the welfare of the King's 'loving' subjects and the 'stay' of his 'unquiet' ones. Moreover, as the chief administrative agency in the realm the council shouldered the enormous burden of enforcing the policy laid down in each case. Not only did the council order action by other officials; it appointed its own members to the execution of vital tasks as well. Lord Herbert of Cherbury's later assessment with reference to the Henrician body neatly fixes the point: 'there were divers able to execute and perform as well as counsell'.[4] Thus in treating of matters of state ('publicq Affaires') the council devised policy and also governed; the dispatch of the King's 'private Affaires' required, as will be seen, that the council occasionally act in the manner of a court.

With a few exceptions – and allowing of course for the conditions of the royal minority – the competence of the privy council in Edward's reign did not exceed that of the late Henrician body. Nevertheless, at the time of Henry's death the procedures for the conduct of government by council – or rather, government under the King-in-council – were neither so well defined nor so firmly fixed that tradition could in every instance serve the new board. A formally established privy council certainly existed in England only from August 1540, and there is little reason to suppose that in February 1547 contemporaries expected the procedures of the early 1540s to cast the dead hand of routine over the new governors. The councillors themselves did not act as if they thought so. In the event, a nearly violent political struggle over the real division of power initially rendered the procedural question academic. Claiming that the Earl of Hertford (later

Duke of Somerset) should be able to order their business for them, the executors, in spite of a dissenting few, acquiesced in his elevation as governor of the King's person and Protector of the realm; for reasons that will be explained, they also thereby agreed to a fundamental alteration of Henry's will. However, in the changes which followed, the Protector retained intact the institution of the privy council, though admittedly that body's functions became somewhat perfunctory after 1547. When the Protector surrendered his offices in 1549, the lords who toppled him, in searching for a constitutional formula to justify their seizure of power, fell back on their technical, corporate responsibilities as Henry VIII's executors – that is, as Edward VI's only true privy councillors. The appearance of tradition at least was maintained: the Earl of Warwick (later Duke of Northumberland) accomplished his subsequent procedural domination of the council through that most formal of Henrician offices, the presidency of the council.

There was, then, an adherence, even if little more than superficial at times, to 'traditional' administrative and constitutional forms. But how effective was rule by council in the effective absence of a king? Some historians, not unsurprisingly, have found in the council's internecine plots, counter-plots, judicial murders, and *coups* prima facie evidence of a general breakdown of government; the councils of Somerset and Northumberland, it has been said, 'hardly belong to a discussion of Tudor methods of government'.[5] Few now remember Dicey's assertion that the administrative methods of the Tudor–Stuart council were most completely expressed by Northumberland's board,[6] an exaggerated notion rightly overruled by subsequent writers. But the current textbook platitude on this point – that constitutionally the period of Dudley's ascendancy cast the darkest shadow over that reign of 'weak and divided' rule[7] – must also be classified among the fossilate remains of Tudor historiography, for it, like much of the work on the Tudor council generally, has preserved either out-dated asumptions or generalisations based only on brief surveys of the major printed sources.[8] Even the latest and most exhaustive study of Edward's reign unintentionally demonstrates how difficult it is to accept even the most confident statements about the Edwardian council: the author has coupled the evidence for Dicey's interpretation with an important but unrelated and erroneously printed source and so, inevitably and unknowingly, has perpetuated an altogether misleading view of the council's size (allegedly forty) and organisation (supposedly a division into permanent 'committees').[9] Such problems obviously can be avoided only by returning to the relevant manuscript materials. One may premise, therefore, that the history of Edward's council necessarily begins with an examination of the extant original sources.

I
Sources

The sources for writing a history of the privy council in the reign of Edward VI fall naturally into three categories: records produced by the council, contemporary references to the council and its work, near-contemporary accounts which incorporate original material no longer available.[1] The first category comprehends by far the most important kind of evidence, the registers which the council ordered to be composed as the official version of its various acts and proceedings. These books, together with officially designated copies of council correspondence, are important not only for what they preserve, but also for what they reflect about contemporary attitudes towards the conduct of government and administration. One of the aims of this study is to show that these attitudes often can be discovered by reconstructing the probable methods of composing such records. Our understanding of the administration of the realm during the Protectorate, for example, is enriched precisely because one of the council books for the period has survived in the meaningfully chaotic form of a rough draft. A descriptive analysis of the composition of that volume alone documents some hitherto unknown aspects of the administrative and political history of that extraordinary regime.

The first category of materials also includes all of the 'real' products of council business, whether officially recorded or not: all original out-letters (including drafts and 'minutes' of many of these), orders, decrees, proclamations (which, although royal in name, originated in council), instructions, agreements, contracts, council warrants for payment, and so on. Agendas, secretaries' notes for meetings, 'remembrances', papers containing 'advice', and 'memorials' constitute yet another source of official (but not public) evidence of matters intended for the council, considered by the council, or concluded at the board. A fourth group of official documents within this category of products of council activity

5

provides evidence that the privy council must on occasion have functioned in a quasi-judicial capacity: the requests, petitions, and bills of supplication addressed to the King's privy council and entertained by privy councillors in regular meetings of the board, meetings not to be confused by this time with sessions of the court of requests or the court of star chamber.

The second category comprises another type of evidence, namely, comments about the council, references to, and accounts and observations of the institution, its members, and their work. There exists no contemporary or near-contemporary description of the privy council under Somerset and Northumberland; a history of the politics, procedure, and business of the institution necessarily must be pieced together from the myriad effects of the council's acts which remain scattered among thousands of items of manuscript evidence. Much of this evidence survives in written form merely as the incidental remark or, more conveniently, the pointed reference. In terms of the commentator's relative proximity to the institution, personnel, or business so described, these materials nominally fall into two groups: privy councillors' own papers and all other sources. The documents in both groups include variously diaries, tracts, chronicles, reports, dispatches, private notebooks and correspondence, letter- and account-books, and so on. Local and central government records which record the receipt of the council's communications, document the execution of council orders, or reflect the influence of privy councillors also fall into this second category; these papers provide a great deal of loose material whose numerous bits of information, when organised topically and chronologically, often resolve otherwise unsolvable mysteries: proof of place, date, authorship, and so forth. One item, William Lord Paget's letter-book in the Northamptonshire Record Office, actually provides much new substantive material, so that it must individually be treated as a singularly authoritative source. Unfortunately, very few similar collections of councillors' papers for the period 1547–53 have survived later fires, rats, dampness, and men. Among those which have, in addition to the Paget Papers at Plas Newydd, Anglesey, and Delapré Abbey, Northampton, are the Cecil Papers at Hatfield House,[2] the Seymour family papers at Longleat,[3] and the Duke of Northumberland's political and administrative correspondence with Cecil and others now to be found among the State Papers in the Public Record Office.[4]

The limitations that the original sources in this second category pose usually are self-evident, but even when one takes into account the author's identity, bias, probable motives, and degree of participation in events, questions often remain which defy resolution. 'For whom was this manuscript intended?' demands a straightforward answer which one cannot always supply even though the recipient's endorsement be subjected to a careful palaeographic analysis.[5] Of course some of the printed sources cited here simply are not available in their original form to students working in England; although, as in the case of the Imperial ambassadors' dispatches, one may check the nineteenth-century transcripts of these foreign language reports in the Public Record Office, there still remains the unalterable fact that these are accounts written by foreigners who, like Scheyfve, could understand very little of the English spoken to them.

In a third category are to be found the accounts of later sixteenth- and early seventeenth-century writers who had access to, consulted, or transcribed materials which no longer exist, and whose writings therefore assume the importance of first-hand documentation. For the study of Edward's council relatively few works actually fall into this category. As the only really authoritative contemporary account of Tudor government, Sir Thomas Smith's *De Republica Anglorum* (1565) ought to have shed strong light on the workings of the privy council, since Smith served the government well as a junior secretary of state under Somerset (1548–9). In fact, Smith says nothing about the institution in particular and very little about the role of privy councillors generally.[6] Although William Mill's and William Hudson's justly important treatises on the court of star chamber draw upon evidence of the judicial activity of the early Tudor council,[7] for Edward's reign their comments are relevant only for the court of star chamber and of course by that time council and star chamber were functionally separate institutions keeping wholly different sets of records. Indeed, the only general statement about the composition, function, and procedure of the sixteenth-century privy council is Sir Julius Caesar's brief essay, 'Concerning the Private Counsell of the most High and Mighty King of Greate Britaine,

ffrance, Scotland, Ireland, etc.'[8] Although he was writing almost
seventy-five years after the event, Caesar's notes make it clear that
he had seen many of the council's records dating from 1545,
before the great fire at Whitehall (1619) consumed the Banqueting House where they lay stacked up in bags and boxes. He mentions specifically certain 'bookes' kept 'in the time of King
Edward the 6' which recorded the council's almost daily reception of letters of all kinds. These registers of incoming correspondence apparently were destroyed in the fire; no other trace of them
remains. But his statements about the conduct of business at the
board and the composition of the privy council registers can be
checked against contemporary sources, with the result that one
may fairly accept Caesar's brief descriptions of the offices of the
clerks, the secretaries, the Lord President, and privy councillors
generally as having a real basis in fact for the reign of Edward VI.
Robert Beale's 'Instructions for a Principall Secretary'[9] (1592) is
rather more a prescription for the way an overworked Elizabethan secretary ought to have organised his time than a description of the way an Edwardian secretary did. Nevertheless, this
treatise by Walsingham's brother-in-law is based on first-hand
acquaintance with the mundane details of the office and certainly
reflects some procedures first defined in practice by Northumberland's great secretary, Sir William Cecil. Beale's knowledge is
particularly helpful, for example, when he refers directly to an
important procedural order 'kept in King Edward's time'.
Among Beale's other papers in the British Museum is a formulary
book for a clerk of the council which contains Beale's transcription
of 'The Othe of a Counsellor tempore Edward 6'.[10] Within this
third category of materials there is also an invaluable early Stuart
transcription of a now lost council letter-book of 1547.[11]

So much, then, for a brief introduction to the range of sources
available for a study of Edward's council. Because of their special
nature, however, several kinds of manuscript evidence warrant a
detailed description and analysis. The original council registers,
letter-books (or evidence of them), signed single copies of out-
letters, docquets, and docquet-books will be considered for the
unique characteristics which they exhibit as deliberately composed records of council activity, and the memoranda and notes of
council meetings, because they provide the best evidence there is

for what really must have happened in 'live' sessions at the board.

Our primary task in the following pages will be to describe as precisely as possible the ways in which the council functioned administratively during a period of war, social rebellion, financial instability, reform in the Church, and potentially violent political change. As one vital aspect of that function was the keeping of an official record of the 'acts' of the King's privy council, it should be important to understand the process by which those proceedings that the council determined should be of permanent record were, in fact, written down. Perhaps the best introduction, therefore, to the books of the acts of the council for this period is a description of the manner in which they must have been composed.

The evidence consists of the three manuscript registers in which are written in clerks' hands most of the known proceedings of the privy council from 31 January 1547 to 16 June 1553. The registers are large volumes, the paper pages in all three measuring approximately $15\frac{1}{2}$ inches by 11 inches. The only surviving example of an early privy council register (1558–9) in its original binding suggests what some of these books really must have been like. It is made up of two distinct bundles of quires sewn together to form a large, soft paper book of blank leaves bound within a flapped leather cover and secured by a strap with a hand-hewn iron buckle sewn to the cover with green ferret lacing.[12] We shall never know the exact appearance of Edward's council books, for sometime after 1832 they were re-bound, their pages having been expertly repaired and uniformly trimmed.[13] In Edward's reign the books were kept in a special chest in the council chamber at Westminster. The register current was also carried about in a travelling coffer with the King and council on progress.[14] One of the registers, almost certainly what is now the first volume, was lost in a fire at Whitehall and discovered only accidentally about 1748 by an historian rummaging about for waste paper at a cheesemonger's in London.[15] Fortunately it survived intact. All three registers in their present bound state are in very good condition.

The first volume contains 592 numbered manuscript pages covering the period from the accession of Edward VI to 4 October 1549. Volume II (150 pages) contains entries from 6 October

1549 to 19 April 1550. Volume III (732 pages) is a record from 19 April 1550 to 16 June 1553.[16] Although the registers were published in 1890 in a series entitled *Acts of the Privy Council of England*, that certainly would not have been the contemporary designation. 'Counsaille Boke' or register is the true name of any one volume. Sixteenth-century councillors produced in their own words 'ordres', 'decrees', and 'determynacions'; only rarely did they find themselves having accomplished an 'Acte'.[17] There is only one gap in this record of 'determynacions', and it is a deliberately created one: the period of twenty days immediately preceding the King's death on 6 July 1553, during which time the council barred from their meetings in a 'secluded chamber' the clerks who normally composed the minutes of the meetings, the councillors swearing among themselves to keep secret the contents of their daily consultations.[18] But these were extraordinary times. The regular procedure, as stated in an order in council of 19 April 1550, was

that there shulde be a Clerke attendaunt upon the said Counsaill to write, enter and register all such decrees, determinacions, and other thinges as he shulde be appointed to enter in a booke, to remaigne alwaies as a leger, aswell for the discharge of the said Counsaillours tooching such thinges as they shulde passe from time to time as also for a memoriall unto them of their own proceedings.[19]

One William Thomas was the clerk thus appointed. In fact, clerks of the council had performed this duty at least since 1540, for the order of 1550 is a verbatim copy of the order appointing William Paget a clerk of the privy council on 10 August 1540, which order was entered in the first privy council register in the series we now possess.[20] However, the rule that the composition of the privy council register alone should be the *sole* responsibility of one of the clerks of the council is a development dating from the reign of Edward VI, when the number of clerks increased from two to three in 1547.[21] The practice was made formal on 20 April 1550, the day after the appointment of William Thomas:

it was agreed that foreasmuch as the due observacion of the Registre of all such thinges as shulde passe by the Ordre of the Counsaill is an office that shall require a speciall diligence, therefore the forenamed Wm Thomas is discharged of all other manner of businesse to thentent that having nothing elles to attend unto he may the better applie his charge to see that nothing worthie to be registred be omitted or lefte unwriten.[22]

This is the earliest direct evidence we have that the clerks of the privy council were distinguished according to function. This specialisation of function must have been observed earlier than 20 April 1550, however, because in March 1550, when Paget set down his rules for the conduct of privy council business, he mentioned 'the Clearke having charge of the counsaill booke' in such a way as to leave no doubt that one clerk had sometime previously assumed specific daily responsibility in connection with the composition of the register.[23] By 1547 all three clerks were known officially as 'Clerkes of the Privey Counseill', thus resolving any question that some might have been clerks of the council while others, more well-defined, were clerks of the privy council.[24] The answer, therefore, as to which of the three clerks of the privy council must have been chosen to compose the register probably can be found by comparing their salaries, for there was a definite distinction made among the clerks on this basis. Pollard suggested that these differences in remuneration marked senior and junior clerkships,[25] but this argument applies essentially to a period when one clerk who was paid 40 marks annually could increasingly be recognised as a clerk of the council in star chamber and the other, paid £20 per annum, a clerk of the privy council.[26] During the reign of Edward VI the three clerks were paid £50, £40, and 50 marks respectively;[27] a comparison of the clerks known to receive these sums and the known hands of clerks responsible for sections of the registers shows that invariably the clerk paid 50 marks was also the one composing the register. Among the three clerks the work of composing the council book doubtless was recognised as a relatively humble professional task. Occasionally, however, the clerks rotated the duties; this is clearly evident from the changes in the hands in the registers. In June 1552 the council also made regular this previously informal practice when

Upon the humble sute of the Clerkes of the Counsell it was accorded by the Lordes that, two of them allwayes remayning and attending at the Courte uppon theyr Lordeshippes, a thyrde of them may allwayes be absent for a fortnight, that is to saye, one of them in course after an other, so as two of them be allwayes present.[28]

In the course of this schedule of attendance upon the council the clerks quarterly received an allowance of 50s. for paper, pens, and ink, and occasionally larger sums, not only for paper but also for 'bookes', 'standishes', 'standeskes', 'certaine catches of iron', and new keys.[29]

The 'bookes' mentioned probably were the 'greate faire paper bookes' described by Sir Julius Caesar,[30] the bound volumes of blank leaves in which the clerks entered all those proceedings which the council commanded to be of permanent record. These proceedings included an almost daily record of the many warrants whose payment the privy council regularly authorised; the text or an abstract of the text of selected letters sent out by the council;[31] notations to the effect that letters had been sent; an official narration, as it were, of important state events, such as Edward VI's coronation and the trial of Thomas Seymour; citations of significant foreign developments which directly touched the government, such as a resumption of war with France; statements recording the appointment of certain officials; notations of the appearance of certain individuals at court; notices of recognizances, usually in an abbreviated form; signed decisions committing councillors or former councillors to the Tower or ordering the execution of a colleague; a specially drafted deposition which was physically inserted into the record; notations of proclamations, orders, and decrees. One does not find in the registers minutes of debates and discussions or accounts of deliberations at the board.

On the basis of a careful examination of the registers, and with information from other sources, it is possible to reconstruct in some detail the procedures which a clerk must have followed when he recorded 'all such . . . thinges as he shulde be appointed to enter' in the council book. Assuming that he was looking at a blank right-hand page in a bound volume of blank leaves, he first folded this page in half by lifting the right-hand edge of the page towards him, placing it in the crevice of the binding and creasing the page down the middle. Then he repeated that motion with the remaining half-page, so that the leaf when unfolded lay equally divided into four vertical sections. The left-hand fold line served as a margin and the centre and right-hand folds served variously as faint guide lines. Almost every page in all three volumes bears the marks of having been folded in such a manner.[32] Furthermore, the centre folds of the folios in the second and third registers are uniformly aligned: these were the leaves of volumes already bound. In the second and third registers the clerk ordinarily noted the place of the meeting, 'At Westminster', for example, at the top of a page in the left-hand margin space and the date at the top right of the page. Often he indicated no place of meeting, merely writing 'Saterday the xvj[th] of November 1549' as a simple heading at the top. Under the heading he entered a neat list of the councillors in attendance that day; if the same councillors were present as had attended the previous meeting, he simply wrote 'Thapparance as before' and then entered the body of proceedings flush against the left-hand margin. In the second volume (October 1549 to April 1550) the clerk reserved a new page for the business of each new meeting, but in the last volume the record is continuous: a new day's proceedings immediately follow the previous day's entries.

The two registers for the period from the *coup d'état* of October 1549 to 16 June 1553 are essentially superb rough copies composed on a day-to-day basis. That is to say, like fair copies they are with a few exceptions neat and carefully written accounts set down by clerks clearly responsible for continuous, identifiable sections of the record. Unlike true fair copies, they were composed not of a piece at some later date in one or more sittings by one or several copyists, but on the same day as, or the day following, the events described. In his cursory examination of Edward's third register, E. R. Adair suggested that this book 'must have been compiled within a very short time of the actual council meetings', but the evidence he offered did not enable him to make a more definite statement.[33] Evidence may now be presented which clearly confirms the daily composition of these two registers. Paget's procedural 'Advise to the Kinges Counsail' implies that before March 1550 the clerk having charge of the council book was daily writing up the business of the most recent meeting 'and the next daye following, at the furst meting, presenting the same by the Secretary (who shall furst consydre wether the entrey be made accordingly) to the boorde, the counsaill shall the furst thing theye do signe the booke of entrees.'[34] Unfortunately the council rarely signed the register after October 1549. On the few occasions when they did so, however, the clerk also recorded the attendances for those meetings and, fortuitously for the administrative historian, a list of the councillors who signed various letters on those dates as well.[35] As some of these meetings fall in a sequence, it is possible to compare the attendances and the signatures, on the one hand, and, on the other, the attendances and the clerk's list of signatories to the letters. Interestingly, such a comparison does not reveal any necessary correlation between the number of councillors in attendance and the number who signed the register. But it does show, in the case of any one councillor's record of attendance and the frequency of his signing the book, that the register was being presented for signatures at the first meeting following the date of the entries thus signed. In other words, the register was being made current before each meeting.[36]

The second of Edward's three registers displays yet another characteristic which enables us to be even more precise about the actual timing of the act of writing up the record. The first nineteen pages of this volume give the appearance of true fair-copy material in the hand of the clerk responsible for all but sixteen pages of the volume. Immediately after the first nineteen pages, however, one begins to notice a distinct discrepancy between the style which the clerk employed for the heading and body of each day's proceedings and the style which he employed for the list of attendances. Consider, for example, page 37.[37] Looking only at the heading, 'Saterday the xvjth of November 1549', and the items of business concluded, one would say from all appearances that the heading and minutes were composed of a piece, at the same time, for both reveal a hand applying uniform pressure to the pen. There is the same regularity, the same angle of stroke which alone produces letters in the same shade of ink. In comparison, the names on the attendance list clearly were written rather quickly by the same hand applying irregular pressure to the pen. The style is identical but exaggerated. In other words, the more hastily written list probably was penned first and the date and minutes of the meeting were carefully entered later.[38] Thus, after noting the attendances in the register, the clerk began taking notes of the proceedings on another sheet of paper, and after the meeting, either the same day or the next, he entered the lords' 'determinations' in full in the register from these notes or perhaps even from memory. If the meeting was closed to him, then he must have quickly checked the attendances, departed from the chamber, and transcribed the proceedings later from notes taken at the board by one of the two principal secretaries. Even had they attended the meetings, it is indeed possible that for the period covered in these two registers the clerks never actually wrote anything at the board other than perhaps the attendances, the secretaries merely handing over to them the drafts of letters, orders, warrants, and so on to be copied into the record. At any rate, the picture we have portrays the clerks standing before their stand-desks in a little room adjoining the council chamber wherever the council were meeting; the great fair paper book lies open before them as the junior clerk or his assistant, at sometime later in the day following the meeting, neatly enters into the register the secretary's notes of bonds, warrants for payment, letters sent, orders, decrees, and special determinations.[39]

Although these suggestions may offer reasonable explanations for the characteristics of the two registers composed after 4 October 1549, the register for the Protectorship of the Duke of Somerset presents so remarkably different an appearance that one may view the volume as a rather extraordinary revelation of certain aspects of Somerset's management of the council and his administration generally. There is no doubt, for example, that the second and third registers provide a continuous record of meetings of the board. With few exceptions we know who attended those meetings. The first register, however, does not necessarily contain a record of business transacted in actual meetings of the council. In fact, it is not necessarily a true record of even the occasions of meetings. Stated more fully, a diplomatic examination of the council book for the period 31 January 1547 to 4 October 1549 reveals that the register of Edward's privy council under the Duke of Somerset contains some material not the product of council sessions, omits any reference whatsoever to some meetings which did take place, and occasionally records regular proceedings under dates on which no meetings were held.

The evidence for these conclusions may be introduced by the fact that this volume was not originally a single volume of blank leaves, but rather a combination of paper books and bundles of loose sheets and quires bound together later. Proof of this is self-evident: the random pages whose fold lines run perpendicular to the spine of the present binding. Sheets folded in this manner clearly cannot originally have been the pages of a bound volume.[40] Of course loose sheets in themselves do not necessarily indicate that sections of the register were arranged deliberately, for a reason; their appearance in the present binding may be the accident of indifferent preservation. But the appearance of one section of unique material preceded by such pages reveals the politically motived insertion of matter which cannot be accepted as a product of a council meeting. This is the famous deposition of February 1547 in which Sir William Paget claimed to have remembered certain of Henry VIII's intentions not contained in the late King's will. Although worded so as to suggest that it was offered in the course of council deliberations and framed as part of the official running business of the council, Paget's testimony clearly was drafted in advance of the day recorded, copied out in a hand not otherwise found in this volume on paper of a different make than the other leaves, and physically inserted into the register.[41] The external origin of this entry and its probable authorship are confirmed by an examination of Paget's letter-book in the Northamptonshire Record Office. The letter-book contains a verbatim copy of the deposition.[42] The appearance *in toto* in Paget's letter-book of this politically important section of the privy council register is prima facie evidence that the section in the register was copied from a draft which originated with Paget. The important point, however, is that the copy in Paget's letter-book is an earlier version of this deposition: the few corrections which it contains were incorporated in the copy intended for the register, and in one case the copy in the letter-book retains an interesting phrase which the council deleted from the text of the deposition planted in the register.[43] Furthermore, an examination of the deposition as it appears in the letter-book shows that this copy may have existed independently, for it seems only later to have been sewn up together with the three other quires of the letter-book the contents of which are of a piece.[44] Thus we have two slightly different copies of a deposition almost certainly drafted by Paget containing what 'the said King Henry VIII devised with me a parte', one of which, in a corrected form, was inserted into the privy council register as what 'we the lord protector and counsaile have thoughte convenient' to do.[45]

In addition to such pre-determined material the extraordinary nature of which required that it be made 'of record', the council also added to the register pre-dated material *ex post facto* in order to justify or explain officially extraordinary events. Such was the case with the action taken against Thomas Seymour, whose alleged crime and punishment required that a specially prepared account be entered in the council book as the official version of the government's destruction of the Lord Admiral. The entries in the register documenting the examination, trial and execution of Seymour demonstrate that the clerks were composing the register weeks later than the events described.[46] We are dealing, then, with a record which could be, and was, artificially arranged to suit the political purposes of the government or facilitate the demands of administration.

On the other hand, there is evidence that the council simply did not record some meetings. A cancelled section of the draft of the entry in the register recording the council's decision of 17 March 1549 to execute Seymour provides a rare glimpse of a second, unrecorded meeting on the seventeenth in which the council considered and refused at least one of Seymour's last requests.[47] That the council should, for high political reasons, have suppressed the record of their own deliberations in so sensitive a matter as the administration of the execution of a colleague is understandable; what is less clear is the omission of any mention of routine meetings. The Imperial ambassador described in some detail a session of the council on 16 June 1547 in which the council appointed Lord St John to deal with Imperial merchants' complaints.[48] The council book, however, contains no entries for 16 June. Paget spoke of a meeting of the French ambassador 'with my lordes of the counsaill' at the court on 30 August 1547, but the register records nothing under that date.[49] As the register contains no minutes of debates or discussions, we should not expect to find even an edited transcript of an audience with a foreign ambassador. Indeed, references to the presence of ambassadors at the board are rare. Nominally, such omissions may have been procedural: the council simply chose not to record conferences with resident ambassadors. But this would not explain why the council before October 1549 often did not record the fact of their own assembly. Indeed, the clerks never recorded attendances and only rarely cited a place of meeting. On the basis of the appearance of the register alone, how is one able to identify a meeting of the privy council when one sees it? To what extent are the entries in this register the products of actual meetings of the board?

To begin with, we may say that the only reliable guide to identifying a meeting of Edward's privy councillors before October 1549 is their own statement to that effect. There seems little doubt, for example, that when the clerk noted 'a deliberacion. . . had in the counsaile Chamber at Grenewiche the xvij[th] of April in the secund yere of his Majestes most gracious Reign', he was referring to a gathering of at least a few councillors, even though no attendance is given and no signatures follow the entry.[50] More specifically, the record may state that 'the ij[de] of Februarie [1547] the saide Lorde Protectour and other his coexecutours whose names be underwritten assembled againe togwither in the Counseill Chambre in the Towre', in which case we may accept the original signatures thereunto subscribed as a true record of actual attendance on that day.[51] But unless so stated, original signatures in this register bear no relation to attendance at a meeting on the day recorded or, for that matter, to physical presence at court for days and weeks afterwards. A case in point is Somerset's signature, which is affixed to four different recorded days' proceedings from 4 to 25 September 1547; at the time, Somerset was in Scotland conducting a military campaign.[52] Paget's procedural rules of 1550 stipulated that spaces be left blank in the register 'for the counsailors absent [to] entre theyre names whenne theye cum',[53] and this Somerset did, in some cases almost two months after the business recorded. The fact that the original signatures in the register do not necessarily prove attendance is also borne out by the fact that not everyone who attended a real meeting at Hampton Court on Sunday, 4 September 1547 signed the council book.[54] Similar circumstances led Pollard to the conclusion that the signatures were merely an official convention and thus had little or no significance.[55] This may be true, for without attendance lists we have no way of knowing who attended meetings, except, as has been seen, in those few instances when the clerk directly referred to councillors meeting in the council chamber. The vital point, however, is not necessarily the non-significance of the signatures or the absence of other signatures, but whether or not the register itself is a true record of even the occasions of meetings.

Now it is true that for the first four months of Edward's reign there are fifty-nine recorded days' proceedings entered in the register and for all but four of these, an average of nine councillors actually signed the book at the foot of each day's entries. Although the number of signatures does not necessarily indicate the number of councillors in attendance, nevertheless, from all appearances, this record of fifty-five days' proceedings doubtless marks approximately the same number of meetings of the privy council. But after 1 June 1547, original signatures, the same six or seven original signatures, appear only after about every fourth recorded day, or on the average, about once a week, and after 7 January 1548 the signatures cease altogether, except for the decision to commit Gardiner to the Tower (30 June 1548) and the confinement (17 January 1549) and execution (17 March 1549) of Thomas Seymour. What are we to say, then, of the seventy-four recorded days from 1 June 1547 to 7 January 1548 and the four hundred recorded days after that (to 4 October 1549) for which no signatures, attendances, and frequently no place, are given?[56] Do these dates record the occasion of 474 meetings of the privy council?

We know that the council often assembled only once a week. Thus, during Somerset's absence from 22 August to 8 October 1547, the register records proceedings under twenty-four different dates when, in fact, as Paget explained to Somerset, the full council were meeting together only on Sundays at court.[57] During October 1548, the plague in London forced King and council to disperse to the country, so that 'when the Protector desired, once a week or so, to hold a Council he caused the members to come to his house'.[58] Nevertheless, the clerks recorded an average of three dates per week during the same month.[59] Additional evidence that the council after 28 May 1547 generally adhered to a once-a-week schedule of meetings during Somerset's Protectorate is provided by the fact that Sunday appears to have been the one day of regularly appointed meeting, in and out of term. On Thursday, 20 October 1547 Somerset wrote Lord Grey that he would 'speke with my lordes of the counsail at our next Assembley apon Sondey coming' in a tone which suggested nothing unusually selective about a meeting of the privy council on Sunday.⁶⁰ Indeed, almost two years later (23 September 1549) it could still be observed that 'the members of the Council only assemble on Sundays at Hampton Court, where the King now is'.⁶¹ Thus, external evidence alone suggests that not every date entered in the register can possibly have marked a council meeting.

The diplomatic of the register also supports this conclusion. Dasent was wrong in saying that the register after 1 January 1548 'appears to have been made up every Sunday'; it is more probable that the frequent and full designation of Sunday alone among all the days of the week merely indicates the regular gathering of the privy council on Sundays; thus the clerks' full notations of several different Sundays (26 February, 1 April, 3 June, 9 September, and 28 October 1548) for which no proceedings are listed, but for at least one of which a location is given (Greenwich, 1 April 1548).⁶² Indeed, the clerks departed from the procedure of listing Sundays fully by name and the other days under abbreviated dates only for the periodic recording of substantive business transacted by the council on a day other than Sunday: witness the unusually explicit reference to the deliberations 'in the counsaile Chamber at Grenewich' on Tuesday, 17 April 1548;⁶³ to proceedings 'in the Counsaile Chambre at Westminster' on Saturday, 5 May 1548;⁶⁴ the hearing 'at the Court at Otelands . . . in the Council Chamber there before the Lord Protectors Grace and Council' on Monday, 27 August 1548;⁶⁵ or the arrest of Thomas Seymour recorded 'At Westmynster on Thurseday the xvijᵗʰ of January 1548 [1549]'.⁶⁶

The rare fullness of such references only makes more pointed the question of how to interpret the 474 other abbreviated dates in this register. The answer must be made from an analysis of the 'business' (indeed, sometimes the only business) recorded under these dates, the notations of thousands of quite ordinary council warrants for payment; an analysis of the warrants as they appear in the register should demonstrate the significance of the clerks' methods of recording them as datable products of council business. An examination of the council book shows that many of these entries actually appear as rough notes of warrants loosely scrawled across the page, as if the clerk had taken them down hurriedly from dictation.[67] One can detect various styles of a single clerk's hand: his 'best copy' hand, routine 'working' hand, and rough, 'note-taking' hand, as it were.[68] Frequently the clerk omitted variously from these notes of warrants the name of payee, payor, messenger, and sum of money involved, and only later filled in the blank spaces in his more composed hand.[69] A single, unexceptional warrant may appear as the only 'business' under an abbreviated date; occasionally, single warrants or groups of warrants comprising part or all of an entire day's proceedings are crossed through with a marginal note to the effect that they have been entered under a later (or earlier) date.[70] Some dates appear twice, both consecutively within the same chronological series[71] and separately within a non-chronological series of dates.[72] And dates not in chronological order appear not only on what were once loose sheets (which may have been jumbled together later), but also within the span of a few days' proceedings copied on to one side of a folio by one clerk.[73]

Thus, merely the appearance of these notations suggests that we are dealing not with the products of dated meetings of the council, but with the rough notes of payments frequently authorised by councillors in or out of meetings. Cancelled, amended, incomplete single warrants hastily jotted down in random chronological order at several different times by several different clerks under haphazardly abbreviated dates clearly were not intended as the record *per se* of formal council meetings. A comparison of dated *original* warrants (or the record of them in detailed treasurers' accounts) and the dates under which the clerks entered notes of the same warrants in the register supports this conclusion. Such a comparison shows, for example, that the clerks frequently recorded warrants in the register under dates *earlier* than the date of the actual warrant.[74] In such cases the date in the register probably marks the day on which a few councillors ordered the warrant to be drawn; perhaps the clerk did not draft the letter until the following day, at which time he also collected the necessary signatures for it, dating it to that day. The note of a warrant in the register, then, may really represent nothing more than the clerk's rough note of an order for payment dictated to him by the secretary (or another ranking councillor), the entry standing, in effect, as the clerk's abbreviated instructions to be fully transcribed later as the formal warrant, or letter, the blank spaces to be filled in with the name of the carrier or treasurer to whom it had been decided the warrant should be directed. The comparison of dates on warrants and the dates in the register also shows, however, that just as frequently the clerks entered notes of warrants in the register under dates *later* than the date on the warrant – later by one day or five weeks.[75] In some of these cases, the date on the warrant does indeed correspond to a date for which there are proceedings entered in the register, but the note of the warrant itself is found in a group of warrants assigned a later date.[76] One may also cite dated original warrants for which nothing exists in the register, neither date nor proceedings of any kind, and yet the notations of these same warrants are found at random under later and earlier dates.[77]

The answer, then, to the question, 'Do the abbreviated dates in the register invariably and truly fix in point of time meetings of the privy council in which such warrants were authorised?' clearly must be 'No'. Of course, some of the dates well may correspond to days on which the council met, including days other than Sunday. The point is simply that we have no way of knowing exactly which dates (other than Sundays) may in fact identify true meetings. The council under Somerset, with a few notable exceptions, chose not to record the fact of their meeting together but, rather, the fact of their having authorised various warrants for payment, and, as has been seen, the clerks followed no fixed procedure in recording the date of that 'collective' act. Thus, whereas every date in the registers for the period after Somerset's fall marks an official meeting of the council, very few of the dates in the register of Somerset's rule identify physical assemblies of privy councillors in session in the council chamber at court. It was noted earlier that most of the entries for the first several months appear to have been the products of actual sessions, although the number of signatures affixed to these entries proves no reliable guide to the number of councillors who may have been present. But after the consolidation of Somerset's power, and especially after January 1548, no attempt was made to show that what the clerks recorded were the products of council meetings. With the exception of the imprisonment of Gardiner and the execution of his own brother, Somerset seems after January 1548 even to have abandoned the pretext which he earlier maintained that the register reflected (in the form of original signatures) the corporate will of a council administering the realm. Until the *coup* of October 1549, the relative lack of any formal procedure governing the composition of a record of the 'determinations' of the council suggests that what we now call the first of Edward's council books often was merely the most convenient place – bundles of loose sheets – for Somerset's clerks to note informally the authorisation of payments made by the Protector's government in the name of the King's whole privy council.

Within the category of primary sources classified as direct products of the council's work, we are also fortunate in possessing for the reign of Edward VI hundreds of examples of council correspondence touching upon almost every aspect of the administration of the realm: letters containing orders, directions, advice, instructions, information, and admonitions from the council to a wide range of officials in the Church and government, persons of every rank, foreign and domestic, in matters great and trivial. Indeed, this is the first reign in English history for which we possess so diverse and so relatively complete a collection of letters originating in the King's council. The letters have survived in three forms: the original signed out-letter, a secretary's or clerk's draft of the original, and a clerk's file copy, in some cases also signed by a clerk and a few councillors. A search of local and private archives occasionally turns up the signed original letter and although further efforts may produce more, in fact very few council letters appear to have survived their reception elsewhere. Some, fortunately, found their way into the British Museum as a result of the deposit there in the nineteenth century of various private collections, but most of the letters have survived among the State Papers in the Public Record Office in the form of rough drafts in the recognisable hands of Edward's principal secretaries (Paget, Petre, Smith, and Cecil). We owe the preservation of these drafts to the fact that they remained in the burgeoning pile of secretaries' papers which formed the bulk of the original collection of documents gathered together in the State Paper Office established in 1578.[78]

The drafts are endorsed typically in a contemporary clerk's

hand as the dated 'minute of a lettre' to the recipient; these 'minutes' of letters are in fact usually the full first drafts complete with corrections, cancellations, and interlineations. Such documents are perhaps more valuable than the dispatched originals, since one can usually identify the hand in question and also roughly follow the development of the author's thought as revealed by his corrections and additions. In certain cases such cancellations and emendations may dimly reflect the results of discussion and debate at the board. Letters carrying instructions or articles sometimes exist in two forms, the secretary's rough first draft and a clerk's wide-spaced, large-writ fair copy of the corrected draft. The wide spaces between the lines allowed the author to make further corrections before the clerks copied out the final version. The clerks also transcribed fair copies of the resulting out-letter, keeping these file copies as official 'office' records of the council's correspondence.[79] Occasionally these file copies (and drafts) bear the original signatures of privy councillors and the transcribing clerk;[80] Edwardian clerks sometimes kept fair copies of council letters to which they added facsimiles of the hands of the councillors who had signed the originals.[81] The retention of this type of record appears to have been unprecedented. The existence of signed copies of council correspondence is unknown for the reign of Henry VII; even contemporary copies of council letters for the reign of Henry VIII certainly are not numerous. Early Tudor secretaries apparently were not in the habit of keeping transcriptions of out-letters for future reference.[82] But the Edwardian privy council even recorded the fact that they were keeping copies of their own letters.[83]

Of course, for some council letters, none of the three forms of manuscript evidence described above has survived, but references of varying fullness to the lost originals are preserved in yet another source produced by the council, a unique register of letters for the period 6 February to 13 June 1547. This register, if one may call it that, actually forms a section of 41 folios at the end of the privy council register covering the last twenty-one months of Henry VIII's reign. A clerk clearly used the blank pages at the end of the old register as a convenient place to record letters sent out by the new council.[84] Technically, these are rough-copy texts, notes, and abstracts of out-letters; the clerk also occasionally included the note of a council warrant for payment. The entries are dated, but the entries within a given month do not always fall in chronological order. A few of the entries correspond to items in the council book but, like the dates of original warrants noted earlier, the dates of such entries in the letter-book frequently precede the date of the entry in the council book. A comparison of such entries suggests first, that the dates in the letter-book are the true dates of the letters and warrants; secondly, that for this early period of the Protectorate, the dates in the council book probably mark true meetings of the council in which councillors were asked to authorise with their signatures the accomplished fact of letters and warrants already dispatched.[85] Dasent thought that the entries in the letter-book were intended by the transcribing clerk 'as a check upon his colleague', a reminder that the letters were to be transcribed later into the council book,[86] but this cannot be true, for the evidence points to the fact that, for a time at least, the council under Somerset were keeping two different sets of registers, the familiar privy council register and an official letter-book distinctly referred to by name in the council book as 'the Register of letters'.[87] Perhaps the folios at the end of the Henrician register make up just this same 'Register of letters'; perhaps the rough entries were transcribed later into a neat, fair-copy register and this volume, now lost, is the register referred to here. In any case, what appears certain is that shortly after the death of Henry VIII the council determined that the council book henceforth was to be reserved primarily for the enregistering of financial warrants, and the register of letters for council correspondence.

This conclusion is supported by two closely related observations: the probable existence after 13 June 1547 (the date of the last entry in the extant letter-book) of another letter-book, and the fact that, whereas before the death of Henry VIII and after the fall of Somerset the clerks daily entered notes and abstracts of the council's current out-letters directly into the council book, for the period of Somerset's Protectorate they almost never did so. A casual comparison of the various council books discloses the second point; the first is confirmed by the survival of a rare seventeenth-century transcript of what must have been a privy council register of letters for the period 13 June 1547 to 8 August 1548, although the copyist, Ralph Starkey, indicated in 1620 that the original volume also contained some council orders and decrees and certain bills of complaint addressed to the council, which he omitted.[88] If official council letter-books existed after 8 August 1548, we should be able to explain the nearly complete absence of any references to letters sent in the first of the three privy council registers for Edward's reign. Such letter-books may have been among the 'great fair paper bookes' wherein were written 'all the Actes of that Counsell . . . and copies of letters', the volumes described by Sir Julius Caesar in 1625, but which perished in the great fire at Whitehall in 1619.[89] Caesar also referred to books dated to the reign of Edward VI which recorded the reception of letters *to* the council, but these privy council registers of letters received also went up in the flames that destroyed the Banqueting House.[90]

It is also necessary to consider here another official ledger, which records not only council out-letters but also certain other important products of the council's work, such as proclamations and warrants for payment. This is an original docquet-book containing 'The note of all the bills Signed by the Kings majestie and the counsaile' from 19 October 1550 to 3 July 1553.[91] Although described in the British Museum catalogue of Royal and King's MSS. as a docquet-book of bills signed as warrants for the great seal, this large volume of 375 paper folios (each measuring 15 inches by $9\frac{1}{2}$ inches) really contains abstracts and notes of a variety of different documents signed by Edward VI, including many which were never presented in chancery as warrants for the great seal. Unfortunately, the act of rebinding these folios destroyed so much of the appearance of the original ledger (or ledgers) that it is impossible to say how the apparent sections of the present volume must originally have been arranged. However, the consistent neatness of the upright secretary hand suggests that we are dealing with the work of one signet clerk who entered into one or two bound blank paper books[92] the note of every document nominally signed by the King during the period indicated, the entries being written down, from all appearances, within a few days of the dates given. The entries are listed chronologically in four columns giving the date, the type of document, the county (that is, the location of a parcel of land if the entry records a grant of purchase; the location of the recipient, if a letter), and the initials of the recipient. The types of bills recorded include grants of offices, leases, purchases, annuities, licences, passports, pardons, proclamations, and royal commissions. Most of these signet bills resulted in letters-patent, and so may be found among the entries on the patent rolls, but some did not, and these include certain types of letters sent out under the signatures of the King (sign manual or stamp) and members of the privy council: letters to English commissioners and ambassadors abroad, instructions, letters of credit, warrants for payment, and in one instance, a letter of rebuke from the council to the Lord Chancellor that Warwick may have persuaded the young King to sign for the emphasis that only the sovereign's own hand could provide.[93]

How did this book come into being? As a ledger of bills passed under the signet, the book officially contains material which initially had required formal Crown approval, and not business more narrowly within the interests of the privy council alone, but of course these were not ordinary times, for during the King's minority every matter requiring the royal sign manual was primarily a privy council matter, and the council under Northumberland, although constitutionally subordinate to the King, in practice wielded full power in the King's name with the dry stamp of the King's signature. As Northumberland's man in the royal household, the Vice-Chamberlain, Sir John Gates, held the stamp, we can appreciate that there must have been some on the council who opposed this blatant political, as opposed to administrative, control of the signet, for the custody of the King's seal fell normally to the King's secretaries. When Northumberland's faction finally persuaded the other councillors on 10 November 1551 to abandon the previous practice of counter-signing all bills passed under the signet, it clearly became necessary to placate those who remembered Somerset's absolutism by arranging that

a brief sum of those bills that shall cumme to his Majesties signature shalbe put in a docquet or codicill, which shalbe signed by the Counselles hands, witnessing that the same commeth to his Majesty by theyr advise, and the same docquet to remayne as a warraunt with those that doo preferre the sayd billes to his Highnes signature.[94]

What is the relationship, then, between the present volume in the British Museum which contains entries as early as October

1550, and the council's order of November 1551 for the composition and filing of separate, signed docquets of signet bills? Fortunately, we possess five of these original docquets for the month of June 1552 and thus clear proof of the implementation of the order of 1551.[95] Each of the docquets originally consisted of a paper sheet folded to form two folios listing in a clerk's hand (as the heading typically reads) the 'Billes to be signed by the Kinges majestie if it may so stande with his hieghnes pleasure' on the date which is included in the heading. A single docquet may contain as many as sixteen items, bills for offices, grants, leases, letters, instructions, commissions, and so on. Each docquet is signed at the foot by five to eleven councillors and endorsed in Cecil's or Petre's hand as a 'docquett'. As the items which appear in the docquets also appear in Royal MS. 18 C. xxiv, we can say that these signed lists of documents requiring the royal sign manual (or stamp) very probably served, for a time at least, as the notes from which the clerk who composed the Museum volume copied his entries. It is reasonable to assume that unsigned docquets existed before November 1551 and that they also provided the chronological notes for the entries in the book from October 1550 to November 1551. Once again, as with the orders for the composition of the privy council registers, the council under Northumberland had formally adopted well-defined procedures for the recording of what was in fact during the King's minority another aspect of the business of the privy council.

There is evidence, however, that the council under Somerset also kept in a docquet book the record of warrants authorised by the privy council as payments made to foreigners employed in the King's service in the North Parts and at Calais.[96] The evidence consists of eight folios of rather full abstracts of such warrants dated from 16 May to 3 July 1549. As the dates are not always in chronological order on any given side of a folio, it is evident that the clerk was entering each abstract informally into a rough copy-book as he received the completed bill. References to some of the warrants listed on these folios are also found in the privy council register.

Thus far the discussion has covered materials which were composed deliberately, to be of record. Consideration will now be given to papers which also provide direct evidence of the council at work but which, because of their highly casual and informal nature, were not meant to be preserved as an official record of that activity – the extant memoranda of matters to be considered and matters concluded in council. There are forty-one of these 'memorials' and 'remembrances', most of them cast in the recognisable hands of two of the principal secretaries of state, Sir William Petre and Sir William Cecil, and at least three clerks, Bernard Hampton, William Thomas, and Sir Thomas Chaloner. As the unbiased products of administrative routine, the papers document precisely the sort of business which must regularly have come to the board, and naturally so, since all of them were turned out in the course of the secretaries' management of that business. This explains why the manuscripts have survived either as part of the original collection of papers gathered into the State Paper Office (and now catalogued in the Public Record Office) or among Cecil's papers preserved at Hatfield House. All forty-one manuscripts are datable to the period September 1551 to June 1553, and all but one to January 1552 to June 1553.[97] Circumstantial evidence explains why it is that the only surviving agendas and notes of business for Edward's council's meetings fall into the last eighteen months of the reign. First, the period is coincident with that of Cecil's greatest administrative activity and it is to his ability as an administrator generally, and his preservation of the papers in the secretary's office specifically, that we owe the existence of relatively so much material for Northumberland's administration. Secondly, the period is also coincident with King Edward's superficial intrusion into the affairs of the council;[98] although Cecil and Petre were not the first Tudor secretaries to draw up agendas for meetings or keep lists of business dispatched, it is the case that in the reign of Edward VI the secretaries were *required* to keep a 'memoriall' of current business before the council and to deliver it each week to His Majesty. As the young King began attending specially staged council meetings by October 1551,[99] the procedure may have been observed earlier than 15 January 1553 when the rule probably was made formal.[100] Of course, it does not necessarily follow that we owe the existence of all the papers cited here to the fact of Edward's attendance at such meetings, or even to his presumed interest (before 15 January 1553) in the council's business; indeed, we should not expect that documents such as these ordinarily came into the King's view. Nevertheless, it is clear that Edward saw some relatively informal notes of council matters and marked them up himself.[101] Whether he demanded to see them is another question.

Twelve of the forty-one manuscripts are lists of items of business dispatched and include only those matters which required formal Crown approval – namely, letters to be sent under the royal sign manual, signet bills and so on.[102] Although headed typically, 'Certen Causes to be moued to the Kinges Majestie', the lists really represent a 'Memorie of matters passed in Counsell', as the endorsement on the same list shows. Together the lists provide clear evidence of the fact that, in spite of the King's appearance of rule, the council under Northumberland firmly controlled the granting of offices, lands, annuities, pensions, and so on in the King's gift.[103]

Compared with these full and fairly neat lists of 'suits', the remaining twenty-nine pieces of evidence in this group of papers present so many individual problems of interpretation that only those characteristics which at least a few of them share in common can be described here. At least seven of the twenty-nine manuscripts almost certainly represent council agendas. All seven bear dates and two of them, a place. Three are in Petre's hand, three in Cecil's, and one in Cecil's and a clerk's hand which resembles that of Sir Thomas Chaloner.[104] However, for three of the dates on these agendas, nothing is recorded in the council book (26 August, 29 September 1552; 29 April 1553) and very little of the business listed appears in the register under later dates. Why is this so? The agendas may have been misdated (improbable); the dates in the register may be wrong (also unlikely). The probable explanation is that Petre and Cecil drew up their agendas the evening before a meeting or even a few days ahead of time.[105] Another possibility is that the agendas in question, and perhaps agendas generally, contained business to be considered not in one meeting alone, but at large, over several meetings. Even those agendas whose dates correspond to dated meetings in the register contain matters recorded in the council book under the dates of later meetings.[106] The fact that some items of business listed on these seven agendas cannot be found in the council book under the same or later dates is to be expected in any case, as the register contains only those items which the lords authorised the clerks to record. The agendas are all the more valuable for that reason: not only do they provide evidence of all the business which came up for discussion, but occasionally they indicate alternatives to some points of business as well.[107]

Another twenty undated lists of business considered in council meetings pose slightly more difficult problems of interpretation than the identifiable agendas. One of the twenty items almost certainly is a hastily jotted list of business for a meeting of 4 March 1552 together with notes probably scribbled down in the course of that meeting.[108] Another one represents a clerk's fuller copy of four selected items of business unquestionably dated to the same day.[109] On a third sheet Cecil quickly noted three hearings to be conducted, with the council's choice of examiners.[110] A fourth paper of 'Matters vnperfected' is a list of warrants to be authorised, offices to be filled, and so on, penned before a meeting by a clerk and then marked up by Cecil and another clerk during or after the meeting (or meetings).[111] A fifth list of business to be dispatched includes all of the items not checked off on an earlier list.[112] The remaining fourteen manuscripts in this group may be described as having been drawn up after a meeting (or series of meetings) for the purpose of noting unresolved affairs generally or drawn up just before a meeting, employed as checklists during the meeting, and then filed, for example, as 'Memorie[s] of matters in Counsell'.[113] Finally, we possess two collections of some 21 pages of notes which Cecil kept as his own casual record of incoming and outgoing correspondence and matters requiring action by the council and the secretaries and clerks.[114]

Within the category of materials produced in the course of the secretaries' management of council business should perhaps be cited two miscellaneous papers composed especially to satisfy the King's youthful interest in matters of state: a brief reminder from Cecil of the council's nominees for several offices and a list of articles concerning Crown revenues.[115] There exist other so-called memoranda of matters of state, such as Cecil's briefs on the King's finances, but neither they nor the two manuscripts just cited should be confused with council agendas or the notes of privy council business taken down as a natural part of the secretaries' day-to-day administration of affairs. We can distinguish the more general 'memoranda' from most of the papers described here on the basis of the reasons for their composition: whereas the former were composed for personal or general reference quite apart from the deliberations of any one council meeting, the latter came into being quite naturally as administrative by-products of particular meetings. The general memoranda concern statements of policy; the papers cited above record the council's consideration of that policy.

There are, however, six memoranda that, although not originating in the secretary's office, nevertheless contain business that at the time the authors – Paget and King Edward – intended for the board's consideration. As the statements of contemporaries close to the council, these papers really fall within the second general category of primary sources, but because they are similar in content to the materials composed by the secretaries and clerks in the service of the council, they will be considered here in that context. Three of the memoranda are in the King's hand and are well known.[116] The other three are entirely fresh documents, providing new evidence for a study of the conduct of Somerset's Protectorate. The originals of these three are probably lost; contemporary transcriptions have survived in the form of dated fair-copy entries in Paget's letter-book.[117] Two of these, a 'Remembraunce' of 2 February 1548 and a 'Memoriall' of 25 January 1549 which Paget had addressed to Somerset, take the form of a set of unnumbered heads of particular matters requiring either a final decision ('To Resolve vpon your procedinges in the parliament for money . . .') or a swift execution ('Item: to set forthe the proclamacion for the callinge in agayne of the testornes'). The third memorandum, entitled 'Certayne poyntes to be resolved vpon in Counsaill', Paget enclosed in a letter to Somerset dated 17 April 1549; Sir William thought the questions raised in his little paper 'were good to be proponed to the hole counsayle, to be with some deliberacion considered, debated and resolued vpon'. One may doubt, however, that Somerset ever allowed Paget's 'poyntes' to be aired at the board. Sir William believed that 'the gouernement vnder the kinge' had followed the wrong course at home and abroad; it would have been most uncharacteristic of Somerset to have tolerated a discussion which presumed the Protectorate to have been a failure. Paget's memoranda may therefore provide evidence of just the sort of business which Somerset did not allow to be raised in council meetings, namely, much of the determination of foreign and domestic policy.

2
Membership

On the death of Henry VIII (28 January 1547), executive power
in England passed, not to his nine-year-old son but to the sixteen
executors of the dead King's will whom Henry had appointed
by authority of an Act of Parliament[1] to be 'Counsaillours of the
Privy Counsail with our sayd Son Prince Edward' and to have
'the Gouvernement' of the young King, his realms, dominions, and
subjects, 'and of all th'Affairs Publicq and Private until he shal
have fully accomplished the eightenth Year of his Age'.[2] Fifteen
days later (12 March) the government of the young King's person
and the responsibility for the protection of his realms, dominions,
and subjects during his minority was transferred by letters-patent
to one of the former executors, Edward Seymour, Duke of Somerset, who was also empowered to select the members of the King's
privy council from among some twenty-six 'counsaillours' nominated in the same patent (or from among 'any others' whom he
should thereafter choose to elevate to the rank of King's 'councillor').[3] Somerset's powers in this regard were reaffirmed in precisely the same terms some nine months later (24 December 1547)
in new letters-patent, which superseded the commission of 12
March; the tenure of Somerset's office, however, was now held to
be at the King's pleasure rather than for the duration of the royal
minority.[4] The terms of this second patent of the Protectorate
remained in force until additional letters-patent dated 13 October
1549 revoked them utterly and completely;[5] the official abolition
of the Protectorate thus restored the conditions of 28 January
1547; once again, Henry's will as authorised by the statute of
1536 formed the constitutional basis of continued government
by council.

In the reign of Edward VI, then, the authority for appointing
privy councillors was derived from two distinct sources, Henry
VIII's last will and testament, as interpreted by the executors

34

TABLE I   *Edward VI's privy council as appointed by Henry VIII*

Thomas Cranmer, Archbishop of Canterbury
William Lord St John, Great Master of the King's household and President of the privy council
John Lord Russell, Keeper of the privy seal
Edward Seymour, Earl of Hertford, Great Chamberlain of England
John Viscount Lisle, High Admiral of England
Cuthbert Tunstal, Bishop of Durham
Sir Anthony Browne, Master of the King's horse
Sir William Paget, one of the King's two principal secretaries of state
Sir Edward North, Chancellor of the court of augmentations
Sir Edward Montagu, Chief Justice of the common pleas
Sir Thomas Bromley, a puisne justice of the King's bench
Sir Anthony Denny, one of the chief gentlemen of the King's privy chamber
Sir William Herbert, one of the chief gentlemen of the King's privy chamber
Sir Edward Wotton, Treasurer at Calais
Dr Nicholas Wotton, Dean of Canterbury and York

before 12 March 1547 and the council generally – under Northumberland's influence, of course – after 13 October 1549, and Somerset's letters-patent of the Protectorate. How such authority was to be exercised remained a purely political question, and one which posed problems for both Somerset and Northumberland, since, as former members of the Henrician council, they each of them understood the particular significance of that one procedure which made membership of Edward's board so distinctive a political calling – the constitutional act of swearing an oath of office.

An oath of membership had been the earliest and most distinctive feature of the medieval council's organisation, for the oath defined a councillor's status and made clear his duties;[6] but whereas the late-medieval oath did not fully define the *council*, in the sense that every man who served as a 'councillor' was necessarily sworn a 'councillor', the oath of a Tudor privy councillor did do so: only he who was sworn a privy councillor could so act in the King's name.[7] Those who took their oaths as privy councillors when that body was first organised under Henry VIII

had thus made a clear break with the late-medieval past. Although the Henrician oath has not survived, we know that by
October 1540 it must have been cast in a characteristic form, for
upon it Sir John Gage 'was then sworn to be one of the Pryvye
Counsaill'.[8] From the record of the Earl of Arundel's swearing-in
on 25 July 1546, we can describe the form of the ceremony itself.
The prospective member was first called to the station of one of
the King's most honourable privy councillors by the King personally in the presence of the King's secretary; the secretary then led
the new appointee from the royal presence into the council chamber and there declared to the Lord Chancellor and the others 'the
kinges Majestes pleasure in that behaulf', whereupon the Lord
Chancellor administered the oath of a privy councillor to the new
man who, after swearing upon a Bible to fulfil his pledge, was
with prescribed formality 'placed at the Counsaill Boorde accordingly'.[9]

Such at least was the procedure in the year before Edward's
accession, but as the new King's council existed only in the terms
of the dead King's will, the question immediately arose as to
whether the executors should first swear an oath 'to mayntaine
the saide laste wille' or swear an oath to their King, Edward VI.
Their decision at the meeting in the Tower on 31 January was
significant: they agreed *first* to Hertford's creation as Protector
and then resolved that 'we shuld forbeare the taking of our othes
to the perfourmance of the wille tille the next morowe, and then
. . . procede furste to the geving of our othes to the Kinges
Majestie, and then to swere to thobservacion of the wille as is
affore saide'.[10] Thus, although the Lord Chancellor received the
great seal from Edward's hands at that meeting, he did not then
proceed to swear in the privy council. It is this fact which makes
the council's 'agreement' of 31 January so interesting: in making
Hertford the King's and England's Protector that day, the council
did not risk violating an oath to Edward; rather, they were up-
holding the succession during his minority according to the understanding allowed them by Henry VIII in his will. Of course they
did finally swear an oath to Edward on 1 February, but they were
doing so still as ministers appointed by Henry VIII. And if there
were doubts about this, they were resolved by Somerset's patents
which prescribed once again that the King's leading men were to

be appointed and sworn the King's own privy councillors, presumably upon the very good assumption that it was better to act
in the name of the reigning King than to bear the imprimatur of
the dead.

This change, however, required that the Henrician oath be
modified in order that it relate to the conditions of rule under a
boy, for the Protector, and after him, the council, embodied the
powers of the Crown *de facto*. One such phrase in the Edwardian
oath certainly reflects this: the appointee swore fidelity to
Edward, his heirs, and successors, kings of England, according
to the 'limitacion' of the Henrician statute of 1536 which established 'his majestes succession in the crowne imperiall of this
realme'.[11] In general, those who took the oath swore[12] to execute
the trust which membership conveyed.

In normal times this trust emanated direct from the Crown;
the adult sovereign chose his men according to 'his Royall will
and pleasure', as Sir Julius Caesar noted,[13] but Edward did not
call, remove, or retain of his privy council whomever he pleased
whenever he so pleased. There is no evidence that Edward in any
way influenced the choice of his councillors either before or after
the *coup* of 1549. This is not to say, however, that Somerset and
Northumberland did not observe formalities; they probably
'sought' and as a matter of form 'received' the King's verbal
assent for promotions to the council. We have no proof of this in
Somerset's case; his patents empowered him officially to make
appointments independent of the Crown. On the other hand, we
know that when Warwick decided in 1549 to pack the council
with new members of reformed religious views, with Cranmer's
help he surrounded the King with supporters who thereafter 'convinced' Edward of the 'necessity' of appointing whomever he and
his 'great frendes' had advised him to.[14] Warwick apparently
thought it necessary to keep the boy's confidence in the matter of
increasing the membership of the council. But we hear nothing
of the King's interest in all of this: only twice during his reign did
he note the addition of a new man to his privy council, and both
times in the passive voice.[15]

If Edward's diary of state affairs makes but scant reference to
newly sworn members, the council's own papers certainly provide
a less than complete record of appointments to the board.

Nothing records the swearing-in of privy councillors under Somerset – with one exception (17 January 1549) we even lack evidence of attendances at meetings after 12 March 1547 – and for half of the men appointed after the *coup* we can only cite the occasion of a member's first known appearance in council (see Table 6, p. 54). A few membership lists have survived, and although these are undeniably valuable (especially for Somerset's administration), they raise as many questions as they answer. Some lack dates; most omit names; none reveals at what times the councillors listed first took their oath of office.

The real difficulty in fixing the board's exact membership lies not so much in the extant lists, however, as in the way in which such materials have been handled. In particular, two mistakes, the one mechanical, the other conceptual, have needlessly obscured the true picture of the council's size and composition. The first has to do with Edward VI's manuscript record of 'The names of the hole councel',[16] printed versions of which are regularly cited as evidence for the view that 'by 1553 the Privy Council numbered . . . forty and included lawyers and lesser administrators'.[17] Invariably, these reprints follow the text of Burnet's seventeenth-century edition (1679–1715),[18] and here is the source of the problem, for when Burnet transcribed the King's list, he assigned numbers to the names of nine men who were not then privy councillors, names which the King had actually penned without numbers under a separate heading in a specially drawn space as merely 'Those that be now callid into commission' to assist the thirty-one privy councillors whom the boy had carefully listed and numbered in another clearly marked section of the same page; these thirty-one men were the unmistakable and only members of the 'hole councel', as Edward's heading for that particular column so plainly indicates. By continuing the King's numbering to include the nine commissioners, however, Burnet created the impression that Northumberland had increased the membership of the 'hole councel' to forty with the addition of a group of lesser officials.[19] Moreover, the list had earlier been bound up in the volume containing the King's 'Chronicle', and as the list follows immediately the last entries of the 'Chronicle' for 28–30 November 1552, Burnet and others after him assumed that the council of forty which they thought the list defined represented the full membership from about December 1552 at the earliest. In fact the paper sets out Edward's privy council of thirty-one members at sometime between 3 and 15 March 1552, an observation based on the diplomatic of the document, the identity of one of the commissioners named, and other pieces of internal and external evidence.[20]

No less misleading than Burnet's transcription is the view of those who have assumed, as Pollard did, that 'the patent which gave Somerset the Protectorship also created a new Privy Council' of twenty-six men 'acting as one body' during the Protectorate,[21] an erroneous notion developed in consequence of repeated failures to read aright the precise terms of the Duke's commission.[22] It will be remembered that by the terms of Somerset's patent of 12 March 1547 Edward VI chose some twenty-six experienced royal servants to be 'our Counsaillours and of our Counsail', a group representing a combination of fourteen of the sixteen executors (Somerset had been elevated and Wriothesley was simply ignored) and twelve others who had been named in Henry's will as 'assistants' to the executors. Of these twenty-six

or of any others which our saide uncle shall hereafter at any tyme take and chose to be our Counsaillour or Counsaillours or of our Counsaille, he our saide uncle shall, may and have autorite by theis presentes, to chose, name, apoincte, use and sweare of Privey Counsaill and to be our Privey Counsaillour or Counsaillours suche and so many as he from tyme to tyme shall thincke convenient.[23]

The fact that Somerset's commission defined no one 'of Privey Counsaill' underscores the historical difference between the King's many and unorganised councillors, on the one hand, and the very select members of his most private council, on the other. Pollard was aware of this distinction, but in the context of the patent of 12 March he seems to have confused the twenty-six nominees as 'councillors' (which they were) with 'the Privy Council thus nominated'[24] (which they were not), for it was precisely this distinction that the patent made clear: Somerset had been granted explicit power to select 'such and so many' of the King's ordinary councillors as he should wish to be 'of Privey Counsaill'. That the twenty-six were not members of 'the Privy Council thus nominated' should have been clear from the fact that no one was to be sworn a privy councillor without also having been appointed a privy councillor by Somerset. The patent of 12 March thus abolished the privy council appointed in the will and in its place established not a new privy council, but merely a group of at least twenty-six councillors eligible for membership of whatever privy council Somerset should decide to call together. Somerset had confirmed himself in office and bound himself to confirm none of his former colleagues in theirs; he had simply spelled out the terms of membership to a board which would in future exist at his convenience.

The following discussion will attempt to identify only those men actually appointed to the King's council. The state of the evidence dictates that this be done by gathering together all records which preserve, in the signed and dated remains of the board's work, proof of an individual's activity as a councillor; by arranging these bits and pieces of evidence in chronological order, it should be possible to build up rosters of members' names for the period of the Protectorate.[25] After the *coup d'état*, the extant official sources allow us to describe Northumberland's appointments more directly. Finally, during each of the three periods when membership underwent dramatic changes – before 12 March 1547, under Somerset, and after his fall – an attempt will be made to describe, where possible, the circumstances of a councillor's appointment or the reason for his selection, and by comparing the background and experience of every councillor, to analyse the composition of the whole board throughout the reign.

From 28 January to 11 March 1547 the privy council consisted theoretically of the sixteen executors of Henry's will; in practice, however, three of these men performed no recorded duties as privy councillors in England. Dr Nicholas Wotton, Dean of Canterbury and York and resident ambassador at the French court at the time, played no part in domestic politics until his return to England over two-and-a-half years later; his brother, Sir Edward Wotton, Treasurer at Calais, remained absent from court (and country, presumably) until about February 1548;[26] Sir Thomas Bromley, a relatively obscure puisne justice of the King's bench, in fact never assumed the office granted him in Henry's will, an interesting failure explained in part, perhaps, by the reportedly marked confusion of his mind.[27] Or was it because he was simply a man of lesser ambitious and traditional catholic sympathies?[28] Whatever the reason, Bromley does not appear to have seized his opportunity for a high political career.

In the Tower on Wednesday, 2 February 1547, at their third official meeting together as the King's privy councillors, the remaining thirteen executors were joined by Sir Thomas Seymour, the Protector's brother. In his will, Henry had named Seymour tenth among twelve royal nominees who were to be 'of Counsail for the aiding and assisting' of the executors whenever the executors should call them so to council.[29] Thus, Seymour's mere presence at this meeting was not, in a strict sense, constitutionally improper; but his official designation by association as one of the executors (and, therefore, privy councillors), and his signature as a privy councillor in the register certainly appear irregular, unless of course, the other executors had recently created him a privy councillor. Had they done so?

We know that Henry had given 'full Powre and Authorite' to the 'most part' at the least (that is, nine) of the executors, when assembled together in council, to 'devise and ordeyn' whatever they thought 'meet, necessary or convenient' for the government of the realm during Edward's minority.[30] Citing this provision in the will as their authority, the executors had, only two days earlier, agreed officially to the election of Edward Seymour (then Earl of Hertford) as Protector.[31] Did the same power enable them to admit one of the twelve assistants 'of Counsail' (or any other) to membership of the privy council?

Although the will did not specifically prohibit an expansion of the membership of the ruling council, certain considerations must surely have weighed against such a move. First, numerous clauses in the will suggest that Henry saw no necessity to replace an executor in the event of death,[32] the implication being that fifteen (or fewer) councillors were fully capable of managing the affairs of government until Edward's eighteenth birthday (12 October 1555). The executors could also draw upon the aid of any of the twelve assistants 'of Counsail' whose 'Assent and Consent' were in fact required under certain circumstances.[33] Furthermore, the executors were well aware of the institutional and constitutional difference between the office of a privy councillor and that of 'the Counsail nat being executours'.[34] Indeed, the appointment of a new privy councillor should have been a difficult one to make, since to be a privy councillor then was by definition to be one of the sixteen executors of Henry's will and it was patently impossible for the executors of the royal will to add other executors to their number. The recent argument that 'the will's lack of provision for replenishing the council may simply be evidence . . . that this was a matter which the Council could deal with itself when the need arose, like any body of executors',[35] ignores the constitutional identity of the offices of privy councillor and executor. Nevertheless, the historical evidence in Thomas Seymour's case is plain enough: within five days of Henry's death Seymour had become the seventeenth privy councillor.[36] How?

TABLE 2   *Privy councillors, 28 January to 11 March 1547*

Edward Seymour, Duke of Somerset, Protector (by agreement) and
    High Treasurer of England (from 10 February)
Thomas Cranmer, Archbishop of Canterbury
Thomas Wriothesley, Earl of Southampton, Chancellor (to 6 March)
William Lord St John, Great Master, President, and Keeper of the
    great seal (from 7 March)
John Lord Russell, Privy Seal
John Dudley, Earl of Warwick, Great Chamberlain of England
Thomas Lord Seymour, High Admiral (from 17 February)
Cuthbert Tunstal, Bishop of Durham
Sir Anthony Browne, Master of the King's horse
Sir William Paget, Secretary
Sir Edward North
Sir Edward Montagu
Sir Thomas Bromley
Sir Anthony Denny
Sir William Herbert
Sir Edward Wotton
Dr Nicholas Wotton

New evidence[37] suggests a possible explanation, that Somerset (then the Earl of Hertford) was forced to create another seat at the board on 1 February as a compromise to his brother's own unexpected demand for the governorship of the King's person. As this evidence also throws new light on the source of the intrigues which eventually destroyed both the Protector and the Lord Admiral, Seymour's bid will be discussed at greater length in the context of the politics of the council.[38] Here it need only be noted that because the will had not named him an executor, Seymour's very real performance of the duties of that office illustrates one of the problems which Somerset's patents were to solve, namely, the ability of the Protector to choose the personnel of Edward's privy council.

By 2 February 1547 the number of active privy councillors thus stood at fourteen. On 6 March the council reduced this to thirteen by ordering the Earl of Southampton (Thomas Wriothesley) to confine himself to his house indefinitely for having improperly delegated his authority as Lord Chancellor.[39] The charge upon which Wriothesley surrendered both the great seal and his seat on the council proved in fact to be merely a technical justification for a more profound political consideration; Somerset forced Wriothesley out of office, not because the earl had remained a Henrician catholic or because the common lawyers may have opposed his practices,[40] but because Wriothesley had from the very beginning opposed Somerset's creation as Protector.[41]

In little more than a month, then, the executors had awarded Somerset 'the furste and chief place amonges us' as Protector, even though, as they admitted, Henry had appointed them 'to be executours with like and equal charge';[42] they had admitted Sir Thomas Seymour to membership or, at the very least, were allowing him to perform an executor's functions; they had deprived the Lord Chancellor of his office and place at the board.[43]

It is in the context of these developments that Wriothesley's opposition to Somerset appears to be all the more significant.[44] Wriothesley had questioned the authority for Somerset's office and exercise of power and in so doing had cast doubt upon the ability of the executors (through Somerset) to modify the terms of the will with respect to membership of the council. The statute of 1536 had given Henry VIII no authority to nominate a protector; unlike Wriothesley who, 'for avoiding of all questions and doubtes', had received the great seal anew from the hands of Edward VI, the privy councillors themselves had been granted no commission by the reigning King to undertake any action during his lifetime. By what authority, then, were the executors empowered to remove from membership of the privy council one so appointed by the will and one whose office by virtue of that appointment rested upon statute law?

Somerset attempted to circumvent this difficulty by securing, upon petition of the council, letters-patent warranted by the King and passed under the great seal on 12 March 1547. By this patent, as it has been seen, the King appointed Somerset Protector of the realm and governor of the royal person (thus confirming the executors' secret agreement of 31 January) and empowered him henceforth to control all admissions to the privy council. Whom did Somerset choose to fill the vacant seats at the board? The signatures in the register show that of the fourteen councillors[45] active before 12 March, he readmitted immediately to membership on 12 March at least six: Cranmer, St John, Russell, Warwick, Paget, and Browne. On the same day, he called to the board for the first time two former 'assistants', the Marquess of Northampton and Sir Thomas Cheyne.[46] In addition to these eight, two others, Sir Anthony Wingfield (an 'assistant') and Sir Edward North (an executor), signed the register during our first period. Somerset probably appointed Wingfield to office before the date on which he first signed the book (2 April 1547);[47] evidence of Wingfield's earlier service does not exist. North, however, had reappeared 'of privy council' by 18 March, together with the Bishop of Durham, Sir Anthony Denny, Sir William Herbert (all of them executors), and Sir William Petre ('assistant').[48]

Of greater interest is the date of the evidence for the appearance of the Earl of Arundel and Sir John Gage, two former privy councillors who, as traditionalists in religion, might have been expected to present some opposition to Somerset. A letter to the council in Ireland shows that both Arundel and Gage were members by 7 April,[49] but it seems that Gage, at least, had fallen under suspicion at the time of Wriothesley's attack upon Somerset, for the Protector had found it necessary to order Gage and Cheyne (also conservative in his religious views) and other unnamed former members of Henry's council who favoured 'the ancient religion' (including Arundel?) to confine themselves to their houses at precisely the time (7 March) when Somerset forced Wriothesley out of office.[50] Did Somerset fear that Southampton might rally 'catholic' opponents of the Protectorate? It would seem so; Wriothesley, deprived of the great seal on 5 March, was dropped from the King's list of twenty-six nominees six days later. On 7 March, then, the lesson for Arundel, Cheyne, and Gage must have been clear: as Lord Chamberlain, Treasurer, and Comptroller, respectively, each of them held claim to a seat on Somerset's reformed privy council, but, like the former Lord Chancellor, they would not be in a position to press their cases should the King find it necessary to appoint others to their household offices. Cheyne, once out of his house, came round quickly; he probably joined the faithful at the council table on 12 March. But Somerset may not have been persuaded of Gage's and Arundel's loyalties much before 7 April, as has been seen.

Following Sir Thomas Seymour's apparent admission to the privy council, it would seem likely that Somerset readmitted his brother to power soon after 12 March, for Seymour was now also Lord Seymour of Sudeley and Lord High Admiral of England, but precisely how soon after 12 March Somerset did so is uncertain; the earliest official evidence for Seymour's membership is his signature on a set of instructions that was sent to the Lord Deputy at Calais sometime in April.[51] Chief Justice Montagu's hand on a council warrant of 26 May fixes his membership of the new council from that same day at the latest.[52]

Two members remain: Richard Lord Rich and Sir Edward Wotton. Rich, an 'assistant' in the will, first appears as one 'of his hieghnes pryvey counsail presently attending on his most royal person' at Hampton Court on 25 September 1547.[53] The date and place identify him thus as one of those remaining in England to administer the realm in Somerset's absence during the campaign in Scotland; Somerset probably appointed him to the privy council for this very purpose. If so, Rich would certainly have been sworn in no later than Somerset's departure from London on 22 August. Whatever the case, no clear evidence exists for his membership from a date earlier than September 1547.[54] The date of Sir Edward Wotton's appointment is perhaps more obscure than that of any other councillor's; his signature on a council warrant addressed to the Treasurer and chamberlains of the exchequer puts him at Somerset Place 23 February 1548;[55] how much earlier than that his duties as treasurer at Calais may have permitted his return to court cannot be known. Although named an executor of Henry's will, he had never been a privy councillor under Henry and there is no evidence, contrary to the implication in the *Dictionary of National Biography*, that he had ever attended a council meeting in England before February 1548.[56]

By March 1548 Somerset had thus chosen twelve former executors and eight 'assistants' to constitute a privy council of twenty-one members including himself.[57] Both the size of this council and the evidence for each councillor's earliest known activity should correct all previous assumptions about the existence of a unified privy council of twenty-six members appointed by letters-patent on 12 March 1547 and 'acting as one body' from that date.

That such a unified group never existed is also proved by a rare, official reference of about July 1548 to the 'lordes and others of the privie counsell'.[58] This schedule shows that at some time following the death on 6 May 1548 of the King's old Master of the horse, Sir Anthony Browne, Somerset reformed his council of 12 March 1547 to early 1548 by dropping five members (Northampton, Tunstal, Gage, Edward Wotton, Montagu) and adding Sir Ralph Sadler, Master of the King's wardrobe, and Sir John Baker, Chancellor of the exchequer and Treasurer of the court of first fruits and tenths. Exactly when these two 'assistants' were sworn in is not known; this list represents the first evidence of their membership.[59]

Of the five members dropped from Somerset's first council, one can merely speculate about the reasons for the exclusion of the Chief Justice of the common pleas. On the one hand, the assertion that 'in the council he [had] acted with the party adverse to Somerset'[60] must remain a statement unsupported by fact; if true, it would appear that Somerset may have expelled Montagu. In any case, Montagu was a political light-weight; nothing in his experience, office, or authority compelled Somerset to retain him.

Now the *Dictionary of National Biography* states that *on becoming* Protector, Somerset expelled Sir John Gage from the privy council and from his office of Comptroller of the household. The patent of 12 March 1547, however, identifies him very clearly as Comptroller; he was also signing council warrants for payments as late as 26 May 1547.[61] But that is the last evidence we have for his membership before 6 October 1549,

TABLE 3   *Privy councillors, 12 March 1547 to May 1548*

Edward Seymour, Duke of Somerset, Protector and High Treasurer
Thomas Cranmer, Archbishop of Canterbury
Richard Lord Rich, Chancellor (from 23 October)
William Lord St John, Great Master and President
John Lord Russell, Privy Seal
William Parr, Marquess of Northampton
John Dudley, Earl of Warwick, Great Chamberlain
Henry Fitz Alan, Earl of Arundel, the King's Chamberlain
Thomas Lord Seymour, High Admiral
Cuthbert Tunstal, Bishop of Durham
Sir Thomas Cheyne, Treasurer of the King's household
Sir John Gage, Comptroller of the King's household (to 29 June
   1547)
Sir Anthony Browne, Master of the King's horse
Sir Anthony Wingfield, Vice-Chamberlain of the King's household
Sir William Paget, Secretary (to 29 June 1547); Comptroller (from
   (from 29 June)
Sir William Petre, Secretary
Sir Thomas Smith, Secretary (from 17 April 1548)
Sir Edward Montagu
Sir Edward North
Sir Anthony Denny
Sir William Herbert
Sir Edward Wotton

and it may be that Somerset was able effectively to 'expel' the
'zealous catholic' by giving the comptrollership to Paget on 29
June 1547.

We may reasonably asume that Sir Edward Wotton's office
(Treasurer at Calais) prevented an active membership for him.
There is nothing to suggest that Somerset dropped or expelled him
from the council after May 1548,[62] but there is also no evidence
that the government considered him to be of the privy council
again until January 1549. It is an interesting fact that although
Wotton was employed as a royal commissioner in England during
July 1548,[63] his name was not included on the list of privy councillors at the same time.

Tunstal's case is equally curious. Although Tunstal spent most
of his time dealing with ecclesiastical and governmental affairs in

his bishopric of Durham, he also attended the sessions of Parliament in London during November–December 1547 and November 1548 to March 1549; his biographer thinks it 'highly improbable' that Tunstal did not also attend at least a few council meetings during those periods of Parliamentary activity.[64] The evidence suggests, however, that he could not have attended any meetings after December 1547 for the apparent reason that Somerset no longer considered him to be 'of privy council'. Indeed, had Tunstal been a privy councillor in 1548, his name would have appeared on the government's list of councillors; had he been a privy councillor while in London on 17 January 1549, the clerk's list of the 'holl Council' of that day would have recorded his membership. In short, there is no documentary evidence for Tunstal's membership from 23 December 1547, when he and six other lords of the council signed the King's general pardon,[65] until 20 November 1549 when his name appears once again on an official list of the full membership.[66] Why was Tunstal not a member of Somerset's council after December 1547? No clear answer exists, but it is evident that the Bishop of Durham opposed Somerset's Scottish and religious policies[67] and this may well explain why the Protector saw no reason to continue him in office.

Finally, the Marquess of Northampton: when they summoned Northampton before them on 28 January 1548, the council ordered him to live apart from his second, secretly married wife, but the fact that he had not yet divorced his first wife probably accounts for his almost certain suspension from membership that day, for the Marquess's continued bigamy, as the council pointed out to him, was creating manifold disorder and inconvenience in the realm.[68] These changes and the death of Sir Anthony Browne are reflected in the resulting total of seventeen members on the list of about July 1548. To these seventeen names must be added another, that of Sir Thomas Smith. Smith had become a privy councillor on 17 April 1548 by virtue of his appointment then as one of the King's two principal secretaries of state.[69] His embassy to the Low Countries during the summer of 1548 probably accounts for the absence of his name from the list.[70]

For this second period of the Protectorate, then, we can identify a privy council of eighteen members including Somerset. That these eighteen and only these eighteen did constitute fully and formally the only true privy council of the time is clearly shown by the separately designated names included in the dossier of July 1548, those of 'The privie chamber and certen of the counsell at large' and 'The lordes'. The Marquess of Northampton and the Earl of Southampton, for example, appear with the fifteen 'lordes'; Sir Richard Southwell and Sir Edmund Peckham, both named in the two patents (12 March and 24 December 1547) and both of them 'assistants' to the former executors are plainly not privy councillors as some have assumed, but merely 'certen of the counsell at large' with twenty-six others.[71]

TABLE 4 *Privy councillors, June to December 1548*

Edward Seymour, Duke of Somerset, Protector and High Treasurer
Thomas Cranmer, Archbishop of Canterbury
Richard Lord Rich, Chancellor
William Lord St John, Great Master and President
John Lord Russell, Privy Seal
John Dudley, Earl of Warwick, Great Chamberlain
Henry Fitz Alan, Earl of Arundel, the King's Chamberlain
Thomas Lord Seymour, High Admiral
Sir Thomas Cheyne, Treasurer
Sir William Paget, Comptroller
Sir Anthony Wingfield, Vice-Chamberlain
Sir William Petre, Secretary
Sir Thomas Smith, Secretary
Sir Anthony Denny
Sir William Herbert
Sir Edward North
Sir John Baker, Chancellor of the exchequer
Sir Ralph Sadler, Master of the King's wardrobe

About the beginning of January 1549, or perhaps a little earlier, Somerset admitted to membership Francis Talbot, fifth Earl of Shrewsbury, and readmitted the Earl of Southampton; both of them signed a privy council letter dated 6 January 1549 at Somerset Place,[72] the earliest documentary proof of their term of service on Somerset's reformed board (that is, the privy council after 12 March 1547). Shrewsbury's rise probably came in reward for his generalship at Haddington – an army of 15,000 under his command had relieved the garrison there in August 1548 – but Wriothesley's reappearance has never really been explained. It will be noticed, however, that the moment of his return corresponds exactly with the council's earliest moves against the Lord Admiral. Wriothesley certainly took a leading part in the investigation of Seymour's alleged conspiracy; perhaps he welcomed this as an opportunity to prove his own political acceptability. Somerset may not have been reluctant to employ him thus, for by doing so the duke was able to shift the onus of the investigation to a former opponent. Perhaps Southampton's reappointment is, therefore, really to be understood in the context of Seymour's fall: in the person of Wriothesley (and Shrewsbury too) Somerset possessed an instrument for the execution of what Paget knowingly termed 'your proceadings with thadmirall',[73] the awkward but necessary business of destroying a brother's influence.

A clerk's list of twenty members of the 'hole Counsail' who met on 17 January 1549 to order the arrest of Seymour[74] reflects the fact that Shrewsbury and Southampton had recently joined the board. The list also shows that Somerset had recalled Chief Justice Montagu and Sir Edward Wotton for this extraordinary meeting; the two of them continued to perform duties as privy councillors throughout the months preceding Somerset's downfall.[75] As a roster of members for the last months of Somerset's administration (January to 5 October 1549), however, this list must be amended to include Sir William Herbert, who was unquestionably a privy councillor, but whose name the clerk seems inadvertently to have omitted; the Marquess of Northampton, whose divorce from his first wife permitted him at last to rejoin his former colleagues at Westminster (probably before 24 July 1549, the date of the earliest extant evidence of his recall);[76] and Thomas Lord Wentworth, a military commander, courtier, and cousin of the King. Traditionally, it has been assumed that Wentworth joined the privy council at the height of the *coup*, the earliest extant evidence of his membership being taken to be the record of his attendance at that extraordinary meeting at the Sheriff of London's house on 9 October 1549.[77] But it is clear that Somerset had appointed Wentworth a privy councillor by 7 August 1549,[78] a fact which has gone unnoticed. The exact date and circumstances of the appointment remain a mystery, however. Thus, with the removal of the Lord Admiral on 17 January, the privy council numbered twenty-one members, rising to twenty-two upon the unknown date of Northampton's resumption of office, and twenty-three upon Wentworth's admission (see Table 5).

TABLE 5 *Privy councillors, January to 5 October 1549*

Edward Seymour, Duke of Somerset, Protector and High Treasurer
Thomas Cranmer, Archbishop of Canterbury
Richard Lord Rich, Chancellor
William Lord St John, Great Master and President
John Lord Russell, Privy Seal
William Parr, Marquess of Northampton
John Dudley, Earl of Warwick, Great Chamberlain
Henry Fitz Alan, Earl of Arundel, the King's Chamberlain
Francis Talbot, Earl of Shrewsbury
Thomas Wriothesley, Earl of Southampton
Thomas Lord Seymour, High Admiral (to 18 January)
Thomas Lord Wentworth
Sir Thomas Cheyne, Treasurer
Sir William Paget, Comptroller
Sir Anthony Wingfield, Vice-Chamberlain
Sir William Petre, Secretary
Sir Thomas Smith, Secretary
Sir Anthony Denny
Sir William Herbert
Sir Ralph Sadler
Sir John Baker
Sir Edward Montagu
Sir Edward North
Sir Edward Wotton

Twenty-seven men who served as privy councillors from 28 January 1547 to 5 October 1549 have been identified: fourteen of the sixteen executors, ten of the twelve 'assistants', and three others (Smith, Shrewsbury, and Wentworth). For the four subperiods described above, we get recognisable privy councils of thirteen to fourteen, twenty-one, eighteen, and twenty-three respectively, or more broadly, a privy council of fourteen members enforcing Henry's will (28 January to 11 March 1547) and a privy council of an average formal size of twenty-one members (including Somerset) operating under the terms of the letters-patent of the Protectorate (12 March 1547 to 5 October 1549). Were these numbers exceptional by earlier Tudor standards? Quite clearly, they were not: Henry VIII's privy council consisted of nineteen members on 10 August 1540, the date of the earliest complete official roster of Tudor privy councillors;[79] six years later the number stood at twenty-one.[80] Somerset's full council was thus not significantly larger than Henry VIII's; indeed, for a time it was actually smaller, considering the fact that membership from about May to December 1548 numbered only eighteen. We can therefore abandon the notion that 'when royal control relaxed after Henry VIII's death numbers [of privy councillors] immediately increased'.[81]

Knowledge of the true membership of Somerset's privy council allows us also to revise Pollard's assertion that 'as a matter of fact Somerset made practically no change in the composition of the Council' and that 'a comparison of the list of councillors at the granting of his patent [12 March 1547] with the number existing at his fall reveals only three additions', Southampton, Shrewsbury, and Smith, and that these additions were 'no doubt designed to supply the places of the three who had meanwhile deceased', Browne, Seymour, and Denny.[82] Now it is true that Somerset added Smith, Wriothesley, and Shrewsbury, but not for the reason claimed. Smith became a member (17 April 1548) before Browne's death (6 May 1548) in order to fill the vacancy in the secretarial office created by Paget's assumption (29 June 1547) of Gage's office; whatever were Somerset's reasons for admitting Southampton and Shrewsbury, he could not have chosen them (by early January 1549) as replacements for dead councillors, as their appointments came at least two-and-a-half months before Seymour's demise (20 March 1549) and eight months before Denny's death (10 September 1549). Secondly, it has already been seen that the council numbered only twenty at most in the weeks following the granting of the patent (Sir Edward Wotton having not yet been appointed) and only twenty-two on the eve of the *coup* (Denny having died), not twenty-seven at both times as Pollard assumed, so that the true comparison is between the twenty actual members of 1547 and the twenty-two in October 1549. Such a comparison reveals not only the addition of Smith and the two earls, but also that of Baker, Sadler, Wotton, and Wentworth. When one takes into account the exclusion of Gage and Tunstal and the deaths of Seymour, Browne, and Denny, the addition of these seven councillors represents, therefore, a turn-over of almost one-third of the membership during Somerset's administration.[83]

Effectively, a date of 5 October 1549 marked the end of Somerset's power, since from that day forward the responsibility for the addition of new members lay with those conspiring against the duke. Forty-three individuals served as privy councillors under Edward VI after that date; nineteen made their first appearance in the period from the *coup d'état* to the King's death (see Table 6). On the eve of Somerset's fall the council numbered twenty-two (Sir Anthony Denny having died on 10 September). While the lords in London were plotting to overthrow the Protector they summoned to office Dr Nicholas Wotton, Sir Richard Southwell, and Sir Edmund Peckham. On 7 October they rallied Sir John Gage, whom Somerset had suspended after June 1547. As an executor of Henry's will, Wotton certainly held a legitimate claim to membership, but throughout the Protectorate, Somerset had employed him as ambassador at the French court; Southwell and Peckham remained the only original 'assistants' whom Somerset had not appointed to the council; Gage, of course, had been a member.

The emergence of Southwell and Peckham as the King's privy councillors in London raises a question of exceptional interest: who had appointed them and by what authority? Only the Protector acting in the King's name should have been able to admit new councillors to the board; King and Protector lay miles away at Windsor Castle. This fact and another consideration would seem to argue against our accepting the former 'assistants' as privy councillors at this time: there exists no record in the council book of their having been sworn to membership and even if such an entry did exist, we should probably have to accept it as merely a later justification for their attendance at those extraordinary meetings.[85]

On the other hand, the members of the London faction stated publicly and in an ostensibly official manner the fact of their acceptance of Peckham and Southwell as colleagues of the council:

TABLE 6   *Privy councillors whose first appearances date to the period 6 October 1549 to 6 July 1553*

	First recorded appearance
Dr Nicholas Wotton	6 October 1549*
Sir Richard Southwell	6 October 1549*
Sir Edmund Peckham	6 October 1549*
Thomas Goodrich, Bishop of Ely	6 November 1549*
Henry Grey, Marquess of Dorset, Duke of Suffolk	28 November 1549*
Walter Devereux, Lord Ferrers, Viscount Hereford[a]	16 January 1550
Sir Thomas Darcy, Lord Darcy	16 January 1550*
Sir John Mason	19 April 1550
Edward Lord Clinton	4 May 1550
George Brooke, Lord Cobham	23 May 1550
Francis Hastings, Earl of Huntingdon	4 September 1550
Sir William Cecil	5 September 1550
Henry Neville, Earl of Westmorland	26 February 1551*
Sir John Gates[b]	10 April 1551*
Edward Stanley, Earl of Derby[c]	9 August 1551
Sir Philip Hoby	16 August 1551*
Sir Robert Bowes	25 September 1551
Sir Richard Cotton	11 May 1552
Sir John Cheke	2 June 1553

* Absence of any record of swearing-in.
[a] Officially sworn 26 January 1550.
[b] Appointed Vice-Chamberlain 8 April 1551 (*Chronicle*, 58).
[c] Specially sworn only for the meeting of 9 August 1551.

on 8 and 10 October the London conspirators published two proclamations, both of which give the names of the 'Lordes and others of his maiesties privey counseill' who had 'subscribed' the contents of the documents; the proclamation of the eighth includes Southwell's name,[86] and that of the tenth, the names of Southwell and Peckham.[87] Both proclamations were 'published under his maiesties seale'[88] and proclaimed in the traditional way throughout London 'and as fast at it myght be thorrow alle Ynglond'.[89] Of course these were council, and not royal, decrees, but the leaders of the London group (who were not, it will be remembered, in possession of the King's person) clearly believed themselves to possess authority enough to require compliance 'in his highnes name and by his graces auctoritie'.[90] On 8 and 10 October the lords at London were thus presenting Somerset with an interpretation of their power equal to his own: the presence of Southwell and Peckham as publicly proclaimed members of the council meant that the lords had determined that they also possessed authority to appoint King Edward's privy councillors. Since by the terms of the second patent of the Protectorship (24 December 1547) Somerset alone possessed that power, these 'appointments' by the London council would appear to be invalid. On 10 October, however, the question was not the legality of the London councillors' moves, but whether in the crisis Somerset would be able to demonstrate that possession of Edward's person could prove more important than the council's control of London and the armed forces; in the event, Somerset fell, and any question of the validity of those appointments became academic.

Upon the abolition of the Protectorate (13 October), responsibility for the government of the realm lay with the original executors of Henry VIII's will; there seems to have been no question that they understood their powers to include that of creating new councillors. Indeed, after 13 October 1549, the Earl of Warwick and his supporters managed to appoint fifteen new privy councillors.[91] From that date they also expelled eight others, including four of Henry's executors (Somerset, Southampton, Tunstal, Paget). These developments and in particular the extraordinary appointments of 6–9 October 1549 are to be explained of course by the council's sudden political realignment, a subject treated more fully below; for the moment it is enough to note that Warwick's decision to side with the left-wing reformers produced, over the next few months, a dramatic turn-over in personnel. In the period before Dudley allowed Somerset to rejoin the council, the controlling clique of lords admitted four new members who held reformed religious views: Thomas Goodrich, Bishop of Ely; Henry Grey, Marquess of Dorset; Walter Devereux, Lord Ferrers, Viscount Hereford from 2 February 1550; and Sir Thomas Darcy.[92]

Although the Bishop of Ely first attended a privy council meeting on 6 November 1549, there is no official evidence of his having been sworn a member.[93] His name does not appear on an official list of the whole council dated 14–20 November 1549, though it is likely that the omission was deliberate, given the nature of the document (a special commission for the signing of council warrants as from 6 October).[94] No mention was ever made of Dorset's swearing-in; his career as a councillor begins officially with his attendance at a meeting on 28 November 1549. Both of the new men were brought into the council precisely for the strength their numbers would bring 'to encounter' the weight of the two recent catholic appointees, Peckham and Southwell, whose addition, together with Smith's and Somerset's removal shifted the numerical balance toward the conservatives.[95] Like Goodrich and Dorset, Lord Ferrers and Darcy rose to prominence in the midst of that 'unrecorded struggle' between Southampton and Warwick for control of the council and the King's government. Unlike the bishop and marquess, however, the appointment of the baron and knight came as a consequence and not in anticipation of Warwick's victory; their sudden appearance on 16 January 1550 (at a meeting for which no place was recorded) confirmed the superior strength of the reformist faction. Warwick's success in securing seats for Goodrich and Dorset during November 1549 illustrated the method of appointment which presumably he followed thereafter, a procedure resting apparently upon his ability to 'persuade' the King of the need to elevate men of his choice. Both the procedure and an explanation of the timing and circumstances of his selection of Goodrich and Dorset are set out explicitly in a contemporary account of the bloodless *coup* by which Warwick purged the council of his catholic opponents. This story is narrated below.[96] No such documentary evidence exists for Ferrers or Darcy (or any other councillor), but the immediacy of the November creations invites comment about the January appointments. It seems likely, for example, that Ferrers, whose first wife, Mary, was Dorset's aunt, simply brought a titled, aged gravity to Warwick's cause: his was the bearing of the noble Henrician courtier-soldier, experienced alike in the King's affairs in Wales (as a member of the council there) and the King's wars in France (with Russell in 1544).[97] His presence in London for the Parliamentary session of 1549–50 suggests his contact with other privy councillors in the House of Lords and may thus explain his informal presence in council ten days before his official swearing-in, since council meetings at this time were occasionally held 'in the Withdrawing Chamber next to the Parliament Chamber in thold Pallays' of Westminster.[98] One assumes that in matters of policy touching the Church, Ferrers, like Darcy, spoke with the voice of one wholly sympathetic to reform. Though he played almost no subsequent part in council affairs,[99] his admission to membership in the context of the events of October 1549 to February 1550 was thus vital to the history of the Reformation in England.

Sir Thomas Darcy's admission to the council probably came in reward for his services on Warwick's behalf in the desperate game of manoeuvre waged by both sides, conservative and reformed, for supreme influence at court. Although outnumbered, Warwick held from the start a significant advantage in this contest for the powers of the Crown, for in October he had been able to place next to the King several trusted adherents.[100] These 'great frendes' almost certainly included Darcy, one of the four new 'principal gentlemen' of the privy chamber who replaced Somerset's men on 15 October 1549. Darcy was to receive £100 per year 'in consideracion of the singular care and travayle that [he] shuld have about his Majestes person'.[101] As an experienced soldier and former gentlemen of Henry VIII's privy chamber,[102] he should have found this responsibility for Edward's security familiar enough; part of his 'travayle' may also have been blatantly political, for it seems unlikely that without friends such as Darcy, Warwick could so easily have organised an effective party in opposition to the conservatives within the very precincts of the royal palace. Ultimately a council order evicting the conservative leaders from court could be executed only because Warwick's men were able to enforce it; surely it was not a coincidence that Darcy was made Vice-Chamberlain of the King's household and captain of the guard on the same day (2 February 1550) that the order was promulgated. By this time Darcy was already a privy councillor. A reasonable assumption, therefore, would be that Darcy's presumed commitment to Dudley's faction had produced the actions expected of him earlier than 16 January 1550. If the additional voices of Goodrich and Dorset had countered the conservatives' policies in council, it may be no less true that the presence of Darcy (and others like him) in the King's chamber had successfully blocked the conservatives' intrigues there during the critical month of November 1549. In the absence of hard evidence this must remain a speculative point; whatever the nature of Darcy's work, it was sufficient to earn for him a place in the counsels of the new regime.

During the period under consideration (13 October 1549 to 2 February 1550) the ruling faction proceeded to intimidate, expel, or suspend from membership four conservatives in religion. The first to go was Sir Edmund Peckham, Treasurer of all the mints. Peckham's tenure as a privy councillor is recorded in his attendance at five meetings of the London council before Somerset's surrender (6, 7, 8, 9, 10 October 1549) and two assemblies at Windsor Castle afterwards (13 and 14 October),[103] and in his subscription to the London council's proclamation of 10 October[104] and a royal proclamation of 30 October 1549.[105] There is no evidence whatsoever for his membership before 6 October 1549; indeed, there is clear proof that he was not a privy councillor before the *coup*.[106] At any rate, as a Henrician catholic, his brief appearance in the circumstances of the *coup* is doubtless explained by his close friendship with his kinsman, the Earl of Southampton, whose executor Peckham became;[107] the manner of his disappearance from the council after 30 October 1549 remains a political mystery.

Sir Richard Southwell's brief career as an Edwardian privy councillor is documented in his attendance at fourteen meetings from 6 October to 29 December 1549;[108] his subscription to the proclamations of 8, 10, and 30 October;[109] and, most importantly, the appearance of his name on the official list of members dated 14–20 November 1549. The wording of the commission of which the list is a part makes it clear that the government regarded Southwell's official membership as having dated from 6 October 1549.[110] At sometime in January 1550, the council ordered Southwell's arrest and imprisonment in the Tower on a charge of having written, as King Edward reported, 'certain bills of sedition'.[111] For this Southwell was fined £500, which bought him, in effect, his pardon; thereafter he played no part in politics. His membership was thus terminated after three months in office.[112]

On or before 14 January 1550, in response to a revealed plot for Warwick's murder, the privy council banned from the court the earls of Arundel and Southampton, ordering them to confine themselves to their houses. For Wriothesley, the order spelled the effective end of his career as a privy councillor. He had in fact ceased to attend meetings after 22 October 1549; ill and sensing defeat, he was able to withdraw in January just before the order to do so reached him. On 2 February the council formally revoked his membership; he died six months later (30 July) at 'Lincolnes place', his residence in Holborn.[113]

Arundel attended meetings through 14 January, but by the eighteenth he had left the court. He too was dismissed from the board on 2 February, and on the twenty-first, for various unstated 'offences', was deprived of his household office as the King's Chamberlain.[114] The King, whose *Chronicle* at this time records information selected for him by the council, dutifully noted that Arundel's 'crimes of suspicion' constituted 'the plucking down of bolts and locks at Westminster, giving of my stuff away, etc.'[115] As the Imperial ambassador repeated a similar version of the story,[116] the council clearly intended that the alleged misconduct explain Arundel's sudden confinement and dismissal. For his complicity in the still-born conspiracy against Warwick, Arundel lay under a potentially graver threat, but as the evidence against him on that count was perhaps open to contradiction, the council offered him the choice of a trial or fine for his unnamed 'offences'. Arundel wisely chose the fine, which the council set at £12,000, a sum perhaps amply projecting the magnitude of the danger which Warwick saw in Arundel's recent activities. Having rendered his opponent powerless at court, Warwick subsequently remitted most of the fine,[117] though not without attaching a conditional test of loyalty: on 8 July 1550 the council instructed Arundel to repair to Sussex and remain in readiness there to serve the King in event of disorder. Arundel replied on the thirteenth that he had 'thought himself restored to the Kinges Majesties favour and to the Counsailes both, which he had derely bought . . . wherfore it seemed straunge unto him nowe to be commaunded into Sussex', but threatened with a trial ('his cace being so apparaunt as it was', in the council's view), he yielded and on 15 July agreed to depart for Sussex.[118]

Arundel attended no recorded meetings of the council thereafter, except for the session of 9 August 1551 for which he was
specially sworn acording to a particular formula.[119] On 8 November 1551, however, he was committed to the Tower for having
been implicated with Somerset in a second plot to kill Northumberland. Sir Thomas Palmer later confessed that this alleged conspiracy was a complete fabrication inspired, if not actually
devised, by Northumberland himself.[120] Even so, Arundel admitted in the Tower that he and Somerset had indeed conferred together (twice – at Somerset Place and Syon House) about
the 'state'; they did not like the order of things and on one occasion actually considered the possibility of 'apprehending' Northumberland and Northampton in the council. No bodily harm was
intended: they meant merely to call the lords to 'answer' for their
conduct of the government and to move them to 'reform' their
actions.[121] As a condition for pardon for this kind of talk, Arundel
'confessed' to the wilder charges, was fined again, and finally
released on 3 December 1552.[122] Scheyfve thought that Northumberland had readmitted Arundel to the council by 21 February
1553,[123] but there is no evidence for this. On the other hand,
Arundel signed at least one privy council letter during the week
before Edward VI's death;[124] perhaps the King's rapidly deterio-
rating health had prompted Northumberland's conciliation of this
great nobleman and Lord Chamberlain to two Tudor Kings.[125]
Whether the duke had modified the formula of 9 August 1551
and admitted Arundel to full membership before 1 July 1553 is
not known.

Taking into account the dismissals of Peckham, Southwell,
Arundel, and Southampton, the arrest of Somerset and Smith at
the height of the *coup*,[126] the recall of Tunstal and Gage,[127] Dr
Wotton's appearance,[128] and the addition of Goodrich, Dorset,
Ferrers, and Darcy, we can identify a privy council of twenty-five
members by the end of February 1550. Officially, Sir Thomas
Bromley was also a member. The formal list of 14–20 November
1549 shows this, and all later lists confirm it, but in fact Bromley
never served King Edward as a privy councillor. How should we
account for his name on all of these lists? It may be that the
government wished to avoid repudiating one of Henry's VIII's
executors without good reason; perhaps Warwick felt that the

formal retention of an executor who was also a legal officer lent greater credibility to his cause. Whatever the case, Bromley's tenure appears to have been purely nominal. His name included, however, the full council thus stood officially at twenty-six members.

It is perhaps the measure of Warwick's power after the purges of 1549–50 that he could both reinstate the Duke of Somerset (10 April 1550) and continue to add his own adherents at will to a council now exceeding thirty members. In fact, as Table 6 shows, by the time of Somerset's second and final fall, Warwick had admitted ten more men to membership, or rather nine permanent members, as the Earl of Derby was admitted to but one meeting (9 August 1551) under a special oath.[129]

The first of the new appointees was Sir John Mason, whose swearing-in (19 April 1550) followed by one day his nomination as ambassador to the French court. The appointment to the council thus added official weight to a diplomatic mission whose chief purpose was to turn to the King's advantage the newly won amity with France. Mason's earlier commission to negotiate that accord (24 March 1550) clearly recommended him, as did his experience (since 1542) as the King's secretary for the French tongue. Politically, Mason's sympathies at home lay with *politiques* like Paget whose protégé he was. Mason stood 'on terms of most intimate friendship' with Paget,[130] and if this helps to explain his advancement to the board, it may additionally suggest a heretofore unnoticed attempt by Paget to moderate the effects of Warwick's packing. What better opportunity to recruit a political centrist than under cover of diplomatic necessity? In fact, Mason's career in council following his return to England (July 1551) appears to have been that of one who sought reward for his co-operation with Northumberland.[131]

Promises of future reward were officially recorded for Edward Lord Clinton upon his appointment (4 May 1550). He became a privy councillor by virtue of his having been made Lord High Admiral, the post which Warwick personally relinquished to him in thanks for the diplomatic surrender of Boulogne (25 April 1550).[132] Clinton's rise to the King's council was a natural one not only because it solved his official unemployment (he had been chief captain of Boulogne since 1548), but also because Warwick's control of the King's ships was thus carried forward by a trusted subordinate and comrade-in-arms (Clinton had served under Dudley at sea in 1544 and 1546).[133] The Imperial ambassador may have exaggerated only a little the claim that Lord Clinton acted as Warwick's 'instrument' for the execution of naval policy, even perhaps to the point of turning piracy to their mutual profit.[134] In politics, the High Admiral held Northumberland's complete trust: on 3 July 1553, when Dudley prepared himself for his last and greatest crisis, he awarded Clinton command of the Tower.[135]

A successful record of military service probably also explains the advancement of George Brooke, ninth Lord Cobham, a former lieutenant-general under Hertford (1546) and, at the time of his appointment (23 May 1550), Lord Deputy at Calais.[136] For Warwick's new French-leaning foreign policy, Cobham's tenure abroad perhaps matched in importance his noble bearing as an old Henrician courtier; on more than one occasion he would act ceremonially as a special envoy to the French.[137] In council he quickly became a trusted member of Dudley's inner ring about the King, regularly signing the most routine of the council warrants[138] as well as the most confidential.[139] If a single reason is to be sought for Cobham's elevation it surely must be that his experience as both captain and administrator marked him as potentially useful for the maintenance of Warwick's power. Like Clinton, Cobham was shortly to be given command of fifty of the council's new horse.[140] Northumberland had found a diplomat and swordsman.

The circumstances of the appointment (4 September 1550) of Francis Hastings, second Earl of Huntingdon, remain less clear. The addition of yet another courtier and aristocratic lieutenant-general (at Boulogne) may have been intended to impress the court of Henry II. If the French respected nobility, they were also to see that the earl's duties as a councillor reflected the government's very real concern for domestic security, for Huntingdon subsequently captained one hundred of the privy council's mounted guard and served as lord lieutenant in Leicestershire and Rutland. Rarely present at court or in council, the Earl of Huntingdon nevertheless represented Northumberland's interests: he had supported the *coup* against Somerset and was later (21

May 1553) to marry his heir to Northumberland's daughter, Katherine.[141]

Sir William Cecil became the junior secretary of state and thus a privy councillor on 5 September 1550. His connections at court, his evident political shrewdness, his familiarity with the administration of council business, all of these made the Protector's able former servant an obvious replacement for Dr Nicholas Wotton. Wotton remained a privy councillor, but his service as one of the two principal secretaries had probably been considered as temporary anyway, since his assumption of the office upon the deposition of Sir Thomas Smith had precluded his expected dispatch as English ambassador to the Emperor. Upon Cecil's advancement, Wotton prepared once more to be posted to the court of Charles V.[142]

The addition of Henry Neville, fifth Earl of Westmorland, further increased the council's group of aristocratic courtier-soldiers. His sudden appearance (26 February 1551) at the age of twenty-seven also marked the official zenith of a most unusual career. Westmorland's fame rested upon dice: it seems that he could neither resist a game nor wager with success. By 1546 his daily losses at 'Domyngoes' in London had plunged him so deeply into debt that only God's holy angels, so he believed, could save him from certain ruin. This was why, as he later explained under arrest, he had commissioned 'a cunning man' to contract their part-time help to fashion for him a lucky ring which would 'ensure his winning'. (The metalwork went slowly, he was told, as angels could be spared for such labour only before matins and after evensong.) Ring in hand, he subsequently lost all in his possession. (His debts to the King alone totalled £437.) Desperation seems then to have unhinged him: while playing tennis at Westminster one day, he concluded (again with his persuasive friend) that only the murder of his father and wife would completely satisfy his creditors. This insane 'unnatural enterprise' was never executed, but word of it cost him six months in the Fleet (October 1546 to March 1547).[143]

Why was the Earl of Westmorland appointed one of Edward's privy councillors? The question may be important for what it reveals of the Earl of Warwick's motives in choosing men of so curious a stamp, for circumstantial evidence allows the speculation

that Neville was meant to be a replacement for Cuthbert
Tunstal, the deposed Bishop of Durham. Until April 1550 Warwick had shown Tunstal marked political favour,[144] but, as will
be seen, the bishop's refusal to bend to the council's new directives
in religion produced his arrest during August of 1550. Tunstal's
refusal coincided with – Dudley may have believed it actually fed
– a new fear, that of a catholic uprising in the North; Dudley
apparently connected this spectre of northern unrest with rumours
of popular support for a revived protectorate under Somerset,
but the government's control of the North was never so certain
that it could expect the power and authority of the council there
to be sufficient for the prevention of even a moderately well-
organised conspiracy. Tunstal's downfall had removed from the
council in the North the presence of one of the King's privy
councillors; Neville was already a member of the northern body
(he had been since May 1549), and it can be believed that this
experience and in particular his active duty against the Scots (1545
and 1548), as well as his brief service under Dudley in France
(1546), had won for him recognition enough to be considered
as an agent for the execution of Warwick's military policy in the
North. To some, therefore, including Scheyfve, it may have come
as no surprise that not only was Westmorland made a privy councillor, he was also immediately dispatched northwards in the company of the Marquess of Dorset with (apparently) secret instructions
to 'keep an eye on' the greatest of the potential leaders of a
northern 'catholic' reaction, the earls of Derby and Shrewsbury.[145]

Politically, Westmorland seems in any case destined to have
been advanced in Northumberland's scheme of things. The earl's
landed position was strengthened upon Somerset's attainder and
several of his debts to Edward VI were forgiven at the time he
was appointed lord lieutenant of the bishopric of Durham.[146]
Neville's local standing had thus been enhanced by the King's
patronage; the council had made resident one of its own members on the northern flank against Scotland. (The next year Westmorland became chief commissioner to treat with the French for
the division of the 'debatable' land there.) The Bishop of Durham
meanwhile lay in the Tower upon Northumberland's suspicion
that he had in some way been connected with northern sympathy
for Somerset (or at least had had knowledge that the North would

support a counter-*coup*); Northumberland was making no secret of the fact that he coveted the palatine jurisdiction of Durham for himself.[147] The government's preoccupation with security in the North seems thus to have reinforced Northumberland's peculiar sense of revenge: Dudley's reply to Tunstal's 'disloyalty' was to deprive the bishop of his offices and powers and raise up in his place as privy councillor the young Earl of Westmorland, a man whose character and career presented a pointed, almost theatrical contrast to that of the imprisoned humanist, scholar, statesman, and cleric.

The first recorded appearance of Sir John Gates at a meeting (10 April 1551) marks a key date in what Pollard might have called the council's 'secret history', for there is now no doubt that Northumberland's control of the King's opinions proceeded in part from information provided daily by Gates.[148] No record of his swearing-in exists, but as the King noted Gates's appointment as Vice-Chamberlain of the royal household on 8 April,[149] we may accept that as the probable official date of his admission to membership, since the Vice-Chamberlain was traditionally a privy councillor *ex officio*. (The vice-chamberlainship had fallen vacant upon Lord Darcy's promotion to the chamberlainship on 5 April.) The recent, disapproving judgement that as a councillor Gates was ruthless, untruthful, and therefore feared,[150] if true, may of course merely describe his mature political virtues. On the other hand, Gates's treason of 1553 cannot be excused; his execution under Mary simply confirmed how foolish he was in thinking that Northumberland's wild last scheme would succeed. In retrospect, the most remarkable thing about Gates down to 1551 is how really representative he was of his class. As the eldest son of an Essex gentleman, he had won royal favour as a J.P., King's commissioner, and gentleman of the privy chamber. Fifteen years of faithful service to the Crown had earned for him some very handsome rewards, especially under Henry VIII, and as Sheriff of Essex in 1550 he had signalled his loyalty to the new regime by enforcing the recent injunctions in religion and assisting in the prevention of Mary's escape to the Netherlands.[151] Such was the apparently unexceptional career of the Henrician servant who, like so many gentlemen at court, had benefited materially from the Reformation.

One small detail in this general picture may suggest why Northumberland found Gates to be a particularly suitable addition to his circle of confidants about the King: this was Gates's brief but extraordinary exposure (31 August 1546 to 27 January 1547) to the administration of business passing under the King's signet. Henry VIII had authorised Gates and two others to sign all royal letters with the stamp of Henry's signature; as noted earlier, Northumberland put this experience to use in 1551 by turning over to the new Vice-Chamberlain the stamp of young Edward's hand. With the King's signet Northumberland virtually possessed the royal will; Gates's selection in turn ensured the protection of this vital instrument: as Vice-Chamberlain, Gates simultaneously became Captain of the King's guard.

The extent of Northumberland's ability to control admissions to the council is best revealed by the unprecedented temporary appointment of Edward Stanley, third Earl of Derby, and the reappointment of the Earl of Arundel. Both were made conditional members on 9 August 1551 by the terms of a specially drafted 'devise', a modification of the regular oath administered to every newly appointed councillor. The exceptional nature of Arundel's and Derby's 'membership' as defined by this device attests not only to Dudley's success in managing the information upon which the King nominally was expected to act, but also to the manner in which, in selecting these two men, he could use the oath of a councillor to achieve his political ends. Arundel and Derby had been summoned to meet the council at Richmond – away from the court, be it noted – on 9 August 1551. There twenty councillors were meeting in extraordinary session.

Before dynner there was a lettre directed from the Boorde unto Mr Vicechamberlayn, being at the Courte, declaring unto him that bicause therles of Arundell and Derbye were comme hither according unto the appoyntement, and unlesse thei were admytted unto the Kinges Majesties Counsaill it was not meete thei shulde be here as Counsaillours; there fore the Lordes thought goode, if it were his Highnes pleasour, that the saied twoo Erles shulde be sworne of his Majesties Counsaill to attende only whan thei or either of them shulde be called unto it, and none otherwise; praieng the saied Master Vicechamberlain so to declare unto the Kinges Highnes, and to retourne aunswere therof hither again after dynner.

After dynner the messenger retourned with aunswer from Mr Vicechamberlayn that the Kinges Majestie was contented the saied Erles of Arundell and Derbie shulde be received as Counsaillours according to the saied devise; whereupon thei were accepted, and so with the rest proceaded unto Counsaill.[152]

Of course Arundel had been a member before, but the addition of the Earl of Derby for one day only, although it illustrates the significance of a councillor's oath, raises some intriguing questions as to the reason for his presence that day at Richmond. Derby was a known opponent of the Reformation: not only by his votes but also by his speeches in the House of Lords he had made clear his sympathy for catholic doctrine. On this ground alone it was thought in January 1550 that he would be made to suffer.[153] It was also rumoured in 1550 that Derby and the earls of Arundel and Shrewsbury were considering joint support for a proposed Parliamentary move to force Warwick's strict adherence to the terms of Henry VIII's will; presumably the plan was designed to halt the reformation of religion during the King's minority.[154] Yet another source of friction between Derby and Warwick during 1550 was Derby's claim to the Isle of Man; it was reported that he had been ordered to relinquish the title but had refused and was preparing to defend it by force if necessary.[155] Beneath these difficulties lay the spark of Warwick's apparent antipathy to the northern earl, his suspicion that if the peasants in the North rose up on Somerset's behalf, Derby and other representatives of the catholic nobility would lend their support.[156] Indeed, as has been seen, it may have been for this reason that the council had sent Westmorland's and Dorset's reconnaissance force north in April 1551, perhaps to intimidate Derby or even arrest him should he provoke a fight.[157] In this war of nerves Derby held his ground. At length, however, he was persuaded to honour the King's summons to repair to London, arriving there on 31 May 1551. By early July he was reported to be going almost daily to court.[158]

What was his business at court and why did his presence there not precipitate the crisis which most observers expected? Scheyfve thought that the council had requested Derby's attendance ostensibly in the interests of the 'welfare of the realm', meaning the peace and tranquillity of the kingdom.[159] In light of the subsequent, officially stressed importance of the 'Decree taken by the whole Counsaill at Richmonde' on 9 August, Scheyfve's observation probably carried much truth, for the council resolved that day to prohibit in the Lady Mary's household the saying of 'any Masse or other Divine Service than is appoincted by the lawes of this realme'.[160] It was a decision of great moment since Charles V might well have found in the prohibition a pretext for intervention in English affairs. This was a threat which Scheyfve himself had earlier communicated to King and council.[161] In February 1549 Paget had warned that war with the Emperor invited a rebellion at home against the further reformation of religion;[162] now it seemed clear that the abolition of Mary's mass might well guarantee the declaration of such a war, and who could deny the possibility of popular support for Mary in the event of her resistance? Doubtless Warwick had hoped to discover more precisely the nature of Derby's loyalties in advance of such a rebellion. If so, the summons to London probably was timed to deprive the commons of a potential leader at a time of reported unrest.[163]

By August 1551, however, Warwick perceived that the war impending between France and the Empire would effectively cancel Charles's earlier threat. If the Habsburg–Valois conflict thus allowed him free time to force uniformity on Mary, he nevertheless saw the dangers inherent in a policy whose unpredictable shock waves could only too easily push men like Derby, Arundel, Shrewsbury, and Somerset together against him. He must therefore make them parties to the council's attack on Mary. But how was this to be done, considering that any final demand made upon the Princess would be issued in the King's name by the body of His Majesty's most honourable privy councillors whose numbers did not include Arundel and Derby? The special oath administered to them at Richmond met this difficulty in the most extraordinary and perhaps only possible manner by conferring membership upon them for the duration of the meeting at which the order was taken. By this means did Warwick effectively secure their complicity as privy councillors in the drafting of the council's 'determinacion at Richemund' and yet prevent them thereafter from acting as privy councillors in the name and on behalf of Edward VI. The importance of the catholic earls' participation in the proceedings of 9 August as well as the fact of their subsequent non-membership was made clear on 23 August in the council's instructions to Rich, Wingfield, and Petre, who were sent to Mary to enforce the Richmond agreement: they were told to remind her that this was the King's policy set out 'of late even with the consent and advise of thole state of his Pryvy Counsell and dyvers others of the nobillity of his realm, whose names ye may repete if you thynke convenyent'.[164] Thus on 23 August 1551 Derby and Arundel clearly were not considered to be of the whole body of privy councillors nor, in retrospect, had they been accepted into full membership on 9 August. The 'devise' had defined their membership as being both temporary and associative.

Beyond the fact of Derby's peculiarly limited membership it is impossible to describe the nature of the political accommodation which the device would seem to reflect. Had Derby been forced under pressure to accept the council's decree against Mary? The council certainly drew Mary's attention to the fact of the conservatives' collaboration at Richmond. Had Warwick purchased Derby's acquiescence in this and other matters with a promise to respect the earl's titles and position? Perhaps so. The Richmond meeting has about it an air of political tension, of calculation; at Richmond Warwick appears to have been gathering and measuring his strength before the sudden last blow at Somerset two months later. Shrewsbury sensed that in February 1551 Warwick had already begun counting allies and neutralists; Derby, like Shrewsbury, may have concluded that in the face of another struggle between Somerset and Warwick he would do nothing himself to imperil the 'quietness, unity, and concord' of the realm.[165] If so, he probably came to this conclusion during June and July, the period of those daily trips to court. The course of events during the year provides circumstantial evidence in support of this: those who were spreading rumours of friction between Derby and the council were being forcibly suppressed in May;[166] Derby was 'sworn' a privy councillor in August; in December he sat among the peers who tried Somerset. At Somerset's death Derby's position as a great catholic magnate stood secure. Very probably he had bought this security at Richmond by supporting the government against the greatest catholic in the realm, the successor to the throne.

It was at the time of the council's enforcement of the decree against Princess Mary that Sir Philip Hoby made his first appearance at the board (16 August 1551). There is no record of his swearing-in. The Emperor's ambassador resident reported that 'Hoby was made a councillor' two or three days before his departure for France as one of the royal commissioners for the negotiation of the proposed marriage between Edward VI and the daughter of Henry II.[167] If this be so, Hoby's appointment would date from about 12–13 May 1551, but there is nothing which corroborates Scheyfve's assertion to that effect. The only certain evidence remains the fact of Hoby's presence in council for the first time at Hampton Court on 16 August and the council's own explicit reference of 16 September 1551 identifying him as 'one of his Majesties Pryvey Counsell'.[168] Unlike the Earl of Derby, Hoby seems not to have been recruited for the support which he might be expected to give to a particular policy. Rather, his evident fluency in several languages and his diplomatic ventures to Spain, Portugal, France, and the Imperial court brought a seasoned expertise to Warwick's councils in matters foreign.[169] Hoby's political credentials were also quite acceptable: he had turned against Somerset in 1549 out of pique, feeling that the Protector had not rewarded his services sufficiently.[170] Moreover, he lacked any sympathy for the conservative cause in religion. As Master of the ordnance, Hoby occupied a not inconsiderable place in the apparatus of Warwick's power. Both this office and his former military experience in France probably explain his captaincy of seventy of the council's élite guard.[171]

The fifth man to be appointed within seven months and the seventh in little more than a year was Sir Robert Bowes (25 September 1551). Trained at law and hardened in battle against both the Scots and the rebels of 1536, Bowes's ancestral ties with the border country had marked him early on for employment in the North.[172] Edward VI retained Bowes as Lord Warden of the East and Middle Marches. After the *coup* of 1549, however, Warwick deemed security along the borders 'so importaunt a matter' that only some 'notable ruler' was to be entrusted with the execution of the King's policy there, the official reasoning being that the French were 'much encreased in aucthoritie and power with the Scottes, having the Scottishe Queene also in their handes'. Consequently, the new Lord President arranged for his own appointment as Lord Warden on 6 April 1550; Bowes; was pensioned off 'untill the Kinges Majestie shulde see a place wheare to emploie him'.[173] The place was found three months later (19 July 1550) when the council decided in the King's name that Bowes should remain Warden of the East and Middle Marches 'as he was before ... forasmuch as it was not thought convenient that therle of Warrewick shulde, according to the former order, go into the Northe, but rather for many consideracions attende on the Kinges person'.[174] This reversal sensibly reinstated a competent administrator and further strengthened Warwick's personal power. As Lord Warden, Bowes became the architect of the legal and geopolitical arrangements by which disputes over the borders between England and Scotland finally were settled; Warwick, in the King's laconic note, simply carried on at court while continuing to receive the compensations of the office granted to him in February – the yearly fee of £1,000 and 'a crewe' of one hundred light horsemen.[175] Transparent though Warwick's designs were, they cannot alter the fact of Bowes's evident competence in the administration of northern affairs. Just before his elevation to the council he was serving as the King's commissioner for the 'limitation' of the Anglo-Scottish border (6 April 1551);[176] as the King's privy councillor, his appointment to fifteen other royal commissions in eighteen months (December 1551 to May 1553) clearly attests to the government's recognition of his abilities.[177]

Bowes, then, was the ninth permanent councillor appointed since Somerset's readmission. During this same period the Bishop of Durham, as already noted, suffered loss of membership. Tunstal had left the court for his bishopric soon after the downfall of the earls of Arundel and Southampton on 2 February 1550 and with his departure his name disappears from the ranks of privy councillors. The true end of his membership dates from about 17 August 1550 when, after being ordered to return to court, he was placed under house arrest at Coldharbour in Thames Street. He never escaped. After a long confinement, he was committed to the Tower (20 December 1551), found guilty of misprision of treason, deprived of his bishopric (14 October 1552), and transferred to the King's Bench Prison in Southwark where he remained until shortly after Mary's accession.[178]

Tunstal's alleged crime was almost certainly a figment of John

Dudley's imagination. The bishop's real offence probably lay in his express opposition to the radical direction of the government's religious programme. In the House of Lords he had earlier voted against the Act abolishing images and probably against that for the authorisation of the *Ordinal*, and when he attacked Knox's preaching in April of that year, the effect of the evangelical's return fire was to throw into even sharper relief Durham's Henrician catholicism.[179] For a bishop also a privy councillor, such doctrinal sympathies were politically untenable in the early months of 1550, for by 2 February Warwick had made of the reformed religion in England an official test of political loyalty.[180] For Tunstal, the test came in August with the summons to London. According to the Imperial ambassador, the bishop was required upon arrival to sign certain 'ordinances' made in respect of religion. What these 'ordinances' were exactly remains unclear; probably they constituted the council's letters ordering the enforcement of the aforesaid Parliamentary acts. At any rate, again according to Scheyfve, Durham several times refused to put his hand to the papers in question, and it was in response to this – and not the later allegation of concealment of treason – that he was ordered to withdraw to his house until further notice.[181]

The chronology of Tunstal's ordeal is important here, for whereas it may be true that his deprivation sprang ultimately from political and administrative decisions rather than matters of faith,[182] in fact it was this initial refusal to sign the council's orders relating to religion which triggered his fall. In the wake of the conservatives' abortive counter-*coup* and especially amidst rumours of a catholic uprising in the North, Warwick's response to Tunstal's defiance of the council's anti-catholic line should have been predictable: he discovered in the bishop's refusal something close to treason. The council dutifully began a search to confirm Dudley's suspicion, but after more than two years of such work the government could neither bring the prelate before a jury nor even attaint him by Act of Parliament and, without clear proof that Tunstal had acted unlawfully, Warwick could not peremptorily dismiss one of Henry VIII's executors from his place at the board. Ultimately, therefore, Tunstal had to be destroyed by the King's lay commissioners on the technical charge that he had delayed in reporting to the whole council rumours of conspiracy and rebellion.[183] Since he had in fact revealed such evidence to Somerset, the commissioners' decision may reflect Dudley's neurotic belief that the former Protector would have exploited a northern revolt and/or Scottish invasion in order to return to power. It is a curious fact that the first mention of Tunstal's misprision of treason came three weeks after Somerset's trial, or sixteen months after the bishop had first declined to affix his signature to the council's religious policy. In order to cover the reason for his confinement from August 1550, therefore, the council found it necessary in December 1551 to make Tunstal's alleged knowledge of 'a conspiratie in the North for the making of a rebellion' retroactive from 'abowt July in *anno* 1550'.[184]

The Bishop of Durham, the earls of Arundel and Southampton, Peckham and Southwell, all were conservatives and all were gone within six months of Warwick's accession to power. This 'chopping and changing' of councillors, noticed publicly even in Rome,[185] reached a climactic and logical end with the beheading of the Duke of Somerset on 22 January 1552. The course of the duke's downfall need not be rehearsed again here,[186] since the axe merely punctuated what his arrest (16 October 1551) had already established, that Dudley ruled as one obsessed by the need to eradicate every source of opposition at the board. Although Somerset posed little threat in council, he remained the one great figure who could rally sufficient strength outside the council to break Dudley's hold on the government. The question which Somerset's trial (1 December 1551) failed to answer, however, was by what means he would have pulled Northumberland down. Contrary to Palmer's testimony, he certainly had not hired an assassin to cut off the heads of Northumberland, Northampton, and Pembroke, nor was there enough evidence to show, as the official indictment put it, that he had gathered an assembly for the purpose of imprisoning the three. Even a packed jury of twenty-six peers refused to believe this and so rightly acquitted Somerset of treason on that count. Equally improbable was a second charge that he had incited the citizens of London to insurrection with drums, trumpets, and shouts of 'Liberty' on 'about St. George's day', 1551. Nevertheless, the jury found him guilty of felony as charged, an offence that carried the death penalty by the terms of 3 & 4 Edward VI, c. 5, the Act of 1550 that the council had rammed through Parliament in response to Wriothesley's abortive counter-*coup*.

Admittedly, Northumberland had fabricated the entire case. He had framed the indictments and at the trial almost certainly persuaded his fellow jurors – they included Northampton and Pembroke – to return a verdict which would ensure Somerset's ruin in spite of evidence as insufficient as it was questionable. Indeed, Northumberland later confessed that he had 'procured his [Somerset's]death unjustly'[187] and that 'nothing had pressed so injuriously upon his conscience as the fraudulent scheme against the Duke of Somerset which would never have come to pass without his authority and favour'.[188] But the irregularities of Somerset's trial have obscured the fact that Northumberland had rightly identified Somerset as the prime mover of a campaign to unseat him. Somerset is usually pictured as the victim of Dudley's clever intrigues in 1551; in fact, according to a member of the French embassy resident in England, Somerset had from the very moment of his release from prison (6 February 1550) deliberately worked behind the scenes to undermine confidence in Warwick's ability to govern.[189] He was motivated by envy and by an intense dislike of the Lord President; the spectacle of Warwick wielding the power he had held tormented him. He simply could not tolerate government under the man who had brought him down. The discontented, the envious, the spiteful – all who hated Dudley's personal reign – were enlisted to support him. His purpose initially was twofold, to acquire the goodwill of the commons and to throw all of the blame for the ill effects of the government's policies on to Warwick. To this end, Somerset's agents – and there were many – gave the people to understand that the debasement of the King's coins in particular had been carried through against Somerset's advice; if only Somerset had been believed, they said, matters would not have proceeded as they had, to the great detriment of the people. There followed, said the observer, a great 'murmure' among the commons.[190] Independent confirmation of the success of Somerset's under-hand activity comes from the Imperial ambassador who described this 'popular murmuring' against the depreciation of the coinage and the council's response to it: the sheriffs were to tell the people that in blaming the Earl of Warwick for this, there were some who were doing him a great injustice.[191]

Meanwhile, wrote the French correspondent, Somerset continued to employ every means possible to make Dudley ever more hated by the nobility and commons. He consulted secretly with those he knew to be discontented and opposed to the ruling junta. Although we are not told the purpose of these clandestine meetings, the Earl of Arundel, as has been seen, revealed under interrogation that he and Somerset had twice met to discuss the possibility of 'apprehending' Warwick; Somerset stated that he had 'contemplated' such action. Contemplation should not have brought him to the block, though it might conceivably have earned for him a Tower cell. In any case, Warwick understood that the threat posed by Somerset was not at first that of a *coup*. The real danger lay in Parliament, a Parliament which could be turned into a forum for the revision of Dudley's rule. This at least was the plan in 1550: in the session that should have been convened that year, Arundel and Somerset's 'party' were ready to demonstrate that 'the kingdom had been very badly governed ... and that those who governed had done everything at will without observing either the forms or procedures laid down in the statutes of the realm'.[192] Warwick knew of the plan and so kept Parliament from sitting, twice proroguing it (1550 and 1551), but not without some difficulty the second time.[193] Somerset's thoughts about the method of supplanting Warwick must therefore have telescoped rapidly in 1551: Warwick's 'apprehension' would have to precede a Parliamentary attack on the legality of his regime. No hard evidence exists of a plot to seize Northumberland's person in advance of such a Parliament, but even before the trial there were those who stated confidentially that that would have been the probable sequence of events had Dudley not acted so swiftly. Somerset's partisans did not intend to have Northumberland killed, according to these sources, but, rather, arrested at a banquet given by Somerset and imprisoned, 'after which they would have summoned Parliament to set everything, religion and the rest, right according to the late King's will'.[194]

Somerset's execution is usually described as deplorable and unnecessary since the 'good duke' presented no danger to the state. But no one can be certain now that Somerset's men would not have attempted Northumberland's seizure, an attempt potentially more divisive in its consequences than the bloodless putsch of 1549. The relevant historical consideration is that Northumberland saw some sort of move coming and struck first. (The creations of 11 October had strengthened his hand; this had been his tactic in 1550.)[195] He also saw that to imprison Somerset was not enough; the duke's supporters would simply have used his incarceration as the pretext for Dudley's removal once Parliament had sat. Somerset *alive* was the danger, whether he lay in the Tower or sat in council, for with Parliament behind him he might be able to dismantle Northumberland's power and restore himself to supreme authority. This, then, is the meaning of the preposterous charges laid against him: he could no longer be tolerated; he had to be eliminated.

The difficulty in assessing Northumberland's action is of course that in order to ensure his political preservation – itself a legitimate concern – he was quite prepared to bend the law. This does not excuse him, rather it explains him. He rightly perceived that the first duty of Tudor government was the preservation of order in the King's realms: the maintenance of the King's estate depended upon it; a council divided jeopardised it. Somerset's mistake in 1549 had been to divide the council by seeming to support the commons; Dudley's mistake was to alienate the commons by forcing upon them the policies of a subservient council. The chief difference between the two men was that Northumberland was the cleverer politician. Indeed, had it not been for Edward's premature death, we might be describing a successful administrator or forceful governor who merely lacked popularity. Admittedly, Northumberland often acted less in the Crown's interests than his own, and never more so than in 1553, but the outrageous character of his scheme for the succession – and all that it suggests about the character of the man – should not obscure the realism of his decision in 1551 to be done with Somerset. Historically, Northumberland defies sympathy because politically he was then both wicked and right.

Considering Tunstal's deprivation, the death of Lord Wentworth (3 March 1551),[196] and Somerset's arrest on 16 October 1551, the council should thus have totalled thirty-three members. A membership list of 2 November 1551 that William Thomas entered into the council's register reveals thirty-two names;[197] the missing councillor is Sir Edward Wotton, who died on 8 November, or six days after the date of Thomas's list.[198] Had Wotton been dropped from membership before his death? There is no positive evidence to confirm such a development. It is a fact that Wotton came to court only very infrequently while Warwick ruled; the council book records his presence but thirteen times during October–November 1549; twice in November 1550; and only three times in December 1550 before his final appearance at a council meeting on 14 December 1550.[199]

Thomas's list includes Paget's name, but on 2 November 1551 Paget lay in the Fleet Prison on suspicion of sympathy for Somerset's cause. Effectively, his loss of membership dates therefore from the day of his arrest (21 October), though in fact he had been ordered to confine himself to his house as early as 2 October.[200] Rumour explained his detainment variously: he had exceeded his powers by earlier promising Charles V that Mary would be allowed to continue in her religious practices (irrelevant); he had revealed Somerset's 'conspiracy' and was being held temporarily in protective custody (incredible); he had plotted with Somerset (improbable).[201] The truth of the matter – that Northumberland meant to deprive the opposition of the shrewdest political head in England – is doubtless revealed by subsequent developments. The council never formally accused Paget of participation in the alleged conspiracy. Rather, they transferred him to the Tower (8 November 1551) and released him (16 or 17 June 1552) only upon his 'confession' (31 May 1552) to a questionable charge of malversation as Chancellor of the Duchy of Lancaster. He lost his offices, titles, and dignity, though much of his £8,000 fine was later forgiven.[202] Although pardoned officially (6 December 1552) 'of all offences and transgressions and other negligences',[203] he did not resume his place at the council table. At some time between 2 November 1551 and 19 January 1552 his name was officially removed from the list of the King's privy councillors.

This fact is evident from two remaining official lists of members' names, one of which, Edward VI's record of 1552, has already been cited. Having dated the King's manuscript and thus identified his thirty-one privy councillors in March 1552 (see Table 7), it remains merely to point out that the 'Mr Controuller' referred to on this list was Sir Anthony Wingfield and not Sir Richard Cotton, as is often thought; Cotton was sworn a privy councillor on 11 May 1952 and became Comptroller of the King's household on 27 August 1552, twelve days after Wingfield's death.[204] Cotton may informally have assumed the Comptroller's duties on 15 August;[205] the charge would have been a natural one, just as the formal appointment itself was, for Cotton had been Comptroller and Cofferer of Prince Edward's household, from 1538 to 1546. To that experience he had added military service in France (1544) and a later post as Treasurer at Boulogne (1547). In what particular way he attracted Northumberland's notice in 1552 is not known, though it may be assumed that his familiarity with the administration of the King's fortifications in the North and at Calais and Guisnes during the period after the *coup* of 1549 amplified the recognition he had already earned 'as a man of singular experience'.[206] Once again Northumberland had brought into the King's council a soldier trained in law and finance.

The second of the two surviving membership lists for the last months of the reign provides 'The Names of the Counsaill' at the beginning of 1553.[207] It includes Justice Bromley, who was not active then, but does not include the Earl of Huntingdon, and he certainly was a privy councillor at that time; the omission is probably a clerical error reflecting the earl's long absence from court.[208] Although the King had not named Huntingdon one of the twenty-two members of the council's committee 'for the state' which was to operate after March 1552,[209] there is no evidence to indicate that Northumberland had modified the terms of Huntingdon's membership as the council had done in the case of Arundel's membership in 1551. Indeed, during the final months of the reign, Huntingdon and Northumberland appear to have been particularly close political friends. With Huntingdon and Bromley, then, the privy council numbered thirty-one official members in January 1553.

The number rose to thirty-two with the addition of Sir John Cheke on 2 June 1553 as one of the King's principal secretaries. Cheke's elevation eludes the obvious explanation – that as a secretary he was entitled to a place in council – for the reason that he became an unprecedented *third* secretary of state. Scheyfve's con-

TABLE 7 *The privy council in March 1552*

Thomas Cranmer, Archbishop of Canterbury
Thomas Goodrich, Bishop of Ely, Chancellor
William Paulet, Marquess of Winchester, High Treasurer
John Dudley, Duke of Northumberland, Great Master and President
John Russell, Earl of Bedford, Privy Seal
Henry Grey, Duke of Suffolk
William Parr, Marquess of Northampton, Great Chamberlain
Francis Talbot, Earl of Shrewsbury
Henry Neville, Earl of Westmorland
Francis Hastings, Earl of Huntingdon
William Herbert, Earl of Pembroke
Walter Devereux, Viscount Hereford
Edward Lord Clinton, High Admiral
Thomas Lord Darcy, Chamberlain
George Brooke, Lord Cobham
Richard Lord Rich
Sir Anthony Wingfield, Comptroller
Sir Thomas Cheyne, Treasurer
Sir John Gates, Vice-Chamberlain
Sir William Petre, Secretary
Sir William Cecil, Secretary
Sir Philip Hoby, Master of the ordnance
Sir Robert Bowes, Master of the rolls
Sir John Gage, Constable of the Tower
Sir John Mason, Secretary for the French tongue
Sir Ralph Sadler, Master of the King's wardrobe
Sir John Baker, Chancellor of the exchequer
Sir Thomas Bromley, a puisne justice of the King's bench
Sir Edward Montagu, Chief Justice of the common pleas
Dr Nicholas Wotton, Dean of Canterbury and York
Sir Edward North

jecture of 11 June, that Cheke replaced Petre, 'who is said to
have demanded permission to retire',[210] is self-contradictory, as
Petre retained his office to the end of the reign. In any case, Petre
was the senior man; had he really stepped down, Cheke would
have replaced Cecil, the junior secretary. The modern suggestion
that Cheke was intended as Cecil's replacement in the latter's
deliberate, politically motivated absence[211] would make sense were
it not for Cecil's attendances during June.[212] Indeed, the hard fact

of the official references to all three men as the King's secretaries
– the only such triplicate appointment under the Tudors – invites
the speculation that on the eve of the King's certain death
Northumberland, appreciating the politic wisdom of old hands
like Cecil and Petre, whose instincts for survival exceeded their
loyalty to treasonous causes, chose to bring in a fresh, eager, ideo-
logically committed recruit to manage the correspondence of
Crown and council during a difficult, anxious time. What better
choice than the King's tutor, a politically uncomplicated academic?

In the course of his rule Northumberland had thus increased
the membership of the early Tudor privy council from an average
of about twenty-one members (twenty-two on the eve of the
coup) to a total of thirty-three by October 1551; saving Cheke's
appointment, he did not thereafter continue to add to these
numbers. After Somerset's arrest and execution, the number
actually fell to thirty-one. We need no longer accept a privy
council of forty by 1553; that body is found only in Burnet's work
and not in the records of the institution.

Now that Edward's only true councillors have been identified,
the next task is to characterise this group of men historically.[213]
Who would be expected, by office and training, to find a place at
the council table? In theory, an adult Edward VI would have
been free to choose whomever he wished to be of his privy council;
in practice, he would probably have followed the Henrician example, a privy council composed of the great officers of state and
household, together with a few outstanding churchmen, nobles,
and commoners of the King's choosing. Henry's council after
1540, for example, included (at least) the following leading men:
the Archbishop of Canterbury, the Chancellor, Treasurer, Great
Master (who was also, *ex officio*, the President of the council),
Privy seal, Great Chamberlain of England, the High Admiral of
England, Chamberlain of the household, Treasurer of the household, Comptroller, Master of the King's horse, Vice-Chamberlain, the King's two secretaries, Chancellor of the augmentations,
and Chancellor of the exchequer. There were others, of course,
including usually two more bishops and later the Master of the
King's wardrobe and the Dean of Canterbury and York. In the

main, one should have expected Henry VIII to have appointed to Edward's privy council either the same leading officers or perhaps all but a few of the same.

That he did not do so is something of a surprise; personalities aside, Edward's first council (January–March 1547) represents a remarkable departure from the Henrician tradition of a privy council composed of the forenamed great figures: although reduced in total numbers by only four, gone nevertheless from the new council were the High Treasurer, the King's Chamberlain, Treasurer, Comptroller, and Vice-Chamberlain, one secretary, the Chancellor of the exchequer, and one of the traditional bishops. Into their places stepped two gentlemen of the privy chamber, the chief justice of the common pleas, a puisne justice of the King's bench and, note, not the Lord Deputy, but merely the Treasurer at Calais. Henry had in his will effected thus a marked alteration of the composition of the Tudor privy council. From this perspective, Somerset's appointments after 12 March 1547 represented a return to the Henrician tradition, for the Protector restored to the council all seventeen of the earlier group of officials of Church, state, and household. In this sense, the effect of the powers granted Somerset in the letters-patent was conservative, not extraordinary: Somerset altered the will and reconstructed the Henrician council.

The real changes came under Northumberland. To the traditional combination of office-holders Dudley had added by 1553 the Constable of the Tower (Gage), the Secretary for the French tongue (Mason), the Master of the rolls (Bowes), and the Master of the ordnance (Hoby); from Edward's first council, he had retained the two justices, as well as Henry's later additions, the Master of the wardrobe and the Dean of Canterbury; to the/ number of all of these he had added finally a relatively large group of non-office-holding peers – one duke, three earls, a viscount, and two barons. This infusion of aristocratic blood represents the most noticeable change that increased numbers wrought on the composition. In 1540 (besides Cranmer, two bishops and eight knights), we can count two dukes, three earls, and three barons. By late 1547, one sees only a slight redistribution of titles: (in addition to the archbishop, one bishop, and now eleven knights) one duke, one marquess, two earls, and four barons. But by 1553 (in addition to the two ecclesiastics, Dr Wotton, and fourteen knights) we

TABLE 8   *Chief officers of state and the King's household,*
1547–53[214]

Chancellor of England[a]

Thomas Wriothesley, Earl of Southampton[b]	to 6 March 1547
William Paulet, Lord St John (Keeper)	7 March 1547
Edward Seymour, Duke of Somerset (Keeper)	6 July 1547
William Paulet, Lord St John (Keeper)	9 July 1547
Richard Lord Rich	23 October 1547
Thomas Goodrich, Bishop of Ely (Keeper)	22 December 1551
Thomas Goodrich Bishop of Ely	19 January 1552

High Treasurer of England

Edward Seymour, Earl of Hertford, Duke of Somerset[c]	10 February 1547 to 11 October 1549
William Paulet, Earl of Wiltshire, Marquess of Winchester	3 February 1550

Great Master of the household and President of the Council

William Paulet, Lord St John	to 3 February 1550
John Dudley, Earl of Warwick	20 February 1550

Keeper of the privy seal

John Russell, Lord Russell, Earl of Bedford	entire reign

Great Chamberlain of England

Edward Seymour, Earl of Hertford	to 15 February 1547
John Dudley, Earl of Warwick	17 February 1547
William Parr, Marquess of Northampton	4 February 1550

The King's Chamberlain

Henry Fitz Alan, Earl of Arundel	to 2 February 1550
Thomas Lord Wentworth	(?) February 1550 to 3 March 1551*
Thomas Lord Darcy	5 April 1551

High Admiral of England

John Dudley, Viscount Lisle, Earl of Warwick	to 17 February 1547
Thomas Lord Seymour[d]	17 February 1547 to 18 January 1549
John Dudley, Earl of Warwick	28 October 1549
Edward Lord Clinton	14 May 1550

Comptroller of the household

Sir John Gage	to 29 June 1547
Sir William Paget	29 June 1547 to 3 December 1549
Sir Anthony Wingfield	by 2 February 1550 to 15 August 1552*
Sir Richard Cotton	27 August 1552

TABLE 8 (*Contd*)

Treasurer of the household

Sir Thomas Cheyne	entire reign

The King's Vice-Chamberlain

Sir Anthony Wingfield	to 2 February 1550
Sir Thomas Darcy	2 February 1550 to 5 April 1551
Sir John Gates	8 April 1551

Master of the King's horse

Sir Anthony Browne	to 8 May 1548*
Sir William Herbert, Earl of Pembroke	2 December 1549
John Dudley, Earl of Warwick[e]	28 April 1552

Principal secretaries of state

Sir William Paget	to 29 June 1547
Sir William Petre	entire reign
Sir Thomas Smith[f]	17 April 1548 to 13 October 1549
Dr Nicholas Wotton	15 October 1549 to 5 September 1550
Sir William Cecil	5 September 1550 to end of reign
Sir John Cheke	2 June 1553 to end of reign

[a] Keepers of the great seal are indicated by 'Keeper' in parentheses.
[b] Confined to his house on 6 March; relinquished the great seal on the 7th.
[c] Arrested by the council on 11 October 1549.
[d] Arrested on 17 January 1549.
[e] John Dudley, the Duke of Northumberland's son; he was not a privy councillor.
[f] Deprived of office on 13 October 1549.
* Died in office.

have two dukes, two marquesses, five earls, a viscount, and four barons. In other words, Northumberland had increased the Henrician and early Edwardian privy council of about nineteen to twenty-one members by adding or keeping on two justices, an average of four lesser administrators, and seven nobles.

In addition to rank, office, and title, a councillor's religious persuasion (or reputed inclinations) would certainly have occupied the interest of his contemporaries. We are able to say that twenty-three councillors held 'reformed' or progressive religious views[215] and that eleven held or at least sympathised with the Henrician catholic position;[216] for the other eleven whose positions are not clear,[217] one can only suggest that they adopted whatever views the times demanded, have left no trace of their true beliefs, or perhaps remained indifferent.

The conservatives, of course, attract obvious attention. Four of the eleven were executors (Browne, Tunstal, N. Wotton, Wriothesley); Browne, Tunstal, and Wriothesley were active under Somerset. Eight of the twenty-seven councillors who were active before October 1549 leaned towards the older religious views,[218] which suggests that Somerset was perhaps more moderate (or fair-minded) than we have supposed, or that he saw in a councillor's religious persuasion less of political significance than did Northumberland. It is a fact, however, that after the purges of the winter of 1549–50, Dudley tolerated the presence of five men of suspected conservative prejudices, Baker, Cheyne, Gage, the Earl of Shrewsbury, and Dr Wotton.[219] The point is that none of them allowed their alleged beliefs to preclude their eligibility for membership of the privy council. It is also true that, saving Dr Wotton (an executor who offered Dudley no pretext for removal), Southwell and Peckham (who probably owed their brief service to Wriothesley and Arundel), and the Earl of Derby (member for a day), all of the members new after 5 October 1549 either adhered to reformed beliefs or acquiesced in the government's official line.

Five of King Edward's forty-five councillors possessed an ecclesiastical training. The Church was represented officially in the person of the Archbishop of Canterbury throughout the reign, by the Bishop of Durham from January to April 1547 and again from October 1549 to February 1550; by the Bishop of Ely from November 1549 (Ely was also Keeper of the great seal from 21 December and Chancellor from 19 January 1552). The other two men, Dr Wotton and Sir John Mason, do not, however, as privy councillors, present the figures of ecclesiastics. Although Wotton held a doctorate in divinity (and civil and canon law) and served as Dean of Canterbury and York, his training had prepared him rather for a career in diplomacy; it seems that contemporaries did not view him as a theologian or man of the spirit. Mason may have set out on a career in the Church, but instead of pursuing it he too found employment in the diplomatic service (from 1537) and later as a clerk of the privy council (1541–5) and the King's French secretary (from 1542).[220] Thus, except for a brief period (December 1549 to December 1550) when Cranmer and the two bishops were active members, this was not a council in which even the reformed Church carried much independent weight. Somerset, it will be remembered, seems to have suspended Tunstal's membership sometime after April 1547 and Warwick secured Goodrich's appointment precisely because the bishop could be expected to support his every move.

To say that this was an almost thoroughly secular council is not to say that all the members were products of the age's new emphasis on learning. From the evidence available for this study, it can be said, however, that a relatively high proportion (nineteen of the forty-five) had been to university. These included eleven of the sixteen executors[221] and nine of the fourteen councillors who were active before 12 March 1547.[222] The most interesting figures are found in comparison of the numbers of university-trained men who served under Somerset, on the one hand, and Dudley, on the other. Thus, whereas fourteen of the twenty-seven (52 per cent) who were members before October 1549 had gone to university,[223] only eighteen of the forty-two (43 per cent) who were active after 5 October had done so, including only five (N. Wotton, Goodrich, Mason, Cecil, Cheke) of the eighteen (not including the Earl of Derby) whose *first* appearances date from that time.

The revealing comparisons in this category are between Somerset's distinct councils and those afterwards: more than one-half (ten, or 55.5 per cent) of the eighteen members of Somerset's second council (May–December 1548) were university men;[224] slightly more than one-third (eleven, or about 37 per cent) of the thirty members of January 1553 fall into the same classification.[225] Somerset's last council (January–October 1549) and Northumberland's select group 'for the state' were of almost equal size, twenty-three and twenty-one members respectively, but whereas thirteen (56.5 per cent) of Somerset's men had been to university,[226] only seven (33 per cent) of the later committee had spent at least some time at Cambridge, Oxford, or a continental institution.[227] Thus, although membership had increased by 50 per cent under Northumberland, the total number of university-educated councillors had actually decreased.

With regard to particular academic and educational achievements, the evidence shows that at least five councillors had studied abroad;[228] they and at least six others could speak at least one foreign language.[229] We know that fourteen of the forty-five had studied civil and/or canon law, including six of the executors,[230] eight of Somerset's appointees,[231] and nine members of the council of January 1553.[232] King Edward could also count five former academics among his councillors.[233]

A formal, higher education certainly prepared a man for service under the King, but experience in the King's affairs was, almost by definition, the prerequisite for membership of the privy council. More than half (twenty-six) of the forty-five, for instance, had seen various kinds of diplomatic service abroad before their appointment to Edward's board. Early on in his career, a man may have assisted another privy councillor or ambassador on a particular mission; at least twelve of our men had done so at one time in the entourage of a King's envoy.[234] Cranmer, Tunstal, Dr Wotton, Paget, Mason, and Hoby had themselves been ambassadors resident abroad. Fully twenty-one men could point to past missions to France or to the English possessions in France;[235] thirteen had held assignments in the field of Anglo-Imperial relations.[236] In a narrower context at least five were particularly experienced in managing English interests in international maritime disputes – that is, in dealing with extraordinary cases of piracy, foreign merchants' claims against English nationals, trade and customs agreements, and so on.[237]

The King's interests often led to war; as responsibility for the organisation and conduct of the necessary military effort fell to the council, we should expect to find among its members several of those lords of the realm who were themselves the King's great military commanders. In addition to Somerset and Northumberland, the Marquess of Northampton, Earl of Arundel, Earl of Shrewsbury, Lord Russell, and Lord Clinton had all of them held important military commands before their admission to Edward's privy council. Somerset, Northumberland, and Russell had also been Lords High Admiral of England under Henry VIII and at least three others (Cheyne, Thomas Seymour, Clinton) had been naval captains.

The surprising fact about the martial composition of the council, however, was the increasingly high proportion of members who had seen active military service. Henry VIII's council of executors included six soldiers (37·5 per cent);[238] Somerset's 'first' council of twenty-one members (March 1547 to April 1548) counted twelve (57 per cent);[239] Northumberland's comrades-in-arms totalled nearly two-thirds of the members (eighteen of the thirty) by 1553.[240] In becoming relatively more aristocratic with fewer university men, the council had also become relatively more 'martial'. Indeed, of the fifteen men appointed by Dudley's favour after October 1549, ten were experienced soldiers.[241]

A man may thus have found his way to the council chamber through war and diplomacy; he may just as well have risen to the top at court. King Edward's councillors (the forty-five active ones) included eleven former gentlemen of the privy chamber.[242] Four of these were executors,[243] six were members of the Protector's first council (March 1547 to April 1548), and seven were members of his 'second' council (May–December 1548).[244] Seven of Northumberland's council of January 1553 could also claim to have been gentlemen of the privy chamber before their admission to the council.[245]

Others may certainly be classified as courtiers too; in fact, at least seventeen of the forty-five had at some time before their appointments as privy councillors held posts (other than that of gentlemen of the King's privy chamber) in the royal household.[246] Into this category fall seven executors,[247] twelve of the twenty-two members of Somerset's council of 1549,[248] and eleven members of the council of 1553.[249] Classifying as courtiers those who had performed essentially ceremonial court duties on special occasions, it is possible to name also another group of at least sixteen individuals for whom this description is true.[250] Altogether, then, just over one-half (twenty-seven) of the privy councillors in the reign of Edward VI may be designated greater or lesser courtiers.

That one type of experience which perhaps prepared a man – great landed noble, lesser courtier, lawyer, bishop – most fully for membership of the King's council was unquestionably the direct experience of administering the multiple affairs of local and central government. What sort of administrative experience had Edward's councillors gained as royal commissioners or as officers before their appointment to the board?

At the local level, nine members had been sheriffs,[251] at least three had held a London City office,[252] four had been (or were at the time of their admission) members of the council in the North (including two presidents of that body),[253] two were former members of the council in the Marches of Wales,[254] and at least eighteen had been named to various commissions for the peace.[255] We may say that at least twenty-seven of Edward's councillors had been involved in local administrative work (including those who had served as commissioners for purely local affairs); in this regard, Somerset's council of 1549 appears to have been relatively more experienced (seventeen of twenty-three members) than Northumberland's council of 1553 (twenty of thirty members.)

The proportion of councillors who are known to have studied Roman and ecclesiastical law has already been noted: they number fourteen of the forty-five, not including Bromley. At least six individuals had also been legal officers in central and local government before their membership of Edward's council.[256] At Westminster, legal training proved to be an excellent qualification for a clerkship in chancery, the privy seal office, for service under the King's two secretaries, or for one of the lesser posts in the royal courts of revenue; these offices in turn led frequently to advanced appointments and membership of an important royal commission. Ten members, for example, had been signet clerks (or special commissioners for the use of the King's stamp), clerks of the privy council, or one of the King's two secretaries.[257] Two others were former Lords Privy Seal;[258] five were certainly familiar with procedure in chancery (as assistants, clerks, Masters of rolls, or Chancellor).[259] A large proportion of Edward's councillors had also had direct experience with the administration of the King's finances; at least sixteen had held a post (including a clerkship) in one of the financial departments or courts of revenue.[260]

At the national level, diverse kinds of administrative activity also followed directly from membership of a royal commission. Noted earlier were those councillors who had been commissioners for various affairs foreign; fourteen (of the forty-five) who had been charged with the administration of the King's wars (organising systems of recruitment, pay, victualling, and so on) can also be named.[261] Another group of at least eight men had sat on several special commissions related to the royal finances.[262] The institution or doctrine of the Church had at various times absorbed the administrative energies of some seventeen members.[263] Into a more general category fall the names of at least sixteen who had been royal commissioners in other causes too numerous to list

separately here.[264] Thus, cutting across the groups of men identified as soldiers, diplomats, courtiers, lawyers, university professors,
and lesser government officials is the experience in administration
that most of them shared. It is perhaps unhistorical to describe
any of these individuals as Tudor 'administrators' in a strict sense,
but it is a fact, as the evidence of their offices and membership of
commissions shows, that all but four of the forty-five men considered here had, before their membership of Edward's council,
performed for the King duties which we should nowadays call
'administrative'.

Finally, it should be significant to note that in respect of their
participation in the great affairs of the realm, at least thirty-eight
of the men under consideration sat in the House of Lords or the
House of Commons before becoming members of Edward VI's
privy council.[265]

Of greater significance even than this observation is the fact
that twenty of the individuals considered here had been privy
councillors under Henry VIII.[266] Putting it another way, twenty
of Edward's councillors were heirs to the great administrative reforms of the 1530s, the inheritors, so to speak, of the rationalised
methods of administration which Cromwell had established only
ten years earlier, and members especially of the institution which
Cromwell had helped to create – the early-modern privy council
which, in the reign of Edward VI, was to rule in the place of a
king. To what extent, however, had the architect of this 'revolution' in Tudor government 'created', in the sense that he had
trained, a group of men who, as *privy councillors*, could be expected to carry through and sustain his reforms? This is one of the
questions that has been asked of Professor Elton's interpretation of
Cromwell's work; upon the answer rides a partial test of Elton's
views and an understanding of the essential composition of
Edward VI's council. 'What really is the evidence for thinking
that Cromwell created the Privy Council of the 1540s?'[267] The
problem is to identify those who were privy councillors under both
Edward VI and Henry VIII and who can also be said without
qualification to have entered Tudor royal government under
Thomas Cromwell's direct influence and/or were subsequently
and unquestionably trained in Cromwell's 'bureaucracy'. The
results of the present study show that seven of King Edward's

forty-seven official councillors were Cromwell's trainees (Wriothesley, Paget, Petre, Sadler, Rich, Cheyne, and Southwell). Six of
these (all but Southwell) had been privy councillors under Henry
VIII. Two (Paget and Wriothesley) were members of the council
of executors; five (all but Southwell and Wriothesley) were members of the council from March 1547 to January 1549; six (all but
Southwell) sat in Somerset's council of January–October 1549; all
seven of them were members by November 1549. In other words,
during the decade of the 1540s, Cromwellian 'administrators'
comprised from slightly less than one-fifth to almost one-third of
the membership of the early Tudor privy council.[268] Only under
Northumberland did this proportion drop before Edward's death.
By 1553 only four (Petre, Sadler, Rich, Cheyne) of the thirty were
products of Cromwell's programmes. Another of the effects of the
increase in membership was thus to weaken relatively the administrative expertise of the King's council. Perhaps the final comment
in respect of Cromwell's impact on the Edwardian council under
Somerset consists merely in pointing out that, like the earlier great
administrator, four, or an average of one-fifth of the later personnel of the council, were or had been the King's secretaries of state
responsible for the administration of council business.

3
The Order for Meetings

The task of reconstructing the methods of government by council during Edward's reign is to a certain extent simplified by the existence of two sets of rules, dated 1550 and 1553, respectively; the earliest of their kind, they together define much of the board's manner of proceeding, from the order for meetings (time, place, frequency, conditions of attendance, and so on) to the secretaries' administration of business in and out of meetings. Some of the rules, however, may never have been observed and others, as the dates suggest, reflect practice only under Northumberland. Although the records of the Protectorate are not so plentiful that we can invariably describe Somerset's methods, the circumstances which produced the rules of 1550 may tell us something about the earlier, more obscure practices.

There are, first, the 'Certein articles deuised and deliuered, by the Kinges Majesti, for the quikker, better, and more orderlie dispatch of causes, by his Majestis preuy counsel', a well-known list of nineteen procedural rules in the King's hand that Secretary Petre endorsed 'For the counsail' on 15 January 1553.[1] Petre also drafted a shorter, rationalised version of these rules;[2] because this manuscript incorporates the corrections which the King made in the royal draft, it has been assumed that the lists together represent a 'plan' devised by Edward VI and Petre for reorganising the council's work.[3] Although it is impossible to say who in fact was the author of this scheme, present opinion suggests that the rules testify to the administrative precociousness of the fifteen-year-old King.[4]

Laying aside for the moment the question of the authorship of the 'Articles', it should be said here that the rules do not necessarily present a guide to the 'reorganisation' of the council's work, nor do they stand as unprecedented orders for the administration of council business, for there exists an earlier but less well-known scheme for the conduct of council affairs, William Lord Paget's 'Advise to the Kinges Counsail' of 23 March 1550.[5]

A comparison of Paget's 'Advise' and Petre's and the King's 'Articles' shows that the two lists (if we may consider Petre's and Edward's as one) consider altogether seven different identifiable subjects, all of them touching upon council procedure. The twelve items of Paget's paper cover four topics: the relations of councillors; attendance and times of meetings; the supervision and direction of the work of the secretaries' staff, especially with respect to the management of council correspondence; the dispatch of suits, requests, and petitions addressed to the King and council. Of these four, the later plan considers the latter three and adds three others: the authorisation of warrants for payment; the secretary's control and review of the agenda; the conduct of debate at the board, including the accommodation of the King at specified times. A collation of the two sets of rules[6] discloses that four of Paget's twelve items encompass ten different points in Petre's and Edward's schedule, and three of Petre's nineteen orders follow closely similar items in Paget's work. Although the similarity of such points in both manuscripts does not necessarily support the view that Paget's 'Advise' served as Petre's (or Edward's) direct guide in composition, strong circumstantial evidence suggests that Paget's paper did in fact serve as the model for the scheme of 1553.

The evidence for this view is related directly to the question of what moved Paget to compose his 'Advise' when he did; as the date and the circumstances of the composition of the document were themselves determined by changes in both the politics and procedure of the privy council, the genesis of Paget's rules in 1550 helps to explain the significance of council procedure under both Somerset and Northumberland.

It will be remembered that Paget had earlier been a clerk of the privy council (1540-3) and a principal secretary of state (1543-7). Even after leaving that office (29 June 1547), however, he continued to manage state business as if he were still the King's chief secretary: during Somerset's Scottish campaign it was Paget (then Comptroller of the household) who directed the affairs of the central government from Hampton Court.[7] 'Everything here', said van der Delft at the time, 'goes through his hands'.[8] An accomplished administrator, Paget was also perhaps the most adroit politician at court. It was Paget who had steered Hertford through the political uncertainties of the succession; the Protectorate itself was essentially Paget's creation.[9] The influence and abilities of this 'master of practices' (as Ponet called him) almost certainly explain how Somerset was able to abolish Henry's council of executors and appoint Edward's councillors at will.[10]

On 23 March 1550, the date of the composition of the manuscript, Somerset lay at Syon House wholly without power; overthrown by his colleagues and only recently released from the Tower, he was still excluded from a board now controlled by the Earl of Warwick. Paget had survived the council's *coup* against Somerset and during February and March 1550 was leading the English delegation in negotiations for peace with France. As he did not return to London from this mission abroad until Saturday, 29 March, we can assume that he composed his 'Advise to the Kinges Counsail' in France.

For whom was the advice intended? Dr Gammon assumed without question that Paget had addressed his paper to Warwick, that 'even while he was yet abroad he favoured the Earl with a lengthy essay on conciliar government'.[11] The recipient's endorsement, 'The remembraunce gyven to my Master by my Lorde Paget xxiij martij 1549', indicates, however, that while in France Paget was able personally to present his memorandum to 'my Master' on the same day as that on which he composed it. The 'Master' of the endorsement, therefore, cannot have been Warwick, for on 23 March 1550 Warwick was in London.

It is almost certain that the 'Master' referred to was another member of that mission to France, Sir William Petre, the chief secretary of state since 1547 and the one man after Paget who was most familiar with the day-to-day routine of council affairs. For six years the two of them had as colleagues shared the secretaries' duties of managing council business. As they prepared to return to London from abroad, amidst reports of the downfall of the earls of Arundel and Southampton, the two administrators may have discussed how the council's activities could be made more regular. Following, as will be seen, the often irregular procedures of Somerset, it would have seemed wholly proper for them to have considered that, by placing the council under uniform administrative practice, they could not only make that body a more efficient instrument of government in uncertain times, but also strengthen its collective authority against the ambition of the Earl of Warwick. We know that Paget was very much concerned that the 'estate of the Realme' be bought to a 'perfait and happy' condition; indeed, on 15 March he had pointedly advised Warwick himself to adopt, with the council, a rational, planned approach to the government of the realm, suggesting that 'the begyning, the progresse, and end of everything be depely forseen considered and provided for'.[12] Clearly, the council could effectively proceed to the formulation of state policy in the manner suggested only if the conduct and administration of its business were made much more regular than had heretofore been the case. As Paget's rules together represent essentially a secretary's guide to the management of that business, it is difficult to escape the conclusion that he gave Petre his 'Advise' while the two of them were working together in France – incidental business from that mission in Petre's hand which has survived in a private collection of Paget's personal papers documents the fact of their close collaboration at the time[13] – and if the secretary kept it for future reference,[14] he must have given it for safe-keeping to his assistant, who clearly endorsed it as the paper given to 'my Master by my Lorde Paget'. In all probability, then, Petre was in possession of Paget's 'Advise' on 23 March 1550.

The tone and form of the paper suggest that the rules constituted more than mere (unsolicited?) advice, that they were, as the recipient knew, a reminder, a remembrance, a memorandum of procedures which had been followed or which, in the light of experience, should be observed. Although the council did not formally accept the 'Advise' *in toto*, as a single set of rules,[15] it did adopt (on 20 April 1550) part of the tenth item which exempted one of the three clerks of all other duties except the keeping of the council register; another order of the day before appointing this clerk (William Thomas) to his post repeated verbatim the order appointing Paget clerk of the privy council ten years earlier.[16] It is equally clear that one other procedure, the signing of the council book, had earlier been followed in precisely the form here given;[17] the rule described what had been done in

1547 as something which ought to be re-adopted in 1550.[18] We also know that Paget's suggested procedure for the secretary's handling of council correspondence reflected contemporary practice.

The rules which raise the most interesting questions concern the time, place, and frequency of meetings, the procedures for attendance, and the composition and number of a quorum. The fact that Paget felt it necessary to remind the council in 1550 that they should meet in the council chamber at court at regularly scheduled times suggests that this is precisely what the council had not always been doing before that time. Indeed, the specificity of the rule points to a more fundamental aspect of procedure than merely place and time of meeting: the authority for calling a meeting.

In his will Henry VIII admitted that he could not 'conveniently prescribe a certain Order or Rule unto our forsayd Counsaillours for their Behavoirs and Procedings'; he could only give them 'or the most part of them, being assembled togirdres in Counsail' the power to devise any 'Maner of Proceding which they shal for the Tyme think meet to use and folow'.[19] It was this lack of procedural order which the executors cited as the primary reason for their creation of a Protector, that 'somme special man . . .

shuld be preferred in name and place before others, to whome as to the state and hedde of the reste all strangers and others might have accesse, and who for his vertue, wisedome and experience in thinges were mete and hable to be a special Remembrancer and to kepe a moste certaine accompte of all our procedinges, which otherwise could not chose within shorte tyme but growe into much disordre and confusion.[20]

In agreeing to allow the Protector to perform the primary tasks of government appointed in Henry VIII's will, the executors (privy councillors) had (or thought they had) also required him to consult formally with them in his execution of those duties.[21] Although this condition may have operated before 24 December 1547, it did not do so afterwards, for in signing Somerset's comprehensive letters-patent of that date, ten – that is, the required 'most part of the hole Nombre' of the original executors – in fact relinquished the council's former right to advise him on questions of policy, as well as the earlier stipulation that he secure their consent to decisions which he should himself make.[22] When, in October 1549, the council recalled that Somerset had broken the promise to which they said he had solemnly sworn 'in open counsell', that he would 'do nothing touching the state of thaffaires of his highnes without thadvise and consent of vs the rest of the counsell',[23] they did not mention that his promise preceded the granting of the first letters-patent of the Protectorate and that in putting their hands to the second patent, they had agreed to a commission to regulate their affairs absolutely: in general, the patent implied that he should be able to establish the order for the council's proceeding; in particular, it authorised him to 'use' only so many privy councillors 'as he shall thincke mete to call unto hym frome tyme to tyme'.[24] In the context of the procedures for meetings, Somerset's patent thus combined both the prerogatives of the Crown and the powers of the Lord President of the privy council: only kings chose councillors and called them to council; in the King's temporary absence, the responsibility for the regulation of meetings fell to the President.

In what has been taken as the definitive account of the office, Pollard thought that 'whatever the president did, he did not preside over the council', that he had no clearly defined duties, that the 'non-existence of any specific functions' suggested that the title was merely honorary.[25] It is clear from Sir Julius Caesar's unknown but careful researches into the history of the office,[26] however, that the President of the early Tudor privy council did have both a specific place and function. It is evident that the Crown conferred the office orally for the duration of the royal pleasure[27] on the Lord Great (or Grand) Master of the King's household.[28] As the great mastership was not granted by patent at this time,[29] it is difficult to fix precisely the dates for the tenures of the early Tudor presidents. We know that by 1540 the Duke of Suffolk was both President and Great Master.[30] It has been thought that William Lord St John became Great Master about November 1545 (that is, on Suffolk's death) and therefore (presumably) Lord President at the same time.[31] Caesar confirms the fact that Henry VIII made St John President, but says that Suffolk continued in that office only until about 1542 at the latest, and that Paulet *as Great Master* was made President by Henry

VIII 'about 34 of his reigne', or sometime in 1543.[32] St John remained Great Master and President until 2 February 1550 when, in a round of new promotions for those who had fallen into line behind Warwick, he was (as Earl of Wiltshire) made High Treasurer.[33] Warwick became Great Master and Lord President on the same day,[34] and held both offices until Edward VI's death.

Following the *coup*, it is not surprising that Dudley should have sought the presidency, for as Caesar knew, the President controlled council procedure: 'the king himself is to set properly with his privy Counsell, or to appoint in his place his lieutenant or president'; 'in the King's absence' the President thus 'directed the business handled and to be handled in the kings Privy Councell and called the Counsell vppon all occasions and when he thought fit, and dissolved it at his pleasure'.[35] In precedence the President (as Great Master) followed the Chancellor and High Treasurer, but as 'lieutenant' of the Crown in council he had the right nevertheless to preside at meetings, so that 'in all times of Counsell [he] sat at the vpper end of the Counsell table' ordering the affairs of the board in the manner described by Caesar.[36] It was 'in warning the Counsellors to mete and disbaring them at his pleasure'[37] that a president under Edward VI was able to exercise the greatest power, and it was this power in particular which Somerset's letters-patent gave to the Protector by allowing him to 'use' only so many councillors as he should occasionally wish, leaving St John, the nominal President, with little more than the title to the office.[38]

Under Somerset, then, the authority for calling meetings rested in a royal commission passed under the great seal and signed by a majority of Henry VIII's executors; as Lord President, Northumberland exercised this authority by virtue of his office. How and to what extent did they use this power?

As the government of the realm lay with the King in his council, so were the acts of his privy council the proceedings of a council at court. In practice this meant that the council book followed the King wherever he might be, since the meetings of the King's privy councillors, by definition, were the meetings of only those 'Lordes and others of the Kinges Majestes privye councell attending upon his highness person at the Corte', to use the contemporary formula.[39] But, as Pollard remarked, by 1540 the King's estate had become the English state and his privy council its government;[40] as the government in England sometimes had to administer the state in the King's absence, it became necessary for the whole council to divide, so that under Henry VIII occasionally we find the 'council in London' corresponding with the 'council at court' and so on.[41] On such occasions, however, we find recorded in the register meetings of 'the privy council' only, no matter which of the two 'councils' possessed the ledger (sometimes the council with the King did not)[42] because there existed but one King's council, although that body might have divided temporarily into two parts or have otherwise found its individual members scattered about the countryside. Such entries reveal merely the essential nature of the privy council: it was a single institution with a fixed membership keeping a distinct set of records; it was essentially bureaucratic because its members could by virtue of their office and with only the slightest changes in procedure continue to administer the realm in the King's name but without his person. This principle of Henrician government the Duke of Somerset nearly destroyed by abandoning even his own reconstructed council; the Duke of Northumberland revived the principle, much to his credit, but applied it so efficiently that he nearly destroyed the Tudors as well.

In the first place, it is true that under both men, just as under Henry VIII, we find the privy council meeting away from the court, but the difference between the Henrician and the later practice is that, whereas under Henry and Dudley (after February 1550: the commencement of his presidency) such meetings are extraordinary and rare, with the Protector they apear to have been the practice. Pollard cited some notable examples before 1547;[43] of 740 recorded meetings from 21 February 1550 to 16 June 1553, only fourteen are certainly not those of councillors 'attendant in the courte'.[44] In other words, ninety-eight of every hundred meetings called by Dudley were convened at court. As Somerset ordered very few meetings to be recorded, we cannot give the exact figures in his case, but it is significant that during the first year of his ascendancy, of the sixty-one references in the register to locations of meetings or places where business was dispatched, fifteen identify the Protector's London residence or his mansion at Sheen near Richmond Park and one cites Thomas Seymour's house 'besides Temple Barre'.[45] Furthermore, the clerk's method of noting place names during this period suggests that almost 40 per cent of the dated 'acts of the privy council' for Somerset's first year in office were accomplished at his house in the Strand.[46] The extant original letters and warrants for this period confirm this observation.[47] Thus, whereas Northumberland's adherents transacted the King's business at court, Somerset dispatched the Crown's affairs from his own household almost as often as from a royal palace, and this he continued to do after 1547;[48] even the suspension from membership of one of the King's councillors was done 'before their Grace and Lordships, being assembled in councile at Somerset Place besides the Straunde' and not in the council chamber at court.[49]

This does not necessarily mean that privy councillors absented themselves from the court during the Protectorate; saving conditions of plague, at least a few councillors were appointed to attend upon the King's person.[50] The point is simply that Somerset was empowered to decide who and how many they should be; during the Scottish campaign of 1547, for example, he appointed a committee of nine privy councillors to remain at London and Hampton Court with the King.[51] Paget kept him informed as to their manner of attendance at court.[52] In this exceptional case, the councillors' duties of attendance on the King's person, as distinct from attendance at meetings, were established informally by the ruling group in Somerset's absence; other than this there seems to have been no fixed procedure before 1550. Some understanding must have existed between Somerset and the rest of the council regarding periodic residence at court, for we know that Philip Manwarynge, a gentleman usher of the King's chamber, and his assistants, one yeoman usher, four yeoman, and three grooms, were occasionally charged with making ready the King's halls 'with my lorde Protectors lodginges and diuerse other lodginges for the Counsaille'.[53] Privy councillors who were also officers of the royal household certainly enjoyed lodgings at court; at any given time we might also find, when business, a court function, reception, or a progress demanded their continual attendance, other greater and lesser state officers and ecclesiastics who were also privy councillors.[54] But unless their attendance had been prearranged in council, Somerset appears simply to have summoned his colleagues to the King only when special business required it and then in letters over his own signature.[55] Although this may have been the regular practice, at least one interesting exception should be noted: on Friday, 3 October 1549, with talk of a conspiracy in the air and his hand no longer a sufficient warrant to order their action, 'lettres were writen in the Kinges name immediately that all the counsell solde be at the courte ['on sonday in the' *crossed out*] on sonday upon their allegiance; so that the same evening there was great cariage came to the courte withall the lordes stuffe against the nexte daye'.[56]

The *coup* of 1549 replaced Somerset's governorship of the King's person and his regulation of the council's residence at court with a procedure whereby at least two of six appointed lords (all privy councillors) were always to be attendant upon the King.[57] The interesting point about this order of October 1549 is that, taking into account the purges of the following winter and the promotions of Warwick's supporters on 2 February 1550, the resulting prescription of lords attendant, with the addition of the Chancellor, matches almost exactly the composition of the quorum for meetings prescribed in Paget's 'Advise'. The effect of the advancements in February was such that, of the High Treasurer (Earl of Wiltshire), Great Chamberlain (Marquess of Northampton), Great Master (Earl of Warwick), Privy Seal (Earl of Bedford), and King's Chamberlain (Lord Wentworth), at least two were to be continually attendant at court. Paget's order required that six privy councillors be 'attendant in the courte', of whom at least two were to be any of these officers including the Chancellor (then Lord Rich) and a third one of the secretaries (Petre or Dr Wotton); the six were to assemble at court for meetings.[58] In establishing a rule which thus explains the almost invariable practice of scheduled meetings at court after February 1550, Paget's 'item' merely reflected recent procedural and political changes. Thereafter, any changes in the conditions of attendance on the King and thus attendance at meetings, made necessary for example by the royal progresses, were arranged in council according to fixed schedules.[59]

The direct procedural relationship between presence at court and attendance at meetings which marks the period of Northumberland's presidency does not characterise practice under Somerset, for although there may have been at least a few councillors continuously at court, the evidence suggests that the Protector called them 'to hym' only very infrequently for what we should accept as an official 'meeting' of the privy council – namely, one convened for the consideration of general affairs or for the hearing of requests, suits, and bills of supplication addressed to the lords of the council.

It should be said first that Sunday may in fact have been the one day of regularly appointed meetings at court, and that these Sunday sessions were reserved primarily for the hearing of suits, and so on; the evidence for this is circumstantial.[60] The point is, however, that with a few exceptions, Somerset chose not to record meetings of the privy council, especially after the consolidation of his power by the terms of the patent of 24 December 1547.[61] As noted earlier, we have no way of knowing whether many of the dates in the register which fall on Sundays (or any other days of the week) really do correspond to days on which the council sat in the council chamber and dispatched the warrants that the clerks so frequently recorded under those dates. The analysis of the register presented in this study proved simply that the dates do not all correspond to council meetings: the government chose to record the fact that some councillors had authorised certain warrants for payment and not whether they had done so in or out of a meeting.

It will be argued here that after December 1547 Somerset ceased to rely on 'meetings' of the council to provide him with whatever advice he may have sought; that during 1548 he began to abandon the council altogether; that events in 1549 (his brother's alleged treason, Ket's rebellion and the Western rising) forced him once again to observe at least the formality of consulting with his colleagues, but that even the few meetings which he did call, whether or not they were ever recorded, were convened merely for the purpose of presenting his already formed views and decisions to the board.

For a start, there is the Protector's attitude towards the official record of what should have been the acts of the council. Before 1 June 1547 the proceedings entered in the register certainly represent the collective work of active privy councillors: forty-six of the fifty-nine days' entries bear a place of origin; an average of nine councillors actually signed the council book at the foot of business for fifty-four of the fifty-five days. After 28 May 1547, however, the same six councillors signed the book only after about every fourth recorded day; these signatures, which before had borne witness to personal authorisation, thus became, as early as June 1547, mere administrative formulas: they do not necessarily correspond to the signatories' physical presence at or near the place of dispatch, on or even close to the dates given in the register,[62] nor do they necessarily signify meetings in which the business so subscribed was passed.[63] Saving four exceptional cases, no signatures appear after 1 January 1548. The council book thus appears to reflect two related facts: meetings became much less frequent after June 1547, and the bulk of the 'business' recorded was not necessarily authorised in meetings of the board. In view of the fact that the executors had charged Somerset specifically with the responsibility for keeping 'a most certaine accompte' of its proceedings,[64] the register would appear here to be a relatively unbiased source for these observations.

In the same context there is, secondly, the council's own version of what they called 'the duke of Somersetes doinges', a letter of 11 October 1549 to English ambassadors abroad presenting the council's case for removing the Protector from office.[65] Stripped of its rhetoric and politically weighted allegations, the letter is remarkable for what it reveals about the probable frequency of meetings and the character of meetings which were called. The councillors admitted that in January 1547 they had thought it necessary procedurally 'to have one as it wer a mouth for the rest' of the council and that they had agreed to Hertford's elevation because he was most qualified by service and blood to head their number. He had not long been in office, however, before he began to dispatch matters of great weight and importance 'by himself alone without calling for any of vs of the counsell many tymes therunto *and if for the name sake* he called any man he ordred the maters as pleased himself refusing to here any mans reason but his own'.[66] They emphasised that Somerset did not proceed in open council. Although we may doubt their ultimate belief that this seditious, outrageous, and detestable man had laboured covertly to plunge the realm into such confusion that he should, when chaos finally reigned, be able somehow to dispose of the King and all of England, nevertheless there is a certain logic to their plea that he had not consulted them in all of this, for had he done so it would now appear that they had in effect consented to his 'naughtie doinges'. Indeed, we need not accept the council's interpretation of Somerset's motives in order to accept their unequivocal statement that he called meetings only very rarely and that when he did so it was merely for the sake of being able to say that he had conferred with the council. Such meetings had become occasional constitutional formalities. Needless to say, perfunctory acceptance and ratification of the Protector's policies under such circumstances was not a manner of proceeding that the council had meant to adopt when they first agreed to Somerset's preferment.

Paget's correspondence with Somerset at this time supports the view that by February 1548 Somerset had effectively abandoned the council as a body of advisers. Nowhere in the extant memoranda which Paget addressed to Somerset[67] does Sir William refer to the government's foreign and domestic policies as matters for the council to deal with; the King's business is always the Protector's *personal* concern. Paget speaks of 'your procedinges in the parliament', 'your determinacions for the yere to come', 'your forrayne affayres', 'your debte', 'your navie', 'your lawe the laste yere for the Sacrament', 'your matters of pollicie', 'your ordre for Religion',[68] and so forth, and always in the context that these are interests for Somerset to resolve, to give order to, to set forth, and so on. In the absence of secretaries' agendas for this period, the very existence of Paget's rather pointed 'remembrances', which are themselves rather like agendas, implies that Somerset alone was weighing policies of his own devising. Perhaps nowhere is this separation of Protector and privy council more directly revealed than in Paget's urgent advice of 25 December 1548 to 'appoint us of the counsaile to attende uppon your grace and discharge us of forreyne offices in particular to thintent we maye be thabler to assist your grace for the oversight of the hole in generall'. The problem, clearly, was that Somerset was attempting to rule without the council; but without the council's advice, as Paget pointed out, 'youe here not all thinges nor all men' with the result that 'youe must often altre your determinacions'.[69]

One point, at least, Somerset accepted; it seems that in 1549 he did resume calling the council together. How frequent were these meetings we cannot know; that Somerset called them merely for the council's unquestioned approval of his policies is evident from several of Paget's private remarks.[70] Furthermore, the fact that Paget had frequently 'to putt your grace in remembrance' of important unresolved business suggests that as late as August 1549 Somerset had, in the absence of the council's regular procedures, still not developed any systematic way of formulating policy and administering the King's multiple affairs.

The relative infrequency of council meetings after June 1547; the probable cessation of meetings during much of 1548; the character of the meetings which were convened; the fact that much of what should have been the council's business at court was handled by the Protector at Somerset Place – against the background of these developments, the restoration of regular council procedures in 1550 appears unquestionably to have been the result of the calculated moves which propelled Dudley into the office of lord president. Indeed, the procedural consequences of Dudley's triumph are apparent in the immediate regularisation of the order for meetings.

The difference in procedure which determined place of meeting before October 1549 and after February 1550 has already been noted; evidence for the period of political manoeuvring in the interim is equally revealing. Thus, although the King was resident at Westminster during November and December 1549 and council letters were dated from there by the clerk, Sir Thomas Chaloner, councillors were in fact meeting regularly at Ely Place, the Earl of Warwick's house in Holborn;[71] but in addition to 'regular' meetings in the council chambers at Westminster, Greenwich, Hampton Court, St James's Palace, and Windsor Castle, clerks also recorded meetings in the star chamber,[72] the 'Dyning Chamber Besydes the Starre Chamber', the 'Withdrawing Chamber next to the Parliament Chamber in thold Pallays' of Westminster,[73] the Sheriff of London's house, and, during the crisis of October 1549, variously at Ely Place, the Guildhall, the Mercers' Hall, and Lord St John's London residence.[74] These at least are official references which hide nothing so colourful as the secret meeting which Thomas Seymour once complained had been convened without him in 'the Gardyn'.[75] But such irregularities passed with the coming of Warwick's presidency; after February 1550, as already stated, the council met almost invariably at court and always recorded the fact.

There is no doubt that Dudley controlled the process by which meetings were called. Consider, for example, the events of 18 January 1552: on that day Northumberland lay at Greenwich where the court had tarried since 23 December. The privy council had last met on 10 January. On the morning of the eighteenth Northumberland received word that the French ambassador would be at the court that afternoon to declare to the council French intentions in the controversy over the location of the border between England and Scotland. This news caught Northumberland somewhat by surprise; the presence of the ambassador in this matter required a full-blown meeting of the board, and on that particular day it is clear that a number of the council were scheduled to sit after dinner in the star chamber. Northumberland wrote immediately to Secretary Cecil in London saying that

eyther the Lordes muste mynde to Come imedyatly after dyner from the start chamber hither or ells he muste haue word respecting his coming till to morro, which, yf the affayres in the start chamber after dyner requirith any tyme, I think yt best to be so. Wherfore I wold you move this to the reste of the Lordes that do sytt todaye there and to send me word yf they wyll haue him deferryd till to morro.

Cecil presented Northumberland's 'choice' to the lords at Westminster and they 'decided' to repair to Greenwich that afternoon, for we know that the meeting with the French ambassador, attended by thirteen privy councillors, took place at court that same day.[76] Thus, when Sir Julius Caesar observed that to the council table the lords 'not lodging in Court, nor Ordinary Greate Officers of the Howsehuld were not accustomed to come, but onely vppon Somons either from the Lord President of the said Counsell, or from one of the Secretaries of Estate; then never to faile in coming thither, or to send a sufficient excuse of their not appearance', he was describing correctly the practice in the reign of Edward VI.[77] 'Lettres to all them of the Counsaill that be absent' from the court frequently went out upon the Lord President's command.[78] In the President's absence the highest ranking privy councillor at court seems also to have possessed the authority to call a meeting if, for example, important intelligence had been received which in his judgement demanded that the councillors assemble themselves 'at what tyme so ever it shallbe'.[79]

Where, exactly, were the council assembling? An analysis of the council's places of meeting from 20 February 1550 to 16 June 1553 shows the board each year to have moved with the court according to the following approximate schedule: Westminster, mid-October to late December; Greenwich, late December to late January; Westminster, late January to late April; Greenwich, late April to late June. During the summer months, if the King did not embark upon a progress, the council moved with the boy in typical fashion from Greenwich to royal apartments at Hampton Court, Windsor, Oatlands Park, and back to Hampton Court again before the return to Westminster. The short progress of 1550 also took part of the council to Guildford, Woking, Nonsuch, and Richmond, whereas that of 1552, which left Greenwich on 16 June and returned to Windsor on 18 September, witnessed meetings at seventeen different locations, including Portsmouth and Salisbury.[80] Although the fact is not recorded, we also know that a few of the council met at Farnham during the King's brief stay there in September 1551.[81]

How frequent were privy council meetings? Paget suggested that the councillors 'attendant in the courte' should assemble together on Tuesday, Thursday, and Saturday (or oftener) from eight in the morning until noon and again from two until four o'clock, and on Sunday from two until four.[82] Although there is no evidence that the council attempted to follow a Tuesday–Thursday–Saturday–Sunday schedule after February 1550,[83] nevertheless it is true that they were holding an average of 4·3 meetings per week until 16 June 1553, when the record ends; this compares with about 3·6 meetings per week after the *coup* and before Northumberland's presidency.[84] The hours of meeting which Paget mentions may well have been the ones observed; it seems likely that he had in mind hours which had been kept at some earlier time when procedure was more regular. One contemporary observer remembered a day when 'all the lordes . . . satt . . . in counsaill from vii of the clocke in the morninge till iiii in the afternoone, and then went to supper',[85] and though this was one of the extraordinary sessions of the London faction on 10 October 1549, the hours of sitting, in the light of Paget's suggested times, seem not so unusual.

Another of the rules of March 1550 would have required the attendance at meetings of at least six of the council at court. Only fifteen times after March 1550 are fewer than six members recorded present – four on four occasions and five at eleven other times. All but one of these meetings occurred before January 1553; it was surely in order to provide for such reduced attendances, especially during a royal progress, that the rule of 1553 prescribed that although four constituted a quorum, six at least were required to make 'a parfaite conclusion and ende of things'.[86] How many members did in fact attend meetings? Perhaps the best approach to a survey of attendances is one which follows the council continuously through one year's business. The year preceding Edward VI's death is a good one for this purpose, for it includes both a royal progress and a Parliamentary session;[87] the number of councillors during this time also remained relatively stable – about thirty members.[88] As Table 9, section A shows, an average of about eleven (10·8) privy councillors attended meetings throughout the year (except for the meetings convened on progress with the King); thus for any one meeting, slightly more than one-third (36 per cent) of the active members were present. Attendance also fell to less than eight (26 per cent) during the progress but rose to an average of almost fourteen councillors (45 per cent) while Parliament was in session. Of course, attendance had always been relatively high at Parliament time; during the winter of 1549–50, for example, when the council numbered twenty-six members,[89] an average of twelve men, or 46 per cent of the membership, were attending meetings (see Table 9, section B).

For the history of the council's procedure the most interesting fact that this survey of attendance reveals is the sudden decline in the average number of members who were meeting in London after April 1552, and especially from October 1552. With the return of the court to Westminster, the commencement of the new legal year, and the consequent resumption of regular government business after the summer, the period from mid-October to late December had every year been one of great activity for the council; one expects that the number of privy councillors in London at this time will certainly be as great as, if not greater than, that at any other time of the year, no matter where the court may lie. Consider, for example, the year 1550, when the average number of councillors who attended 116 meetings from 2 February (the first day after the prorogation of Parliament) to 22 July did not exceed 11·1, or 40 per cent of a total membership of twenty-eight.[90] During the progress of that year average attendance dropped to 6·5. But at Westminster after 16 October, the figure rose sharply to 13·8, which meant that at a given meeting we could expect to find almost half (46 per cent) of a council numbering thirty members in the council chamber.

For the same period (18 October to 29 December) in 1549, average attendance (12·8) represented an even higher proportion of total membership, 49 per cent of twenty-six, a figure partly explained by the fact that meetings at this time also fell during the Parliamentary session after the *coup*. In 1551, when no Parliament sat, however, a high average number of councillors (fourteen) were also attending meetings at Westminster, although Somerset's alleged conspiracy and arrest then must certainly have accounted for the sustained presence of some of these men. Nevertheless, these fourteen, on the average, represented almost 47 per cent of a membership of thirty. In the light of attendance at Westminster in 1549, 1550, and 1551, the figure of 10·8 for the autumn of 1552 thus marks a decline of more than one-fifth (23 per cent) in the average number of privy councillors who were assembling for meetings. As the average level of attendance then was the same as for the entire year after April 1552, it is apparent that although membership had increased by over 13 per cent (from twenty-six to thirty) since 1549, the *proportion* of the total number of members who were attending meetings had actually decreased in that time.

As President, Northumberland could warn the council to meet; could he also, to use Caesar's phrase, disbar them at his pleasure? On the one hand, it is not apparent that he was refusing individual councillors admission to meetings; on the other hand, it does seem that by the end of the Parliamentary session of 1552, Northumberland had changed the conditions of certain councillors' attendance. The effects of these changes (see Table 10) were,

TABLE 9

Place	Date	No. of meet-ings	Range of attend-ance	Average	Total member-ship
A. *Attendance at meetings 18 April 1552 to 10 April 1553*[91]					
Westminster	18–29 April	10	6–16	13·1	30
Greenwich	1 May to 8 July	40	5–21	10·8	31
(Progress) Windsor/	9 July to 14 Sept.	33[a]	6–12	7·7	31
Hampton Court	18 Sept. to 9 Oct.	16	6–13	9·6	30
Westminster	11 Oct. to 18 Dec.	55	6–15	10·8	30
Greenwich	27 Dec. to 22 Jan.	13	5–15	10·5	30
Westminster	26 Jan. to 10 April	50	8–19	10·8	30
Total		184[b]	5–21	10·8	30
B. *Attendance at meetings during sessions of Parliament*					
Westminster[c]	4 Nov. 1549 to 1 Feb. 1550	38[d]	7–16	12·0	26
Westminster[e]	23 Jan. to 15 April 1552	61	5–19	12·4	30
Westminster	1–31 March 1553	20	9–19	13·6	30
C. *Attendance at meetings on progress with the King*					
Guildford[f] etc.	14 Aug. to 14 Oct. 1550	41	4–10	6·5	30
Oatlands[g] etc.	9 July to 14 Sept. 1552	33[h]	6–12	7·7	31
D. *Attendance at Westminster during the autumn*					
	18 Oct. to 29 Dec. 1549	35[i]	9–21	12·8	26
	16 Oct. to 21 Dec. 1550	39	6–20	13·8	30
	16 Oct. to 21 Dec. 1551	55	7–21	14·0	30
	11 Oct. to 18 Dec. 1552	55	6–15	10·8	30

[a] The clerk recorded 34 meetings during this period but did not give attendances at the meeting at Oatlands, 9 July 1552.

[b] This total does not include the 33 meetings with the King on progress.

[c] Westminster is given as the location of 7 meetings; the old Palace of Westminster for 2 meetings; star chamber for 1; no place is given for the other meetings.

[d] Although there were 41 meetings, attendances are given for only 38.

[e] The star chamber is given as the location of 1 meeting and the 'Parliament Howse' for another.

[f] Guildford, Woking, Oatlands Park, Nonsuch Palace, Richmond.

[g] See p. 305, n. 80.

[h] See note [a] above.

[i] Westminster is given as the location for only 12 meetings during this period; no location is given for 23 meetings. The number 35 does not include probable meetings on 7 and 9 November for which no attendances are given, or the possibility that additional meetings may have been held on 23 October and 12 November.

firstly, to establish a circle of fourteen privy councillors who were regularly attending half (actually 46 per cent) or more of the number of all meetings at Westminster, Greenwich, Hampton Court, and Windsor, and, secondly, to reduce the King's privy council of thirty-one official members to a total of about twenty-one truly active members – namely, those who were attending about one-fifth or more of all meetings. Is there an explanation for this?

It is a curious fact that about this time (March 1552) King Edward named his special council 'for the state' and it was almost precisely those councillors not members of this committee who attended very few meetings thereafter.[92] It is true that several of the prominent members of the committee (including Cranmer) fall outside this group of twenty-one active councillors, but, as an attempt will be made to show later, the committee, or so-called council 'for the state', was probably an honorific group which merely excluded none of the great officers of state and household. Even so, it is also probable that the King's appointment of the twenty-one members of the committee essentially reflected Northumberland's political calculations – he had restricted the circle of his close political friends – a fact which the figures of attendance clearly seem to confirm. Indeed, not including Northumberland, twelve of the other twenty members of the committee 'for the state' were Northumberland's appointees and twelve of the other twenty 'active' members were similarly new after October 1549. More pointedly, of the other thirteen very active councillors (those attending about half or more of all meetings), eleven had been named to the committee; nine of the thirteen had been appointed by Northumberland. It is surely no coincidence that after April 1552 the King's committee – with the exception of Cranmer, Hereford, and Westmorland, whose infrequent attendances can be explained[93] – consisted entirely of those privy councillors who were regularly administering affairs at London (although, as will be seen, the committee itself exercised no real power). The important point is that whereas Northumberland had certainly increased the membership of Edward's privy council, he had also effectively created a smaller, 'working' group of about the same size as the full councils of the period 1536–49. Numerically the privy council of 1553 was in practice no more unwieldy than Henry VIII's privy council.

TABLE 10   *Attendance at council meetings, 18 April 1552 to 16 June 1553*[94]

	Number of attendances	Percentage of total no. of meetings (218)
*Darcy	189	87
*Cotton	158	79**
*Winchester	170	78
*Cecil	162	74
*Bedford	150	69
*Petre	139	64
Mason	135	62
*Gates	123	56
*Clinton	112	51
*Goodrich	111	51
*Northumberland	110	50
*Northampton	108	49
*Bowes	106	48
Cobham	100	46
*Shrewsbury	75	34
*Suffolk	75	34
*Cheyne	64	29
*Hoby	56	26
*Pembroke	54	25
*Dr Wotton	46	21
Huntingdon	41	18
Baker	34	16
North	28	14
*Cranmer	18	8
Sadler	7	3
*Hereford	7	3
*Westmorland	6	3
Rich	6	3
Montague	5	2
Gage	0	—
Bromley	0	—

* Members of council 'for the state'.
** 79 per cent of 199 meetings from 11 May 1552 when Cotton became a privy councillor.

4
The Conduct of Business

The source of most of the information upon which the council acted consisted in letters to the board 'from all partes of the kingdome, of the weekly states of the markets, and provisions or wants of the Countries, and of all Intelligences of busnes both at home and abroade'.[1] The opening of such correspondence was as much a political as an administrative act since the information received could conceivably have proved useful to those in opposition to the ruling faction. Somerset and Northumberland found it necessary, therefore, to ensure not only that the secretaries keep them closely informed of the reception of letters, but also that a group of adherents be present to receive dispatches. The opening of letters addressed to Protector and council occasionally became a notable administrative ritual: from the court at Windsor on 25 September 1548 the council explained to a correspondent that they were able to reply in the terms given only because Somerset had made special arrangements for them to open letters in his absence.[2] That may have been an extraordinary measure, but Northumberland, before he was able finally to destroy Somerset's influence, ruled that all vital incoming correspondence be received in council before at least a few of his men: on 10 January 1551 'it was ordred that no lettres of importaunce concerning thastate shulde be broken up but at the Borde whan the Counsaill is assembled'.[3] Sir Julius Caesar remembered having seen several volumes of council records, and 'by some of those bookes it appeareth that in the time of King Edward the 6 and before, and after, it was accustomed that some of the said Counsell met almost every day to recive letters'.[4] As none of the extant registers records the regular *reception* of letters, Caesar can only have been referring to a series of now lost registers of in-letters. As it was apparent from the ledgers themselves that a few councillors were assembling to open correspondence, the books must have recorded the lords' attendance at the time of opening or perhaps have displayed their signatures in witness of the council's reception of the day's post.

We do not know when or for how long during Edward's reign this informal 'committee' of councillors may have observed the procedure of collective reception of letters; we do know that many packets were delivered first to the secretaries, who turned them over direct to Somerset and Northumberland. In practice, this meant that in the period before October 1549 letters intended for the council passed first through the hands of Paget and Sir John Thynne, steward of Somerset's household;[5] after 1550 the letters went frequently from Cecil to Northumberland and then back to Cecil and Northumberland's men with the King, Thomas Lord Darcy, the King's Chamberlain, and Sir John Gates, Vice-Chamberlain, for selective presentation to Edward VI and the other councillors.[6] After the consolidation of their power Somerset and Northumberland attempted to pre-empt the council's reception of letters by having English ambassadors and officials address their letters personally to Protector and President or send two letters, one to the head and one to the body of the council.[7] Edward VI saw the council's letters only at Cecil's discretion or upon Northumberland's specific command.[8]

Whatever the source of business – letter, bill, presentation, appearance, and so on – it became the duty of the senior secretary at court (or the junior in his absence) to present to the board all such particular matters which required the council's full attention – namely, those which required the verbal and/or written consent of at least a few lords in order to be resolved. The secretary's task under model conditions of governmental routine was thus to organise this multitude of affairs in terms of items of business on an agenda which he could then read out at a meeting. (Lack of time and cost of paper would have prohibited the distribution of advance copies.) The agenda of letters to be read, warrants to be signed, matters to be discussed, and so on represented the administrative centre-piece of the council's work: control of the formulation of the agenda provided a powerful means of regulating almost every aspect of the council's activity. Indeed, formulation of the agenda has been described as perhaps the most important way in which Cromwell had come to dominate Henry's council;[9] after 1540 Tudor secretaries of state assumed this aspect of the management of the council's work as part of their normal duties.

It is surely significant, therefore, to observe that in the whole lot of extant state papers for the period of the Protectorate not a single agenda has survived as an informal, 'natural' product of the secretaries' management of business. The lack of such documentary evidence suggests that the papers were not lost: they may never have existed. The only extant papers that resemble agendas are the private memoranda which Paget addressed to Somerset from, as it were, outside the secretaries' regular channels of communication. As noted earlier, the very fact that Paget felt bound to remind Somerset of such ordinary kinds of business in schedules of that type suggests strongly that the secretaries were not actually composing agendas, either for the consideration of the board or the duke's perusal. How, then, should we describe the procedures for the conduct and administration of privy council business during the Protectorate?

It has been stated earlier that Somerset sought to control certain kinds of business by denying to his colleagues access to incoming correspondence. A description of how this was done on one occasion illustrates how it could regularly have been accomplished and how, using similar methods, Somerset was able to act independently of the council in other matters. It seems that Somerset had instructed the clerks to be on the watch for particular kinds of letters to the board, for on Saturday morning, 19 May 1548, when Armagil Waad discovered a letter touching upon the government's religious policy – a letter that in the eyes of an observer tended to a 'seditious uproar' – he turned it over to the Protector and quickly dismissed the bearer, who might otherwise have attracted attention waiting for a reply. Somerset read the letter privately and then told Waad to keep the entire matter close to himself.[10] The point is that, as the council did not sit on 19 May 1548[11] or on very many days thereafter, there arose few occasions when this and other missives could have been laid before the board; it should have been convenient for such a letter to have 'disappeared' among all of the other papers collected into Somerset's hands. In this, as probably in similar matters, the clerks of the council worked directly from Somerset's personal instructions; the Protector could thus act independently of the council and the secretaries when it served his purpose.

Diverse kinds of contemporary evidence suggest that the incident cited here was not exceptional; that such procedures frequently characterised the Protector's methods; that he did often bypass the secretaries in the management of other kinds of business; that the Protector's own servants often assumed some of the regular functions of the salaried clerks of the privy council. The 'disappearance' of council documents, for example, clearly points to the fact that Somerset viewed what should have been the council's work as his own, to be supervised by himself: Petre regularly turned over to him council records that should properly have been filed at Westminster. It was thought that Somerset's servants had simply 'not looked after' these and other records, but after the *coup* Petre revealed that such carelessness had been deliberate: as secretary he had been forced to surrender state papers 'to such as were great then abowte' Somerset; 'having bine sins in some trouble', they scattered the writing abroad. The council authorised a search, but admitted in 1550 that none of the originals could be found.[12]

We should expect that these documents included copies and drafts of out-letters written in the name of the Protector and privy council; the fact that relatively few such copies exist is almost certainly explained by Petre's admission. The nature of a few extant examples reveals more than merely the way in which they may have been lost, however. It is apparent, first, that Somerset wrote directly to English ambassadors and officials in letters which should have appeared over the signatures of a number of the council; such letters appear variously in the hand of a clerk of the privy council, a secretary, or Paget (after he became comptroller),[13] and are dated typically from the duke's residences.[14] In other words, we have here what were in effect council letters drafted by the council's 'administrative staff', letters in practice being sent out in the Protector's name. These letters and others like them document the essentially administrative nature of the Protectorate: as the King's affairs of state had increasingly become Somerset's own business, so had the King's secretaries of state and the clerks of the privy council become Somerset's administrative assistants working from within the organisation of the Protector's own 'court'. Although Petre and Paget were executing what we should normally describe as the routine of the secretary's office, nevertheless, such procedures had effectively become aspects of the administration of the Protector's household.

Nowhere is this more apparent than in the case of letters drafted jointly by a secretary of state (or Paget) and a member of Somerset's household staff, letters which, although written in the Protector's name, should nevertheless have come to us as examples of the council's correspondence. There are, for example, Paget's additions to draft instructions in Thynne's hand, as well as similar papers in Petre's hand which Thynne endorsed.[15] In correcting one of Thynne's drafts, Paget may inadvertently have revealed how far removed was the council from the co-ordination of Somerset's policy in particular and the administration of the realm generally.[16] Of course we do possess letters from the Protector and council, and in Somerset's absence, from a few councillors on behalf of the whole council;[17] however, few things could have been accomplished without Somerset's signature and nothing without his knowledge or direct approval. The council's charge of October 1549 stated simply that he had dispatched business of real importance without their participation. We have already seen how he managed to do so outside the framework of scheduled meetings; the evidence for a reconstruction of other administrative procedures lends further support to the council's contention.

Consider the informal procedures by which the Protector dealt privately with foreign ambassadors. In this, as in the conduct of the council's business generally, the pattern of Somerset's behaviour appears to have followed a now familiar pattern: he began by working through the council, but then gradually assumed a separate and total control of affairs. At first, continental envoys enjoyed scheduled audiences before the assembled board; appointments are reported to have been arranged and conveyed in an established way by the secretaries, clerks, and council messengers.[18] In his detailed dispatches, van der Delft frequently mentioned the fact that he had appeared before the Protector and council or simply the council;[19] though he might have taken Somerset aside for confidential remarks, there is no question that in this early period (to 10 July 1547 at least) the envoy also conversed with, heard from, and took his leave of 'all the members of the Council'.[20] But by May 1548 his references to audiences with Edward VI's council cease; we read instead of presentations to and appointed conversations with the Protector alone, at court, and at his home, even though the nature of the business so discussed remained the same.[21] Somerset told van der Delft that no matter whether the Protector alone or Protector and council jointly should answer the Emperor's claims, he (Somerset) 'thought better to communicate them to the Council [himself]'. Van der Delft caught the point: 'This was meant to convey to me that I ought not so persistently seek audience of the Council, but should discuss my affairs with him personally.'[22] The ambassador would be able to quote Somerset again in respect of the council's continued exclusion from consultations.[23] In March 1550, in the kind of meeting from which they had earlier been barred, the triumphant faction reminded van der Delft of this practice by holding themselves not responsible for business transacted specifically in those sessions.[24] Even the council's formal relationship with ambassadors had been altered, as the clerk's record of the French declaration of war of 8 August 1549 shows: to Whitehall came the French envoy with a herald and trumpeter and there in the afternoon he 'declared his revocacion and the openyng of the warres, to my Lordes grace', without recourse to the privy council.[25]

Procedurally, the council may have referred all representations of foreign ambassadors to the Protector, but the council also expected Somerset to keep them fully informed as to the content of those discussions and this Somerset clearly did not always do. The rumours of 1549 that he had agreed secretly to betray Boulogne to France arose directly from his 'often priuie conference with the ffrench Ambassador and the french Ambassadors secretary sent from the others of the King's majesties Counsall'.[26] Although some of the council's allegations of October 1549 smack of propaganda, the article stating that Somerset had improperly discussed matters alone with foreign ambassadors carried a charge both substantial and true.[27] The council had certainly thought it desirable that the Protector should act 'as it wer a mouth for the rest' in answering ambassadors, but this was to have been a representative function, as ambassadors, like other suitors, were to be considered essentially as ones having 'to do with thole body

of the counsell'.[28] After the *coup* the principle was embodied
in procedure: once again foreign envoys met with the council
assembled.[29] Only when the King's death became a real possibility
did Northumberland in feverish preparation for the new reign
meet secretly with the French, whose diplomatic weight he was
thus able to throw against Mary's Imperial friends.[30]

Somerset's control of the information upon which the council
might act; the method of his employment of the King's secretaries
and clerks; the conduct of council business in his household; the
fact of the administration of some of this business by the Protector's servants; the manner of his dealing with ambassadors; his
employment, as will be seen later, of the royal stamp and signet
– all such procedures bear further witness to the course of Somerset's administration, an administration divorced from the secretaries' traditional means of organising the council's work.

How irregular was Somerset's management of the King's business – quite apart from the fact of his abandonment of council
meetings – becomes apparent upon the resumption of rule by the
whole board. The formulation of agendas provides perhaps the
best evidence of the re-establishment of an ordered administration
of the King's affairs. The earliest extant agenda for the period of
Northumberland's presidency dates from September 1551, but
there seems little doubt that from October 1549 the secretaries
had once again taken up the management of council business in
a manner similar to that which the extant agendas show them
later to have followed. Although Paget's 'Advise' makes no mention of the drafting of agendas – perhaps he knew that Petre and
Wotton accepted the task as fundamental and routine – the rules
of 1553 assume the formulation of them to have been a regular
part of the secretaries' duties.

Indeed, by 1553 the only novel element regarding the use of
the council's agenda concerned the King: the rules suggest that
Edward VI had become – or had been persuaded that he ought
to become – interested in these lists of current business. According
to one of the rules, a secretary was to present to the King on
Sunday evening a memorandum of the business to be considered
by the council during the forthcoming week; the King was to
assign particular kinds of business to certain days. It has been
assumed that the introduction of this Sunday evening agenda and

the presumed subsequent distribution of business over the following week represented a novel procedure which served as the basis
for a reorganisation of the council's work. In fact, familiarity
with the extant agendas suggests that only the form of the weekly
list was to be changed: what had constituted the secretaries'
rough notes would become a clerk's fair-copy 'memoriall' to be
delivered to His Majesty.

Nor was the assignment of business to several days of the week
a new procedure. In 1550 Paget would have reserved Sundays
for petitions, and so on, and a minimum of three other days
(Tuesday, Thursday, and Saturday) for the 'Kinges affaires'
generally ('thaffairs occurrent'); Edward VI and Petre would
simply have heard 'sutes, petitions, and commen warrauntis' on
Monday ('that day, and none others be assigned to that purpos'),
leaving Monday afternoon to Friday morning open for the debating of what the King called 'the great affaires', or Petre,
'matters of state'. Thus in assigning business to different days, the
later procedures merely recognised the distinction between everyday matters of 'publique' administration and the King's great
policy concerns.

Were these procedures followed? Neither the council registers
nor the extant agendas reveal the consideration of business on
Sundays, Mondays, and so on according to the divisions noted
here. The entries in the register for a given day are similar to those
for any other day; even the dated agendas after January 1553
mix warrants, appointments, foreign affairs, and other matters
indiscriminately.[31] There appears to be no foundation in fact for
the supposition that these rules of 1553 served as the procedural
basis for a 'reorganisation' of the council's work; councillors
under Northumberland seem to have considered foreign and
domestic points of business after January 1553 in just the same
way as they had done for many months before that time. It is
possible, as already stated, that Edward VI's 'interest' in council
procedure accounts for the survival of some of the papers classified
as agendas: in addition to the Sunday evening 'memoriall' the
King would also have required the secretaries to compose on
Friday afternoons a list of 'such things as have been done the four
days past', including not only matters concluded, but also 'how
many [articles] they have debatid, but not ended and how many

the time suffered not to peruse . . .', and this 'collection' they were to present to him on Saturday mornings.[32] Secretary Petre's 'Memoriall of matter to be considered' of 29 April 1553[33] falls on a Saturday for which there is no record of a meeting and so may have been one of a number of similar but now lost briefs produced in direct response to the procedure cited.[34] Of course these are just the kind of notes a good secretary should ordinarily have kept; the difference is that such jottings, rather than going into the waste paper basket, may also have been informally duplicated for the King and for this reason retained by Cecil.

To what extent was Edward VI involved in the real business of the council? Professor Jordan has ascribed to the boy the 'precocious maturity' and critical independence of a fourteen-year-old administrative genius who framed 'in his own mind' a programme calling for 'a major reorganisation of the Council and its conduct of business';[35] the popular view has the young King of England attending council meetings and, 'as his custom was', preparing the agenda for the next day's session.[36] Although the contents of the King's education in politics may be fairly clear,[37] the nature and degree of his participation in the real work of government and administration are perhaps open to question.

As early as 14 August 1551 Edward could record that it had been 'appointed that I should come to, and sit at, Council, when great matters were in debating or when [ever?] I would'.[38] Later, at some time from 3 to 15 March 1552, when the King composed the names of his committee 'for the state' he wrote: 'Theis [councillors] to attend the matters of the state I wil site with them ons a weke to here the debating of thinges of most importaunce,'[39] and indeed, Scheyfve reported on 30 March 1552 that 'the King is usually present at Council meetings now, especially when state business is being transacted', adding that Edward VI 'began attending a little before the Duke of Somerset was arrested'.[40] The rules of 1553 also made provision for the King's appearance in council: Edward was to be free 'to hyre the debating of any matters' at his pleasure,[41] but the royal pleasure was operative, as the King himself knew, only 'if ther rise . . . mater of waight . . .', *in which case* 'warning shal be gieuen whearby the more may be at the debating of it'.[42] Against these statements must be placed the hard fact that the clerks of the privy council never recorded the King's presence at any of the meetings included in the government's official record of its sessions. Why?

The answer almost certainly is that the meetings which Scheyfve mentioned and those to which Edward referred were not bona fide meetings of the privy council – that is to say, they were not actual working sessions of the council. We may assume that when the King heard the debating of matters of 'waight' after January 1553 he was attending the same sort of meeting held presumably once a week by his committee 'for the state' after March 1552. An independent official reference to the committee fixes its existence as certain in 1552.[43] The point is, however, that although the committee was made up of many of the most active privy councillors, its sessions did not constitute meetings of the privy council, just as the sessions of other committees did not constitute official assemblies of the whole board. Scheyfve was certainly correct in reporting Edward VI's attendance at 'meetings', but he could not have known (nor have later writers understood) that these were extraordinary committee, and not council, meetings – conferences staged especially for the King's benefit to which additional councillors were called and for which special 'warning' was given. In any case, the council determined in advance of such meetings with what business the King would be made privy, when and how to introduce it to him, and what the council's position would be in respect of the matters discussed. It is likely that what Edward thought was the 'debating' of state affairs represented rather a periodic way of enlightening the young Prince as to the reasons for his privy council's already formed decisions. But even this procedure was not new in 1552; the council was in the habit of 'informing' Edward VI of their decisions and of persuading him 'for his satisfaction in point of conscience' why he should 'condescend' to their way of thinking.[44]

Nevertheless, three memoranda in Edward's hand[45] have suggested to others a second way in which the King participated in the conduct of business, namely, that he was himself drafting his council's agendas. It is true that on 18 January 1552, for instance, the young King in the presence of sixteen of his privy council personally handed over to the Marquess of Winchester a set of nine points of business 'to be immediately concluded on by my counsell'; the occasion cited, however, was an audience in 'his Majestes Inner prive Chamber' at Greenwich and not a privy council meeting.[46] There is no evidence that the council moved then or shortly thereafter to a consideration of Edward's agenda; in fact, the document shows that one of the issues listed had already been decided upon[47] while others which had been raised some months earlier were to lie unresolved for many months thereafter.[48] More importantly, it may be asked precisely how Edward VI was able to produce a paper which at first glance suggests a secretary's sense of the ordering of business. Had the young King assumed the administrative duties of the office of a principal secretary? The best reconstruction of what essentially must have been a procedural formality shows the King receiving from the secretaries lists of current heads of unresolved business; these he transcribed in his own fashion, perhaps combining the items of several back-lists, and 'submitted' them to his council. The business listed on the resulting agendas certainly was real, but the agendas themselves were not, since they reflected the secretaries' management of affairs and not Edward VI's. The eighth of Edward's rules of 1553 leaves little doubt, in fact, as to the origin of the King's 'agendas': 'on sonday night again his Majesti hauing receiued of the secretaries such new matter as hath arisen upon new occasion, with such matters as his counsel haue left som not determined, and sum not debatid'.[49] This is not to say that the King did not understand the nature of the business noted, but only to point out that his written exercises are not evidence of a regulation of affairs which only the act of drafting an original agenda provides. King Edward's agendas thus contradict the view that the boy really ordered the council's work. Rather, they bear witness to the early operation of one of the rules of 1553, the provision that the secretary supply the King with a brief of forthcoming business; indeed, as early as September 1551 the secretaries (and/or clerks) were presenting Edward with notes of business to be concluded.[50] On this point, then, the rule of 1553 could hardly have formed part of a reorganisation of council procedure; on the contrary, the rule merely recognised an informal, but established, procedure.

That the King's initiation of business was an act carefully directed by those around him, that his apparently mature grasp of governmental affairs actually marked Northumberland's ability to control the lad's opinions and decrees, are borne out by a contemporary witness whose frank remarks throw new light on the nature of politics at the very centre of Edward's court. Northumberland, according to the French official probably attached (after July 1551) to Boisdauphin's embassy,

had given such an opinion of himself to the young King that he [the King] revered him as if he were himself one of his subjects – so much so that the things which he knew to be desired by Northumberland he himself decreed in order to please the Duke and also to prevent the envy which would have been produced had it been known that it was he [the duke] who had suggested these things to the King. He [Northumberland] had placed [in the King's household] a chamberlain, Master Gaz [Gates] who was his intimate friend and [the] principal instrument which he used in order to induce the King to [do] something when he did not want it to be known that it had proceeded from himself; [it was Gates] who was to report back to him everything said to the King, for this Gates was continually in the [King's privy] Chamber . . . All of the others who were in the Chamber of the said [King] were creatures of the Duke. [Sir Henry] Sidney was his son-in-law and it can be said that he had acquired so great an influence near the King that he was able to make all of his notions conform to those of the Duke. When there was anything of importance which he [Northumberland] wanted to be done or said by the King without it being known that it had proceeded by his motion, he visited the King secretly at night in the King's Chamber, unseen by anyone, after all were asleep. The next day the young Prince came to his council and proposed matters as if they were his own; consequently, everyone was amazed, thinking that they proceeded from his mind and by his invention.[51]

The picture of Northumberland drawn here appears to be incredible in certain respects. Those clandestine conferences at night in the royal apartments well fulfil the requirements of the Renaissance political narrative; but such an embellishment, typical of the genre, does not undermine the convincing explanation of how the King regularly became familiar with state business and, more importantly, came to accept and support Northumberland's policies, even the reckless ones, and especially the last one whereby the boy, near death, was persuaded to rob Mary of her right to succeed him. (Gates was said by this observer to have been 'one of the principals who induced the King to make out his will to the prejudice of the Lady Mary'.[52]) Northumberland obviously nurtured and played upon Edward's respect for the Lord Great Master; more useful was the King's genuine affection for Sir Henry Sidney, just eight years older than the King and perhaps the King's psychological older brother. Sidney was one of the King's closest boyhood friends and thus one of the true favourites at court; a gentleman of the privy chamber (from 18 April 1550), and from 22 July 1551 one of the four 'principal' gentlemen there; the King's companion who in March 1551 married Northumberland's daughter, Mary, and who for his services and support was knighted precisely at the time (11 October 1551) when Northumberland decided to eliminate Somerset.[53] Occasionally Dudley himself probably persuaded the King to move business 'in council' on the morrow; frequently the duke need not have been at court since Cecil or Gates, working with Sidney, should easily have been able to win the King's confidence in a matter. The efforts of Cecil, Gates, and Darcy in this respect are clearly documented,[54] and as the King trusted Sidney completely, the young Sir Henry could not have refused a request from Gates, for example, to inform Edward of the council's and Northumberland's purposes. Northumberland shrewdly perceived that Edward's intelligence was that of the bright, bookish pedant, the student who delighted in exercises, rules, enumerated items, and lists. For the King, administration consisted in agendas. So long as he copied out notes and agendas of council business he could believe that what was happening in council, and particularly in the 'meetings' staged especially for him, was real, that his councillors really were engaged in the debating of affairs of state which he himself had put forward. But the King's 'agendas' alone provide no proof of an administrative genius at work. If the contemporary observation recorded here is substantially correct, the agendas as well as the royal appearances 'in council' actually show just how far removed the King stood from a true exercise of power; how effectively Northumberland had covered himself with the King's legitimacy; how politically skilful was Northumberland's rule as President of the King's council.

With agenda in hand and a meeting brought to order by the Lord President or ranking councillor, one of the King's secretaries, 'standing at the vpper end of the table', as Sir Julius Caesar remembered it, 'acquainted the rest of the Board with all occurences' of state.[55] reading out the contents of letters received and enumerating the items of business requiring both a 'hasty expedition' as well as a careful weighing. Under Northumberland as few as four or five councillors were able then to proceed to a discussion of the agenda; officially, six at least must have been present to conclude a matter.[56] Paget's rule to the effect that the six 'shall have theyre procedinges ratefyed by the rest whenne theye cum'[57] implied that 'the rest' were bound as a matter of course to adhere to the decisions of the ruling rump. However, one of the rules of 1553 enabled fewer than four councillors to 'declare' to the King that a specific piece of business required 'wonderful haste', – namely, immediate dispatch;[58] three councillors need only have brought the matter to the King 'and before him debat it'. As the purpose of the ensuing 'debate' was to persuade the boy of the need for quick action, the procedure should effectively have permitted Northumberland's clique at times to act without the council.

One of the rules of 1553 would have committed 'long, tedious, and busie' matters to informal committees of one, two, or three councillors, the purpose being, as Petre phrased it, 'to hire and rough hew' the difficult questions; after preliminary study, the committees were to report the matters back to the council for a final discussion and resolution.[59] An official reference of 11 May 1550, recorded during a meeting at Greenwich, shows the rule in operation:

Upon rehersall of the Kinges Majesties debtes and deviseng howe it might be discharged, it was agreed that his whole revenewes shulde be certainely knowen; for thexaminacion whereof the Lord Chauncellour, the Lord Threasorer, the Lord Pagett, Mr. Sadler and Mr. Northe were appoincted to call thofficers of all Courtes before them, commaunding them by a daie to make their perfect declaracion, that they having taken the same may accordinglie make relacion thereof to the Counsaill.[60]

The note of a letter of 13 September 1551 'directed to the Lord Treasurer, the Lord Great Master, and the Master of the Horse, to meet at London for the ordering of my [Edward VI's] coin and the payment of my debts' fixes the existence of another of these informal committees; after Wiltshire, Warwick, and Herbert had sketched out the council's monetary and financial policies, they were 'to return and make report of their proceedings' to the rest of the council at the court at Farnham.[61] The dates of these three committees and the purpose of their work demonstrate quite clearly that the rule of 1553 recognised what must frequently have been the practice; the rule obviously did not represent a reorganisation of procedure as from January 1553.

A wholly different and unprecedented method for handling certain kinds of business is found in Sir Thomas Smith's plan of 1549 'ffor the Coledge of the Civilians taddend [*sic*: to attend] vpon the Cownsell, the L. Chauncelor, and other the Kyngs Majesties affaires'.[62] This proposal would have created a body of eleven doctors of civil law to serve as the council's permanent staff of legal advisers.[63] Although the idea failed eventually – Smith wanted to dissolve two Cambridge colleges and erect in their stead a new college of civil law to train the non-existent doctors[64] – it represents nevertheless a Tudor secretary's highly original attempt to relieve the privy council of much of its technical work.

Once a matter had been introduced, the council spoke to the question in ascending order of rank.[65] In practice this meant that the secretary was usually the first to offer his opinion. The procedure always favoured the ruling faction since the secretaries, in following Northumberland's lead, thus introduced both the agenda and the government's position on a given question. The other councillors should not have missed the cue.

Of the procedures governing debate we have very little evidence. Motions clearly were in order; a wholly unique reference to one introduced by the Marquess of Northampton in a meeting at Greenwich on Sunday, 11 May 1550, gives us a rare glimpse of an otherwise unknown aspect of procedure.[66] The secretaries may have kept abstracts of arguments raised for and against questions which had been temporarily suspended so that 'when the matter is treated or spoken of again, it may the soner and easlier come to conclusion'.[67] Unfortunately, nothing of this sort has survived. Edward VI is known to have kept in his private chest the 'reason and cause of every thing' preferred by his council,[68] but these were papers drafted probably by the secretaries for the King personally in order to persuade him of the justice of the actions of a council controlled by Northumberland.

As to the conduct of debate itself, we know that discussion often proved lively, growing at times to heated and violent argument. Dudley reportedly struck Gardiner a blow with his fist during a meeting at Windsor in October 1546;[69] as Protector, Somerset interrupted speakers, cut off debate, and sharply rebuked councillors to their faces.[70] (In his more restrained moments he merely dismissed opinions contrary to his own.) It was against this background that Paget in framing his 'Advise' urged 'the counsaille to love one another as brethren or deere freendes', appealing to every man to 'speake in convenable maner . . . in matters opened at the Counsaill boorde without reproufe, checke, or displeasur'.[71]

How the council proceeded to the resolution of a point in difference remains an intriguing question. Did they vote and, if so, in what way? The Tudors would not have counted ballots; rather, they would have heard the 'voices' to a question. In theory, all councillors were equal[72] but the voice of a great lord must in the balance have been heard above that of a knight.[73] Shouting often filled the council chamber;[74] whether volume alone decided matters of policy remains a part of the council's secret history. Both Somerset and Northumberland probably sought unanimity from the council in decisions of state, but neither man achieved it. Indeed, Somerset actually ignored the united opposition of the council on several questions (the defence of Boulogne and his social policy in 1549),[75] and his own refusal to consent to Edward VI's betrothal to Elizabeth of France did not stop Warwick from pursuing negotiations with Henry II.[76] The point is really academic, since, as Protector, Somerset thought himself in all things able 'to act by himself if he pleased, according to his own discretion',[77] while by 1552 Northumberland had simply purged the board of all opponents.

In another context, however, the privy council under Northumberland may well have 'tryed' numerically the 'voyces' for and against the several kinds of private suits which could only be heard at the board, the petitions for offices, pensions, benefits, and licences in the King's gift as well as certain extraordinary requests addressed typically not to the King but to the 'Lordes of the Kinges Majesties most honorable privie Councell' or occasionally to the Lord President, 'the right high and mightie prynce the Duke of Northumberlandes grace'.[78] The President was to present these suits to the board for a secret vote every Sunday afternoon from two to four. Did the council employ Paget's interesting procedural device of dropping black and white balls into a pot bearing the suitor's name, 'the sute to take place if theyre shalbe putt more white thenne blacke balles'?[79] Paget's biographer thinks not, claiming that Northumberland normally 'desired to know the actions of every councillor'.[80] On the other hand Paget had with good reason devoted the greatest and most detailed portion of his memorandum to these procedures: he sought to make regular and formal the methods used in council to bestow the King's gifts, for by subjecting the process to organised, collective control he hoped to avoid the divisions and resentment which Somerset had created by concentrating the powers of royal patronage in his own hands. Indeed, Somerset's monopoly had served as the council's rallying cry against the Protector when they first moved to destroy his office.[81] But it remained no less true after the *coup* that he who controlled the King's person and powers of patronage also controlled the council; hence Paget's detailed concern that the administration of this power be made subject in practice to a majority vote of the King's privy council. Although Paget's method of 'trying' the voices to a question may have been novel, his assumption of the necessity to do so rested on the obvious example – the circumstances of Henry VI's minority. In fact, his method of breaking a tie ('If theye be founde equall white balles . . . then the lorde presydent to preferre the sute') recalls that of 1426.[82]

Now it may have been the case that the young King did occasionally exercise the Crown's prerogative in granting suits for lands, and so on, but it would also seem that at least one privy councillor must have been a witness to the boy's verbal and written act in order to prevent another councillor from securing the lad's signature to a blank bill. Northumberland once pleaded that he obtained the King's assent to a lease for a client in the presence of the King's Chamberlain, but as that officer was Darcy, another of Northumberland's plants at court, the duke's argument carries a hollow ring,[83] and doubly so, since Dudley's move violated an earlier order in council which had temporarily prohibited such suits.[84] At most times, however, Northumberland

and the others submitted their own suits to their colleagues for approval.[85] In respect of suits generally, and especially grants in the King's gift, the council plainly recorded the fact of their control; the King formally acceded to the council's decision in such cases.[86]

It has been noted that Edward VI's 'attendance' at 'meetings' and his drafting of 'agendas' represented the form but not the substance of a true participation in council affairs; there is similarly no evidence that he played any substantive part in the conclusion of business. Northumberland and the council could claim that they had referred to the King for a decision or that they were merely executing the King's own judgement in a matter, but such statements can be exposed as patently false or as transparent attempts to evade responsibility by cloaking their moves with the mantle of the Crown's prerogative.[87] That Edward VI took his cue literally and directly from the Duke of Northumberland the King in any case boyishly revealed.[88]

For the execution and administration of certain resolutions, the council appointed from time to time *ad hoc* committees of its own members. One of these was the committee of nine which Somerset named in August 1547 to govern the realm from London while the Protector and the others conducted the invasion of Scotland.[89] Under Paget's direction the committee divided itself into 'two bandes' in order to share the duties of attendance upon the King at Hampton Court; Paget arranged a schedule such that 'one Band shall wayte contynually one weke and the other band the other weke and upon Sondayes to be alwais together at the Courte'.[90] The committee assumed the council's regular administrative duties (authorising warrants, and so on) and initiated some surprising executive action as well (ordering the arrest and imprisonment of Bonner and Gardiner).[91] In advance of Somerset's departure Paget had also drawn up a list of tasks to be performed in support of the Scottish campaign; in preserving a record of the appointment of individual councillors to these tasks (the supervision of supply and recruitment), the document is unique among extant council papers. It illustrates just as well the secretary's method of co-ordinating such business (in this case Paget, as Comptroller, fulfilled the function of the King's chief secretary).[92] The nature of the work undertaken by the councillors suggests that the board (that is, Paget during the early period; the President with the secretaries later) frequently assigned to individual members the responsibility for discharging specific administrative duties. In some cases, such responsibilities represented a standing charge. The Earl of Warwick, for example, from about July 1550 assumed responsibility for all 'Thinges to be considered for Ireland' – the number of men who were to be sent there, the provision of artillery and munitions for the garrisons, the supervision of the King's revenues, the ordering of the mint and the mines, and so forth; from time to time he was to report his needs to the council.[93]

Ordinarily, standing committees of the privy council handled just the sort of duties that Warwick here discharged personally. In fact, the supervision of fortifications and expenses relative to Ireland the council had earlier assigned to the Great Master and the Master of the King's horse. A reference to them and to six other committees, dated late October 1549, provides the earliest evidence of the existence of standing committees of the privy council under Edward VI.[94] The date and the function of the seven (one was a committee of the whole) suggest that the board probably set up such machinery then precisely in response to the deepening financial crisis generated by the ex-Protector's military policy. After throwing Somerset over, the new leadership awarded to the Earl of Arundel, Sir Edward Wotton, and Sir John Gage responsibility for the supervision of affairs relating to Boulogne and Calais. (Arundel's name was later crossed through.) Ireland, as noted, received the attention of Lord St John and Sir William Herbert. Sir Richard Cotton and the cofferer of the household (neither of them privy councillors at this time) assisted Paget and the Earl of Shrewsbury in the task of overseeing the supply of the northern garrisons. Sir Richard Southwell and Sir Edward North devoted themselves similarly to Scilly and Alderney. The council gave to the Lord Admiral the power to appoint men to assist him in 'the charge of victualling of the sea'. 'Thorder of the myntes' went to Wriothesley. Most important was 'the forsight for money'; this burden the whole council assumed 'by reaport of the treasourers euery wyke'.

No trace of the work of these committees remains, but an explicit reference of 30 October 1549 to 'thorder for division of severall maters to severall of the counsellors', in laying down standing orders for Southwell and North, suggests how the others must have proceeded. The council had instructed the captain of the Isles of Scilly to send all requests for his wants and furnishings to the two councillors named who in turn were to organise and clarify the information so that 'the rest of the counsell here' could give further order for the provisioning of the island. The council's letter of 26 October 1549 to the Earl of Rutland refers similarly to the standing responsibilities of Shrewsbury and Paget with regard to the supply of men, money and munitions in the North. Rutland was required to credit the committee's instructions in the same way that he would letters from the whole board.[95] How long these committees continued to operate, even with different personnel, is unknown. Certainly the one for Ireland disappeared after about July 1550. Of course the Lord Admiral could always be expected to report his needs to the council; no mention of the other committees after 1549 has been found. It may be that in the wake of Somerset's failures the board simply erected these standing bodies as temporary instruments for the reorganisation of the King's finances and military supplies. An exception was the committee of the whole which continued to receive the treasurers' weekly reports.

When, on 17 July 1550, the clerks recorded that 'bicause his Majestie and the Counsaill be alwaies at London or nighe theraboutes, his Majestie will alwaies appoint twoo of the Counsaill to understande and determyne all complaintes of the Frenche Kinges subjects',[96] we know that the council had thus established another of its few 'standing committees'. The board had earlier decided to appoint, or perhaps have the King commission, two non-privy councillors for the same purpose;[97] later it was thought that the discussion of foreign claims against English nationals was a matter best handled by two privy councillors. The two who filled the appointment were Secretary Petre and Dr Wotton.[98] At one point Sir Philip Hoby and Sir John Mason seem regularly to have managed the council's formal representations to the Imperial ambassador resident in London; whether, in fact, the council had actually determined that two of their number were 'alwaies' to constitute such a group remains unclear.[99]

There is finally King Edward's well-known council 'for the

state' of March 1552 which appears to fill exactly the modern prescription for a formal standing committee.[100] Its establishment, membership and existence raise little question; less clear, however, are the reasons for its formation and the nature of its function. It is tempting to think that this group of twenty-one privy councillors represents an 'inner ring' of the board, a contraction made necessary both by the presumed unwieldy size of a council grown large[101] as well as by the dictates of Northumberland's control. This understanding rests upon the assumption that because the committee concerned itself with the formulation of state policy, its deliberations essentially replaced the meetings of a larger privy council. Is this so?

In the first place, it cannot now reasonably be argued that 'attempts to solve the problems posed by its [the council's] size naturally led to committee-making',[102] since this was to reason from that non-existent council of forty. There is no evidence that contemporaries thought a council of thirty-one too large or, more importantly, that a reduction from thirty-one to twenty-one members would have solved such a problem had it existed. Indeed, fewer than twenty-one would seem to have represented more manageable numbers.

Secondly, the interpretation of the proper or, it might be said, probable, function of the committee has been made unnecessarily complex by those who see its formation as part of the first stage of a plan to reorganise the council. In this view, the committee stands as but one of five committees to emerge from attempts in March 1552 to make the council's work more efficient. The 'Articles' of 1553, it is thought, completed the effort by reforming the council's procedure.[103] This attempt to view the royal commissions of March 1552 as committees of the privy council has merely confused the issue. Committees of the council, it should be said, were composed entirely of privy councillors and were appointed informally (but nonetheless officially) by the board for the purpose of handling what were essentially aspects of the council's own business; committees found their life in the council, they possessed no power independent of the council, they were responsible to the council (technically, to the King-in-council) only. They were, as all committees are, essential parts of the larger body's internal administrative machinery. Royal commissioners, on the other hand, derived their specified powers from the King in letters-patent under the great seal. Thus we find in Edward VI's famous brief of March 1552 not five new council committees but rather four perfectly well-defined royal commissions and one committee, the King's so-called council for the state.

One approach to an understanding of the function of Edward's group lies in its procedural relationship to two royal commissions. One of these was appointed on 13 July 1552 for calling in the King's debts. The commissioners – six of the nine were privy councillors – were required to bring to the attention of the council 'for the state' the most 'desperate' of the sums of money remaining due to the Crown.[104] The reference is clear enough; we may imagine that the committee 'for the state' was to consider what action was to be taken against recalcitrant debtors. But as the committee was named about four months before the appointment of this commission, we should expect the committee's competence, as first conceived, to have been greater than merely the consideration of proceedings against the worst of the King's debtors. The text of an earlier royal commission, that of 9 March 1552 for the hearing of requests, does indeed suggest that the committee enjoyed greater responsibilities. The commissioners of 9 March were to hear all suits which the King or 'the privie Counsell for the State' should deliver to the 'Master of the Requests' (who was himself a commissioner); those suits which concerned the King or which 'ought to be kept secreate' were to be referred back to 'the priuie Counsell assembled for the State'.[105]

The function of the committee for the state as defined by the commission of 9 March poses something of a puzzle, however, since the committee was to perform precisely those duties which the whole privy council had always performed – or at least had attempted regularly to perform as early as March 1550 when Paget first spelled them out in his 'Advise'; 'all billes of supplicacion to the Kinges Majeste or the counsaill shalbe delyvered to the Master of the requestes and he delyver to the lorde presydent all suche that conteign mattier that cannot be determyned butt by the King or his prevey counsaill'.[106] Thus, councillors who had assembled 'for the state' were in this instance considering precisely the kind of business which they might just as well have considered at a regular meeting. And of course the whole council had always met to consider the reports of the various financial commissions.

Is there any evidence that the committee 'for the state' actually met? Of the 245 recorded meetings of the privy council from 9 March 1552 to 16 June 1553, 43 were attended by from five to twelve members of the committee only (average attendance: 7.8, or about one-third less than that for all other meetings), but this proves nothing, since, for example one-third (14) of these meetings fell during the progress-time – 10 during August 1552 alone – while none occurred in November 1552 and February and March 1553. Moreover, the business recorded under those 43 dates is essentially the same as that of all other meetings. It will be remembered that the King had said that he would sit with his committee once a week to hear the debating of the most important 'matters of state'; while we should not expect the proceedings entered on those 43 days (or any other days) to include the minutes of debates, nevertheless it *is* surprising to find that none of these entries records the King's presence, even at the time of the royal progress.

What kind of a committee was it, then, whose membership comprised twenty-one privy councillors; whose sessions were attended by the King possibly once a week and were never recorded; whose members when assembled 'for the state' were able not only to hear and dispatch the kinds of suits which the whole council of thirty-one members had previously entertained, but also to consider the reports of the commissioners investigating the Crown's debts, as well as discuss the great affairs of the realm; whose membership excluded two of the most active councillors, Sir John Mason and George Lord Cobham, and another of Northumberland's loyal supporters, the Earl of Huntingdon, also a privy councillor?

The suspicion that the powers of King Edward's council 'for the state' were perhaps more nominal than real is reinforced by an examination of the size and composition of the group. It would seem that for the hearing of suits within its competence and the consideration of financial reports, the board should have divided itself into several committees, each smaller than the one of twenty-one members which was to sit for both these and presumably other 'matters of state'. At twenty-one the committee seems unnecessarily large – indeed, too large – for the performance of specialised duties. Does the committee's size reflect therefore perhaps something of a different character? In this regard, it is worth noting that the King (or whoever may have directed his formation of the committee) intended originally that only four-teen privy councillors and two lesser officials should stand 'for the state'; the King's manuscript notes of the proposal show that sometime after composing this mixed group of sixteen, he dropped the two minor officers and added the names of seven other privy councillors, giving us the resulting large committee. These additions and two other corrections in Edward's paper appear to reflect a change in the author's conception of the group, from that of a royal commission to simply a larger body of privy councillors which excluded none of the officers of state and house-hold.[107] This transformation would also imply a change in intended function, from the specialised to the general, or, more importantly, a change in essential character, from that of a truly functional body (of whatever competence) to one of which membership was a mere formality.

Considering that the author enlarged and significantly altered the composition of the group for the state; considering, also, that the competence of the resulting large committee of privy councillors apparently equalled that of the whole board; considering, moreover, that the rules of 1553 provided for the King's presence at a particular kind of meeting under certain conditions – how should one describe the probable historical role of the council for the state? The most likely conclusion is that the council for the state was brought into existence primarily to accommodate the King's person at 'meetings' staged especially for him, sessions for which special 'warning' was to be given so that 'the more' could be 'at the debating' of affairs. If such meetings served merely to introduce the boy to the council's already formed decisions or to persuade him of the necessity for planned action, one should understand the total lack of evidence of the committee's work: such meetings presented to the King only the form and not the reality of the true meetings which have remained of record. To this may be added a final observation. It was pointed out earlier that with a few exceptions, the twenty-one most active members of the privy council after March 1552 happen also to have been

members of the King's committee;[108] as the committee was
formed at a time when Northumberland almost certainly determined the extent of each councillor's participation in affairs, we
should probably be able to say that as the committee itself constituted a purely nominal body, the composition of the group
would seem therefore to mirror rather more accurately the Lord
President's political alliances than the administrative reforms of a
royal genius.

A discussion of the conduct of the council's business would not
be complete without an examination of the procedures observed
during a royal progress. When the King moved about the country,
we may distinguish between the 'council at court' and the
'council at London'. These were not two committees of the council, but merely some privy councillors attending upon Edward's
person at, say, Plymouth or Reading, and others at London, all of
them transacting the King's affairs.[109] (Individual councillors, as
will be seen, often shuttled between Westminster – or Northumberland's house in Chelsea – and the peripatetic court.) The official difference lay in the fact that the councillors with the King
as a rule possessed the register, so that their proceedings became
the recorded acts of the privy council.[110]

With the King went, typically, the High Treasurer, Lord Privy
Seal, Great Chamberlain, the King's Chamberlain, Vice-Chamberlain, and the Treasurer, the chief secretary, and others of the
appointed lords and councillors (such as the Duke of Suffolk,
Lord Cobham, and Sir John Gage in 1552).[111] Dudley, the President, disdained meetings on progress, preferring his Chelsea residence or a good ride into the North parts.[112] One clerk of the
council stayed at Westminster and two rode with the court, one
looking after the register and the other writing letters. The council's administrative entourage would also have included several
clerks of the signet and a number of under-clerks and assistants.
At Guildford and Waltham in July and August 1552 we also find
the busy John Cox, a Master of the court of requests, receiving
supplications to the King and council.[113] The Lord Chancellor
invariably remained at London with the Archbishop of Canterbury, the second secretary, and four to six of the lesser figures
(such as Bowes, Mason, North, and Dr Wotton in 1552).[114]

The interest in the meetings on progress lies not so much in the

sessions themselves as in the way in which the council at court
co-ordinated the business of administering the realm with the
council at London, for although the sovereign power moved with
the court, the government's administrative machinery remained
centred upon Westminster. On Friday, 26 August 1552 for
example, when Northumberland joined the King at Salisbury,
Cecil drew up for him an agenda of urgent business, noting
among others things that some order was to be taken regarding
'the pyrattes at Callice and Douer'.[115] It was decided without a
meeting that the Lord Chancellor should make out commissions
of oyer and terminer and send them, together with a list of persons
recommended for the commissions, to the deputy of the Lord
Warden of the Cinque Ports at Dover. These instructions Cecil
ordered the clerk with the council on progress, William Thomas,
to set out in a letter to the Chancellor (Goodrich, Bishop of Ely)
in London. Thomas drafted the letter the next day, being careful
to authenticate it with his own signature in fulfilment of a council
order passed one year earlier to the effect, 'that no lettre nor
other writing shuld passe at the Boorde to synge by them [the privy
council] but that first the same shuld be subscribed by oone of the
two Pryncipall Secretaries or one of the Clerkes of the Counsell',
and dispatched it to the Lord Chancellor.[116] Thus was an executive decision of the council at Salisbury transmitted to and
administered by the council at London.

As the bulk of the intelligence addressed to the council arrived
at London, the lords there would consider it, send to the court
the most important originals, and report the contents of the rest.[117]
At Chelsea the Lord Treasurer (this time not at court) and Great
Master once received a letter from the German Count Palatine;
they enclosed it in a letter to Cecil at the court at Farnham requiring him to cause a certain 'pact and conventyon made with the duc
Philip to be sought' – a clerk would probably have had to look for
it among the state papers in the travelling royal coffers – and
thereupon to return word, advising them what answer they should
be able to give within the 'tenor of the sayd pact'.[118]

But while the earls of Wiltshire and Warwick may occasionally
have relied upon Cecil for their understanding of the King's
foreign policy, at the same time Cecil necessarily awaited the great
lords' decision in all matters of policy: only two days earlier (13

September 1551) he had written in the King's name on behalf of the councillors at Farnham directing Wiltshire, Warwick, and the Master of the horse (Herbert) to 'meet at London for the ordering of [the King's] coin and the payment of [his] debts; which done, to return and make report of their proceedings'.[119] Wiltshire and Herbert conferred with the council at London[120] and then returned to Farnham for a meeting with Cecil and the others at court on the sixteenth.[121] On the eighteenth the King moved to Windsor[122] but Wiltshire (at least) kept going, rejoining the 'Lords at London' who, in good empirical fashion, were trying 'all kinds of stamping' in order to decide on the new fineness for silver coin.[123] Leaving the King at Windsor with the Lord Privy Seal (Bedford), the Great Chamberlain (Northampton), the Chamberlain (Darcy), the Vice-Chamberlain (Gates), the Comptroller (Wingfield), and the Earl of Huntingdon,[124] Cecil, Hoby, and Herbert also departed for London on the twentieth in order to assist Wiltshire and Warwick in the matter of deciding how best to proceed against the bishops of Chichester, Worcester, and Durham.[125] But as the secretary carried with him the privy council register, the six councillors at 'Chelsey' on 22 September 1551 (Wiltshire, Warwick, Herbert, Cecil, Mason, Hoby) were now the ones producing the 'acts' of the privy council.[126]

The record of this session at the Earl of Warwick's house preserves thus one of the few instances during a royal progress of a meeting held neither at court nor at Westminster. It was probably for this reason and also because they had ordered the recommittal of the Bishop of Worcester to the Fleet following his appearance before them that day that the council at Chelsea actually signed the entries of the register for 22 September,[127] a notable example of a procedure which they had earlier abandoned, and were never to observe thereafter. In fact, 'the lordes and thothers' at London had the day before assembled for a meeting but, uncertain perhaps that their determinations should stand as the acts of the whole privy council under such circumstances – or perhaps lacking a quorum – they had ordered the clerk to break off his transcription, leaving only the date, an unfinished sentence, and a blank page as mute testimony to the fact of their division.[128] On the twenty-third the King and the council attendant moved from Windsor to Oatlands;[129] Wiltshire,

Warwick, Herbert, Cecil and Hoby left Chelsea to meet them there, bringing in their train the great council book, so that the meeting of the two groups at Oatlands on the twenty-fourth became once again that of the privy council at court. The London lords also brought with them a new clerk of the council whose swearing-in on the twenty-fourth at Oatlands marked him as responsible for the composition of the register thereafter.[130]

The truly exceptional nature of the procedures on progress with the King in Edward's reign is only partly revealed, however, in the peregrinations of councillors at court and at London. Inevitably, the administrative requirements of rule by a council were adjusted – or interpreted – so as to express the political demands of the dominant faction. As late as September 1551, for example, Dudley had yet to secure colleagues who, when appointed to remain as the council at Westminster during a progress, could be trusted to execute unquestioningly and unfailingly the administrative orders of the council with the King and the register. It will be remembered that the conference of the six councillors at Chelsea on the twenty-first and the twenty-second had not included the Chancellor, Rich; consequently, Rich was not a party to the decision which was almost certainly made then to proceed against Heath and Day by a royal commission of lawyers.[131] It remained merely for the reunited councillors at Oatlands to settle upon the personnel of the commission, and this they accomplished at some time between the twenty-fourth and the twenty-eighth, Cecil having informed Edward VI of the council's nominees in a brief memorandum.[132] In the meantime, the King was moved to Hampton Court where, on the morning of the twenty-eighth, ten privy councillors at a meeting of the board authorised the appointment of the commissioners.[133] After the meeting the clerks at court copied out the commission in the form of a warrant, which Edward VI and an unknown number of the councillors at Hampton Court signed.[134] Then, at a second, separate and officially recorded meeting later that same day (28 September 1551), eight privy councillors authorised two letters from the board, one to the Lord Chancellor at Westminster instructing him to send the signed commission 'to suche of the Counsell as ar at or nere London whose handes be not thereto that they may signe it, and then to seale it and send it with a [second]lettre from the sayd Lordes, sent hym included within his, to the sayd Commissioners'.[135] Several of the council signed this second letter, the letter advising the commissioners how to proceed in 'the causes' of the bishops of Worcester and Chichester, and dispatched it to Westminster in the council's packet containing Rich's instructions and the King's commission.

True to his instructions, Rich collected the signatures of the London councillors to the King's bill, affixing to it the great seal of England.[136] But in an unprecedented move he returned to Warwick (at Hampton Court) the council's letter of the twenty-eighth to the commissioners, explaining that it required more than the eight signatures which it now displayed.[137] We can only imagine Warwick's reaction to Rich's rebuff. Was the Lord Chancellor of England, himself a baron, telling his lordship, the Earl of Warwick, Lord President of the privy council, that eight of the King's most honourable privy councillors carried insufficient authority to issue directions under their own hands to the recipients of a royal commission, a commission which Rich himself had signed? Warwick's reply took the form of a signet-letter from Edward VI:

we think our authorite to be such that what so euer we shall do by the advise of the numbre of our Counsell attending vpon our person, although theye be much fewer than viij, without accepting of any persone, the same to have more strength and efficacye than to be put into question or doubt of the validite therof; for in dede we think your Lordship not ignorant hereof that the nombre of our counsellors or any parte of them maketh not our authorite, although in dede there advise and good counsell necessarely becometh the same wherunto also we will euer inclyne our selfe, and therfore if yow or any other shuld be of other opinion, as in a sorte maye be collected coniecturally by your lettre, the same is not convenient, but might be in sondrye cases too hurtefull where often tymes our affayres for lack of spedye expedition vpon the expectation of other nombers of counsellors than chanceth sometyme to be present with vs might take grete detryment.[138]

As a straightforward interpretation of the constitutional relationship between the Crown and the council in the reign of Edward VI, Warwick's statement would be no less revealing if it did not also reflect what, in the context of the letter which provoked it, must have been the real issue raised by the Lord Chancellor: Dudley's answer shows Rich and the council at London to have been concerned not with the number who had finally signed the letter to the commissioners – it carried two signatures more than the number required for the conclusion of business – but rather with the number of councillors *at Hampton Court* who had first subscribed it, as well as the identity of those who had *not*, for a number 'much fewer than viij' had probably first set their hands to the missive and, in all probability, the Earl of Warwick was not one of them.[139] Rich may have known that on 22 September, with part of the council at court (Windsor Castle) and part at Westminster, Warwick and five others at Chelsea had decided to appoint a commission of lawyers not merely to 'hear and determine' the case against Heath, but in all likelihood, to deprive him of the bishopric of Worcester in any event.[140] Rich and the London council may or may not have agreed with this policy; the point is simply that they had taken no part in its formulation, and yet on the twenty-eighth they were being asked for the execution of that decision to add their own hands to the signatures of but a few of Warwick's supporters[141] – including perhaps that of Bowes, who was sworn a member at Oatlands only as late as the twenty-fifth.[142] It was as if a minor faction of the council at Hampton Court was requiring the councillors at London to adhere to a decision which yet a third part of the council had earlier taken at Chelsea. To the Lord Chancellor, the precedent must have appeared a dubious one, that he and not the man responsible for the move should sign the effective order for Heath's deprivation. Technically, there was nothing irregular in Dudley's action; he had simply bent to his own purposes the administrative procedures of the council on progress.

Nevertheless, the co-ordination of work between the two parts of the council at such times placed an undeniable burden on both councillors and clerks. The schedule of a progress clearly did not lend itself either to efficient, centralised control of the machinery of government (witness the delay in the execution of the above commission caused by Rich's protest[143]) or to the regularity of attention which external events sometimes required. Indeed, the progress of 1552 artificially delayed the council's consideration of its foreign policy *vis-à-vis* the Emperor;[144] Northumberland expressed himself glad finally to understand on 3 September 'that the Kinges majestie by thadvyce of my lordes, cutteth of[f] parte

of this superfluus progress wherby my lordes of his majestes councell may the more gravelie and deliberatlye and in better tyme
attend to his highnes wayghtie affaires in theis troubelsome
dayes'.[145] His remark recalls the arrangements for moving Edward
VI from Hampton Court to Westminster on 15 October 1551,
'because it was thought', to use the King's words in reference to
Somerset's alleged conspiracy, that 'this matter might easilier and
surelier be dispatched there, and likewise all other [matters]'.[146]

Whether councillors were meeting at or away from London,
Northumberland's control of the dispatch of affairs rested essentially upon the efforts of his favourites about the King who also
sat at the board, in particular, Cecil, the King's secretary, and
the King's Chamberlain and Vice-Chamberlain, Darcy and
Gates. Cecil's efficient handling of business explains in part the
effectiveness of a large and potentially nebulous body of royal
advisers; to his and the other secretaries' procedures for the
administration of the council's work attention will be turned
shortly. Here it is intended to examine the methods by which
Northumberland can be said to have effected his will in council,
the means by which he secured even during his absences the
resolution of particular items of business as well as the adoption
of general matters of policy.

Frequently we find the President discovering a matter of 'suche
moment' that he must require Cecil 'instantlye and earnestlie' to
solicit the lords for their 'indelayde' resolution of the question.[147]
In directing an item to be placed on the agenda for the council's
immediate consideration, rarely did Northumberland fail to suggest precisely how he thought it should be ordered,[148] and
although Cecil could hardly have mistaken his meaning in most
instances, nevertheless in the dispatch of suits especially Northumberland stood ready to remind Cecil of the government's procedural façade, 'that in thaunswer yt wold please my lordes to
haue consideracon that he [a suitor, Lord Willoughby, who had
asked licence to tarry at Calais] and others may knowe that those
weightie offices ys Ruled by the hole bourd'.[149]

The bulk of Northumberland's correspondence, however, cor-
rects the notion that in great matters the whole board really did
'rule'. It is true that Northumberland disdained the tedium of
regular meetings – he attended about half of all sessions after

March 1552 – and that some accused him even of neglecting the government of the realm.[150] However, although he may have left to the council's discretion the conclusion of routine and relatively unimportant business,[151] it seems equally clear that even from his sick-bed he maintained through Cecil, whom Scheyfve called 'the duke of Northumberland's man',[152] his control of the agenda and thus his supervision of really important business, including directions for the government's programme of Parliamentary legislation in general[153] and a bill for a subsidy in particular;[154] an appointment to a vacant bishopric;[155] the coining of new monies;[156] the investigation of allegedly treasonous actions;[157] and so on. Northumberland's apparent disinclination to attend meetings meant that at least a few councillors found themselves travelling back and forth from Chelsea to assemblies of the board at Westminster[158] – in March 1550 by water daily between Whitehall and Greenwich where Warwick had isolated himself in the King's palace[159] – in order to effect his instructions in council. Occasionally Northumberland essentially concluded matters himself: we find him (a) sending Cecil a letter of interest, (b) instructing that the council reply in a letter over their signatures, (c) enclosing his own personally drafted abstract of the recommended text, and (d) awaiting the finished product in order to sign it.[160] At other times he depended upon Cecil to open matters of high priority to the King alone and a chosen few of the duke's closest supporters; in this way did clandestine negotiations between the Merchant Adventurers and Northumberland's group result in the council's procurement of a loan for the King of £40,000. The agreement was signed by seven members of the ruling faction in a secret, unrecorded meeting.[161]

One measure of Northumberland's control lay in the relative ease with which he obtained the King's signature to a host of letters, warrants, and bills. The act was accomplished most frequently not by Cecil, but upon Northumberland's orders which Cecil conveyed to Darcy and Gates. Thus when the Lord President wished to see Knox appointed Bishop of Rochester in October 1552, he wrote to Cecil, praying 'you desyer my Lord chamberleyn and mr vicechamberleyn to helpe towardes this good act',[162] and although this particular example documents a notable failure, nevertheless Dudley's plea illustrates the informal procedure which so often produced the grant of an office, lease, licence, or reward. Knowledgeable suitors who had to do with the whole board knew that Darcy spoke for Northumberland.[163] We find the Lord Chamberlain 'settinge forth [a] sute to the Kinges majeste';[164] helping Cecil 'preferr the signyture' of suits granted orally by Edward VI on Darcy's recommendation;[165] instructing the King as to Northumberland's candidate for Speaker of the Commons, and so on.[166] Indeed, it would appear from Dudley's letters that just as Cecil organised the matters to be discussed, so did Darcy and Gates represent Northumberland's interests both in council and before the King; 'thadvyse and consent of som others of my lordes of the privie councell' might technically have been required, but Cecil was charged invariably to confer with Darcy in a matter,[167] to give the enclosed various letters to the Chamberlain and Vice-Chamberlain[168] or, to quote Dudley himself in the context of a specific case, to work with 'my lorde chamberlein and master vicechamberleyn my speciall frendes for theyre helpe and furderaunce toptayne me A warrante ffrom the borde . . . to be furnishid with soche termes and wordes as may sirue my purpos'.[169]

5
The Authorisation and Administration of Business

Whatever passed the board must have been authenticated as a valid act of council; that is, it must have carried the signatures of at least a few councillors. Throughout the reign of Edward VI privy councillors subscribed one and sometimes both forms of the documents which embodied the council's acts – the original, which the board dispatched, and the record of the original, which it retained.[1]

The significance of the signatures in the privy council's registers has already been discussed: by 1 June 1547 the signatures had become mere administrative formulas.[2] Before June 1547 and after January 1548 the political nature of the proceedings subscribed by the council surely bears witness to the government's attempt during the royal minority to secure the allegiance of its supporters by recording their complicity in acts which might later be regarded as 'crimes';[3] the repetition between those dates of the same six or seven hands in the book probably illustrates the informal procedural convention which stipulated that for an act to have been valid six councillors at the least must have authorised it or consented to its passage. In fact, there existed no formal procedure during the Protectorate which required that a specific (minimum) number of councillors sign the government's acts. That varying numbers of privy councillors at different times did sign letters, signet bills, proclamations, and the council's copies of all of these suggests, however, that, in spite of the broad personal power which his patents had granted him, Somerset was concerned officially to show that he governed with his colleagues' assent.

In practice, letters from the council exhibited any number of signatures. During the brief period of rule by Henry VIII's executors, almost all of those first present in the Tower and at Westminster regularly gave evidence of their new authority;[4] in accordance with the will, 'All, or the most part of them' (that is, at least nine), continued to do so until 12 March 1547. Under Somerset, however, as few as three (Somerset, Rich, and Southampton) once issued orders,[5] and it was not unusual for Somerset and three others similarly to order action on the King's behalf.[6] But the appearance of even a few signatures in addition to Somerset's autograph may actually have represented a change in the Protector's procedural intentions: upon Paget's advice, Somerset may have altered the form of a number of letters from the first person singular to the first person plural, so that letters from the Protector became letters from the board – for the effect that the council's assent could be presumed to have upon certain recipients.[7] The Protector apparently thought it expedient to collect as many signatures as possible to the council's letters to Princess Mary, for example.[8] In Somerset's absence not fewer than five privy councillors sent out commands on behalf of the Crown in the name of the whole council.[9] After the *coup* (6 October 1549) the council almost invariably followed the unwritten rule that six or more members were to sign all letters from the board;[10] operating on the theory that greater numbers lent greater credence, twenty-three councillors signed a letter of 1 July 1553 contradicting the rumour that Edward VI had died.[11]

It was noted earlier that the council probably signed the register of letters received; they certainly put their hands to the entries in the registers of letters sent. This fact is not evident from the unique rough copy of the only original letter-book which we possess,[12] but we know that the clerks composed a series of what were probably fair-copy registers[13] and these they presented to the lords for their signatures: on 30 August 1550 the clerk noted in the council book 'A lettre to Sir Morice Denys . . . the copie of which lettre appeareth in the booke of the first entreys';[14] Robert Beale's 'Instructions for a Principal Secretarie' (1592) recorded the fact of 'the order kept in K. Edward's time, the next daye after their Lordships had signed the lettres, to sett their hands to the entries of the booke'.[15] However, we do not know exactly when and for how long the council subscribed the entries of the letter-books; the purpose of the procedure was to fix corporate responsibility for the acts of the government and to authenticate the council's record of its correspondence, but Somerset and Northumberland also accomplished these objects by having their colleagues sign the original drafts of some letters[16] and single fair copies of others.[17]

By warrant of the authority of letters over their own signatures, the council also regularly ordered the officers of the various courts of revenue to make expenditure. These council warrants for payment fall into two categories: (*a*) orders to the officers of one financial department to make payment or delivery to another royal official for further disbursement; (*b*) orders for payments to be made direct to the recipient by way of the King's reward or for services rendered in the King's affairs. By letters-patent of 16 October 1546 Henry VIII had empowered any six of his privy council to issue warrants under the stamp of the King's signature for payments in the King's affairs; expenditures for the King's garrisons and fortifications especially might otherwise have been delayed had the warrants for them awaited his own signing.[18] The commission lapsed, of course, upon Henry's death; Somerset did not seek a similar one. When Northumberland (as Earl of Warwick) resumed the late Henrician practice, he found it convenient to make one change: he persuaded Edward VI to grant letters-patent authorising every privy councillor and at least six of them to address warrants over their own signatures only to the treasurers and receivers of the King's revenue courts for payments to be made in the King's affairs.[19] With a few exceptions, all of the surviving original council warrants after that time bear at least six of the council's hands.[20] An order of 20 April 1550 also decreed that treasurers were to honour no warrant so signed unless it also bore the signature of the clerk having charge of the register;[21] the purpose of the rule was to ensure that 'no warraunt shulde escape unregistered', but it also had the effect of assuring Northumberland's control of the spending of money, since the clerks were directly responsible to the secretaries, and the secretaries to Dudley. (It also assured the clerks of their fees.)

Nevertheless, the commission of 1549 set no limit to the amount of money which six councillors could thus order any treasurer to pay whether in reward or for services rendered ostensibly to the

King, a situation which on one occasion allowed Northumberland to order up more than £2,000 by way of encouragement to his French friends.[22] One of the rules of January 1553 effectively amended the commission by specifying that the King's rewards in excess of £40 and all general payments for 'his busines or affaires' above £100 were thereafter to pass under the royal sign manual.[23] That all such extant warrants after that date bear the King's signature documents the council's adoption of the procedure.[24]

The essential regularity of the procedures for the authorisation of the council's warrants after Somerset's fall stands in sharp contrast to practice during the Protectorate. Warrants of the first type – (a) above – addressed to Sir Edmund Peckham (Treasurer of the mints) in amounts up to £1,000 exhibit as few as three hands.[25] Four and five signatures to council warrants are common enough;[26] we know of at least one instance when Somerset alone issued a warrant to the Treasurer and Chamberlains of the exchequer.[27]

In view of the fact that Northumberland sought a commission under the great seal for the specific purpose of authorising the council to issue warrants, it may be asked by what authority even a few councillors under Somerset were able to order payments by their signatures. It seems that having been appointed privy councillors by Somerset according to the terms of his patents, the council understood, or thought they understood, themselves as sharing in the Protector's powers whenever they ordered action under their own hands.[28] In any case, in an ancient court of record such as the exchequer, the signatures of privy councillors alone did not stand as a sufficient warrant for action by the treasurer and chamberlains – the exchequer normally received orders for the kind of payments discussed here by privy seal[29] – and yet Somerset's council frequently ordered the exchequer to make sizeable payments of various kinds upon receipt of the council's letters only.[30] In this particular case, therefore, Somerset found it necessary periodically to direct to the exchequer a blanket writ of privy seal for the discharge of all council warrants addressed to that court during a six-month period.[31] In all other cases not governed as this was by 'the old auncyent course of [the King's] seid Courte', the question of the council's authority to order action by another department merely illustrates the technical problem that the King's privy council encountered generally at this time: as an institution it possessed no seal with which to authenticate its business.

To contemporaries, the question of obvious interest concerned the King's letters. What, the French ambassador wanted to know immediately upon Henry's death, would be the procedure for signing royal letters in the new reign? Paget's reply, that the King himself would certainly sign all letters that should in future bear the royal seal, was meant to imply that Edward's autograph would carry authority independent of the Protector's countersignature, which had also appeared on the first royal missives to the French King.[32] Certainly nothing was to pass under the King's signature without Somerset's having first subscribed it: this was the Protector's express order to the King's tutors and also presumably to the secretaries and clerks.[33] In practice, a few of the council (and as many as ten) signed the King's official letters,[34] and in Somerset's pre-arranged absence, at least six.[35]

In addition to authenticating the King's domestic correspondence (including letters to sheriffs, justices of the peace, the Lord Deputy and Council in Ireland, and so on), the signet also served, of course, as the seal of warranty to other departments of state, directing further action under another seal (as a warrant for the privy seal or great seal) or simply ordering an official to act directly, as in the case of warrants for expenditure addressed to household officials.[36] Research for this study revealed only one original warrant of the latter type for the period of the Protectorate, and the six signatures that it displays in addition to the sign manual suggest that at least a few councillors probably regularly authorised warrants of this kind.[37] As for the former type, the evidence is clear enough: both the executors before 12 March 1547 and the privy council afterwards signed the King's bills as warrants for the great seal.[38]

Of particular interest, however, in respect of the uses to which the King's hand might be put is the fact that by 14 July 1547 Somerset had assumed sole responsibility for the witnessing of a certain type of royal letter – the King's directives for the raising of troops.[39] What is more, these were letters bearing not Edward VI's sign manual, but rather the dry stamp of his signature.[40]

Somerset continued to wield the stamp until the *coup* of 1549.[41]
Of course in the exercise of his office the Protector could always
claim to be acting in Edward's name for the theoretical surety of
the realm. Somerset's second patent specifically empowered him,
whenever he should deem it expedient, to raise troops foreign and
domestic for the defence of the King's subjects.[42] But the independent use of the stamp of Edward's hand permitted Somerset to
enjoy a constitutional state of being that the privy council did not
accept as having been expressed in the terms of the patent. In
fact, the council interpreted Somerset's ability to raise troops
under signet-letters in order to protect the King against Ket[43] as
an exercise of the royal prerogative but one step away from the
'protection' of the King against themselves.[44] It was for this
reason that when the London council moved against Somerset in
October 1549 they sought first to nullify the validity of signet-
letters: 'Foras much as the Duke of Somerset abusing the Kinges
Majestes hand, stamp, and Signet, and with out the aduise of
vs of his highnes counsaill hath sent forth diuers and sundry
writinges to levye the Kinges Majestes subgetz', the council therefore commanded sheriffs and justices of the peace to levy no man
'by force of any such writting whatsoeuer xcept thandes of vs of
his Majestes pryvey counsail or the more part of vs shalbe subscribed to the same'.[45] The conspirators aimed not merely to overthrow the duke's person but also to re-establish the council's
control of the administrative process that in this case had enabled
Somerset to prepare pre-stamped copies of signet warrants in
which spaces for the recipient's name, the date, and the number
of men to be raised had been left blank, to be filled in as circumstances required.[46]

After the *coup*, the council resumed the earlier procedure by
which at least six members counter-signed all letters dispatched
under the sign manual or stamp.[47] By 10 November 1551, however, with his dukedom secure, the council purged, the stamp in
his hands, and the young King in his confidence, so sure was
Northumberland of his political control that he could flatter the
King officially by asserting that it seemed 'summe derogacion to
his Majesties honour and royall autorite' for the council to sign
signet bills; the procedure was to be dropped in order that 'his
Majesties doinges may appere to the worlde to be, as they are in

dede, of such force as nedeth not to be either authorised or directed by any other'.[48] So transparent and bald a constitutional fiction was nevertheless covered by a brilliant administrative manoeuvre: henceforth at least five members of Northumberland's inner group at the board would sign docquets of the King's bills in witness to their having been stamped by Gates, Northumberland's man in Edward's household.[49]

The Act of Parliament 31 Henry VIII, c. 8 also required that Edward VI's proclamations 'import or bear underwritten the full names of such of the King's honorable council then being as shall be the devisers or setters forth of the same'.[50] The prescription seemed clear enough, but the same Act also supplied the titles of some twenty-six officers who were in fact to constitute this 'council'; all 'or at least the more part' of these twenty-six were the ones thus required to sign Edward's proclamations.

It has been suggested that Somerset secured the repeal of the statute in 1547[51] for the very good reason that to every proclamation that the government wished to make, he thus had to collect the signatures of twelve other members of the mixed 'council' named in the Act, a task as administratively troublesome as it was politically inhibiting.[52] In practice, however, the statutory regulation seems not to have discouraged Somerset. Before repeal, the government made twenty proclamations;[53] during a comparable ten-month period following repeal, it made twenty-one.[54] Moreover, we possess clear evidence – the signed bills which were presented in chancery as immediate warrants for the great seal – that the councillors were signing proclamations both during and after the period in which the Act operated. The stamped immediate warrant for the proclamation of 31 January 1547 (declaring Edward's accession) bears the original autographs of nine privy councillors and two assistants to the executors;[55] similarly, the warrants for proclamations made after 1547 and before October 1549 show that as many as six privy councillors were assenting to the government's edicts.[56] It would appear that Somerset wished also to preserve his own record of the council's complicity in some of these acts: the council's draft of the 'proclamacion for stay of the peoples attemptates about breaking vp of pales diches hedges etc. xxij° maij 1549' carries his own and four other hands.[57] Although we have clear evidence of the collective authorisation of royal proclamations for the whole of the Protectorate, it is interesting to note, however, that during the time in which the Act of 1539 remained in force (to December 1547), the council seems to have been not especially concerned to fulfil the letter of the Henrician statute: of the eleven signatories to the proclamation of 31 January 1547, for example, only seven represented offices prescribed by the Act.[58] Even so, the necessity of collecting signatures to these royal orders appears not to have been the reason why Somerset repealed the statute; in most cases he seems actually to have sought at least a few signatures – the twelve that the Act required were in any case never found – as a record of the council's consent. As to the real reasons for the Act's repeal, it can only be suggested that that mixed body of officials should probably have found it difficult properly to meet in order to hear cases within their competence: the awkward machinery that they represented made the Act difficult to enforce in practice.

In the context of the council's assent to royal proclamations, the evidence of one made on 11 August 1549 suggests an additional point which to the author's knowledge has never before been noticed, the fact that the final version of some of these decrees, the document which the common criers (or other officials) read out in public, also bore signatories' names. The source for this proclamation (which set regulations for the provisioning of soldiers in London) is now to be found in the MS. Journals of the common council of the City of London; a clerk of the court of aldermen indicated that four privy councillors signed the foot of the bill.[59] As Grafton did not print this particular royal order, the clerk can only have taken the names from an official manuscript version; whether his source exhibited autographs or merely the names of those who authorised the proclamation cannot be known. Interestingly, there is no extant chancery warrant for this proclamation.[60]

The evidence of a second proclamation of 11 August 1549, which prohibited hunting and hawking at Whitehall, shows that only the Protector's name appeared on the original public version.[61] A comparison of the text of this and the other one made the same day reveals, furthermore, that whereas the King with the advice of Somerset and the privy council made the first, for the provisioning of soldiers, the King with only Somerset's advice made the second. The stated procedural difference would appear to be significant here: the exercise of the royal prerogative to prohibit hunting within the precincts of a royal palace was a matter which the Protector alone might regulate, but in order to fix the price of meals which the owners of lodging-houses in London could charge the bands of 'noblemen and gentlemen appointed to attend upon the King's Majesty's most royal person',[62] the government officially sought the council's assent for the satisfaction of those to whom the order was first directed – the mayor and aldermen of the City.

It is impossible to calculate in how many cases the number of signatures to the original proclamations thus may accurately have reflected the source of the 'advice' (that is, the fact of assent) cited in the official formula. The government under Somerset made seventy-four proclamations,[63] fifty-five by advice of Somerset and the privy council;[64] three on the Protector's advice alone;[65] four by the advice of the privy council during Somerset's official absences;[66] and eleven without any reference to the advice or consent of Protector and council.[67] Substantively, these last eleven involved no important use of the prerogative, most of them being declaratory in authority or administrative in purpose; of the two made on Somerset's advice that have not been cited, one ordered soldiers to their garrisons[68] and the other merely informed religious pensioners where they might collect their stipends.[69] The great bulk of Somerset's pronouncements, therefore, including all of the really important ones, rested procedurally upon the stated formal consent of the privy council; in practice, of course, the policies which his edicts pronounced can only very rarely have been the collective work of the board. Considering his virtual abandonment of the council in most matters, as well as his self-assumed style ('Edward by the grace of god Duke of Somersett . . . .')[70] in government, we are probably on safe ground in assuming that in most cases the decision to proceed in a matter by royal proclamation was a decision which Somerset made.

Upon the abolition of the Protectorate, evidence of the council's collective authorship and authorisation of proclamations becomes substantially clearer. We have the Earl of Warwick's own description of the making of a proclamation which prohibited the export of victual except to Calais. Writing to Secretary Cecil at the court at some time from 14 to 18 September 1550, he wondered why the proclamation could not have been concluded according to the 'devise' which they had earlier discussed with the Lord Chancellor; in any case, he would be at the court in the afternoon: 'Looke what my Lord of Somersett, the master of the horsse [Herbert] and yow with others do resolve in yt and then send me the instrument yf it nede my hand And I wyll subscrybe to yt as they do this for noon.'[71] Six at the least having signed the 'instrument' – that was the rule: all bills presented for the King's signature before 10 November 1551 were to carry at least six hands – the proclamation was authorised at a meeting at Oatlands on the twenty-second and proclaimed on the twenty-fourth.[72] We also have the signed bills (that is, immediate warrants) for a number of proclamations, and these display the council's original autographs.[73] Independent contemporary copies of proclamations of 30 October 1549, 11 June 1550, and 20 July 1550 suggest once again that signatories' names (at least) appeared on the final form of some of the documents which were publicly proclaimed.[74]

By the order of 10 November 1551 the council ceased signing all bills presented for the King's signature. Dudley's purpose – to give the impression of an Edward VI enjoying full sovereignty – is also reflected in the formulas of the later proclamations: increasingly the King alone makes a commandment and not, as before, 'by the advice of his privy council'. Indeed, one-third (twelve) of the thirty-five proclamations issued after 5 October 1549 make no mention of the council's advice or consent,[75] and of these, four represent significant exercises of the prerogative power.[76] Procedurally, Northumberland's proclamations therefore conceal what Somerset's orders usually falsely proclaim, a power wielded with the council's consent, the irony of course being that Dudley controlled a packed board whose methods after November 1551 were perhaps no less autocratic than those of the Protector.

Proclamations based on the prerogative power which omitted any procedural reference to the council's assent in one sense mark the official zenith of Dudley's career, a career that had begun when he secured the office of the presidency in 1550. Dudley had seen then that the potential powers of that office, once fully applied, would enable him to capture procedural control of the council and that this control, coupled with his ascendancy at court – either in person or through his 'great frendes abowte the king' – would ensure his political pre-eminence. The slight but revealing changes in the council's procedural formalities alone record both Edward VI's graduation to the mere appearance of rule and the success of Dudley's very real use of the royal power: the deletion of the phrase 'by the advise of the Counsaile' from 'all warraunts, billes to be signed, and all such writinges as shall pass in the Kinges Majesties name';[77] the order that nothing was to pass the lords' signatures unless first subscribed by a secretary or clerk, a procedure designed to make the council's administrative staff directly responsible to the President and thus ensure his control of affairs; the disappearance of the council's hands to bills sealed with a signet also now in Northumberland's control, the arrangement of 14 December 1551 whereby the King formally allowed Gates 'to seale all such warraunts as shall passe vnder the king's priuie seale without other more speciall warrant',[78] official recognition of Northumberland's ability to order action in the royal name.

Having thus laboured carefully to mask the council's supremacy with the King's sovereignty, it remained only for Dudley to attempt finally to reinforce his position with an Act of Parliament. The incident is obscure and may well have been short-lived, but Charles V's ambassador in London can hardly have mistaken the gist of a report to the effect that 'The King of England's Council are trying to pass an act giving all orders of the Council the same force as acts of Parliament. The knights and commons, the second order of Parliament, refuse their consent to this.[79]

Neither the Lords' nor Commons' Journals mention even a first reading of such a bill; the author has found no other reference to it in any contemporary source. If the report was true, and it would seem that at the very least some sort of government proposal had been bruited about, we can only suppose that as a foreigner, Scheyfve had confused council orders with proclamations which, as everyone knew, were ordered in council. One might read any number of things into Scheyfve's dispatch, not the least of which is that the privy council had drafted a bill which would have given proclamations the force of statute, and for this reason his version of the report must be treated with caution.

Even if grounded upon rumour, however, Scheyfve's statement still reflects something of the contemporary reaction to the procedural trend which characterised Northumberland's administration.

In this account of the conduct of business occasional mention has been made of the council's administrative staff – the two principal secretaries, the secretaries for the French and Latin tongues, four clerks of the signet, three clerks of the privy council, and an unknown number of clerks' assistants. Our task here will be to complete the picture of the council's administrative machinery by describing the methods employed by the secretaries and clerks in the dispatch of the board's affairs.

The responsibility for the organisation of this work fell to the secretaries who, although attached to the royal household, were nevertheless the chief administrative officers of state. As privy councillors *ex officio* they carried less official weight than the ranking lords, but two administrative tasks determined that they were the most informed and therefore potentially the most important members – the formulation of agendas and, as Paget put it, the 'keping of all lettres, minutes of lettres to and from the King or the counsaill, Instructions, and suche other writings as shalbe treated upon by the counsaill'.[80]

One such letter to the board is of exceptional interest, for the clerks' and secretaries' record of its management allows us to follow the way in which the council's consideration of its contents was translated into executive action. At Carlisle on 20 February 1547 Thomas Lord Wharton, Warden of the West Marches, dispatched his son to Westminster 'to attend and knowe my Lordes of the counsailles pleasure vpon' nine particulars contained in a written inquiry.[81] When this letter reached the court it was delivered to the secretaries, whose assistants filed it with other current business as being 'For Sir Thos. Whartons depech'. Sometime early in April one of the council, perhaps Paget, turned his attention to Wharton's detailed requests, noting in the margins of the original what was to be done to satisfy the Warden's interests. Among other things, the council was to write letters of thanks to several gentlemen serving the King on the borders.[82] The officer responsible for these marginal reminders then composed an abstract of Wharton's headings, again noting after each the requisite action.[83] This abstract served a double purpose, as the secretaries' list of business to be authorised by the council and, once the 'aunsweres' to Wharton's points had been agreed upon, as a kind of master sheet of instructions to the clerks and their assistants for the drafting of the required documents.[84] 'Whartons depech' was apparently accomplished at one stroke in council on 12 April 1547, for a clerk entered a full copy of the council's abstract of Wharton's headings together with the council's abbreviated 'aunsweres' into the council's register of *out*-letters (not the book of proceedings) under that date.[85] In response to one of the headings cited here, the council had also ordered the secretaries specifically to draft unaddressed form-letters of thanks to the gentlemen serving with Wharton so that when he received the resulting packet of duplicates he could fill in the appropriate names himself; the secretary's final draft of this letter stood as the 'master' from which the clerks transcribed the fair copies sent to Wharton.[86] On 12 April 1547 the lords signed the copies and the clerks duly entered into the privy council register of letters the full text of the correspondence thus dispatched.[87]

The clerks also regularly endorsed the secretaries' drafts as 'minutes' of the letters sent (or to be sent) and filed them away singly; indeed, by August 1550 the council may have discontinued the register of out-letters, retaining instead the full 'minute' and recording that fact in the council book.[88] Under Northumberland, the secretaries advanced this procedure one step further by retaining not merely rough – or fair-copy – 'minutes', but *signed* fair copies of certain letters.[89] In general, however, the retention of unsigned fair copies of out-letters appears to have been the rule, but this fact in itself establishes the procedure as a unique development in the history of Tudor administration, for it bears witness to the almost 'modern' sophistication of the management of council business under Northumberland, in this case the secretaries' organised supervision of the clerks' work of copying at least two different forms of the same letter, the original copy to be sent, and what one might call a 'staff' copy for the reference of the secretary and council.[90]

To take the place of registers of letters, the secretaries may have kept calendars of in-coming and out-going dispatches. This was the later practice, apparently;[91] it would not have been a novel procedure for Cecil to have followed after 1550, nor would it have been unusual for him to have required the council's messengers to return certificates of receipt from those to whom the council's letters were directed.[92] The rule of 1547 which provided for the certification of clerks' copies of entries from the register – the copies were to bear 'theis speciall wourdes in thende, *concordat ad originali* [*sic*]'[93] – almost certainly determined that the clerks, like their Elizabethan successors, kept little books of record showing who had received an official copy of a letter or, just as importantly, who at the court might have asked for the original copy or the 'minute' thereof;[94] we know that the council sometimes sent to the mayor and aldermen of the City copies of the council's letters to the sheriffs of various counties.[95]

When the council required that unaddressed fair copies of letters (or simply numerous copies of the same letter) be sent to specified persons in every shire, the clerks and under-clerks, to handle the task of duplicating documents quickly, organised themselves into teams for the distribution of such routine labours.[96] Circumstances permitting, the secretaries also collected signatures to these undated circulars, holding the copies in reserve until the day of dispatch,[97] at which time the clerks pulled out the requisite master check-list of recipients' names – the secretary indicating the names to be omitted or included in a particular batch – and filled in the proper addresses.[98] One of these master-lists for 'Lettres to be written to the lordes of Ireland' exhibits either a Tudor administrator's deft sense of protocol or what, for the time, appears to have been an uncommon grasp of the realities of Irish political life: eighteen letters were to be addressed to seventeen lords and the wife of one other since, as the clerks' instructions explain, she was the one 'by whome he is moste rulid'.[99] For other types of business which required the production of letters having a standard form – warrants, recognizances, and so on – the clerks probably were able to refer to a formulary book for the needed text,[100] or certainly to office copies of letters which preserved the preferred texts;[101] otherwise the secretary wrote out the form to be observed and from this the clerks copied the final version, filling in specific bits of information supplied to them separately.[102]

In practice the secretaries could hardly have found enough time to draft all letters, nor could they have possessed the often specialised knowledge demanded in a reply. The alternatives were obvious: they instructed the clerks to collect the necessary information (or resolutions) from other councillors[103] and draft the reply themselves;[104] they referred the work directly to another councillor.[105] In fact, much of the work of formulating the substance of the council's important letters actually fell to the clerks, the secretary adding his corrections both to the clerk's first rough draft as well as to what frequently took shape as a clerk's second, wide-spaced fair copy; from this, a final version was copied out by an under-clerk and presented to the board for signing.[106] In one extraordinary case the council's final draft of a letter recommending Paget to the Emperor was presented to the Princess Mary for copying, on the assumption that a letter in her hand and name would carry greater conviction than one from the King in a secretary's hand,[107] a procedure as politically transparent as it was administratively inefficient.

It should not be thought, however, that even the regular procedures for framing council letters characterised a particularly responsive governing board, for delay followed inevitably upon the clerks' method of having to collect the lords' opinions to a matter and draft and re-draft them in terms acceptable to the whole board. A clerk of the privy council once found himself on the receiving end of this process. As one of the King's commissioners in Scotland, he marvelled that 'of all our lettres sent to the courte we haue received none aunswer'; since 'in xj dayes nothing is retourned', he had begun to wonder 'how our doinges ar taken with my lordes'.[108] The fault, however, lay not so much with Cecil, unquestionably one of the best-organised men of the sixteenth century, as with the inability of the lords to put their heads together conclusively. Northumberland abhorred indecision. He wanted nothing more than a firm administrative hand;

. . . wherefor in my opynyon, when soche aduertisementes shall come whiche requier resolution and answer from the councell as matters insydent to theyr lordships only to meddyll with, yt sholde be A great redynes to your mynisters there to worke by yf that they may perceve aunswer . . . for yf I were there present I wold thinke yt mete , , , to haue theyr lordships opynyons and advyces.[109]

. . . the grettist lakk that ys in our doinges ys delaying of thinges when theyr restythe no more to be don but even to gyve order.[110]

An answer formulated; a letter drawn, corrected, copied and sent; the fact of the resolution recorded and the text of the dispatch itself placed on record – after all of this, the clerks finally arranged for the systematic filing of the documents thus produced. The current registers of in-letters and out-letters as well as single copies of current out-going correspondence they kept locked up in 'the Counsaill Chest', a great coffer standing in a little room adjoining the council chamber at Westminster. Into its myriad trays and drawers also went fresh recognizances, signed bills, reports, account-books, depositions, contracts, and even bags of money,[111] the whole lot looked after by one called appropriately 'the keap[er] of the Counsell chest', who produced the books and writings upon the council's demand.[112]

The records stored in the council chest, however, represented but a small part of what had become by the end of Henry VIII's reign a casual but nonetheless distinctly recognisable collection of privy council documents – essentially, the council's archives. At some time after the establishment of the privy council (*c.* 1536) and before October 1540, it became the custom of the secretaries to give over to a clerk or clerk's assistant the informal charge of keeping this small but steadily growing mass of letters and papers in some order. Before he became a clerk of the privy council, Paget assumed these duties; we know that Cecil, while still a clerk in Somerset's household, did likewise.[113] In the earlier period the responsibilities probably were slight, but by 1547 the collections had filled up a little room at Westminster – the 'studie' where they were housed – to such an extent that an inventory of at least the most important items was needed for the council's information.[114] This list, in Sir Ralph Sadler's hand and dated to Edward's reign, shows that the clerk having charge of the papers arranged the records relating to domestic affairs by subject ('the seas', '. . . the Matyer of the last Quene attaynted', 'The boke of entrees of warrants for Money') and foreign correspondence by geographic category. In the latter case, the clerks filed the original in-letters together with copies of the council's replies in bags and boxes marked according to the country (or sovereign power) to which the contents related; these 'Bagges of bokes, Lettres and other writenges' were then stashed away in 'the Cupbordes and tilles in the studie'.[115] Had one browsed through the foreign section of the study in King Edward's time one would have seen

A greate bag of Lettres etc. to and from Thambassadors with Themperor writen vpon it THEMPEROR

A greate bagge of Lettres etc. touching germany
A greate bagge of matiers of ffraunce
A bag of Matiers of Scotland
A bag of Matiers of fflaundres
A litle bagge of mattiers of venyce
A great bagge of Mattiers of Calays

and so on.

Like many late Henrician practices, the systematic organisation of the council's papers – a characteristic procedure of the new, essentially bureaucratic institution – broke down during the Protectorate. The breakdown is explained by Somerset's virtual abandonment of the council; by the dislocation of the secretaries' management of council business; by the consequent loss of letters and other documents. Somerset may have confiscated some of the papers; he certainly put one of his own servants, and not one of the council's staff, in charge of their keeping. That his was a period of personal rule the gaps in the council's records silently confirm.

Regularly employed about the council chamber were a few functionaries who, although not directly connected with the administration of business, nevertheless deserve to be mentioned here. In addition to the guardian of the great council chest there was Peter Saxon, the 'keeper of the Counsaile Chamber' who was paid £10 per annum 'for his attendaunce in keeping the Counsaill chamber and providing of necessarie for the same.'[117] In the pay of the Lord President there was also a 'dore keaper of the Counsell chamber',[118] a servant whose well-defined powers incidentally failed him one day at Oatlands in September 1551 when the Earl of Wiltshire discovered one Thomas Trowghton 'putting a bill seditiously vnder the Counsaile chamber durre'.[119] 'Attendaunt alwaies at the . . . Courte uppon the kinges most honorable Counsaille' for the purpose of 'beyng sent at soundry and dyverse tymes for money' was a certain Robert Olyver who, although officially a deputy to the Treasurer of the Chamber, nevertheless found his usual employment at the council's hands, riding in the King's affairs with letters and warrants from the board.[120] The council frequently paid the King's messengers for similar duties;[121] like Olyver, they were attached to the chamber, but unlike him they did not enjoy a fixed and full-time responsibility to the privy council.

Of course, the clerks of the council also left their writing-desks to deliver the council's written and verbal instructions, but these often were authoritative missions requiring an experienced servant second only to a principal secretary in both knowledge and official capacity. De Selve reported that 'le protecteur a envoyé le secretaire du conseil Honning' to him to explain an aspect of English policy in respect of Boulogne.[122] Waad, an Oxford B.A. who probably spoke several languages, certainly served often enough as the council's channel of communication with the French, Portuguese, and Imperial ambassadors.[123] As the 'gentleman who understood Spanish', Chaloner was once sent to listen to Sebastian Cabot's interview with van der Delft.[124] William Thomas should understandably have had many contacts with Venetian officials in London: already the author of a *Historie of Italy* (1548), he finished his *Principal Rules of the Italian Grammar* just a year before becoming a clerk.[125]

It is not surprising therefore to find the clerks on diplomatic missions abroad; Thomas accompanied the Marquess of Northampton's embassy to France in 1551,[126] and Bernard Hampton served with Hoby in Flanders in 1552.[127] At home their varied activities comprehended the examination of accused persons (Waad, in the Countess of Sussex's case)[128] and mustering bands of foreign mercenaries.[129] Work often proved tedious (Chaloner once took an inventory of the contents of Sudeley Castle)[130] and downright laborious (the council ordered Honyngs to 'seale up the durres' to the Bishop of Winchester's house),[131] but the salary, the very handsome occasional fees[132] and the inevitable Crown favours at this time made the office very rewarding indeed.[133] With ability and the right connections, clerks could become councillors, but during Edward's reign especially the politics of the board seeded every connection with potential disaster. Honyngs may have attempted to help Wriothesley and the conservatives swing the council's case against Gardiner by stealing the judges' opinions in the matter;[134] whether guilty or not, he was implicated in the theft, and when Wriothesley went Honyngs lost his job too. Access to privileged information also rendered the clerks' position useful to various parties outside the government. The merchant brothers Johnson, always interested in the council's thinking on trade policy, might just as well have resided in the council chamber, so close was their understanding with Armagil Waad ('good Armigall our old and assured frend').[135] Unlike Honyngs, however, Waad remained professionally discreet and politically non-partisan; like Chaloner he was a very capable administrative assistant, precisely the kind of servant that the King's new privy council required.

Such then, were the procedures, formal and informal, by which the privy council ordered its meetings, concluded its business, and provided for the administration of its work. In reconstructing the methods of government by council under Somerset and Northumberland, an attempt has been made to demonstrate the extent to which Paget's 'Advise' of 1550 and the 'Articles' of 1553 either reflected earlier practice or served as a basis for subsequent action. It should now be possible to view the two sets of rules in their proper historical perspective.

Paget had drawn a model, based certainly upon informal precedent, for the time, place, and frequency of meetings, and the number and composition of a quorum; essentially the council adhered to this scheme. He suggested specifically that the council revive one of the practices of 1547 – the signing of the register; the council did so, but observed the rule only for a short time. For the dispatch of suits he attempted to define for the first time regular – and with respect to the labelled pots and black and white balls – novel procedures. In the wake of the *coup* of 1549 and the threat of civil war, not to mention the deposition of Wriothesley and Arundel, he urged his colleagues, unaccustomed as they were to doing so, to treat one another fairly, equally, and openly, at least during meetings. Coming as it did at the end of a political settlement which had re-established rule by council under a president, Paget's paper served both as a reminder of and a guide to the way in which that rule ought to be administered in the council chamber. In 1550 his advice represented a combination of precedent, practice, and new proposals.

The 'Articles' of 1553, on the other hand, assumed rule by council; they were intended primarily for the secretary and not the council, a secretary who was to keep the King informed of the state of the council's work. But, as was seen, only one of the orders stood as altogether new in 1553, the prescription that warrants for payment above certain amounts (£40 for reward and £100 for general affairs) were to pass the King's signature. Indeed, the other rules either modified earlier practice (the assignment of business to particular days of the week, a rule which apparently was not adopted) or recognised procedures which had been followed. Far from representing part of a plan to reorganise the council's work, Petre's and Edward VI's rules essentially described the *status quo* in procedure. The rules were thus not original with Edward VI. One can only speculate as to the reasons why the King thought of the 'Articles' as having been 'devised' by himself. It will be remembered that other documents in Edward's hand having to do with council matters do not necessarily present evidence of original authorship. There is no evidence that Petre thought of his version as a summary of the King's original work.[136]

We may, therefore, abandon the notion that the period March 1552 to January 1553 witnessed a reform of the council's procedure. In Edward's reign, the true reorganisation of the conduct and administration of council business occurred in February and March 1550 with the advent of Warwick's presidency and the definition of fundamental procedure contained in Paget's 'Advise to the Kinges Counsail'. The Articles of 1553 must be viewed against that background. As Paget had originally given his 'Advise' to Petre in France in 1550, we may suggest that Petre's well-known scheme finds its direct precedent in his colleague's earlier, more comprehensive, and historically more important set of rules. Some of Paget's rules merely confirmed what had been informal practice since the time of Thomas Cromwell; some were devised for the purposes of government during a royal minority; some were drafted in particular response to the breakdown of rule by council under Somerset; all of them testify to the fact that in 1550 the council was first made subject to a fixed administrative routine.

6
Governing the Realm

Reference was made earlier to the theoretical omni-competence of Edward's council, and it was stated that to the council during the royal minority fell the charge of governing the whole realm. Functionally, the board fashioned policy, executed and administered that policy, and, though it was not a judicial tribunal, sometimes acted in the manner of a court by arbitrating disputes between two parties. Substantively, the King's councillors' work touched every aspect of the Crown's 'public' affairs (that is, state business) and its 'private' matters (suits, petitions, and so on), as well as the affairs of individual Englishmen. Generally, *what* happened in respect of the great acts of state – the reformation of religion, the debasement of the currency, and so forth – is well known. It comes as no surprise to learn that the council stood at the centre of such matters, formulating policy and ordering action. The range of *types* of activity is also familiar: we know that in the King's name the council was able to fix the price of meat or close the ports, to cite merely two of its options within the economic sphere alone. The purpose here, therefore, is not to present summary 'histories' of, say, finance or religion in Edward's reign, nor merely to catalogue what the council did in those several areas, but rather to document where possible the decisive fact of the council's consideration of policy and by way of representative examples to illustrate the administrative and executive actions of privy councillors themselves. Examination will also be made of the evidence for the council's quasi-judicial activities.

It is about the first and arguably the most important of the council's functions, the formulation of state policy, that we are the least well-informed. To be able to know who and how many of the council were responsible for the decisions taken; to discover the contents of the deliberations which preceded the announcement of policies; to understand the true reasons or motives for the substantive acts of the government – to have such evidence would be to possess something close to the 'real' history of the council's administration of the realm under Edward VI. Rarely does one find this sort of information; the official sources only occasionally record the fact that considered policies actually emerged from discussions at the council table.

Lacking official accounts of the making of policy, we can at times piece together the fact of the council's responsibility for measures not ordinarily cited by the clerks in the council book. The board played an original role, for instance, in framing legislative programmes for Parliament and drafting particular bills. The council's schedule of proposed bills naturally embodied much of the Crown's 'public' policy, and the centre-piece of this Parliamentary agenda was usually a bill for a subsidy. Thus when the King, echoing the results of a council debate, wondered 'What nombre of actes are thought best to passe this parliement [of 1553] and which', his immediate response – 'What kind of ayde or subsidie' was to be required of his subjects – naturally reflected the government's priorities.[1] Nevertheless, asking the Commons 'to burden theyr myndes and hartes' with the King's 'extreme debtes and necessite' had the effect that year of drawing members' attention to the whole range of the government's policies and actions, and this was precisely what Northumberland wished to prevent. As he confided to Darcy, in drafting arguments in favour of a requested subsidy, the council should not seem to present itself as having 'to make a counte to the Comons' for royal policy, policy which in the eyes of some served merely to enrich the nobility.[2] Who was to 'pen the book' of the subsidy thus became an unusually sensitive matter in 1553, since it was indeed in the language of such a bill that the council would have to justify its demand for additional revenue.

Of course both Somerset and Northumberland constantly concerned themselves with money matters, and necessarily so, since their expenditures regularly exceeded Edward VI's ordinary income: from beginning to end their plans required the King's receipt of extraordinary revenue. Royal indebtedness limited personal ambition; the prospect of the collapse of their programmes reminded Somerset and Northumberland of the primacy of fiscal policy. The full story of Edward VI's finances has yet to be written; without it, the history of government action during his reign remains admittedly a story of parts only partly understood. As the paucity of the official records frustrates any attempt to reconstruct the council's financial debates, one can only hope to illustrate the obviously important connection between the King's revenues and the government's ability to formulate policy generally. This task is rendered less arduous by the existence of Paget's letter-book, a first-hand source the contents of which make it naturally convenient here to examine the policy-making function during the Protectorate, reserving chiefly for the period after 1549, when the relevant sources are more numerous, a discussion of the execution of the council's directives.

Paget's 'memorials' detail an extraordinary view of Somerset's attempts to construct workable foreign and domestic policies. Devising policy acceptable to the council proved difficult enough for him; the impact abroad of domestic action further complicated a deepening crisis at home. Paget's correspondence suggests that in the beginning – that is about December 1547, when the Protector consolidated his position – what debate there was on matters of policy remained private, engaging only Paget, the duke, and perhaps one or two others, but that during the spring and summer of 1549, in stormy sessions at the board, an increasingly dissident council several times took issue with Somerset's programmes. In revealing all of this, Sir William's papers essentially document a case for the Lord Protector's mismanagement of the realm, a development which Paget rightly understood to have followed directly upon the consequences of his invasion of Scotland. The Scots adventure, as Sir William repeatedly warned his master after 1547, would only serve to undermine the King's finances, the government's authority, the Protector's power and position, and ultimately the security of the whole realm.

Events of course confirmed the predicted failure of the 'good' duke's efforts to govern England. But Paget's prediction did not stand alone, for he had also spelled out alternative policies, suggestions which followed naturally upon his analysis of the interrelated character of all policy. Religion, trade, foreign war, domestic tranquillity – all, in Paget's view, were of a piece, and the Protector's ability to finance his programmes in any one field rested upon his ability to finance his programmes in every field.

Somerset fell, not simply because he alienated his powerful colleagues, but because he could not continue arrogantly to ride over them with bankrupt policies.

Neither bankruptcy nor political ruin could have been foreseen in 1547. Indeed, to his initial credit, Somerset had followed up victory at Pinkie with a shrewd financial bargain at home. The King's subjects, as the council book recorded it, were frankly 'induced' in Parliament that year to grant to the Crown all colleges, free chapels, chantries, and so on; it was intended that the income from these expropriations should relieve the same subjects 'of the continuall charge of taxes, contributions, lones and subsedies, the whiche by reason of warres they were constreyned . . . to abyde' under Henry VIII.[3] The cost of occupying Scotland could thus be met without recourse to further Parliamentary grants.

However, to the Scottish 'charges and expences, which do dayly growe and increase by reason of diverse and sundry fortifycations, garrisons, levying of men and soldiours', was added in 1548 the cost of preparing English defences against France. On top of this, wrecking every government's financial estimates, was a relentless, quite extraordinary inflation of prices. Of course Somerset cannot have foreseen or understood the price revolution in England, though his debasement of the King's coins undoubtedly contributed to it, but the question arises whether, at the beginning of 1548, he understood by how much the battle of Pinkie had advanced the probable day of reckoning with France and thus generated the inevitably greater debt which a French war would bring. We know in fact that the wider consequences of his military policy in Scotland had been made plain to him in 1547 by no less a person than Henry II himself, as Paget was to remind Somerset and the council two years later: 'whenne we beganne warre firste with scotlande the ffrench kinge said he wolde rather lose his realme then leave them [the Scots].'[4] And it had been no idle threat. 'The frenche men', Paget drily remarked to Somerset on 2 February 1548, 'sende no small ayde to them.'[5]

The possibility of war with France revealed the full dimensions of the financial crisis in England. The 'said Lord Protectour and others his Majestes Counsaile do plainely perceave nothing to be so myche lacking as money' was an official statement probably based in part on the reports of Lord St John and Secretary Petre who had earlier been commissioned to survey the various courts of revenue for the purpose of ascertaining what moneys these were expected to yield during 1548.[8] Noting that without money 'no defence can be had', the council seized upon one of the obvious short-term solutions and on 16 April 1548 decided to sell expropriated chantries to the annual value of £5,000. The commissioners who acted upon this decision worked with unusual speed, presenting complete accounts by 20 July; from the immediate sale of almost half of the recently acquired possessions the council realised £110,486. The profits of the mint, meanwhile, were bringing in an average of about £11,187 per month.[7]

But it was not enough. In February Paget had urged Somerset to order up estimates of only the *ordinary* charges of the King's garrisons for the calendar year 1548 with the recommendation that Somerset 'for goddes sake . . . passe ouer thys Sommer without newe fortificacions' in the North. The King's indebtedness dictated a policy of defence in Scotland: better that well-placed horse and foot protect what had already been won there than that Somerset should build ten new fortresses and 'vpon the commynge of ffraunce to lose but one'.[8] As it happened, mounting military expenditures forced Somerset towards the end of 1548 to do precisely what he earlier had admitted he could not do that year 'without great difficulte, daunger and grudge' – seek financial relief in Parliament. Even the sales of expropriated chantries and so on could not keep pace with average charges of about £200,000 per year in Scotland alone, a figure representing about half of the Protector's average yearly outlay for all military purposes.[9]

In the Parliamentary session which was convened on 24 November 1548, however, a bill for a subsidy was not forthcoming nor had one been introduced by Christmas, although 'indede if your grace be remembred, it [a subsidy] was the onelie cause why the parliament was called before Christmas'. The Commons, said Paget on 25 December, expected 'to paie a subsedie and speake it and thought it the furst thinge that shuld haue come in parliament'.[10] These remarks clearly imply that the Protector had failed to draft a bill for a subsidy in advance of the session and, worse, had apparently not yet taken into account the sort of

survey of the government's financial position from which the estimates for a subsidy should have been made. (We do know that
the next year Somerset ignored Sir Thomas Smith's recommen-
dations based upon just such a survey.)[11] The Protector's administrative failings in this respect moved Paget to evaluate not only his
financial reckonings but also the direction of policies the success
of which assumed adequate funding from the start.

It was necessary first, suggested Paget in the confidential note
(25 December 1548) already cited, to consider 'whether at your
first setting forward youe toke not a wronge waye, as . . . I thincke
you did', for

If your grace loke backewarde, then shall youe se that at the fyrst
entre of your waye, being but in an entree to Warre with scotlande,
[you were] in peax with fraunce, in amitie with thempereur, and in
an indifferent concorde with all the rest of the world (except Rome).
Youe are nowe in open warre with Scotland, entringe into warre
with fraunce, readie to haue thempereur falle out with you, and in
discord with all the reste of the World, besides discension at home . . .
And to mainteyne with all your doinges, loke where youe are nowe,
and whereaboutes in your waye: youe are in beggerye, in debte, In
scarsitie of men to serve, In vnwillingnes of men to serve, in doubte
to aske aide at home for your reliefe.[12]

How dangerous it would be to wait upon events or to think that
aid either material or diplomatic might be found abroad. No,
'youe haue no helpe but by reliefe at their handes that are bounde
to aide youe', the body of the realm in Parliament, 'whose welfare
youe have to hert and whose protection youe haue in speciall
care, and they had never more moneye amonge them then they
haue at this daye if youe thincke youe maye be bolde to aske it'.
Admittedly, a protector might not be able to ask for as much in
the way of a subsidy as Henry VIII could have done, but, Paget
thought, a subsidy 'is the onely and readie helpe that yow have'
and without it 'youe shall want in the myddes of all youre
affayres'. It was necessary, therefore, to appoint immediately to
'your money and victualles matiers men that will thoroughly
wade to the bottom in them and that will in good ordre, when
youe aske, make youe vnderstande the certayne state of them. And
abide to be reasoned with concerninge the same'.[13]

If there were those who found Somerset deaf to reason in such matters, others, like Paget, understood that part of the difficulty in formulating the right sort of request for assistance in Parliament lay in the duke's sensitivity to adverse popular criticism: 'ffor youe haue cared to content all men and be lothe or rather afrayd to offende any'. If Somerset's reluctance to burden the laity with new taxes was genuine, his procrastination in financial affairs did not speak well of his executive abilities. By 25 January 1549 Paget was urging him still 'to Resolve upon your procedinges in the parliament for money out of hand, for the tyme goeth away an yt had bene meter to have bene nowe in levienge of yt then about to aske yt'.[14] When the government's tax bill finally appeared – convocation was also persuaded to grant a subsidy – it was, as Professor Dietz once said, a curious measure in that it provided an indirect levy on sheep, wool, and wool cloth instead of a direct tax on land. This may have reflected Somerset's spirit of agrarian reform, but the relief (as it was called) finally brought in less money (£54,000 in 1549 and £47,500 in 1550) than Henry VIII's later subsidies, though it was supposed to yield up to £156,000 a year.[15] The relative paucity of the return thus bore out Paget's earlier argument in favour of the subsidy that Somerset had rejected: 'for your graces devises for moneye of Shepe and clothe will amount to nothinge in comparison'.[16]

If Somerset thought that a tax on sheep and wool offered the politically safer course at home, Paget was quick nonetheless to point out the relationship between the Protector's uncertain foreign policy and his ability to collect the proposed levy:

youe are in playne warre with the Scottes, and even ready to enter the same with the french. There is cause to doubte themperor abrode and lykewyse some of your owne at home. This your grace seith at hand. Nowe maye it please your grace to loke farre from yow. I meane, what will happen hereof if foresighte be not vsed? . . . Certayne and undoubted ruyne and destruction to the hole realme and to your selfe ioyned with an infamy. What reamedye? Let vs see what our force ys. ffurste, we have no money at all to speake of in a kinges case. No, but, youe saye, we shall nowe have yt of the subiectz. But if thempereur Jarre with youe there can be none levied, ffor the merchaunt shall haue no vent, The clothier shall haue no vent, nor your Shepeman no vent of his wolle.[17]

The disruption of English exports of wool to the Netherlands; the consequent diminution of the chief source of revenue envisaged by the 'relief'; bankruptcy in the event of an Anglo-Imperial war; these were calculations perhaps rendered academic by a simpler, rhetorical question – whether, as Paget phrased it, 'our force were of yt selfe . . . sufficient to withstand Scotland ffraunce Thempereur and the Romyshe' combined.[18] At the very least, England must be assured of Charles' neutrality; at best, it could be hoped that the alliance of 1543 by which Charles was pledged to defend English dominions[19] might be extended to cover Boulogne, where French pressure was greatest. Excepting one issue, the agreement of Habsburg and Tudor on this point was not inconceivable, but that issue was religion and upon it even France calculated its gain: 'ffraunce', said Paget, 'seith nowe a most propice tyme to falle oute with youe, consideringe that thempereur will not in respecte of our new devises [in religion] have any greate lyste to here youe.'[20]

That remark was made at Christmas 1548. In the face of almost certain war with Henry II – on 3 October 1548 the council had actually debated the wisdom of a pre-emptive English declaration[21] – there developed among Somerset's colleagues a concerted effort to persuade him to attempt at least to discover Imperial intentions. On 24 January 1549 Paget could

> beseche your grace to calle to remembraunce how that youe have bene moved diuerse tymes, not onelie by me but also by sondry others of the counsaill, to send to discipher thempereur, which your grace hath consented to be a thinge necessarye and yet haue semed to differ [i.e. defer] yt for want of good occasion . . . Sir, occasion ys bawld behind.[22]

Doubts about the Emperor's designs as well as the council's preoccupation with domestic order during the winter of 1548–9 forced not only a reassessment of Anglo-Imperial relations, but also, of necessity, of the political implications of the government's reformation of religion in England. The threat here was not only that Somerset's religious policy invited Charles V's attack, but that in the event of an Anglo-Imperial war, 'here at home some thinckinge yt [the war] to be for religion, will peraduenture thincke yt also their duetie for suerty of the Kinge and the realme to take his [the Emperor's] parte'. Seeing that 'your force at home ys too weake' to put down a rebellion of the King's catholic subjects, 'abroad consider your grace what help youe shall have. If youe say in almayne, I aske from whome there.' The Landgrave Frederick of Saxony, the Duke of Württemberg, the Count Palatine – all 'be as prinsoners to thempereur'. Maurice of Saxony, the dukes of Bavaria, and the Marquess of Brandenburg 'be firmelie knit' with him too, 'and so is also Denmarke'. 'Prusse ys pore.' The cities maritime, impoverished and afraid of Imperial might, offered no help either. The King of Poland lay too far away. 'Yet myght we for religions sake make a goode partie with some of thalmayns yf we had good store of Money.' Lacking funds, the cause of reformed religion would not prove great enough, however, to keep the Germans in league with Edward VI.

And though there were suche a league for religion, yet your grace knoweth that thempereur Can devise some other cause to falle out (when he lyste) [and] to stoppe theyr mouthes abrode. And nevertheles some here at home will thincke yt to be (and in dede their is none other cause) for cause of religion.[23]

Considering the King's financial insecurity; the possibility of war with the catholic powers; the unlikely prospect of foreign military assistance; the spectre of a rebellion in support of the old religion: 'What then saythe your grace all in desperacon?' The answer, Paget offered, lay not with force but diplomacy ('where strength fayleth assaye what arte wyll do'), for the Protector could, by the careful management of one issue, extricate himself from potentially dangerous circumstances. Religion, or rather the form of religion in England, could be made to serve the King's needs.

Wherfore me thought yesternight your grace beganne to devise well, to fayne frendeshippe with thempereur, to seme to yeld to hym, to dalye withe hym, to wynne tyme of hym by puttynge him in hope that youe will geve eare to hym, and youe haue good meanes to do yt yet. ffor the thinges that hetherto youe have passed be but formes and Facions of Service and mynistracon of the Sacramentes, which ys and hath bene dyverse in dyverse places in Christ churche and ordered and altered as pleaseth the governours. So as there ys no cause why thempereur shold be in dede offended with this, yf the matter were well debated with hym. And therfore haue youe hereby (yf youe staie goinge further) good meanes to practyse with hym and to enduce hym to thincke that as youe myght alter these ceremonyes from their former facion to this they be nowe at, so he maye fortune to enduce youe to alter them from this facion to that they were at before.[24]

Thus, by 1 February 1549 Somerset had accepted the argument that his religious policy risked alienating the Emperor at the King's peril and was evidently seeking to assure Charles V of the King's moderation. But did Somerset ever seriously consider re-establishing the ceremonies of the Henrician Church? Two years later, upon his readmission to the council, it was rumoured that Somerset held no objections to abandoning the new religion and taking up the old again.[25] This is hardly credible, though in 1551 he would probably have liked to moderate Dudley's extremism. More to the point is Somerset's own remark of 1552. Head on the block, he then stated with some pride and no equivocation that as Protector he had been the principal 'agent' behind the reformation of religion. During that period (1547–9) we know that Paget, in conversations with the Emperor's ambassadors, had consistently exaggerated Somerset's moderation as a reformist in religion.[26] Even so, in respect of his toleration of Mary's mass, the record is clear: Somerset's very real moderation on this point was to a certain extent geared to considerations foreign. He and the council had overlooked the lady's weakness 'partly to gratifie themperor'.[27] To what further lengths the Protector might have been willing to go to placate Charles V remains an open question. In his own person, Somerset stood sincerely with the ranks of the reformed.

Technically amicable relations between England and the Empire in 1548–9 masked fundamental differences in spirit; each side understood the other's true purpose. Though, as Paget said, Charles seems 'to favour yow for his owne commoditie, yet vndoubtedly he is in his herte displeased with your procedinges in religion'. Having grown great, Paget observed, and seeing England's 'decaye', the Emperor could find little satisfaction in a friendship feigned, since there were other princes who 'neyther pretende so myche trust in his frendshippe as we do, nor haue so myche nede of it as we haue'. There yet remained the danger of a secret Franco-Imperial accord 'contrarye to our procedinge[s] nowe' with Charles V.[28]

If Somerset's formulation of religious policy hinged in part on the possible consequences of that policy abroad, his chief consideration must surely first have been the concord and unity of Englishmen. Not all of the evident 'discension at home' had grown from diversity of religious opinion and practice, but the government naturally assumed that without uniformity of accepted belief the commons' political obedience could not be assured. Actually, Somerset and the council knew that they held the governance of a people whose religious unity they did not command. This was never expressed officially, but the tone and substance of another of Paget's references to the European scene suggests that this was in fact the view which contemporaries held of the religious life of England under Protector Somerset even before the troubles of 1549. Paget thought, for example, that the kingdoms of England and Poland might well be compared on this point, as 'the kinge of poole ys . . . but newlie come into his kingdome, and not yet fully established. If yt be said yet, for religion he will Joyne with youe [against Charles V], I answere that [he will not] thoughe . . . he had his kingdome vnited with hym wholly as he hath not, but is therin in the same case and worse then we be.'[29] Unlike Sigismund II, Somerset of course did not also have 'the muscovites at his backe to troble him daylye'. Nevertheless, the Protector's task in England stood clearly before him, to see the laws in respect of religion executed without remission, 'ffor so shall youe bringe in agayn obedience which nowe ys clean gone'. By 'takinge all disputacions from vs other then by the lawes ys apointed', domestic quiet shall ensue. Paget had earlier feared the possibly uncontrollable effects of religious disputation among the people; 'your ordre for Religion beinge yet in your hands' at Christmas 1548, he had thought it best then to 'waye well' any further reformation of the Church. But by 2 February 1549, when it was clear that the statutory reformation would go forward, he could anticipate the day when 'we shall no more saie thow papist and thoue heretique, for your lawe the laste yere for the Sacrament and this yere for the ceremonies will helpe moche the matter yf they be well executed'.[30]

The very decision to proceed by statute in the matter of the form and content of reformed belief in England reflected a deeper calculation. Certainly before a date not later than 2 February 1548 Somerset had resolved to continue the reformation of the doctrine and institution of the Church by royal proclamation and not by statute: on 25 December 1548 Paget recalled that 'as for matters of religion your grace thought they might if nede were be ordered by the Kinges majestes authoritie and so youe determined ones and in suche sorte to haue them sette forthe'.[31] But earlier, on 2 February 1548, he had cautioned against the intended application of the prerogative power; he had reminded Somerset then to

appointe the nombre of learned men as well for the consideracon of the lawes, which to be contynued and which be abrogated, as also for the decent ordres to be observed in the church; and stayenge all thinges unto the parliament tyme, then with advise and consent of the bodye of the realme and the learned men to contynewe or alter suche thinges as upon great and depe consideracon and foresight shalbe thought convenient and agreable bothe to goddes Lawe and to preservacon of the pollicie of the realm . . . otherwaies be vncertayne subdayne [sudden] and daungerous to youe and yours.[32]

Thus, if we are to believe Paget, Somerset had not in fact intended to convene the session of Parliament which sat from 24 November 1548 to 14 March 1549 for the purpose of submitting the government's religious policies to the 'body of the realme'; the 'onelie cause' why Parliament then sat was, as earlier noted, for the consideration of what the Commons had assumed would be the council's request for a subsidy. The fact that Parliament did proceed to a consideration of the 'ordres to be observed in the church' during that momentous session suggests that by November Somerset had agreed to what, under the circumstances, was obviously the more advisable course of reform by statute and not by royal proclamations based only upon the technical consent of the privy council.

Whereas the various proclamations of 1548 (for the removal of images and the disuse of holy water, and so on) had not reduced the tension of religious debate, the Act of Uniformity of 1549 failed immediately to produce an order acceptable to all. Usage of the Prayer Book authorised by the Act sparked a rebellion in Devon and Cornwall in precise confirmation of Paget's earlier description of a people divided in their loyalty to the reformed faith and a Protector responsible for ordering their adherence to it. The Parliamentary session of 1548–9 appears therefore to mark a turning point in Somerset's administration. It was a session called for the authorisation of extraordinary revenue for the funding of an adventurist military policy in Scotland, but the occupation of Scotland, as it happened, also guaranteed war with France. The prospect of an Anglo-French war eventually moved the government to prevent by diplomacy an armed Imperial response which, it was feared, would invite English conservatives to resist the authority of King and council. To forestall rebellion and provide in the first instance for the right ordering of society both religious and civil, a Parliamentary reformation establishing religious uniformity was pushed through; it was a reformation neither so extreme that it provoked international destruction of the trade upon which England's taxable wealth was in part based, nor so moderate that it compromised the genuine impulses for reform at home. What was not foreseen in advance of this session was the financial and political cost of the Scottish campaign; what few then appreciated was the absence of a resolute hand to manage the policies and personnel of the government.

Certainly the Protector delayed in suppressing the revolts of 1549. His famed 'liberality' probably explains his unwillingness initially to take up the sword against the King's poor but rebellious subjects, but the council did not find in such noble restraint a prescription for England's survival, and when they deposed him they acted in concert behind Ket's ruthless, more decisive conqueror. Historically, however, Somerset's politically ineffective idealism, no matter how attractive the social conscience behind it, does not explain why he fell into such clear administrative difficulties by the end of 1548. That his colleagues dumped him on account of his allegedly liberal outlook is not the whole case: Warwick and the others did not finally decide to make war on England's Protector simply because a few of their parks had been enthusiastically ploughed under by those who found inspiration in what they believed to be Somerset's sense of a 'common wealth'. Rather, the privy council deposed the Protector of the realm because of the administrative incompetence of his regime. Though admittedly driven by selfish political interests, the conspirators stood united on the question of the duke's inability to manage the King's men and money.

Certain of the administrative irregularities of the Protectorate have already been noted; the official records themselves barely mask Somerset's methods. But Paget's letters stand as a rather more pointed description of the administrative character of the regime, for the author, at once adviser and intimate, was uniquely placed to assess both Somerset the man and Somerset the governor of the realm.

Somerset's 'official' personality is on the one hand described by his troublesome manner of dealing with colleagues. So abrupt, abrasive, and rebuking had the duke's private manner become that 'no man', lamented Paget, 'shall dare speake to youe what he thinckes, though yt were never so necessarye for youe to knowe yt'. Especially grievous to those councillors of experience and competence were Somerset's 'great colericke facions' which blew up 'when so ever youe are contraried in . . . that which youe haue conceaved in your heade'.[33] It was necessary 'before your grace shewe your owne opinion in matters, to here other mens', otherwise, by his sharpness the Protector prejudiced men who were loath to offend him. The result, predictably, was that under pretence of faithful service, but really in order to escape the duke's ill-humour, men sought 'to make your grace beleve thinges to be other than they are and abuse your grace, which is daungerous for the prince'. A diversity of opinion expressed by those able to weigh the great affairs of state brought credit to the prince who wished to govern well, 'but alas Sir', complained Paget, 'youe here not all thinges nor all men'.[34] A king discouraged frank advice at the peril of his realm, 'but a subiecte in great aucthoritie (as your grace ys) vsinge such facion ys like to fall into great daunger and peryll, of his owne person besides that to the common Wealth'.[35] In particular, therefore, did Paget urge Somerset 'to discipher' the lords of the council 'as ones you did', to seek again their regular assistance in the formulation of state policy,[36] bearing in mind that 'when the hole counsayll shall move youe or geve youe aduise in a matter (like as they did of late for sendinge of men to bulloyne) to folowe the same and to relent sometime from your owne opinion'.[37]

Tact, however, seldom veiled the Protector's insistence on getting his own way. For the others at the board in 1549 it was a maddening but typical experience 'when the hole counsaill shall Joyne in a matter, and your grace travayle to out reason them in yt, and wraste them by reason of your aucthoritie to bowe to yt'.[38]

Rigid adherence to his own opinions complicated an already awkward situation, since his stubbornness often blinded him to business of a more immediate and important nature. The solution in
part was 'not so sone to beleve the thinges to be trewe that your
self desyreth', an attitude 'which many times may cause your
grace to leave vndone thinges that nedethe'.[39] And

ffor goddes sake Sir followe thinges when tyme requireth and whiles
tyme Serveth ... I amongest others thincke yt my duetie to put your
grace in remembraunce of thinges necessary to be done, beschinge
your grace when yow are put in remembraunce of them to waye
whether the thinges be mete to be done or no, and if youe thincke
them so mete, then to folowe the remembraunces and do the same
without delaye.[40]

The duke's inertia in such instances annoyed Paget only a little
less than the fact of his master's inattention to his detailed memoranda. Had not the Protector, in a secret conference in the gallery
at Westminster within hours of Henry VIII's death, promised
during Edward's minority to follow Paget's advice 'more than
any other mans'?[41] For his part, Paget had certainly brought to
the duke's administration, 'in sondry consultacions aparte with
your grace' down to the end of 1548, the voice of knowledgeable
counsel. The evidence of a 'Scedule' addressed to Somerset on 2
January 1549,[42] however, may point to a decline in the adviser's
real influence at the centre; in lieu of a New Year's gift Paget
could pen merely 'a token of my herte' – a list of maxims or rules
for the right conduct of a prince, every one of which Somerset had
already violated. Had the author couched the rules in a negative,
descriptive form, the schedule would in fact stand as an abstract
of Somerset's alleged administrative failings – his inability, according to Paget, to maintain 'wise men' under him, his reluctance or
refusal to follow advice in council, his difficulty in forging
balanced decisions and executing them promptly, his unwillingness to punish the disobedient and rebellious according to prevailing standards of justice. It was on this last point that Somerset
drew Paget's most forthright criticism. A laxness in the proper
execution of the laws and a hesitancy to enforce the peace of the
realm – these in Sir William's mind constituted the Protector's
chief shortcomings, weaknesses which, as much as his Scottish and
financial policies, were contributing to the evident 'subuersion of

the noble Realme of england and the ruyne of your grace', not to
mention the destruction of the young King.[48]

The root of the problem lay in Somerset's attitude towards
'liberty', the liberty of the subject to speak and write about
government policy. On 9 November 1547 Somerset told van der
Delft that the King's councillors had earlier decided 'to abolish
and to modify' several laws which they felt were too severe and so
give to Englishmen 'a little more reasonable liberty'. According to
Somerset, this could be done 'without in any way releasing them
from the restraints of proper order and obedience'.[44] Writing one
year later (25 December 1548), Paget conceded that men might
disagree as to what should have been the right course of action,
but in repealing Henry VIII's treason and heresy laws – the
Protector himself had probably drafted the great Act of 1547[45]
– Somerset had wrongly endeavoured from the start to please
every camp. Not only was this universally impossible, but in
England especially was such an attitude misplaced: historically,
Paget argued, Englishmen had been bound by such rigid legal
restraints under Henry that 'beinge subiectes in suche a subiection
as they were lefte' at the time of his death, it was foolish to expect
uniformity of behaviour and belief now that those bonds had been
removed. Under Henry words and actions frequently endangered
the author, 'though the meaninge were not evill'; under Edward
VI men spoke and acted too freely, with too great a liberty and
without fear of punishment. 'Then all thinges were too straight
and now they are too loose . . . What are and were the causes?'
Henry VIII clearly thought it 'not convenient for the subiecte to
Judge or to dispute or talke of the soverayne his matters and had
learned of his father to kepe them in dewe obedience by thad-
ministracion of Justice vnder the Law'. But Edward VI's ministers seemed to 'mislyke not' the fact that men judged and
disputed their doings, 'vpon supposall that all men shalbe
pleased'. The result was that 'as the people (which be most incon-
staunt, incertayne and flexible) varie their sayenges and shewe
them selfz to lyke or myslyke, So do the mynisters chaung their
determinacions contrarie to all the rules of pollicies'.[46] Inconsist-
ency and laxness at the top had bred unruliness and presumption
below. The nobility were held up to contempt and gentlemen
generally were despised, while politically, people no longer feared

their governor. Domestic dissension, which under Henry's rule 'was by feare kepte in and constrayned', threatened now 'to burste out'.[47]

Paget and Somerset no doubt once believed that volatile religious opinion, too often the fuel of political conflagration, would be contained by the Act of Uniformity. But Paget had come to feel that the duke's concern for his reputation among the commons had weakened a traditional, legally grounded respect for the King, the King's laws, and those charged with the administration of the law. In rebelling, the King's subjects, caring neither for Protector nor King, had taken advantage of Somerset's 'lenytie', his 'softenes', and his 'opinion to be good to the pore'. The compassionate prince, implied Paget, courted ruin unless his laws, firmly applied, expressed a will to preserve order, for 'society in a realm', he said, in a phrase familiar to students of the Tudor political mind, 'dothe consiste and is mainteyned by fearefull love to god and the prince which procedeth by meane of religion and lawe'. The lack of one or the other or both destroyed virtue, justice, and thus government and society. ('Farewell kinge' in such circumstances.) It therefore grieved Paget deeply to look upon a kingdom such as England where the use of the old religion was lawfully forbidden but the use of the new had not yet taken hold, where the law was almost everywhere ignored and the prince as a consequence nowhere feared.[48]

An anonymous contemporary statement of 'Certain enormyties in the comyn welth to be reformed',[49] although dated October 1550, describes just as well this prevailing disregard for law and law enforcement under Somerset. The author, himself probably a government official, was particularly concerned about the political implications of an officially tolerated but technically unlicensed expression of opinion. 'The learned men disagree in sundrye pointes of the use of ceremonies and so preache diverslye'; most of the clergy lacked discretion, and being inconsiderate of the times and of the disposition of the common people, by their preaching had actually increased 'presumptuous Iudgementes in the people against their magistrates withe a contempte of ye same'. The results could everywhere be seen:

The players playe abrode in everye place everye lewde, sediciouse fellowse devise, to the daungier of the Kynge and his counsaylle.

The mooste parte of the people telles tales, devisethe lyes, spredds rumors of the Kynge, his counsaillors, and ministers, discoursing of thaffaires of estate at theire libertye.[50]

Paget too thought that 'The common people [had become] too liberall in speche, too bolde and . . . too wise and well learned in their owne conceytes'[51] and so warned Somerset of the obvious, namely, that with such base 'comunalitie' came in all sorts of unreasoning mischief and vice. But 'I was a Cassandra, I told your grace the truthe and was not beleved.' As late as 17 April 1549 it could be seen that 'all thinges were in maner goinge backewarde'; by 7 July Ket and the Westerners had turned the Tudor polity upside down: 'the comyns is become a kinge appointing conditions and lawes to the governours.'

Complaints about the high price of food and the enclosure of common pasturage were frequent and understandable, he continued, but did such talk really identify the true causes of England's disorder? He thought not. Rather, the fault lay in the very nature of Somerset's method of government: the Protector had promulgated too many policies and was effectively executing none. Commissions for this, new laws for that, and proclamations for yet other matters taxed the energies and attention of those who were also asked to support with their taxes the war against France and Scotland. Under attack from the commons, the gentry were concerned less with service than survival, or as Paget had put it in April, were content merely 'to endure'. Somerset's leniency had contributed to this administrative paralysis: in tolerating the commons' discussion of Crown affairs, he had allowed the King's lesser subjects to overstep their place. On top of this, he had committed a great tactical blunder: at 'the furste sturre' of rebellion, the right way had been to follow the matter hotly and strike down the leaders 'to the terrour' of the others. Pardons then should have been in order. But the duke's policy of granting pardons 'owt of course' had merely emboldened the rabble to act upon hope of future forgiveness. Nevertheless, the Protector enjoyed a king's power, and events demanded that he reduce Edward's subjects to their proper station. 'Take a noble courage to youe', Paget urged in the midst of strife, and follow Henry VIII's example of the King who kept well his subjects in their right degrees, highest to lowest, by 'the onely maintenaunce of Justyce in dewe course'. The example of Somerset's German contemporaries was by contrast to be avoided: in 'the very lyke tumult to this', the 'spiced consciences' of certain of the German princes had moved them to accept the rebellious peasants there as their poor Christian brethren, that is, as their implied social equals. Such misplaced 'womanly pitie', Paget reckoned, had cost the princes much grief, not to mention perhaps one hundred thousand German lives. The lessons were clear. England's erroneous course could not be corrected except by the immediate application of force. Swift military action against an insurgent commons would alone deliver to the King an obedient realm. 'By this meanes youe shall be dradde which hetherto youe are not.'[52]

If the duke's name roused rather more love than fear among the commons, he had by February 1549 lost the respect of a council who found his handling of affairs to be inept and perilously slow. Occasionally this was so with respect to administrative appointments; increasingly it was the case in fiscal affairs. The really urgent questions at the turn of the year had to do not so much with policy as executive action – ordering the collection of revenue, suppressing disorder, and defending the realm against the French. 'As sone as the parliament ys done', Paget had advised him then, send some notable man northward, another into the Marches, and others into Kent, Suffolk, Norfolk, Sussex, Wiltshire, and the West.

Let them be well enformed . . . of your advice, bothe for the staye of their countreys, and also for the levienge of the relief. Let proclamations be sente forthe, declaringe and settinge forthe the gratuities the kinge gevith now to his subiectes. (ffor their kindenes in releasinge the purveyours and the reste of the thinges.)[53]

In addition to the enforcement of statutes made in respect of religion, Somerset was reminded to commission able gentlemen for musters and beacons. There was finally Paget's particularly emphatic recommendation to 'appoint Sir Edward Wotton (yf he be able to lie at london as I thincke he be aswell as at his house) and Sir Walter Myldemaye to assyste for the money matters'.

Somerset acted upon some of these points; although he did not resort to the use of the royal proclaiming power, he and the council in letters over their hands eventually instructed the commissioners for the collection of the relief to induce payment by

emphasising the great benefits which the commons had received
during that Parliamentary session, including, for example, a
general pardon as well as the King's acceptance of several bills
requested by the lower house (for escheators, the 'ease' of sheriffs,
discharge of purveyors, and so on).[54] But such administrative
action came on 22 March, nearly seven weeks after Paget's
insistent reminder and eight days after the end of a Parliament
which Paget thought Somerset had needlessly kept in session. On
12 March Sir William had noted with some irritation his master's
refusal to prorogue a Parliament which 'both houses saye stayes
only vpon your graces pleaser' – a neat slap at Somerset's determination to win Parliamentary approval for the government's bill
of attainder against his brother, the Lord Admiral. Paget's plea
was

> for gods sake to end the parlyament, to the entente youe maye
> provide for your owtwarde thinges in tyme, whereof youe haue
> greate nede, and so muche as I never sawe in my tyme. All the noble
> men and others do desire it, and for my parte, I thinke it hadde been
> best if it hadde been ended before Christmas, for thenne your grace
> shulde haue hadde leasour in the deade tyme of the yere (which is
> now past) in making actes not so necessarie, butt they might haue
> been differed till a more quyet tyme, to provide for the thinges that
> shalbe nedefull in somer.[55]

If by 12 March Somerset had already judged Thomas Seymour's attainder and execution to be politically expedient –
French agents in England had been instructed to promote the
Admiral's faction in hopes of promoting a civil war[56] – no doubt
he also saw in his brother's fall the King's financial gain, for 'the
thinges' to which he knew Paget referred were military preparations in Scotland and at Boulogne, and in the spring of 1549 the
cost of defending the garrisons there was beginning to test the Protector's very ability to survive. Defeat in the North and overseas
would pose such a danger 'as my harte bledes to thinke vpon',
said Paget; to be defeated for lack of money 'woolde touche your
graces credit at home and the credite of all the rest of the counsaill'. What to do? 'Your grace knowes myn opinion already':
Wotton and Mildmay should be given full authority to

> make of the mynte, of the sales, of the Admyralles, of Sheringtons
> money and plate, and of the kinges plate cummyng to the towre,

all . . . the money theye can possible, and make what shifte theye can
devise for more, by which I thinke . . . maye be made fourty thow-
sand powndes.[57]

Wriothesley's experience in such matters also came to mind: if he
were asked 'to take paynes therein', Paget opined, 'you might
slepe the quietlyer'. There remained the terrible distraction of
domestic unrest. For the suppression of rebellion, the chief lords
of the council were most qualified to act by virtue of office and
training. St John, Paget offered, should be able to oversee victualling; Warwick should welcome command of the North; Russell
'semes not to mislike' the prospect of being sent into the West
Country so long as he has help. But it was Somerset's responsibility to require such service of them and to do so without delay,
especially in the face of the King's growing financial distress.

And in this case, Sir, and also for the sending of a speciall man
northwardes, your grace must not sticke to use auctoritie, thoughe
sum men will not (peraduenture specially for the money mattiers) be
best contented; butt for gods sake, Sir, spare no man so the king
maye be well served, and appoynt men to sirve that can serve, what
soever this man or that man abrode saye.[58]

At that late date (12 March 1549) Somerset's most important task
yet remained the appointment of the forenamed 'freshe men' to
direct the government's financial affairs, 'for if youe do not, your
grace shall shortly se dangier followe'.

We do not know what role, if any, Wotton, Mildmay, and
Wriothesley may have played after 12 March 1549 in ordering
Somerset's 'money mattiers'. Sir Thomas Smith certainly studied
the Crown's fiscal problems in 1549, but his suggestions – selling
more Crown land and borrowing anew – offered nothing in the
way of a solution to the King's chronic indebtedness. One can
only say that the £40,000 which Paget thought might be
squeezed from various sources could hardly have done more than
cover immediate demands for cash. In the absence of some sort of
crude 'budgetary' planning of the sort, for example, that Cecil
would later undertake, the Protector had no way of knowing how
much money he would need to pay his mounting expenses. Necessarily he relied on temporary solutions, such as loans and the
debasement of the coinage, to achieve short-term relief. The sale
of chantry property and the profits of the mints enabled him to

stay afloat during the spring of 1549, but by the beginning of the summer all supplies of ready cash had been exhausted. The government quite literally was operating from one shipment of bullion to the next: payment of the troops under Russell awaited each new batch of debased coins.[59]

The flow of bullion to the mints, however, was slowing to a trickle, and as few testons were being received, even the government's cut from the conversion of these coins was fast disappearing. The mints, said Smith to Somerset on 22 June, simply could no longer generate revenue in the amounts which had previously been delivered. Equally uncertain were the prospects for revenue from other sources during the months ahead. The first part of the 'relief' had been paid, but of course it had already been accounted for; income from the levy on sheep could not be expected before winter, and that upon cloth not before the year's end. The first instalment of the subsidy granted by the clergy – the rate was six shillings in the pound of the yearly value of all livings – was not payable before October 1549, although Smith speculated that the spirituality 'wold not mych stick to anticipate the payment of their subsidie' ahead of schedule. A few 'earnest lettres to the busshops', he thought, should produce the required payments by mid-August. If so, July at least could be seen through, provided, he said, that the government step up the pace of the sales 'or make som Anticipacion or lone. Or els bend hole upon that to prepare bollion by all meanes and reiect all olde dettes and all other paymentes which possibly may be sparid till wynter'.[60]

Sir Thomas Smith was probably not one of Paget's hoped-for 'freshe men' whose financial expertise might yet save the ailing Protectorate. In one respect, however, Smith looked at finance in a way that Paget did not. Paget criticised expensive military policies because they increased Crown debts; indebtedness weakened the government's ability to provide for the maintenance of public order. Smith, on the other hand, hinted at the domestic impact of the methods employed to raise money in the first place: he understood clearly that debasement was an inflationary fiscal policy[61] and that rising prices depressed the poor, creating the sort of distress which led to disorder. Thus Smith's unheeded advice of 1549 to convert base testons into smaller denominations was really a device 'to ease the pore people'.[62]

Royal finances and the economic conditions of the poor: though the two were causally linked, neither had absorbed Somerset's attention as much as military strategy abroad, for during the first few months of the new year his chief concern had been to hold off France and yet hold on to Scotland, even though, as Paget continually reminded him, the Scots war alone threatened to make it financially impossible for him to govern, let alone wage a second war. The situation appeared to be so grave and Somerset's response so dilatory that Paget felt himself able no longer to proffer advice to his master alone. With one last plea ('for goddes sake in tyme devise for remedie'), he addressed himself to his colleagues on 17 April in terms of 'Certayne poyntes to be resolved vpon in Counsaill'. The fundamental questions were, firstly, whether to continue to prosecute the war with Scotland 'or rather . . . to shyfte of the warre either vtterlye or at the leaste for a tyme', and, secondly, with regard to the French, whether to break with them and by force bring them to reason; to negotiate with them for some more 'honorable and suer staye'; or to continue in the present 'vncertaine termes'. There seemed little choice except to terminate the war with the Scots and come to peaceable terms with the French. The King's finances decreed it: 'We owe more then we be nowe hable to paye thoughe we had nothinge elles to employe our money vppon but our debtz and ordenarie charges in tyme of peaxe. We have not nowe nor shall not haue this yere sufficient money to mainteyne vs in the warre honorablie.'[63]

Within two months Somerset had assumed the charges of war on a second, domestic front. Now he faced the ultimate dilemma: on principle he could not bow to the demands of Ket and the Westerners, but neither could he really afford to pay mercenaries to suppress both them and the Scots and still meet the expense of a French attack. Still fulfilling the role of the seasoned adviser, Paget surveyed 'these melancholy matters' from his chamber at court on 6 August. 'Because I se your grace so muche troubled . . . I haue thought it my deutie . . . to laye before your eyes the state which youe stand in, at this present. And what will by all lykelihode folowe . . .':

Youe haue to maintayne contynually duringe the warres great nombers of men against Scotland, great garrison against fraunce both by land and Sea, and no small power thorough your Realme for the reducynge of the same to the kinges obedience. All which can not be furnished without great sommes of money . . . But if you want (which I feare) then for goddes sake caste your charges aforehand and take such wayes, vpon depe consideracion of the matter, as if youe shall se that youe shall not be able to go throughe with the maintenaunce of all that youe haue begonne . . . and aboue all thinges regard the kepinge safe of the state at home, how soeuer for necessitie youe do with thinges abrode.[64]

Paget appreciated that there were two 'thinges abrode' which touched Somerset's honour directly, Scotland and Boulogne; having revived the Henrician policy of conquest in Scotland, Somerset could no more retire from the field of battle there than admit the evident superiority of Henry II in France. When Boulogne was won, Paget reflected, victory had seemed honourable indeed, as did Somerset's triumph at Pinkie, but Boulogne and Scotland were in 1549 dragging England towards the abyss. Had not the King of France himself proclaimed that he would never agree to terms of peace which did not also comprehend the Scots? 'Without peace with scotlande I beleve that the ffrench kinge will neuer be at peace with englonde.' Somerset had rejected Paget's reasoning in April, but the logic of Sir William's position in late August was more powerful: 'yf warre with scotlande bringe warre with fraunce', it would be well to consider, he mused, whether England were able by continual combat to weary the French of their Scottish friends. Paget entertained few doubts. As England held no power to force them apart – 'youe do consider, I am suer, how great a prince the ffrench king ys' – Somerset was asked to contemplate the consequences of further hostilities. The probability was that after much waste and loss and expense, in the end he would have to forfeit that which had earlier been gained. Newhaven, only recently lost to the French King's men, offered 'profe' of this, and Paget feared the 'like experience of Bulloygne'. Moreover, the financial drain would present Edward VI with 'his oune realme in mysery and beggerye' very nearly at the moment 'when he shall enter him selfe to governement', a 'certayne and inevitable dishonor in the Judgement of the worlde'.[65]

Surely Somerset, as much as Paget (who, after all, was the one

who had originally devised 'the place which youe nowe occupie'),
understood the trust implicit in the charge to a protector of the
King's estate:

The poynte as I take it whereunto your grace directeth your course
in service, vntill the Kinges majeste be readie to receve thadministra-
cion of his owne thinges, is to leave unto his Majeste his realme as
florishinge and as welthy bothe at home and outwardly as his father
lefte yt or bettre yf it maye well be. But at the leste no worse, for that
will not well be answered.[66]

But by 28 August 1549 it seemed that there was little anyone
could do 'as will suffice to preserve the kinges Majestie and the
Realme from civile spoile and ravyn'. The Scots campaign had
been a prescription for national disaster. As Edward's England lay
'exhausted and worne to the bones with these eight yeres warres',
the abandonment of so ruinous a course should therefore be considered a decision no less honourable than wise. Henry VIII
served once again as a model of princely conduct: 'vpon consideracon of his estate and condition at home', he found it 'in his
herte to forbeare the warres with scotland, havinge the same
querell that we pretend nowe, and yet was yt no dishonor to him
at all'. Amidst rebellion and war, Paget's last hope was that
Somerset recall the Scottish garrisons, shore up Boulogne, and then

transpose all the rest of your care, studie, travaile and expences this
wynter ceason to the conservacon of the state of the realm here at
home. ffor what availeth yt to seke to wynne foreyne realmes, and to
lose your owne wherein youe dwell or to seke to be conquerors of
other dominions abrode, and to be made slaves and bonde in your
owne countrey of your owne subiectz?[67]

The French war remained, but Somerset must first be able to
command rebellious Englishmen

and that must be done by force and terrour . . . then may youe consider what is expedient for the comyn wealth . . . then maye youe
aske of them suche ayde, as wherwith youe maye the better be able
to mayntaine the warre, or elles making peace this winter season . . .
establish in perfection your pollicie, paye your debtes . . . and wynne
to your selfe throughe the world great credit with the reputacon of
wysedome for your good procedinges.[68]

The fact of the collapse of Somerset's measures need not be of
concern here. Paget's letters furnish evidence enough of the little-
known fact that the Protector had at hand periodic analyses of

his actions and plans, frank appraisals which occasionally carried stunningly prophetic statements of developments in consequence of the duke's designs. Formally, it seems that on most of these matters Somerset heard the opinions of others at the board during 1549; constitutionally, the others certainly felt duty bound to debate England's course of action because Somerset's failures were discrediting them too. There appears to be little if any evidence, however, that the privy council actually assisted him in devising his programmes. If it was not to be the business of the council to share this function, Somerset must surely bear the greatest part of the responsibility for the events of 1549, for he possessed and usually ignored what he most needed, an administrative adviser who proved also to be a creative source of ideas for the formulation of state policy.

As the chief administrative agency in the realm, Edward's council enforced policy, either by appointing its own members to various tasks or by ordering the necessary action in letters to local officials. The extent of this responsibility is well illustrated by the contents of agendas. We possess several good examples of these, of which Paget's 'Memoriall' to the Duke of Somerset of 25 January 1549[69] is unique, preserving as it does a record of business for an administration that sought to circumvent government by council. Paget reminded the Protector then to make 'the Decre and other ordres for the committinge of thadmirall and his complices'; to make final arrangements for the 'Depeche for Bulloygne', which included appointing someone 'in lieu of thadmirall' to execute the orders and to inquire of the Lord Great Master (St John) 'how farre forthe he is for money' for the project; to decide upon the final disposition of the King's forces in the North parts, a matter which similarly required the naming of someone, 'to go thyder', an estimation of the number of men required, and the charges for their provisions; 'To Resolve for the ordringe of your navie in cases'; to collect intelligence through the employment of spies, 'or otherwise by your embassadours', '. . . of the proceedinges of fraunce'; to submit to Parliament a bill for a subsidy; 'To geve ordre for the staye of belles Leade, and other ornaments and goodes of churches'; 'To aunswer the fyrste request of the comynes for the Sherifes and thexchetors cases et cetera';[70] to send out commissions for the visitation of hospitals, cathedral churches, and universities; 'To geve ordre for the spedie printinge and settinge forth of the Service with speciall charge to see yt trewly printed'; to grant the King's general pardon.

Although this was an agenda of Somerset's concerns (the Lord Admiral's arrest took first place), the categories of council business detailed are familiar: affairs Parliamentary, financial, and foreign; matters military; orders executive and administrative touching society and the economy. Reference has already been made to the council's policy-making role *vis-à-vis* Parliament in the period after 1549: much of the Crown's public policy the council embodied in legislative programmes for Parliament. Thus, on 15 December 1551, just one month in advance of the fourth session of Edward's first Parliament, the King noted that 'there were certain devices for laws delivered to my learned Council to pen, as by a schedule appeareth'.[71] The privy council, of course, and not the officers of the council learned in the law, had in the first instance decided upon the contents of the schedule.[72]

Outside pressure occasionally moved the council to sponsor a particular bill. After an interview with the London clothiers in the star chamber on 28 April 1550 the council 'concluded that some devise shulde be had for a lawe that none shulde meddle with clothemaking but such as had been prentises to thoccupacion'.[73] This decision resulted in 'An Acte lymiting what Parsons shall weave or make broade Wollen Clothe'.[74] The draft of another bill among the secretaries' papers and the fact of its subsequent enactment also document the government's hand at work in the business of Parliament.[75] Occasionally a private bill signed by Edward VI was introduced into Parliament; as the council necessarily authorised everything presented for the King's signature, all such bills (in the form of petitions to the Crown) must at some point have come up for consideration at the board, and, indeed, the appearance on a council agenda of precisely this kind of business substantiates the point.[76] Although this particular bill was not enacted, another to the King from the mayor and aldermen of the City was, and we know from other sources that the council authorised the introduction of the petition into the House of Lords and assented to the engrossed version of the resulting bill 'For thassuraunce of certaine Landes solde by the

Kynges Majestie to the Mayor and Citie of London'.[77] These last two bills incorporated private business put forward by non-privy councillors; business originating in council which closely affected the royal prerogative would also in some form have required the council's hands. Thus do the original bills of the King's general pardon, for example, bear the signatures of as many as seventeen privy councillors.[78] (During the Protectorate Somerset alone countersigned such bills after 1547.)[79] General pardons, of course, were predictable and followed a familiar form, but the 'Act touching the Fyne and Rawnsome of the Duke of Somersett' of 1550 presents the interesting example of a policy which was itself the product of the council's internal political factiousness, a policy which the triumphant faction translated into state business by embodying it in an Act of Parliament to which the fallen duke, his wife, the King's Attorney- and Solicitor-general, and twenty-three members of the board were asked to put their signatures.[80]

Whatever the policy, the council wished always to secure the Commons' consent to the measures introduced. This the board attempted to do in two ways, by securing the election of members who could be expected to support the government's programme, and by directing the management of the Commons' business. The council's official attempts to recommend particular candidates – and pack the Commons generally in 1553 – are well known: there is the evidence of the council's letters in this regard,[81] and the fact that one or more councillors – Paget in 1547 – actually set about the task of co-ordinating the government's efforts.[82] In October 1551 the council ordered Rich 'to cause serche to be made howe manie of the Parliament House be deade syns the last session [4 November 1549 to 1 February 1550] to thintent that grave and wyse men might be elected to supplie theyr places';[83] this systematic attempt to swamp the by-elections failed at Reading, and so the board wrote to the officials there to elect a new burgess in the place of the one they had chosen.[84] These, of course, were official acts; individual councillors built up their own following in the House – witness the twelve members of Parliament who can be identified with the Seymour family interests in Wiltshire in 1547.[85]

Acting in the King's name the council chose the Speaker of the Commons; in Edward's first Parliament he was Sir John Baker, also a privy councillor. Technically, the nomination came from the Treasurer of the King's household, who always sat in the lower house in the sixteenth century and was its usual leader;[86] the Treasurer in Edward's reign was Sir Thomas Cheyne and he too was a privy councillor. Paget, as Comptroller of the household, appears in practice to have been the real leader of the Commons under Somerset.[87] In any case, the Speaker, as everyone knew, expressed the council's official thinking.[88] Moreover, the council was effectively represented as an institution within the Commons: the *Commons' Journals* identify the 'King's Privy Council in this House' as a group of individuals who sat together and even acted together in the chamber in a distinct manner.[89] Nine of the council worked in this fashion during the second session of the first Parliament; at least seven did so in 1553.[90] At regular council meetings the board issued these members with specific instructions as to how to proceed with a given matter in the Lower House – the famous directions for the handling of the burgesses of Coventry and Lynn represent a case in point.[91] And, of course, the bills which were frequently committed to privy councillors may have come up for discussion at the board. There is little doubt that the privy council, acting as the King's chief instrument of government, became very much involved in the business of Parliament. Foreign observers could well note that during a session at Westminster, the councillors – including, of course, those who sat in the Lords – appeared to be 'constantly occupied with their Parliament'.[92]

The council's chief responsibility was to supervise the maintenance of order and stability and provide for the defence and security of the realm. In order to fulfil this dual charge, the board at London needed information, information of the state of the King's garrisons and the readiness of shire levies, intelligence as well of the possibility of local unrest. The bulk of the council's correspondence with local authorities was in fact drafted in response to the request that such information be provided regularly: with the new commissions of the peace upon Edward's accession went a standing order that every six weeks the justices of the peace were to 'wryte to us the sayd Lord Protector and others of the privye Councell in what state that shere standythe'.[93] This incoming intelligence of local conditions and the 'provisions or wants of the Counties' has not survived,[94] but upon its original receipt the council at London issued, among other directives, orders for the enforcement of the law, proclamations ordering obedience to the King's statutes and commands, and tactical advice to gentlemen who found themselves ill-prepared to cope with unusual or unexpected developments.

The independent record of a letter of the type now lost suggests the sort of information which must often have prompted the government's action. On 25 September 1550 the mayor and aldermen of the City informed the board that the bands of vagrant soldiers who had come to London after the dissolution of the English garrisons overseas were threatening to muster at Finsbury Field for the purpose of sacking citizens' homes.[95] The mayor and his brethren urged the council to give the matter their immediate attention. We do not possess the council's response to this particular letter, though similar warnings from the City had probably produced the proclamation of July 1550, which in fact had ordered disbanded soldiers to leave London.[96] The proclamation, however, represented nothing more than an attempt to transfer London's problem to the localities. How indeed were these soldiers to be absorbed in the counties? The council's little-known answer (July 1550) was to reorganise some of them into floating contingents of troops – one hundred to a group in Dorset, Hampshire, Kent, and Suffolk, and two hundred each in Sussex and Essex – and to require the chief gentlemen in those places 'to keep them in order' for future use.[97]

This *ad hoc* solution to the problem of demobilising the Boulogne garrison thus effectively created a small *guarde mobile*, insurance perhaps against French intentions (the treaty notwithstanding) and a useful force in the event of popular revolt. Insurrection was very much the council's concern that summer as it had been since 1548; national defence was always of the highest priority. A circular of May 1548 provides a good example of the dual nature of the council's standing charge to local officials in such matters.[98] Coastal defence certainly ranked first – tending the beacons and equipping the levies for eight days' minimum service was the usual requirement – but the 'doinges of the common people' were nearly as important, given the authorities' fear of riot and unlawful assembly. In 1548 the idle servants of clothiers and artificers especially were to be watched; by 1550 it seems that the commons generally were feared. When in May 1550 the Sheriff of Kent described in his letters to the council a conspiracy among the common sort in that shire and Sussex, the board's immediate, almost reflexive response was to order him to assemble his forces on Whit Sunday following.[99] Vagabonds and raucous games were covered by Acts of Parliament whose enforcement the council had only the month before impressed upon every justice of the peace in the realm;[100] the investigation of assemblies outlawed by various statutes the council continually urged upon gentlemen everywhere.

Especially feared was the inflammatory power of the printed word. From the council's point of view, printing presses inevitably spurred suspicious activity: there was official concern, for example, over certain foot-loose 'light fellows' in Suffolk whose inspired thirst had driven them to 'drynke all day and looke uppon bookes in the night'.[101] Censorship was accepted as necessary in order to choke off sedition at its source, a principle Somerset adopted rather late in the day. On 13 August 1549 he ordered printers to submit to Petre, Smith, or Cecil (not then a privy councillor) all works in English; any one of the three could thereafter prohibit the publication or sale of any book in England.[102] Northumberland stipulated in a proclamation of 28 April 1551 that permission to print would be granted only in letters signed by the King or at least six of the council,[103] a rule designed to combat what an anonymous observer had earlier discovered (October 1550), that 'the prynters do printe abrode what so ever any fond man devisethe be yt never so folishe so sedicious or daungerouse for the people to knowe'.[104] Riotous action and reports of treasonous tracts and speeches councillors themselves occasionally followed up for evidence of rebellion – Gates, Bowes, Hoby, Sir Edward Wotton, and the Earl of Westmorland did so[105] – though the usual prescription, as in the case of the Suffolk readers, was to order local agents to examine the matter first.

Outright rebellion demanded that councillors like Northampton, Dorset, Warwick, Russell, Herbert, and Wingfield actually lead military operations against the King's lesser subjects. The lords remaining at London supervised the recruitment, supply, and payment of the foreign mercenaries and shire levies used in such emergencies. Rebellion of course tested to the limits the council's ability to co-ordinate the efforts of English officials charged with preserving the peace of the realm. On the one hand, safeguarding London raised relatively few administrative problems: on behalf of the mayor and aldermen, the recorder of the common council himself usually moved the board for exact instructions relative (for example) to the placement of ordnance – a privy council warrant was necessary for the movement of the City's twelve pieces from the Tower – the time and places of the suburban watch, and so on.[106] At other times (as in April 1551, when 'conspiracy' was in the air), the council spelled out its demands verbally before the lord mayor in the council chamber.[107]

Communicating with justices of the peace, sheriffs, and lords-lieutenant posed problems of a different sort. The familiar circulars dispatched to the shires in times of trouble naturally recited what the council expected to be done, but such letters merely prepared the ground for the real tasks of government during a crisis. Consider the council's administrative response to the riots in Hampshire in 1549, for instance.[108] On 15 May the board sent out a general order to the sheriffs and justices of the peace of that county to hold their forces in readiness to suppress troublemakers. In the meantime the council assigned to select gentlemen in Hampshire the jurisdiction of a chosen number of hundreds there; on the twenty-sixth, St John and Wriothesley instructed the mayor of Southampton (who fell within the territory of their administrative jurisdiction) to call together the constables of the hundreds allotted to him and issue them the enclosed special orders. The constables in turn were to give order to the men of every parish; the constables were to be told that they could seek aid directly from the council as circumstances required. Enclosed was a 'paper' of the division of the shire for the mayor's further information.[109]

Adequate though such arrangements may have seemed at the time, the lethargy and even opposition of local officials had yet to be overcome. The co-operation of the constables in Hampshire in 1549 contrasts sharply with the actions of their counterparts in Nottingham who reportedly rode about actually trying to raise a revolt in 1550.[110] Somerset understood the difficulty of persuading these unsalaried agents to comply with his orders, but he seems also to have believed that the King's proclamations would triumph where his own letters had failed. By their very nature, he thought, royal proclamations should overawe the commons and 'sett a terror and dyvysyon' among rebels.[111]

The council issued proclamations for the maintenance of public order (fifteen of Somerset's seventy-four and six of Northumberland's thirty-five were so related[112]) and national defence (seven under the Protector and two after him[113]), and sent out detailed orders for the enforcement of the law, but in fact the King's decrees and the council's orders often had little effect: proclamations (when not in the hands of councillors) went unproclaimed in the outlying areas; during 1549 some justices of the peace and sheriffs simply ignored instructions dated at Westminster or Somerset Place. The unsettled circumstances at points distant from London rendered such acts intolerable. The authority of the central government and the security of the realm would collapse unless local authorities could be made to obey administrative orders originating in council.

That this was particularly so in 1549 is evident from Grafton's text of a speech delivered by the Lord Chancellor (Rich) in the star chamber the day after the term following the close of Parliament.[114] The occasion for this sort of speech was traditional; typically, the Chancellor addressed the council, the judges, and such justices of the peace as could be found. In Elizabeth's time the speeches often were official pronouncements which combined statements of royal policy, 'political discourses upon contemporary circumstances', and 'wholesome advice'.[115] In 1549, however, the substance, tone, and purpose of the Chancellor's remarks appear to have been rather different. Speaking on behalf of the Lord Protector and 'the rest of the Kinges priuie and learned counsaile being present in the starr Chamber', Rich addressed the assembled justices of the peace and knights of the shire as those 'to whome we are wont to direct our writinges, and to whose trust and charge the Kings Maiestie hath committed the execution of all his Proclamations, of his actes of Parliament, and of his laws'. Citing the breakdown of order in the realm, Rich upbraided them for their slack execution of the King's proclamations and the 'orders taken by the Counsaile (as we are aduertised)', noting that in some shires it appeared that 'the people haue neuer heard of diuers of his Maiesties Proclamations'. And if they had heard of them, the justices of the peace too often rested content to wink at violations. The Chancellor therefore was issuing detailed instructions for the right ordering of all the shires. *Inter alia*, the gentlemen were to look properly to their duties at quarter sessions, see to the punishment of malefactors according to the law, apprehend tale-tellers and those who preached without licence, and so on; they were charged especially to notify the privy council of any who stirred up 'rowtes or ryots' or unlawful assemblies, seditious meetings, uproars, and uprisings; they were asked to fire the beacons in the event that anyone maintained by a 'forreine power and the Bishop of Rome' should land on the King's shores. And, of course, they were always to follow the council's written instructions and enforce the King's proclamations.

Sir Richard's remarks, though slightly formulistic, serve to remind us of the essential character of English government in the early-modern age. However much we may be able to document increasingly bureaucratic procedures at Westminster – one must except the Protectorate – the fact remains that kingly power grew weaker with distance precisely because it was personal power which rested upon the co-operation of lesser persons in their several 'countries'. Because, during Edward VI's minority, the authority of the government did not in practice reside in the boy's person, it was clearly necessary that power at the centre – the power exercised by the Protector and after him the council – be made unusually personal at times. The occasion of the Lord Chancellor's speech enabled Somerset and the King's councillors to affirm by the sheer gravity of their presence what they had so often expressed merely in written formulae to their unseen correspondents – a personal and thus a more 'presyse warnyng and knowledge of the premysses'.[116]

It is true that rebellion and war together in 1549 presented the government with extraordinary problems of law enforcement, security, and defence, but the end of French hostility did not also mark the commencement of domestic tranquillity, for the spectre of popular rebellion did not disappear with Ket and the westerners. On 1 February 1550, having heard reports of the likelihood of a new 'comocion' in the country, the great lords of the council, in order to 'provide the better agaynst all such inconvenients', privately resolved 'to breake up the parliament this day and to send the gentlemen home . . . with such powers and comyssion and such hope of assistance from us yf nede be, as we trust shalbe able to . . . stay the malice of such yll disposed people, as otherwise wold lightlye be sturred and induced to ryse agayne'.[117]

What sort of assistance the council then contemplated is not clear. We know only that local disturbances became more widespread during the course of 1550 and that by 20 December Warwick had abandoned the notion that local authorities could, upon the mere hope of the council's ill-defined support, effectively check such incipient unrest. Because direct action from the court was required, 'there was appointed' then, as Edward VI recorded it,[118] 'a band of horsemen' whose apparent *raison d'être* was to extinguish these brush fires of revolt. Members of the nobility, said the King, were to lead the crack troops.

In reality, 20 December 1550 fixes the date, not of the establishment of a royal gendarmerie as the King thought, but of the advancement of the view (no doubt Dudley's) that if such a force were created it would be captained by privy councillors in particular and not noblemen generally, for the fundamental question was actually settled on 26 February 1551 when

it was debated wheather it were convenyent the Kinges Majestie shulde have a nombre of men-of-arms in ordynarie, aswell for the suertie of his Majesties parson as for the staie of the unquiet subjectes, and for other services in all eventes; which aftre long disputacion was thought and concluded upon as a thing very necessarie.[119]

Twelve trained bands totalling 850 cavalry paid at the King's expense were mustered; the commands of ten of the twelve bands went to select members of the board.[120]

The decision to create the nucleus of a standing army in England was a historic one. It was not, however, a proposal novel to the period of Northumberland's rule. In 1549 Sir Thomas Wyatt placed before Somerset and the council a scheme for the creation of 'a power of the choise of the King's most able and trusty subjects'. Though some councillors (according to Wyatt's son) had a 'greate likinge' for it, others must have contested the idea sharply, for we know that 'this thinge' of Wyatt's sparked a really divisive debate, 'some divition then beinge amongst thes that bare the sway, some hindered that that others liked of'. Somerset dropped the project 'either for the newnes of the thinge, or for that it was not at that season thought so convenient to have the subietes armed', a remark based on the assumption that a majority of Englishmen were 'evel affected' to the government's reformation of religion.[121]

Wyatt's plan would have established local militias, whereas the measure actually adopted set up an élite guard retained by the privy council. In part, the gendarmes find their origin in the traditional security arrangements referred to by Paget when he reminded Somerset on 2 February 1548 to determine how many horsemen and footmen those at the board, in the chamber, and at court could muster for service 'either about the kinges majestes person' or in the field against a foreign foe.[122] In retrospect, the positioning of bands of one hundred and two hundred members of the Boulogne garrison in a coastal arc around London (July 1550) appears to have been a more deliberate step in the direction of creating a standing army ready to serve at quick notice. Even so, there is no evidence that those men from Boulogne were intended to be stationed permanently on English soil; privy councillors certainly did not retain them.

The horsemen of 1551 represented a rather different conception of the need for security at home, as they were designed to deter 'eventes' other than invasion and rebellion. What other events? A counter-*coup*? It is easy enough to see in the King's cavalry Northumberland's private guard. Perhaps the duke and his supporters simply judged a gendarmerie to be 'a thing very necessarie' for their political survival. But Somerset also participated in the 'long disputacion' preceding the gendarmes' appointment. Are we really to believe that he voted to arm Dudley so? Perhaps not, though the price of Somerset's support may initially have been command of one of the new bands.[123] Northumberland, however, was not so foolish as to place a sword in his rival's hand and he did not do so; although Somerset received payment for his troops' wages, the King was technically empowered to order musters of these men and he did not do so before 8 October 1551 – that is, not until one day after Sir Thomas Palmer had 'revealed' to Northumberland the existence of the 'good' duke's allegedly treasonous designs.[124] When the council's new horsemen finally went on parade (7 December), Somerset lay behind Tower bars. Scheyfve was probably not alone in thinking that the gendarmes were brought out then in order to intimidate a populace angered by Somerset's arrest and imprisonment.[125] Ironically, when Northumberland's test came in July 1553 he found that he had disarmed himself upon his own command. At Michaelmas 1552 he had ordered the men-at-arms disbanded for lack of money.[126]

Short-lived though they were, the Tudors' only gendarmes identify the men on whom Northumberland had come to rely for the maintenance of his position, for, saving one or two others such as Cecil and Gates, it was the captains of these bands who were paid in effect to protect him from just the sort of blow he had directed at Somerset. For the support of one hundred horsemen, Suffolk, Winchester, Northampton, Bedford, and Pembroke each received £2,000 per annum; Northumberland collected the same amount for fifty horse; Darcy, Clinton, Cobham, Hoby (who was also Master of the ordnance) and the earls of Rutland and Warwick (Northumberland's son and Master of the King's horse) were granted £1,000 each for their fifty men-at-arms.[127] For the £18,000 thus charged to him annually, what services if any did the King receive from these men? Except for the occasional martial display, none, it seems: musters were supposed to have been held every three months, and though two are recorded – 7 December 1551 and 16 May 1552[128] – nothing testifies to the use of the gendarmes in the manner ostensibly prescribed by the order of February 1551 – namely, for the suppression of rioting and so on in the country. In short, Edward VI's new horse appears to constitute yet another device by which Northumberland sought to assure himself of the security required by one whose authority, unlike Somerset's, was not that of a protector of the realm. As President of the council, it was natural that he should seek through that office to control the gendarmes; as captains of this force, privy councillors formed a natural entourage, united perhaps as much by avarice as by the power of the office and the dignity of the titles most of them already owed to his favour.

If the council's cavalry were not employed as shock troops to crush rebellions in the shires, how did Northumberland deal with the rural disorders referred to? Regarding the executive action required, the answer seems reasonably clear: he directed certain privy councillors to station themselves in their 'countries' and elsewhere in order to prevent, as contemporaries put it, the inconstant disposition of the commons. Bedford and Herbert were specially dispatched to Wiltshire, the West, and Wales for this purpose in April 1550; during February 1551 Westmorland left London for his lands with similar instructions to stand ready 'in all events'.[129] By 1551 it appears that the lords-lieutenant received standing orders to the same effect; as lords-lieutenant, privy councillors were expected as a matter of course to contain the domestic unrest so much feared at court. Under Northumberland, sixteen or seventeen privy councillors, almost all of them veterans of combat, regularly secured posts as lieutenants. In 1552, for example, councillors held or shared all but five of the twenty-two jurisdictions in England.[130] Most privy councillors nominally held commissions of the peace, but the duties of the lords-lieutenant were very real and, if not always martial, at least demanded an attention to administrative detail which must at times have been burdensome. Darcy and Gates, for example, spent very little time away from the court, so that we are probably correct in describing as administrative their responsibilities in Essex when, as lords-lieutenant of that county, the two of them were required by the council (15 June 1552) to search for several men suspected of counterfeiting the King's coins.[131] In this instance, the two councillors probably supervised the justices of the peace and others who actually conducted the search.

The activities of privy councillors as lords-lieutenant thus illustrate the council's dual job of enforcing order – an executive action – and ordering the enforcement of the King's and the council's commands – an administrative function. One comment on the importance that the council attached to the administrative function – an official statement essentially describing the nature of the government's problem in this respect – is the commission of 9 March 1552 'for the execution of penal laws'.[132] Ten appointees (including seven privy councillors) were charged to consider which statutes and proclamations were indispensable for the maintenance of order in the realm; to identify, apprehend, and 'reform' the chief offenders; to determine how the pertinent acts and decrees were so to be advertised that their enforcement by royal officials might thereby be expedited. Completing the instructions was an exhortation 'to use all good means' to ensure that every official concerned, from the barons of the exchequer to justices of the peace, sheriffs, escheators, and coroners, actually performed the duties prescribed by their offices relative to the enforcement of statutes within their jurisdictions. Of the ten commissioners, the earls of Bedford and Pembroke certainly brought considerable 'field' experience to this task, whereas Petre, Baker, Hoby, Bowes, and the King's solicitors, Gosnalde and Griffyn, together added legal and administrative expertise. Politically, Lord Darcy and Sir Thomas Wroth provided a liaison with Northumberland.

Although gaps in the evidence have left the commission's efforts veiled in obscurity, the reason for such an investigation was underscored by that anonymous source close to the council who, in speaking of certain political 'enormyties' to be reformed in 1550, noted as a matter beyond dispute that justices of the peace and others had failed to see 'those statutes observed whiche be within the lymytts of theire Commission', and that upon one excuse or another, ministers of the law generally were themselves not proceeding according to the due course of the law.[133] The commission thus stands as one measure of the council's attempt to revitalise and rationalise law enforcement at all levels. If acts of Parliament were to be obeyed, if proclamations were yet to have effect, the King's officials and others were going to have to adhere more closely to the council's administrative decrees. At stake was the privy council's ability, through these men, to govern the realm.

Equally important was Northumberland's determination to arrest the King's recurrent slide towards bankruptcy. In fact, a shortage of ready cash as much as popular disregard for the law determined that one of the most important tasks of the commissioners for the execution of the penal laws would be the enforcement of statutes, and so on, whose violation, when successfully prosecuted, might be expected to yield to the King a wealth of fines and forfeitures. 'For calling of forfeites done against the lawes' was what Edward VI, parroting no doubt Northumberland's view, originally conceived the commissioners' work to be early in March 1552.[134] When, at a secret council meeting at

Syon on 3 October 1552, Northumberland, Suffolk, Bedford, Northampton, Cobham, Darcy, and Cecil discussed, as Cecil recorded it, 'The Kynges Majestes Dettes with some devise towardes ye discharge of ye same', their lordships soberly agreed that one way to augment royal income was 'to procure the Recovery of forfetures of peynall lawes'.[135] Empson's and Dudley's methods apart, Northumberland's most important means of raising additional money in 1552 included the sale of Crown land and confiscated lead, the coining of bullion melted down from ecclesiastical plate, and the negotiation of loans from foreign bankers and domestic merchants. In 1553 the request for a Parliamentary grant coincided with Sir Thomas Gresham's brilliantly succesful manipulation of the foreign exchange market, so that the reduction of Edward's debts 'external' was matched by the prospect of extraordinary revenue at home. The council in the meantime had stabilised English currency and begun to reduce all sorts of superfluous household and governmental expenses. Central to this policy were Northumberland's plans for reorganising the courts of revenue.[136]

'Heroic' and 'honest' are words which some modern historians have used to describe these programmes as well as the intentions of the men who ordered and executed them.[137] Of course Northumberland perceived that the preservation of the estate royal was the *sine qua non* of his own tenure in office. That he was forced to sacrifice the one weapon which might have ensured his survival – the gendarmes with which he might have beaten back Mary – shows just how cruel were the realities of royal finance in 1552. Insolvency had ruined Somerset, and Northumberland was prepared to take almost any step to avoid spending sums of money which even in peace-time were transforming expected surpluses into intolerable deficits. Blockhouses were abandoned and provisions for table at court were curtailed; even the sale of the King's ships was proposed (although the protection of English vessels against French pirates was one argument advanced to justify the need for a subsidy).[138] Pruning expenses was one thing; paying off the King's debts (over £132,372 in Flanders and £108,800 in England[139]) was quite another matter, and yet Northumberland did to a degree accomplish the improbable – he liquidated the whole of the overseas debt before the end of the reign. The success

of this and other aspects of his financial policy excuses neither his
political adventurism nor his greed, but it would be wrong to say
that he did not genuinely mean to put right as well as reform
the administration of Tudor government finance.

Northumberland had certainly formed distinct views about the
financial requirements of national policy; he reversed decisions of
council majorities when he thought their judgements unaccept-
able, even in those cases where he had specifically left the settlement of a financial matter to their collective wisdom. As he once
put it bluntly in a letter to his colleagues, he thought that he alone
held 'final experience' in matters of very great importance, such
as government finance.[140] Unlike Somerset, however, who was
among those to whom he had addressed that remark, he proved to
be willing eventually to follow the advice of, and delegate
authority to, men like Cecil, Mildmay, and Gresham, who were
more expert than he in matters financial. Debasement of the
currency stands as a case in point. As a way of writing off the
King's debts, debasement offered temptations at first too great to
resist. Even when the council, mindful of popular disaffection,
began to turn away from debasement in June 1551 – in Warwick's absence they resolved to mint but half of an amount of
£160,000 they had earlier decided upon – Dudley thought this
'not the way but rather to plounge us in furder care and
soro[w]'.[141] Apparently he was determined to squeeze as much
profit as possible from the mints before coins of a new standard
were issued, and in the short run he got his way. Profits of about
£114,00 were realised before the end of July 1551, but at this
point he abandoned debasement and moved the council to restore
the fineness of English coins. Technically, this attempt to reform
the coinage failed. As a deflationary tactic to raise the value of
money, however, it was more successful than historians have been
willing to admit,[142] and this deflationary policy Northumberland
almost certainly adopted upon Cecil's persuasion.

It has been said that Northumberland's methods were both
shrewd and unjust, that he sought to pay the King's debts with
debased coins while demanding silver of the new standard from
the King's debtors.[143] But is it the case that in 1551 this particular
scheme was 'typical of Northumberland'[144] or merely a device
dictated as much by contemporary standards of political conduct

as the government's need to ease a debilitating burden of debt?[145]
One can condemn his political treachery as well as commend his
fiscal resolve: in 1551 Northumberland sought sensibly and not
irresponsibly to liquidate Edward VI's short-term obligations.
Other, less calculable motives produced the somewhat paranoiac
style of his politics. It is often forgotten, for example, that the
hoarding of coin in the Tower served Gresham's officially backed
policy of driving up the price of English money on the Antwerp
exchange and not Northumberland's supposedly ambitious
designs. Moreover, there were some keen-minded contemporaries
who correctly predicted that one result of the government's efforts
in this regard would be to drive *down* the price of victuals,[146] a
not inconsiderable feat in a fiercely inflationary age.

The true purpose of the government's financial policy Northumberland himself stated clearly on 16 June 1551. The time had
come, he said, when the King should live 'of his own'.[147] The
council had already decided (two months earlier) to create an
extraordinary privy purse (or 'treasure') for the King, an emer-
gency fund of £40,000 in cash reserves to be laid aside 'for all
events'.[148] Profits at the mint were earmarked initially for this
purpose, but in the larger view it was thought that more efficient
methods of revenue collection provided the only basis both for
replenishing this 'treasure' as well as supplying the King with a
sufficient ordinary income. Close supervision of the operations
within the various courts of revenue was clearly required; it
was necessary that the council possess up-to-date accounts of
receipts and expenditures. Citing Somerset's lax administration
of the King's money, the board had almost immediately upon the
Protector's fall (18 October 1549) ordered the treasurers to certify
the 'states of their offices' and especially the debts due within the
same.[149] So vital was the regular reception of such information; so
important (in theory) was the principle of collective control of
finance that the board at about the same time (that is, late
October 1549) constituted itself, as noted earlier, a committee of
the whole for the 'forsight for money', receiving each week
from the treasurers the aforementioned reports.[150] After 11 May
1550 the council considered these declarations by report from a
council committee composed initially of the Lord Chancellor, the
Lord Treasurer, Paget, Sadler, and North. All officers of the

revenue courts were henceforth to be called before the committee to make written statements of account.[151]

The committee illustrates quite well the organised supervision of finance under Northumberland as well as the council's pre-occupation with royal indebtedness, for the appointment of these five members had come 'upon rehearsal' of the King's debts at a time when the council was actively 'devising' how foreign and domestic obligations might quickly be discharged.[152] That was in May 1550, and there can be little doubt that if council agendas had survived for that year and the year following, they would probably record what Cecil's notes consistently reveal on those extant for 1552, namely, that financial affairs topped the list of the council's concerns and that the problem of discharging the debt took first place among such 'money matters'.[153] 'I am suer you wold be gladd to haue his Majestie out of debt,' said Northumberland to the others in June 1551, and though at that date disagreement reigned as to the proper means of achieving it, Dudley reminded his colleagues that it was their responsibility not only to wish it so but to endeavour 'to bringe yt to pas'.[154] Northumberland's insistence that the council work successfully to reduce debts internal and external was translated into action towards the end of 1551, when Edward VI appointed the first of a series of *ad hoc* commissions on finance, commissions engaged (to say it once again) not in privy council business as such but in the King's personal (financial) affairs. It was natural that privy councillors officially should take the leading parts in this activity and be assisted by legal and financial experts outside the council chamber. Dealing as they were with Crown lands and goods, the commissioners necessarily enjoyed the protection of the great seal in their work, and this, as much as the need to bring in non-conciliar personnel, determined that these would be royally certified bodies and not informally appointed committees of the privy council.

Although by the end of 1551 Northumberland had decided in principle upon a thorough-going reform of the financial machinery, a reform which, it was hoped, would in future enable the King to live 'of his own', the duke's immediate aim was to raise cash. The financial commissions of 1552-3 variously served this end; together they represented a fast-paced attempt to fill the treasuries and pay off his debts. The intensity of the council's efforts in this regard can be gauged by the fact that for the period after 6 October 1549, the *Calendar of Patent Rolls, Edward VI* lists thirty-three commissions of which privy councillors were members, and of the twenty-four which in some way touched finance, twenty were named during the last eighteen months of the reign. Sixteen of these twenty constituted, as it were, Northumberland's crash programme in finance, a partial outline of which is to be found among Cecil's papers.[155]

One method of increasing receipts was to force Crown debtors to pay off their obligations immediately. The first of the new financial commissions (dated 2 January 1552, although the membership was fixed by 30 December 1551) charged the Lord Chancellor (Goodrich), the Lord Privy Seal (Bedford), Gates, Petre, Bowes, and Mildmay to 'call in' all debts due to the King.[156] The powers of a reinforced commission on debts of 13 July 1552 – Hoby and the bishops of London and Norwich joined the earlier group – reflected Northumberland's pressing desire to tighten up the internal administration of finance. The commissioners were instructed to inform that ephemeral council 'for the state' of the most 'desperate' of the sums due; commit to ward officials who, in the commissioners' judgement, had failed to account for certain debts (various sums and arrears having grown by default of the auditors); upon survey of the treasurers' books write letters to debtors commanding payment.[157] Two further commissions (7 December 1552 and 12 January 1553) examined in particular debts arising from the previous sale of Crown land.[158]

Between 23 May 1552 and 15 March 1553 five distinct commissions authorised the nominees – Gates, Bowes, and Hoby almost invariably represented the council – to sell Crown land and so immediately raise cash.[159] Noting that the King was by various statutes entitled to a great store of ecclesiastical lead, bell metal, plate, jewels, and so on, the council named eight of its members and three others on 12 December 1552 to inquire how much of such precious stuff ought to have come to the Crown, how much had been sold (and for how much and by what authority), and how much remained unsold and where, the idea being to get existing caches of these goods to the jewel house and mints as promptly as possible.[160] Five lesser councillors (Cotton,

Gates, Bowes, Baker, Mason) and three officials were subsequently asked (16 January 1553) to collect the reports of this commission and set up administrative procedures for the collection and delivery (primarily to Sir Edmund Peckham, High Treasurer of all the mints) of discovered stores of ornament and such-like.[161] The appointment of nineteen privy councillors to an identical commission of 3 March 1553 emphasised just how serious were the physical problems of securing these valuables: the commissioners were able on their own authority to imprison anyone who disobeyed their orders relative to the collection, storage, and transportation of plate, bells, ready money, and so on.[162] The evident embezzlement of goods already accounted for produced two further commissions, one of which (undated, but probably after 16 January 1553) required twenty-four of the council to take a full view and inventory of all known stores of church plate in England and compare the resulting lists with the inventories of earlier, similar commissions.[163] The Earl of Pembroke, as President of the council in Wales, represented the privy council on a similar commission for Wales (29 May 1553).[164]

As the work of these groups went forward, the council redoubled its efforts to gather exact information about the state of the King's treasuries. The well-known commission for the survey of the revenue courts (23 March 1552),[165] upon making a complete account of all 'certainties' and 'causualities' for the year ending Michaelmas 1551, deposed on 10 December 1552 that the government during that time should have enjoyed a surplus of receipts over expenditures in the amount of £36,513. Actually, the cost of defending Calais and Ireland alone, not to mention other, inestimable charges in the household and the admiralty (for example), more than devoured that theoretical sum, creating yearly a governmental deficit predictable in fact but never in amount.[166] Pressure to reduce current expenses probably explains why at about the same time (12 December 1552) nine councillors and three others were commissioned to make comprehensive inquiry into all receipts and expenditures.[167] More specifically, the members were required to establish exactly how much money the council had authorised to be spent on behalf of Edward VI. Such information should have provided some basis for estimating future spending; it also gave the council ammunition against peculators.

In another section of the report of 10 December 1552, the commissioners surveying the revenue courts recommended a reorganisation of the structure of financial administration. Their purpose reflected the aim of Northumberland's policy, 'to devise vppon a certayn yerelie Revenue' sufficient for the maintenance of the King's estate, but in the end their conclusions reflected the influence of conservative exchequer officials, for this proposed yearly income and also the special reserve (or 'treasure') were still each to be drawn from designated, fixed sources (lands). Here was a plan based on the ancient system 'of allocating specific revenues for specific purposes', and not the more recent and more flexible method practised by Henry VII and Thomas Cromwell whereby departmental surpluses were pooled into a single fund.[168] Northumberland probably wanted to revive Cromwell's methods, but Edward's death cut short any hope of seeing the young King live 'of his own' by charging up expenses against a single, sufficient governmental reserve.

However, the duke did realise one of his self-professed goals of June 1551. Between January 1552 and May 1553 he was able, through the council, to order the treasurers of the revenue courts to channel a total of £39,948 into the King's 'priuie cofers', and this money he spent during that time in Edward's very 'special affairs' – for rewards, fortifications, and gendarmes, household expenses (during the progress of 1552), and the repayment of certain foreign loans. Peter Osborne, nominally a 'clerk' to the four principal gentlemen of the privy chamber – a position that Osborne probably owed to the influence of his friend, Sir John Cheke, the King's tutor – served as treasurer of this fund, acting in effect, though not in office, as keeper of the privy purse (or rather a special privy purse).[169] Council warrants directed to the exchequer indicate that receipts from the Parliamentary 'relief' of 1547–8 were being diverted to Osborne as soon as they were received in that court; the Lord Treasurer (Winchester) was asked on 14 May 1552 to 'expedite' collection of 'relief money' not yet paid into the exchequer.[170] Earlier, on 8 February, the council had ordered the treasurers of the revenue courts to pay weekly to Osborne the arrears and debts which were being 'called in' by the various commissioners.[171] Osborne also received advances from the under-treasurer of the mint, kick-backs from officials who owed their promotions to Northumberland's favour, and miscellaneous sums paid directly into the King's hands by the grateful recipients of Crown grants.[172] Payments made out of Osborne's account were never authorised 'for any respect but by speciall ordre from his Majestie of [*sic*] theyr Lordshippes',[173] and the surviving original warrants, when matched up with the council's record of their dispatch, show just how direct was Northumberland's management of this money. On 25 May 1552 at Greenwich, for instance, eight councillors (Goodrich, Winchester, Cobham, Wingfield, Darcy, Mason, Hoby, and Bowes) commanded Osborne to turn over to Sir Thomas Eliot, a London mercer, £7,000 to be delivered by way of exchange to Sir Thomas Gresham at Antwerp towards repayment of Jasper Shetz, one of the King's creditors.[174] At the same time the council ordered Gates, the one privy councillor who more than any other was identified with Northumberland's purposes, to arrange for the actual transfer of the money from Osborne's hands.[175] For a time, therefore, Osborne's account served effectively as the council's own treasury, allowing Northumberland the convenience of being able to make certain payments with unusual speed.

It was probably the not-so-secret activity of Gates, however, which prompted Scheyfve to remark that by January 1553 Northumberland's handling of royal finance had become very close and 'suspicious'. 'The King's moneys', observed the envoy,

which used to be under the direct control of the Lord High Treasurer and the receivers who managed the finances, are now being taken either to the Tower or to the [jewel] house at Westminster, and only one or two intimate friends of the Duke are given access to them. The Treasurer is excluded and this has been going on for some time past.[176]

Although parts of his report were true – money was being laid up in the Tower – the ambassador misunderstood the significance of the whole picture. He seems, for example, to have mistaken some of Osborne's disbursements for an attempt to rob the King. In any case, he wrongly assumed that the Lord Treasurer took no part in the management of Edward's money late in the reign. Although Winchester had never formally directed royal finance in the way that Scheyfve thought, he certainly was privy to the allocation of funds in the King's special treasury: he regularly signed privy council warrants to Peter Osborne.[177] More importantly, Paulet had from the beginning played a remarkably busy and very diverse role in many aspects of the King's finances. As Lord Treasurer (from 3 February 1550) Winchester nominally supervised the exchequer; until 1554 we cannot call him what he then effectively became, England's first minister of finance.[178] If anyone set national financial policy under Northumberland it was probably Cecil, with, of course, the duke's approval and Mildmay's and Gresham's advice, but historically, the Marian reforms recognised what Winchester was in any case doing administratively in the reign of Edward VI – supervising and co-ordinating the work of the various financial agencies and using his office as privy councillor to execute the council's administrative orders in finance.

Paulet's tenure as Edward's Lord Treasurer requires research beyond the limits of this study, but some idea of his varied efforts as a councillor can briefly be sketched out here. As noted earlier, he sat on the committee which weekly received the treasurers' reports, a position which probably allowed him to act as a sort of minister of financial information to the whole board. Predictably enough, one finds him transmitting to the treasurers the council's orders for extraordinary declarations of account.[179] That he possessed some technical ability is suggested by the council's charge to him of 6 May 1550, that he 'take order' for the renegotiation (extension) of foreign loans in the amount of £54,800.[180] It was the Lord Treasurer who once collected all gold crosses, images, and plate in the Tower and melted them down into 'wedges readie for suche further purpose' as the council should appoint,[181] the purpose invariably being that he deliver such wedges to Peckham for conversion into coin and then honour warrants drawn against money thus coined.[182] Other metals came to Winchester's hands: upon the council's request he supervised collections of the lead so desperately sought by the Crown; he assisted in establishing the silver content of English coins; he sold the King's stores of copper.[183] His role as a royal commissioner for financial matters is well documented;[184] lacking hard evidence of his contribution to these bodies, we may fairly assume that his administrative experience as much as his office made him indispensable to their work. Few privy councillors can have discharged as many duties in the administration of finance; no one except Darcy attended more council meetings; probably no one signed as many privy council warrants for payment.

The evidence of Winchester's signature on so many warrants reminds us of the essential nature of much of the council's business. Talk of reformation and rebellion might often have resounded in the chamber, but the task of authorising thousands of payments unquestionably occupied the greatest part of the council's labour. The act of subscribing warrants illustrates, of course, how direct was a councillor's financial authority; that such warrants allowed the King to purchase Christmas gifts as well as hire Albanian mercenaries shows how very extensive was the council's obligation to pay the Crown's public and private bills.[185]

Reference has so far been made to the executive and administrative actions of councillors in only three areas where the board's authority was so direct – Parliamentary affairs, domestic security, and finance. The privy council also embodied the supreme headship of the Church and spoke with the voice of a king in the social and economic life of the nation; on issues secular and ecclesiastical, national and local, the King's councillors were accustomed to act. The council's religious policy needs no elaboration here, and although work remains to be done on social and economic problems, the techniques of administration in each case can be documented by way of example. In letters and proclamations the council spelled out the relevant policy and requisite action, demanding obedience of subject and official alike; upon order from the board or in commission, individual councillors enforced these decrees.

If we are to believe the reports of the Emperor's ambassador, the King's policy in religion was merely that which Henry VIII would have laid down had he lived. Somerset allegedly made Henry the author of the injunctions of 1547; Northumberland reportedly believed himself to know how the old King's mind would have worked on questions of religious doctrine in 1551.[186] That Edward's councillors and not the spirit of a dead sovereign really ruled the Church was plain to see: by council decree Secretary Petre was empowered to seal instruments for the enabling of bishops, and so on; upon 'commandement from the councelle'

altars were moved and vestments changed.[187] As the authors of
the proclamation of 31 July 1547, the lords of the council also
sought to 'to plant true religion' in England,[188] but the enforced
reading of the injunctions prescribed by the proclamation stands
as Somerset's sole attempt to define doctrine by the use of the
King's prerogative. Royal proclamations constituted the most
powerful public method of regulation by administrative fiat, and
the Protector regularly used it: the eleven remaining decrees in
the ecclesiastical realm – he issued seventy-four of all types – were
procedural or administrative, as they provided information for
religious pensioners, set prices for the Book of Common Prayer,
ordered punishments for assaults on the clergy, and so on.[189] Two
of Northumberland's three proclamations on the subject of religion and the religious can also be described as administrative in
nature, but the third and last one, declaring the true meaning of
kneeling at the communion service, yet survives as the council's
most famous extra-Parliamentary attempt to alter the meaning of
the reformed faith.[190]

Not every ecclesiastic agreed that it lay within the council's
power to legislate on points of doctrine. Gardiner told Mason
that he had found the injunctions of 1547 contrary to Henry
VIII's instructions and determinations as confirmed by act of
Parliament;[191] both he and Bonner doubted that innovations in
religion could be undertaken during the royal minority. Politically, the point was academic. Before his deprivation Bonner was
asked whether he was aware of Dr Cox's denunciation of Gardiner for having denied Edward VI's authority,[192] a form of
pressure only a little less direct than that used against Gardiner
himself. Once the judges had confirmed the council's right to
order a reformation of the faith, the fate of such opponents was
fairly certain. Deputations of councillors examined them in
prison, while someone like Cecil or Petre prepared the case for the
prosecution. Royal commissions which included privy councillors
– Cranmer, Petre, and Smith in Bonner's case (17 September
1549) and Cranmer, Goodrich, and Petre at Gardiner's trial (15
December 1550)[193] – heard the charges against them; the Archbishop of Canterbury pronounced sentence of deprivation; the
whole council confirmed Cranmer's action. Recalcitrant clerics
could be removed with little political difficulty when, as in Bon-

ner's case, the council knew that their action enjoyed the support of powerful, progressive interests in the City: 'the Citie of London', noted Thomas Seymour to his brother on 15 September 1547, 'is verye glad to hire tell of the Busshop theire pastor being in the Flete.'[194]

Less manageable was the popular response to evident religious change. When sermons at St Paul's were suspended in October 1548, the council had to rely upon the members of the London companies to restrain the curious among their apprentices and servants who ran aimlessly 'to poules A gasying and a gapynge' at the empty pulpits.[195] The popular destruction of images in London required closer attention. In Somerset's absence (14 September 1547), it was decided that Lord St John should take order with the mayor and aldermen for the restoration of images and punishment of image-breakers. St John conveyed to the mayor the council's prescription, which, incidentally, added a government order for the alteration of 'stories made in glasse wyndows'. Windows portraying Thomas Beckett were to be changed with as little noticeable effect as possible, but in the case of those picturing the Bishop of Rome, if the change required more than simply painting over his crown, the entire glass was to be coloured over. 'If any doute Ryse', said St John, 'take aduyce of me or some other of the Councell . . . I pray you Wryte me your mynde And I shall Answer you to bring this matter to good order.'[196] In the meantime, popular demands for the removal of other images grew, and the council, while still pressing for the punishment of wrongdoers, halted the order for restoration until Somerset's return.[197]

Requests for assistance in the maintenance of public order also went out to clerics. In fact, most of the council's administrative efforts in religious affairs seem to have been directed at the preachers whose sermons were expected to reinforce the government's demand for obedience in Church and state. The politics of church attendance were not lost on the bishops who promulgated to the clergy the council's latest word on the subject.[198] It was the message in the sermons, however, that mattered, and the council frequently interviewed London preachers during the week before the delivery of their Sunday sermons.[199] The board's power to license preachers did not prevent a verbally seditious gloss on a

scriptural lesson; the two privy councillors who were also ecclesiastics more than once examined loose-tongued preachers upon
Northumberland's wrathful order.[200] It was not a sermon, but the
'naughtie conversacion' of one John Goodale that moved the
council to ask the Dean and Chapter of Westminster to remove
him as appointee to the stewardship of St Martin's and name
'some meater man to the rome'.[201] A more positive act, such as
Bucer's Cambridge appointment, records the board's influence
just as well, though Goodale's obscure fate, deserved or not, marks
the everyday reality of the council's administrative tyranny in
religious affairs.

In the King's highest causes, privy councillors served under the
protection of the great seal: a bishop's denial of Edward's authority, as has been seen, required a trial before royal commissioners.
Excluding surveys of ecclesiastical property, however, relatively
few privy councillors were in fact ever commissioned to deal with
matters religious. During Somerset's Protectorate, Cranmer,
Petre, and Smith once inquired into heresy;[202] clerical position
and legal training just as obviously explain the composition of two
later commissions on heresy[203] and two for the examination of
ecclesiastical laws,[204] the four of which together named seven of
our men – Cranmer (four times), Goodrich, Petre, Dr Wotton,
and Cecil (thrice each), and Baker and Bromley (once each).

Similarly, only three commissions in Somerset's time involved
privy councillors in what might broadly be termed the social and
economic welfare of the realm. Sewers once drew the attention of
four members (Rich, North, Petre, and Thomas Seymour);[205] Sir
Edward North was twice (March 1547 and March 1548) named
with other non-councillors to survey the accounts of cathedral and
collegiate institutions, founded by royalty, whose endowments
allowed yearly distributions of money for the relief of poor folk
and the repair of highways. Declarations of such required disbursements were to be made in augmentations; North, as chancellor of that court, was empowered to enforce the provision by
calling before him the deans or provosts of the colleges in
question.[206]

North's commission is not evidence that the council possessed a
'social conscience'. Far from it: the board once told the chancellor
of augmentations that the sum of £40 which Henry VIII had

conferred upon the newly erected college at Chester for yearly 'deeds of charretie' was to be turned over to the mayor there for the construction of a new quay and harbour.[207] The poor of Chester who were thereby denied collegiate charity would not have appreciated this as an example of governmental investment in public works rather similar in kind to the council's payment of £200 to the burgesses of Scarborough for the repair of the pier and haven there.[208] If the poor were sometimes forgotten, the idle and foreign were driven beforehand. In November 1552 the council asked Sir Edward North to co-ordinate the efforts of the justices of the peace 'abowt hym' in the matter of deporting certain 'Egiptians'; he was to assist officials in Buckinghamshire, Bedfordshire, Norfolk, and Suffolk in conveying these gypsies from place to place until they reached the nearest port.[209] London's ordinary vagabonds were not deported, of course; they were, according to the terms of an Edwardian statute, simply ordered out of the metropolis to their native 'countries' or place of most recent residence. If some of them had not heard of this Act or the most recent proclamations to that effect,[210] they may in any event have felt the boot or the whip of the men who were told to enforce it.

Proclamations ordering vagabonds out of London, like the decrees prohibiting 'lewd' plays and interludes, were police measures, however, and not social devices. The idle poor really bear witness to the ill-understood dislocations of the Tudor economy; they were the social consequences of the economic anarchy in early-modern transport, trade, and industry. Proclamations – proclamations based upon regulatory statutes – provided the only really powerful tool at hand for ordering the economy on an *ad hoc* basis. It is a measure of the importance of such royal instruments that thirty-one of Somerset's seventy-four proclamations and twenty-one of Northumberland's thirty-five dealt with what might arbitrarily be called society and the economy (excluding pronouncements that were essentially police directives for the maintenance of law and public order). The coinage and other financial problems (holding subsidy collectors accountable for their returns, restricting the export of money, and so on) account for the bulk of these throughout the reign (eight during the Protectorate and eleven thereafter),[211] although attempts to regulate trade provide almost as many examples – twelve under Somerset and four under his successor.[212] The remaining proclamations dealt variously with hunting and the royal forests (four),[213] urinating and casting 'annoyances' at court (one),[214] enclosure inquiries (two),[215] the manufacture of wool cloth (two),[216] the price of victuals (four),[217] and the distribution of grain and food supplies (five).[218]

For the commons, the price and availability of food were too often related directly to the council's deliberate alteration of the value of English coins; merchants, upon foreknowledge of the 'abatement' of the shilling (to 9d, for example), pushed up prices to a 'marvelous' reckoning; growers and middlemen hid their stocks until the higher prices ensured greater profits. It was a vicious circle which the council tried to break by fiat – by ordering merchants and shopkeepers to adhere to schedules of prices fixed by proclamation (or by justices of the peace and others specially commissioned for that purpose) and by commanding the lords-lieutenant and justices of the peace to search in barns and country buildings for caches of grain.[219] The urgency of the situation sometimes called for the council's 'letters of second charge' to these officials.[220] We hear very little about privy councillors personally pursuing forestallers and regrators – a commission of 4 December 1551 identifies seven doing so[221] – but we know that the council's regular demands for information regarding the state of the local markets enabled the King's men in London to distinguish between a case of illegal hoarding and the natural, but no less damaging, problem of maldistribution of supplies in times of want. Thus did the council in 1551 discover the plight of the inhabitants of Southwold in Suffolk who, 'being in great misery', apparently possessed the money but not the food to relieve their starvation.[222] It was not unusual for the board to stipulate to shipowners and customs officials that deliveries of wheat, beans, herring, and so on be re-routed or speeded up,[223] but the surviving evidence of this sort of administrative activity refers to requisitions for London during Parliament time, and not distressed rural areas at other times.

As high prices and short supplies in London hit the council directly, we should expect to find evidence of the board's direct interference in the workings of the market there. Perhaps no better example of this exists than the meeting of 8 June 1552, when fifteen privy councillors sat in the Guildhall and threatened to relieve the City of its liberties unless the wardens of the various companies (a) agreed to sell goods at a loss in order to keep prices down, and (b) admitted that they should be glad to do so on such terms, as there existed no other remedy to the contrary.[224] For their part, the mercers had earlier stated (8 July 1551) that they had been forced to raise prices of imported goods in order to make up losses incurred abroad in the sale of high-priced English exports.[225] How many of the council were persuaded by this as an explanation of the relatively high cost of all goods sold in England is not known. It is worth recording that in 1547 English merchants had successfully petitioned the council to dispense with statutory provisions prohibiting the export of English cloth above certain prices.[226]

Temporary restraints of trade in certain goods were common enough, though the reasons for such actions varied from the economically necessary to the politically retaliatory. Exemptions from arbitrarily imposed restraints were occasionally granted, in which case the council instructed the customers, comptrollers, and searchers of the port of London to allow merchants thus favoured a quiet, free, or secret passage.[227] Confusion of such orders was perhaps not uncommon when the customs officials had to distinguish between merchants of various nationalities. Mistakes landed the inspectors before a council both irate and embarrassed, for the ambassadors of maritime nations not favoured often demanded the government's apologies.[228] Handling the problems arising from restraints of trade fell in *ad hoc* fashion to a designated councillor. The Marquess of Winchester and the Earl of Bedford several times assumed such responsibilities upon Somerset's and the council's request.[229] Essentially, the council served as a national board of trade, allowing and disallowing trade at will. Reason and economic self-interest do not invariably explain the council's actions; no one should suppose that it was the welfare of English merchants that the council always favoured. However, the settlement of claims against foreign shippers sometimes provides the only clue as to why, for example, Newcastle was permitted after a season to resume the Danish trade.[230] Unsettled relations with France, by contrast, explain why in August 1548 the board secretly licensed anyone and everyone in Devon and Cornwall who were 'willinge to gooe to the seas at that theyre owne aventure' to seize the French fishing fleet coming from Newfoundland.[281]

Licence to undertake profitable, non-piratical commercial and industrial activity was granted to men such as the Earl of Bedford, who, from 13 December 1550, was free to dig iron ore from the earth beneath several royal forests, so long as he yielded to the Crown 6s 8d on every ton of metal he could thereafter smelt in his newly erected mills.[232] As a privy councillor himself, Bedford marks well the connections between government and early-modern capitalist enterprise in England. If such a connection existed in the following venture, it has been lost to history: on 13 March 1553 the council allowed one Thomas Galiard to ship overseas, presumably for quick sale in a ready market, some 200,000 pairs of old shoes.[233] Of course, anyone's movement overseas, with or without such a haul, required a passport approved at the board, signifing yet again how really broad was the council's executive and administrative authority. Indeed, it has already been shown that this authority was in practice almost without limit; it certainly ran unchecked by the reigning King. In this sense, the board's ability to order and to act was unique among Tudor privy councils, because historically it knew only temporal boundaries – the accession and death of a boy in whose name the council ruled.

The council devised policy; the council governed. Functionally, the council also acted in a quasi-judicial manner; although not a court of law, the King's chief ministers of state did occasionally proceed by arbitration in a matter at variance between party and party as well as examine, commit, and punish individuals in matters affecting the King's peace, person, and interests. But in all such actions, privy councillors sat as privy councillors and not as members of the court of star chamber, the court of requests, or as royal commissioners for requests. We know that by August 1540 at the latest, the privy council and the court of star chamber were distinct and separate institutions keeping different sets of records and performing different functions, while in the reign of Edward VI, the court of requests (known officially and variously as 'the Kinges Honorable Counsaill *of* his Courte of Requestes', 'the Kinges Counsaill *in* his Courte of Requestes', and 'the Kinges honorable Courte of Requestes in the Whyte Halle at West-minster'[234]) consisted of two masters of requests, neither of whom was a privy councillor. Having said this, it is also true to say that the privy council did consider bills of supplication which stated complaints or alleged offences between party and party and Crown and party. The important difference, however, is that in none of this did the privy council ordinarily render a verdict of judicial guilt or innocence or impose a sentence; it tried nothing: it was not a court.[235] These were privy councillors sitting not as judges but as the King's chief ministers of state.

Theoretically, the council entertained only those suits touching matters of 'estate', that is, having to do with the King's business, public or private. Such was never the whole case, for at times the board also took, as will be shown, an almost paternal interest in the private lives of individual Englishmen. Paget once revealed to the Bishop of Arras something of the actual practice under Somer-set – in this instance, as it concerned foreigners' complaints against English subjects. D'Arras had contended on behalf of Charles V that in England justice had too frequently been denied to Imperial subjects acting as plaintiffs in maritime disputes. To the bishop it seemed that as all business in the realm passed through Somerset's hands, Imperial merchants, when of necessity forced to turn to the duke for redress of wrongs, found him too busy to hear their pleas. Paget replied that 'my Lord Protecteur nor none of the pryvey Counsaill medle with no priuate mater whose soever it be but only with maters of estate, leaving all other things to their ordinary course of Justice', adding snappishly that the cases which Somerset had personally settled in the interests of Anglo-Imperial amity seemed thus to have been very little con-sidered at Charles's court. Sir William swore by St Mary that in future he would advise Somerset to refer all such petitions to the course of 'commyn Justice', meaning the admiralty.[236]

Paget's remark in fact confirms official but documentary evi-dence now lost of the council's quasi-judicial activity, evidence which a seventeenth-century copyist had seen. In 1620 Ralph Starkey transcribed what he called 'the most materiall matteres contained in the booke of Acts of Councell . . . Entered by the

Clarke of the Councell at the Councell Table' from 6 February 1547. Starkey laboured to preserve the entries 'senceirely as they are in the origenall booke', and indeed he did so, including items from a now-vanished letter-book, but he also deliberately omitted, as 'unnecesari thinges not worth the observacion . . . Complaintes made by Strangeres againste our men of warre at the Seas, for goods and shippes taken by them at the Seas with the Counseles orderes therin'. Moreover, such a register of complaints and decrees in maritime cases took its place beside other papers record-ing quite distinctly the 'Complaints of privat persones'.[237] As Starkey cannot have confused the latter petitions with star cham-ber bills of pleading – the complaints together with the other entries formed a single heap of the council's proceedings, not the court's – what we have therefore is pretty clear proof that the council's arbitration of disputes between party and party had by 1547 become a regularly recorded aspect of its quasi-judicial function and that for a time this activity comprehended (irregu-larly under Somerset) the settlement of Anglo-Imperial maritime suits.

The existence of books, now lost, registering in particular the council's arbitration of disputes between private parties should explain the rarity of such entries in the extant privy council volumes. More to the point, however, is the observation that Somerset probably heard many such cases and recorded them separately, whereas under Northumberland the number actually settled at the board decreased sharply. This fact simply reflects the tighter, more efficient management of privy council business after 23 March 1550: the council probably adopted Paget's pro-cedure governing the council's reception of supplications, and if so, many suits although addressed to the council, were properly referred to the ordinary and prerogative courts.

One must remember that the council was every day pestered by a horde of suitors seeking swift redress to a variety of griev-ances. The total number of requests, complaints, petitions, bills of supplication, and so on, addressed to King and council had increased so much by this time that both the council (alone) and the masters of requests (sitting as the court of requests) faced an impossible burden of work. By 10 November 1549 the council had already begun to reorganise the procedures for hearing miscellaneous supplications; on 14 November they agreed to entertain these on Wednesday afternoons, but only those which Sir Nicholas Hare, a master of requests, had first determined were important enough to warrant the board's consideration. Typically, the clerk noticed the fact that Hare had 'had accesse to the Lordes, uppon whose declaracion of the contentes of several complaincts order was taken as followeth . . .'.[238] In 1550 Paget spelled out what probably became the settled routine: all supplications were delivered to the master of requests, who then turned over to the Lord President 'all suche that conteign mattier that can not be determyned butt by the King or his prevey counsaill . . .'; all bills of complaint were remitted 'to the law or courtes of conscience' as the case required.[239] By March 1552 four privy councillors, the two masters of requests, and one other had been appointed royal commissioners to hear requests;[240] all suits were to be turned over to one of the masters of requests for the commissioners' consideration but, as already shown, he was to return to the King's secretaries 'enie that seme to concern the state of the Kings majestie or that is or ought to be kept private'.[241] It will be remembered that the commissioners of 1552 did not constitute a committee of the privy council; their task was simply to sort out the bills which suitors daily were submitting to the board and to hear and determine those which could not otherwise be referred to courts of equity or to specially appointed commissioners in the counties.[242] The royal commissioners of requests constituted in effect an expanded court of requests. The council had relinquished none of its powers to the commissioners; the commissioners simply shielded the board from the daily bombardment of superfluous petitions.

The petitions addressed to Edward's privy council are diverse both in terms of the stated complaint and the remedy sought. Edward Lord Grey bemoaned the fact that his lately divorced wife had taken up with ruffians and desperate men who now threatened to murder him; he requested that the council punish the woman and her friends according to their demerits.[243] The inhabitants of the town of Staines implored the council to revoke Somerset's earlier order 'to pluck upp the Comen bridge at Stayns'; realising that the decision had been made in the interests of defence against the rebels of 1549, the townspeople suggested that if the bridge were left untouched, they would promise 'to sende oute A Scowte to discrye of any Armye [that] be comyng that waie'.[244] Ann Paget petitioned the lords to show mercy to her husband, William Lord Paget, upon the occasion of his arrest and imprisonment.[245] Henry Pony, in a bill addressed to Somerset alone, asked to be restored to his ale house, the Pye, which Alice Dacres had somehow managed to take from him.[246] And in an unusual case involving a claim against the Crown, a Venetian merchant pleaded that he had been appointed by the Lord Treasurer to import bullion for the King's use; that although he had successfully delivered 15,000 lb weight of fine silver, he had also been robbed by one William Piers at the mouth of the Thames of eight pieces worth £2,700; and that the stolen metal had been sold and occupied to His Majesty's use and profit at the King's mint in Ireland. In consideration of the premises, the merchant sought recompense from the Crown at the lords' convenience; in lieu of ready money from the King, he would accept licence to buy bell-metal or lead.[247]

In the cases cited, we have only the petitions and not the fact of the council's action. An unusually detailed narrative of a hitherto unknown meeting at Somerset Place on 3 July 1547, however, reveals the Protector and privy council proceeding to the arbitration of a matter at variance between the City of London and the admiralty.[248] The question at issue concerned the conservancy of a portion of the River Thames, the City alleging violation of their claim (based upon statute) by the admiralty (whose claim rested in a later commission). After counsel for both parties had expounded the merits of their clients' cases, the two chief justices and the King's learned council in the law, upon an examination of the validity of the admiralty's commission, deposed that as it bore a later date and had been granted during the royal pleasure, it did not stand in force in respect of the earlier statutes. At this, both parties and their counsel withdrew to a separate chamber, leaving the Protector and privy council alone to discuss the issues privately. The clerk taking the minutes of this secret deliberation – it is significant that minutes were kept – noted perhaps unintentionally the lords' true line of reasoning as well as their later publicly declared opinion. At first he recorded that the board resolved not to give a perfect and absolute judgement *against* the admiralty, for in time the admiralty officials might perhaps find more substantial evidence in support of their claim; realising the suggested partiality of the statement, the clerk crossed out 'against the admiralty' and 'they might perhaps find' so that his final version had the council delaying an absolute decision since, in time, other matter might arise for the full maintenance of *either* claim. Whereupon, the council called in the mayor and others, and Somerset declared that both parties were for the moment to continue their accustomed order for 'conservatie' of the Thames until the next term when some determinate order should be given.

Following Somerset's announcement, the mayor and his colleagues brought forth a second suit, this one for the unrestricted government of a fair in Southwark, but as the King held title to the lands and possessions therein, the Lord Great Master (St John) was appointed to go to Southwark to 'vieu and consider' with whom the right of the ordering of the fair belonged; upon his further information a determination would be made at a later time.[249] The narrative ends there, but the full text of the order and decree in this case has survived in another place;[250] the privy council resolved that the mayor and aldermen were to be allowed to continue to hold the fair, but the King, contrary to the City's suit, was to continue to enjoy the profits thereof.

The record of this meeting at Somerset Place is wholly unique: it is the only extant piece of evidence providing a reasonably complete view of the sort of meeting which must regularly have occurred throughout the reign. (Somerset, it seems, also acted alone at times, settling arguments at will.) The privy council's briefly noticed action of 7 February 1550 at the star chamber documents the only other instance when, upon receipt of a designated 'Bill of Compaint . . ., the matter therin conteyned . . . [was] comytted unto us of his [Majesty's] Privie Counceill to be harde, examyned and finally ordered'; the board did then 'order and decree' a settlement in a dispute between two claimants to an office in the King's gift.[251] Upon order from the board individual councillors and committees of the council also examined complaints, the results being reported to the full membership for confirmation in the name of the King's whole council.[252]

It has already been stated that the council was technically not a judicial court of record, that it did not judge guilt or innocence or impose sentence. But did it, in addition to the regular quasi-judicial functions described here, also at times *effectively* exercise judicial functions? Dr A. G. R. Smith thinks so, finding in Professor Elton's view of the Elizabethan board – that it 'was not a court in any real sense and had no judicial functions' – an interpretation which 'puts an intolerable strain upon the evidence'.[253] The example which Smith cites,[254] however, actually proves Elton's point that the council settled disputes between parties without formally assigning guilt. Neither the arbitrary imprisonment of one of the parties nor the levying of a fine – all for the non-performance of the council's order in the case cited by Smith – alters the fact that in deciding the matter in the first place the council was acting not as a court of law but in the manner of a board of arbitration. The means which it used to enforce the settlement were quasi-judicial.

Proof that a distinction between judicial and quasi-judicial functions still applies to the Elizabethan board can be found in Edward's reign when on one occasion it seems that the council under Northumberland did indeed render a verdict and impose a sentence. On 3 July 1551 at Greenwich the privy council heard the complaint of one Wilkes who contended that Sir Thomas Newneham had assaulted (made 'a fraye' upon) him at Coventry; the council summoned Newneham before them, found him 'faultie' as charged and so ordered him committed to the Fleet.[255] The council's settlement of Wilkes's case appears to document a true judicial function, an example as extraordinary as it is rare, since the evidence (apparently) comprehends an allegation that the defendant, acting alone, attacked the plaintiff's person with intent to do bodily harm, an allegation which on the face of it should have been heard at common law. Since neither riot nor unlawful assembly was mentioned, *Wilkes* v. *Newneham* may be a case which did not fall within the recognised competence of the King's council.

On 5 June 1550, upon information of a great riot and unlawful assembly made by the Lord Sturton upon William Hartgill, the council ordered both parties to appear before them in the council chamber at Westminster; the matter being examined, Sturton was committed to the Fleet and bound in recognizance of

500 marks that his men and friends should keep the peace against Hartgill.[256] The council's quasi-judicial action in this case reminds us once again of that body's responsibility to suppress disorder, though Sturton might be allowed to wonder posthumously how he had managed to escape process in star chamber.

If *Hartgill* v. *Sturton* smacks of similar proceedings before the lords in the court of star chamber, it is probable that three of the currently classified star chamber bills of pleading were considered by privy councillors as members of the council and not judges of the court. The three supplications are addressed not to the King according to the formula normally employed in that court, but to Somerset and 'the rest of his Majestes most honorable prive Counsell'[257] or simply 'to the Kinges Majestes most honorable Counsell'.[258] Technically, irregular forms of address do not necessarily mark extraordinary cases;[259] altogether, thirty-three of the 621 extant bills datable to Edward's reign are addressed to persons other than the King.[260] All but four of these thirty-three alleged offences fell unquestionably within the purview of the court; these twenty-nine bills were first received by the lords of the privy council (or the others to whom they are addressed) and then directed 'to the sterre chamber' as the endorsements on some so plainly show.[261] One is not a star chamber case and was properly referred to the masters of the court of requests.[262] In the three remaining cases, the plaintiffs – a Portuguese merchant, the Fuggers' London agent, and the tenants of the King's manor of Stockwell in Surrey – sought the council's assistance in disputes with royal officials, the King's customers and controllers in two instances and the chancellor of the court of augmentations in a third;[263] the nature of the complaints lodged and the remedies sought should have required arbitration at the board and not a judgement in the court of star chamber.

Confusion on this point arises from the fact that privy councillors often heard complaints or examined suspects 'at the Sterre Chambre' as the clerk of the privy council recorded it,[264] but, as stated earlier, this was the *inner* 'starred' chamber at Westminster, not the *outer* room where the same councillors and the judges might the same day have sat in session as the court of star chamber. Privy council proceedings recorded in or at the (inner) star chamber might or might not include quasi-judicial business;[265]

business recorded at other places of meeting often does include such matters.[266] When Richard Grafton mentioned that 'the Lordes sate . . . in counsayle in the Starre Chamber'[267] on 9 October 1549, he knew that this was a privy council meeting of great political moment; he may not have known that it was one of two meetings of the London council that day and was never recorded.[268] Politics figured very prominently in the case of John Beaumont, but when the privy council wrote to the Duke of Northumberland on 20 June 1552 that Beaumont 'this day has been before us in the Star Chamber', the councillors were referring to an otherwise unrecorded session of the court[269] and to their own duties as judges therein. Essentially, the court of star chamber was the King's council in judicial session; the presence of the other law officers as members of the court did not alter the fact that the great lords of the privy council could stop, delay, or expedite actions before the court for any reason, political or otherwise. Indeed, the privy council regularly concerned itself with proceedings of the court; in fact, it is probably true to say that the council effectively managed much of the business of the court by ordering appearances there[270] as well as reviewing 'the bookes' of cases before the judges in the star chamber.[271] Nevertheless, council and court remained separate institutions.

The council also detained, examined, and committed persons upon the frequent allegation of treasonous activity or slanderous speech. It was Somerset's policy in fact to order committal 'for a season' as a means of chastising persons he considered to be actually or potentially disorderly ('lewd'), 'for', as he put it, 'Such is the obstynacye of many people that without sharpenes they will not amende.'[272] Harmless misbehaviour, on the other hand, brought only a paternalistic slap, as when Sir George Norton was asked to redirect the attentions which the Countess of Oxford found so vexatious and troublesome.[273] Though Norton's fervour might have been flagitious, it posed no danger to the state. Had he spoken ill of King or council, his words, if reported, would have brought him some more severe punishment. Slanderous speakers in particular suffered sharp discomfort: a miller's servant at Battlesbridge was once set upon the pillory and had both ears cut off – 'by the Counselles commaundement' – for speaking seditious words against the Duke of Somerset.[274] One William Tomson may have gone the same way for singing a song of his own making.[275] Edward's councillors seem never to have been well liked by the commons; the members of the board knew themselves to be the subject of many a crude market and ale-house story. Rumour vied with ballad and cheap dramatic device to discredit men who in the popular imagination seemed brazenly eager to ride the King's own steed: Paget had heard one tale which likened the government to a 'fayre goodly' horse which all of the council had sought at once to mount – with predictable results for the beast.[276]

This was loose, common talk. More noticeable were the words and actions of those who, according to an anonymous court official, spoke too freely of 'thaffaires of estate' and so 'brekes lawes'. Of course, informers reported these allegedly treasonous activities – Northumberland used royal proclamations to advertise cash rewards for such work[277] – so that 'by this meane [was] the counsaill troubled withe . . . many sutes'. Nevertheless, in Edward's reign, said this observer, a well-placed suspect could 'hope by freendship of one or other in the counsaill directlye or indirectlye eyther to have pardon or to be wynked at'.[278]

Less fortunate, naturally, were the poorer sort: they were tortured. In October 1552 the council committed one Hawkyns to the Tower after he had confessed to having forged the Archbishop of Canterbury's signature with the alleged 'intent to haue Styrred A Rebellyon and comotion'. Northumberland then suggested to Cecil that the board appoint 'some discrete persons . . . to haue thexamynacon of hym and eyther, by fayre meanes or fowle to caus hym to declare his councellors'.[279] It is not surprising that the council should have employed torture as a means of extracting information from Hawkyns; to the council fell the awesome responsibility for the security of the realm, and contemporaries certainly would not have denied to the board its power of investigation in a matter so serious as a plot to foment rebellion by the authority of Cranmer's forged hand. Neither was it unusual for the council to direct its own members to employ 'such sharpe sorte of handlinges, either by threatning of torture or otherwise as . . . may best serve for the boltinge out of the truthe' when a suspect's allegiance to the Crown lay in question.[280] Royal commissioners, some of them privy councillors, once received standing orders from the board to torture prisoners in the Tower at their discretion.[281] This foul business had to do with the council's 'investigation' of Somerset's alleged conspiracy to murder Northumberland. Somewhat more surprising is the council's practice of ordering torture in the cases of suspects accused of criminal acts not connected with rebellion or disloyalty. The council instructed Sir Anthony Hungerford to proceed 'by the law' against a certain Reede suspected of numerous robberies; if Reed feared that course, he was to be sent to Westminster to be put to torment.[282] Under suspicion of a particularly heinous murder, one Willson and one Warren similarly underwent a racking ordeal at the council's command.[283] Northumberland did not stick at the thought of ordering torture in other cases,[284] nor did Cranmer himself once in the case of two men charged with stealing three hawks.[285] Examination by torture appears thus to have been one of the council's routine measures. It may be important to note, however, that although the lords ordered suspects such as Willson and Warren 'to be put to the tortours' fairly frequently, the same councillors probably did not wish their reputations to rest upon even the infrequent use of the rack. As Northumberland said, the rough handling of Hawkyns was a matter to be 'kept very close and secret'.

In addition to the arbitration of disputes at the board, and the examination of suspects, the council supervised the functioning of the entire judicial system. To document the essential aspects of this activity would be merely to repeat what has already been well described elsewhere. The privy council's instructions to and relations with the councils in the North[286] and the Marches of Wales;[287] the council's interference in the conduct of cases before the various courts[288] – these and other aspects of its quasi-judicial activity[289] are corroborated by the evidence for the period under consideration. In such instances, the competence of the King's council in the reign of Edward VI did not differ essentially from that of the Tudor privy council either before or after that time.

7
Politics

Recent interpretations of the events of January 1547 agree on one apparently vital point, that whatever one may say about the validity of the moves which overthrew the provisions of Henry's will, they were actions which received the full support of the late King's executors: in the Tower on 31 January 1547, the council appointed by Henry VIII 'voted unanimously'[1] to make the Earl of Hertford Protector of the realm and Governor of the King's person. An older view, that Wriothesley alone had opposed the 'agreement' of 31 January and that his opposition brought his removal on 6 March, is now discredited; in the latest account, the possibility of Wriothesley's opposition is not even mentioned, since the Chancellor's fall, it is argued, was really caused by a justifiable attack by the common lawyers on a technical charge that the council and even Wriothesley accepted.[2] Indeed, it is now thought that in the weeks following Edward's accession, the council governed in a spirit of co-operation and unanimity; the relation of the Protector to his colleagues appears to have been 'unexceptionable'.[3]

Fresh evidence – a contemporary account by a clerk in Somerset's household who was an eye-witness to these events[4] – makes it plain, however, that within four days of Henry's death, an unexpected bid for a direct share of the Protector's power nearly wrecked the executors' secret agreement, and that after weathering this crisis, Somerset was forced to remove Wriothesley, who had in the meantime emerged as the leader of a potential opposition party seeking to prevent the confirmation of that agreement. It will be argued here that these two developments not only influenced Somerset's decision to secure firm authority for the exercise of his office, but almost certainly determined that the terms of his letters-patent would also enable him personally to choose the members of the King's council.

The considerations which were to influence the form of Somerset's patents found their origin in the first instance in the circumstances of Sir Thomas Seymour's appointment to the privy council. Earlier it was observed that by 2 February 1547 Seymour had somehow become identified with the body of Henry VIII's executors, that officially he had become a privy councillor although the will had not named him one. There is no doubt that Seymour's admission to an otherwise closed circle of advisers represented an accomplished fact on 2 February, but it is the only fact which the council's records reveal; the suddenness of his appearance is as remarkable as the silence of the register on the question of the manner of his appointment. As it happened, the author of the 'Notes of the controversy' between Somerset and Northumberland was present in the Tower when Seymour made his first appearance in the council chamber there; the 'Notes' allow a reconstruction of the events that must have produced the appointment.

It will be remembered that Seymour had only just been appointed a privy councillor on 23 January 1547, or five days before Henry's death.[5] The King's demise had thus put an abrupt end to a very promising career. More importantly, Seymour played no part in the secret moves of 28–31 January that assured his brother's control of King and council. As one of twelve mere 'assistants' to the executors, he stood excluded from membership of Edward VI's privy council. Consequently, he was barred from the executors' first meeting in the Tower on 31 January, and thus from the proceedings which ratified Hertford's elevation to the dual office of Protector of the realm and Governor of the King's person. On 1 February, following the second council meeting, Seymour and the other assistants were summoned to the Tower and there informed by the executors of the previous day's agreement and the contents of the will.[6]

At some time after the meeting of the thirty-first, and just before that of 1 February, however, John Dudley, the Viscount Lisle, approached Seymour privately and informed him not that it had been 'secretly agried' that Hertford should have both the governorship of the young King and the protectorship of the realm, but rather that Hertford should be Protector, and Seymour Governor. It was, of course, a deliberate lie: in the words of the narrator, Lisle told Seymour 'not what was concluded, but what he ment.'[7] Implying that the executors had not made a final decision about the division of the two offices, Lisle urged Seymour to 'haue his voyse to be the governor of the kinges person', thinking it right that Seymour 'shold haue all the furtheraunce he colde make' in obtaining the governorship. Seymour rejoiced. He gave Lisle 'great thankes and prayed him that he wolde move it at the Counselles boorde'. Lisle 'Answered that he thoughte [that] not beste to do nor any other elles but only [Seymour] him self', adding that 'it was so reasonable a request that he knewe no man wolde denye it him. Wheare vpon the nexte day the borde being full . . . Sir Thomas came in and made his demande and showed his [r]eason; which being ended was nevre aunswered, but straight the counsell roose vp and departed [from] the Counselles chamber.' Lisle, seeing that Hertford was highly irritated by Seymour's performance, went to him

and tolde him my lord did not I tell you ever that he wolde with stande all your intentes and purposes and he only wolde envye your state and calling to this Rome; his harte being so bidge [*sic*] that he will never rest till he do owt throwe you agayne if you give him never so smale accountenaunce.[8]

Two years later, at the height of Seymour's quarrel with Somerset, and before the Lord Admiral's arrest on charges of treason, Warwick is alleged to have reminded him that he owed his high position as a privy councillor and great officer of state to the favour of Somerset and the council 'who had admitted him among their number against the late King's wish'. Indeed, it was said, so strongly had Henry VIII opposed the idea of Seymour's appointment to the council of executors, that being upon his death-bed and hearing Seymour's name 'among those elected to the council,' the King had 'cried out, "No, no," though his breath was failing him'.[9] But on 2 February 1547, Seymour, having lost his bid to be Governor, did in fact assume for the first time the duties of an Edwardian privy councillor. What had happened in the interval between the dramatic confrontation at the board and his admission to membership of the council against Henry VIII's expressed command, and in violation of the will?

The most likely explanation is that Hertford had accommodated his brother's bold demand for the governorship of Edward

VI by awarding Seymour merely a place on the ruling council. At the time of the sensational meeting – 1 February at the latest – Hertford's very real control of the King's person represented a *fait accompli* to which the other executors had already 'secretly agried'; there seemed little chance that at the moment of triumph he would surrender the fruits of a carefully planned and wholly successful *coup*. But, as the narrator of this account points out, the executors had not yet 'promiced' Hertford his prize,[10] an act which the will specifically required them to do in writing.[11] Faced with such a direct and unexpected challenge to the settlement of 31 January, Hertford may have been forced to seek some sort of compromise. At any rate, admitting Seymour to membership held advantages for both men: it restored Seymour's earlier, short-lived career as a privy councillor, and it left intact the Protector's own position as Governor. In provoking Seymour's open bid for a direct share of power, Lisle's treachery had precipitated a political and constitutional crisis that Hertford appears thus to have solved by creating another seat at the board. Whether or how the executors justified this action according to the terms of the will cannot be known.

Seymour's appointment, however, had set an important precedent. Were there not other members of Henry VIII's council who, on 2 February, by reason of rank or service, could put forward a better claim to the office of a privy councillor in Edward's reign – the Earl of Arundel, Henry's Lord Chamberlain; the Earl of Essex; Cheyne, the King's Treasurer; Gage, the Comptroller; Wingfield, Vice-Chamberlain; Petre, a principal secretary? The will had excluded all of them from membership of Edward's privy council, and yet the acceptance of Seymour in the office which even Henry had denied him would make it difficult for the executors to refuse another determined bid for membership from, say, the Earl of Arundel. After 2 February, therefore, the need to expand the membership of Edward's privy council may well have weighed heavily in the Protector's political calculations: the excluded officers of Henry's last council might find the advancement of Sir Thomas Seymour an event increasingly intolerable to bear.

A second, concurrent development probably convinced Somerset of the necessity to re-define the conditions of membership of Edward's council – the Lord Chancellor's open resistance to the agreement of 31 January. Grafton said flatly that Somerset's advancement 'was well allowed of al the noble men sauying of Thomas Wriothesley';[12] Froude even had Wriothesley speaking out against Hertford's elevation at the executors' first meeting at the Tower.[13] Pollard questioned Froude's authority for the speech, but was inclined to believe that, in any case, the Chancellor probably had opposed the creation of the Protectorate on the thirty-first.[14] Even so, had Wriothesley's sentiments moved the Protector to expel the Chancellor from his office and seat at the board? Two months after his fall, Wriothesley himself told van der Delft that his misfortunes sprang from the 'enmity' which Somerset had borne against him 'for a long time past'.[15] Somerset, according to Wriothesley, had not obtained by the terms of the will the titles which he had expected Henry to grant him, and the Protector ascribed this to the 'influence' of the Lord Chancellor.[16] There is no way, of course, to verify an allegation which Wriothesley attributed to Somerset, but there would have been no reason for Wriothesley to have falsified the statement which he made to van der Delft on or before 16 June 1547 to the effect that he had refused to 'consent to any innovations in the matter of government beyond the provisions of the will'.[17] The Imperial ambassador remained convinced that as a consequence of this, Somerset, who had had Warwick and Paget 'on his side,' unseated the Lord Chancellor.[18]

It is true that Wriothesley had surrendered the great seal in the face of the common lawyers' charge that he had improperly delegated his authority as Chancellor; this, at least, forms part of the official explanation which was recorded in the council book. Professor Jordan, who follows Pollard's view, thinks that the council agreed with the charge and so unanimously asked Wriothesley to step down.[19] Technically, the lawyers' charge was true, and it proved in fact to provide a convenient justification for Wriothesley's removal: although his delegation of authority by commission under the great seal rested on good precedent, the Chancellor had failed to consult his fellow executors for permission to grant the commission to himself in Edward's name.[20] Under most other circumstances, the executors should have welcomed the commission, for it released their colleague from some of his duties in chancery for a more active role at the council table. In view of the fact that the council did not consider itself competent to determine Wriothesley's case – the council's first draft of the proceedings against him stated this, but the relevant phrases were omitted from the final version copied into the register[21] – it may be asked why, then, the board proceeded to support what Wriothesley called Somerset's 'contention' in the matter[22] and relieve him of the great seal and his membership of the council.[23] The answer, as the author of the 'Notes' said, was 'by cause he being lord Chauncellor of England at the death of King Henry the viijth was sore against him [Somerset, then Earl of Hertford] to be made protector . . . Wheare vpon', he added, 'he was put from his office'.[24]

At the time of the Lord Chancellor's arrest, Somerset's authority for the exercise of his new office rested on nothing more than the executors' 'agreement'. As has been seen, the executors probably stood on safe ground when they interpreted Henry VIII's will as enabling them to create Hertford Protector, but at the same time, the new Protector, unlike the Lord Chancellor, possessed no authority from the reigning King to undertake any action; his powers were ill defined, his tenure remained a mystery, his ability to act in the King's name appeared questionable to foreign ambassadors. For these reasons, it was inevitable that Somerset would seek firm authority for the exercise of his office; short of an act of Parliament, a royal commission was required. If there was one executor, therefore, whose opposition Somerset should have found intolerable, it was the Lord Chancellor, the Keeper of the great seal. We have no hard evidence that Wriothesley specifically refused, or said that he would refuse, to affix the great seal to letters confirming Somerset's elevation, but the timing of his fall, the date of the resulting patent, and the testimony of Somerset's servant certainly suggest Wriothesley's open resistance: *because* Wriothesley was Lord Chancellor *and* 'was sore against' Somerset's elevation, 'he was put from his office'.

Somerset's desire to receive authoritative confirmation of the executors' agreement was not the only reason why he sought the King's letters-patent; he needed also to be able to control the membership of the privy council. Wriothesley's opposition made this plain; as suggested earlier, the deposed Lord Chancellor might well ask by what authority the executors were empowered to remove from membership of the body of executors and privy councillors one so appointed by authority of the Act of Parliament of 1536. Somerset's patent attempted to get round this problem by granting to the Protector alone the absolute power to appoint the full membership of the board from 12 March. This power also effectively quashed any real or potential opposition which Somerset faced: his opponents among the executors who were privy councillors before 12 March might simply find themselves, like Wriothesley, out of office after that date, and those among the assistant executors who aspired to membership could not expect to be appointed if they stood opposed to a protectorate.

That Somerset's power to choose Edward's privy councillors was designed in part to throttle potential political opposition at the board is further suggested by the fact that Wriothesley was not alone in criticising the agreement of 31 January. We do not know who or how many may have joined him in opposing Hertford's elevation; we know only that a few others sympathised, at least, with his stand, and that their sentiments seriously endangered their positions. Indeed, Wriothesley, so the account runs, 'submitte[d] him selfe for the safetie of the rest'.[25] Whether this observer meant that Wriothesley was willing under the circumstances to surrender, or was left with no alternative but to do so, remains an intriguing question. It is unlikely, as Pollard has said, that Wriothesley's presumed Henrician catholicism weighed heavily against him;[26] nevertheless, it is true, as already noted, that Somerset ordered several of the known conservatives – Cheyne and Gage, at least – to confine themselves to their houses at the moment of the Chancellor's arrest.[27] It may be that when the observer referred to 'the rest' whose 'safetie' was assured by Wriothesley's fall, he meant the conservatives who had been privy councillors under Henry VIII but who were not members of the new council. Like Gardiner, and perhaps Arundel, these were men who, as van der Delft said, were 'known to be opposed to any change in their ancient religion'[28] and who could look to Wriothesley as the only councillor then in a position to alter the course of the new regime. The fact that one of Somerset's clerks pointed to 'the rest' as an identifiable group suggests that the government was prepared to believe that there existed a party capable of exerting some influence even in council. It seems that as late as 29 May 1547, the ruling faction remained sensitive to the consolidation of a party of disaffected lords: the council was not allowing Wriothesley to leave London for his estate near Southampton; as Gardiner had earlier retired to Southampton, van der Delft thought it 'quite probable' that the council wanted 'to prevent these two men from meeting'.[29]

We may, therefore, suggest that three considerations influenced the form which Somerset's letters-patent of the Protectorate were to assume on 12 March 1547. In the first instance, he and his fifteen (twelve active) co-executors desired that the King, as a technical matter of course, confirm them in their offices as his privy councillors in order that they might proceed to the governing of the realm 'with more ample autorite' than that provided them by their own agreement, based as it was upon the authority which they understood Henry to have granted them in his will. The resulting commission, when signed by Edward VI, would serve, they said, as a 'testimonie of *thundoubted* powre and sufficiencie of the saide Lorde Protectour and Counsail to treate and conclude apon any matter wherein they shuld have to do on his Hieghness behaulf'.[30] This, at least, stood on 13 March as the council's official justification for the commission. Thus far, there was nothing to suggest that anything had been changed except the status of one of the sixteen executors who was now Lord Protector; the commission – the terms of which the council first recorded only on 21 March – recognised his titled pre-eminence, defined his powers, and established his tenure. Ostensibly, the commission should also have recognised Henry's fifteen other executors as Edward's privy councillors.

That it did not do so was determined by Thomas Seymour's action on 1 February: his admission made inevitable an expansion of the council of executors. The commission of 12 March, therefore, had to be phrased so as to permit the Protector and the executors to add to their number. At this point, however, Wriothesley's opposition, and the consequent possibility that others would join him in attempting to overthrow the agreement of 31 January, introduced a new consideration: if the provisions for membership of Edward's council were to be modified, they had now to be phrased so as to enable Somerset to deal with existing or future political opponents. This could be done only by revamping completely the terms of membership: no one was to be confirmed in the office of a privy councillor; from 12 March, Somerset was to be able personally to select every member of the council.

Neither the informal creation of a Protector by the terms of the executors' agreement nor the granting of a patent which recognised Hertford's accession to the office violated Henry VIII's will; a Protector of the realm and Governor of Edward VI's person would in any case have been appointed by letters-patent and not by a royal will.[31] Indeed, Henry VIII himself may actually have granted Hertford – or instructed him to secure – such a patent.[32] But there was nothing in the actual granting of the office that required Somerset to destroy the privy council which Henry was empowered to appoint and did appoint in his will. To believe that Henry really did mean Hertford to tear up the provisions of the will on this point is to believe the incredible – that the King had no faith in his ability to prescribe government by council during his son's minority; that the composition of the council which he did finally name was merely incidental, if not irrelevant, to his thinking; that his apparently vehement opposition to Seymour's membership in particular stood as a gesture both empty and feigned. Even before the breath was out of Henry's body, Paget and Hertford had devised a protectorate, but there is no evidence that they had also plotted to break up Edward's first privy council. Dramatic and unforeseen political developments made it necessary for them to do so by 12 March.

The immediate impact of Lisle's duplicity, Seymour's boldness, and Wriothesley's opposition was thus to transform fundamentally the conditions of membership of Edward VI's council; and the repercussions were felt long afterwards. Seymour was re-sworn of the new council, but he yearned yet to win the governorship of the King's person; his efforts brought him finally to the block. The Protector readmitted Wriothesley to the board in time to help with the council's proceedings against Seymour; and Lisle, now Earl of Warwick, seems during the two years before Seymour's death to have pressed forward his efforts to drive ever more deeply a wedge of distrust between the two brothers. Foxe spoke of the 'slanderous tongues' that sowed hatred and suspicion between Seymour and Somerset;[33] Queen Elizabeth later remarked that there were those who had deliberately prevented the possibility of a reconciliation between the two and so hastened the Admiral's execution;[34] Ponet pointedly referred to 'those that conspired the deathe of the two brethren';[35] Antonio de Guaras held no doubts that the animosity between Somerset and Seymour was originally produced 'by the contrivance of Northumberland'.[36] And the account given by the author of the 'Notes', allowing for a few embellishments, certainly confirms Guaras' belief, itself a reflection of opinion at Mary's court, as well as the early-seventeenth-century judgement that 'the Earle of Warwicke had his finger in the business' that brought Seymour to ruin.[37]

This is not to imply that Warwick personally brought about the Admiral's death. Seymour's flamboyance, his arrogant daring, and his apparently intense ambition to be Governor of the King's person; the Protector's uncompromising, high-minded pride on this point; even the Duchess of Somerset's intervention against the Admiral at the last hour[38] – all of these contributed to Seymour's demise. But if we accept as given the fact of Warwick's lust for power as well, Ponet's observation stands as an arresting comment on the depth of Warwick's involvement. It appears, in fact, that from the very beginning – January 1547 – Warwick conceived of removing both Seymour and Somerset from the arena of political activity. Indeed, to achieve real power for himself, he needed to isolate not one but both of the King's uncles. It is probable that at the moment of Henry's death Dudley actually feared that there existed an alliance between the two; a Seymour–Somerset pact would effectively have driven Dudley to a position of much diminished importance. It is true that the brothers were friends at the time, and to the author of the 'Notes' it appeared that Dudley 'feared muche the amitie betwene the twoo britherin'; Dudley sought with 'all diligence to understand their humors; and so by lytell and a lytell to compasse them bothe'.[39]

It was foolish for him to begin by attacking openly the settlement of 31 January, since his unquestioned confidence with Seymour and Somerset – even his enemies knew that he 'was familiar with the bothe and loved of them both and trusted of the both'[40] – rendered them vulnerable to his intrigues from within. Warwick's genius for political manoeuvre seems to have consisted in part in an unusual ability to play upon the weaknesses of others. It appears that he began by playing upon Seymour's frustration and reckless ambition. At the moment of execution, Guaras found Northumberland a man of 'great courage' who had triumphed in 1549 because he had recognised in Somerset an opponent lacking both in nerve and force of character.[41] The contemporary French observer who wrote 'Quelques particularitez d'Angleterre du temps du Roy Edouard et de la Reine Marie' thought that Warwick's apparently attractive qualities – his great presence, his strength of character, even what some called his 'liberality' to others – were artfully contrived in order especially 'to acquire the favour of those who could either serve or harm him'.[42] Wriothesley was one whose favour Warwick appears certainly to have gained by 6 October 1549; he may have done so deliberately because he saw that Wriothesley could serve the purpose which we have assumed Warwick had for some time held – Somerset's overthrow. On the eve of Wriothesley's fall in January 1550, Princess Mary described Warwick as the most 'unstable' man in England;[43] what she perceived as instability, however, was probably a depth of cunning which made him seem to be two different persons. Outwardly, said the Frenchman, Warwick's speech matched his composure; he was affable, gracious, and kind. But within was a man vindictive, disloyal, and proud, a man whose courtesies cloaked an arrogant contempt for those who stood in his way.[44] The recognition of this aspect of Warwick's character may well have been in the minds of the many who felt that Seymour's execution had also marked Somerset's destruction.[45]

The circumstances of the *coup* of 1549 which brought Somerset down are familiar enough. We are concerned, rather, to discover why Warwick moved so suddenly after the *coup* to purge the board of its 'catholic'[46] members and back the left-wing extremists in religion. The blow against the Protector had been the united effort of sixteen members of the London faction of the council, but upon Somerset's committal to the Tower the conspirators' solidarity disintegrated. The subsequent 'unrecorded struggle' between the party of the earls of Arundel and Southampton on the one hand, and Warwick's faction on the other, marked, as Pollard said, a turning point in English history,[47] for

Warwick's victory in January 1550 was followed immediately by the introduction of the protestant Reformation into England.

The usual explanation of these events rests upon the view that Warwick had taken the lead in organising those who opposed Somerset's rule; that he had gained the support of a group of catholic privy councillors – Wriothesley, the Earl of Arundel, Peckham, Southwell – by offering them hopes of a conservative settlement in religion after the *coup*;[48] that he used these dupes merely to topple the Protector so that he could seize power for himself and push forward a protestant revolution that would reward him with the property of a reformed Church.

There is much in this explanation which is attractive because of its known or apparent truth. Of Warwick's ability to conceive of such a strategy there seems to be no question. 'He had', said Sir Richard Morison, 'such a head that he seldom went about anything but he conceived first three or four purposes beforehand.' It has been aptly remarked that Morison meant by this perhaps three or four alternative plans or an equal number of double-bluffs.[49] It is true, of course, that Warwick figured prominently as one of the leaders of the conspiracy; although he was not alone in delivering the blow, he was certainly instrumental in directing it. Contemporaries accepted both Warwick's apparent catholicism and the rumours that the new government would restore the older practices in religion; Gardiner expected to be released from the Tower, and Hooper began preparing himself mentally even for death in the reaction which he thought would follow the conservatives' triumph.[50] Warwick's switch, if it can be called that, was no less astonishing than the speed with which he effected it: by March he had become Hooper's 'intrepid soldier of Christ';[51] he had ousted the catholic councillors; he had packed the board with those who could be expected to support his radical faith. And no one can deny the fact of Warwick's subsequent gains at the expense of the Church.

There remain, however, some doubts and not a few unanswered questions. Are we really to believe that in September 1549 Warwick conceived of a plan whereby he would use Arundel and Wriothesley as his tools in a plot to drive Somerset from office, and then, somehow, after a successfully faked restoration of catholic rule, evict them from their seats at the board? That before overthrowing them both, he would allow them to share the charge of governing the King's person? That if he secretly intended in September 1549 to back a thorough-going protestant revolution, he would permit not only the placement of the catholic earls about the King, but also the addition to the council of two known conservatives, Southwell and Peckham, as well as allow Smith's vacant position to be filled by Dr Wotton, one who could hardly be termed a zealous reformer? How, in the space of little more than three months, were four new members appointed, all of them of reformed views? Why did Warwick feel that he must take the drastic step of removing the catholic councillors from membership? And by what means, precisely, were Wriothesley, Arundel, and Southwell expelled with such apparent ease? Can it be believed that Warwick alone conducted these intrigues, that he was able single-handed to dismiss his enemies and appoint his friends at will?

There is, first, the question of Warwick's motive. After February 1550, Hooper believed Warwick to be the fearless instrument of the word of God. Did Warwick see himself in this light? The day before his death 'he desired to here masse, and to receave the sacrament, according to the olde accustumed maner', by which 'I lett you all to understande that I do most faithfullie belyve this is the very right and true waie, oute of the which true religion . . . I have ben seduced theis xvj yeres past.'[52] Privately, he may really have believed this, but by his confession he was also admitting that he had throughout Edward's reign accepted the royal supremacy in England, and since, through a pliant council, he himself had exercised that power, the question really becomes one of self-interest. He realised that others thought him a 'dissembler' in religion, but when in 1552 he said that 'I have for xx yere stand to oon kynd of religion in the same which I doo nowe profes, and have I thanke the lorde past no smalle daungers for yt',[53] he probably meant that he had always accepted the King's religion because it had assured his preservation. In one sense, the confession of August 1553, therefore, was quite logical: effectively he had recognised Mary's supremacy and could suppose that at the last hour she might spare his life. His earlier, seemingly contradictory and varied expressions of faith can be viewed in the same way. Thus, before Henry's death, it was observed that in matters of faith Dudley stood 'neither on the one side nor on the other'; he had done and would continue to do only what was 'agreeable to the King's Majesty's pleasure'.[54]

What would be the royal pleasure in the new reign? In one sense, the question was irrelevant; until the King's eighteenth year the council embodied the royal will and in exercising the supremacy during the royal minority the assembled councillors were able legally to make new orders in religion. The judges' unanimous decision to this effect[55] had cleared the way for Somerset, and Warwick could expect to wield the same power once he had gained control of the council. But he could not ignore altogether Edward VI's personal beliefs, and it has been asserted that because the boy was a devoted adherent of the reformed faith, Warwick adopted the same faith as an obvious means to royal favour.[56] The French, who seem to have understood Warwick better than most, found him essentially indifferent to the religious opinions of the age; he had declared for the reformers, said one, in order really to win the favour of the commons who were already well disposed towards them.[57] This judgement, however, was made after Warwick had seized power (that is, after January 1550), and so does not explain how, in the period immediately following the *coup*, when he shared the control of Edward's person, he was able to engineer the dismissal of the catholics. Moreover, after the conservatives were gone, his retention of the royal favour did not require that he move sharply to the left of the King in doctrine. During September and early October 1549 it had been in his interests to pose as one willing to accept a return to orthodox practices; as late as 17 October it could be observed that although he was not yet a self-confessed believer, he had nevertheless taken up certain of the old observances.[58] Information received at the French court and recorded some years later (1606) by Jacques August de Thou indicated that Warwick had gained the conservatives' support 'by pretending a secret Inclination to restore the antient way of Worship';[59] Burnet understood this to mean that Warwick had given the catholics 'secret assurances'.[60]

Some sort of understanding between Warwick and the conservatives had been reached before the *coup*; the Venetian ambassador at the Emperor's court even spoke of the existence of one between Warwick and the Emperor, and Charles V himself later (24 November 1551) referred to Warwick as one who had once desired 'to restore religion to its original condition'.[61] We can appreciate that Warwick's sham catholicism was motivated by his immediate political requirement – conservative support for the blow against Somerset. But the presumed need to secure the royal favour or even the favour of most of the commons after 17 October does not explain how, merely by dropping his pretended sympathies, he was able, against a conservative majority, to begin adding reformist councillors (Goodrich and Dorset) in November. Indeed, none of the motives which may be ascribed to Warwick – that he was greedy beyond measure for Church lands; that as a man of the 'new learning', he had decided at the moment of Henry's death systematically to stamp out catholic doctrine;[62] that he perceived, perhaps unconsciously, that a violent revolution offered the best chance to establish the dictatorship to which he aspired;[63] that he sought the advancement of his family and so could not allow the political restoration of the old, essentially catholic nobility whose presence should have greatly diminished the lustre of his more recent dignity;[64] that there was a 'fatal taint of crooked self-seeking' in his family's blood that drove him inevitably towards desperate measures[65] – really explains how and why he was able to do what he did between October 1549 and February 1550.

It is probable that the key to understanding the events of this period lies not in the discovery of his political or religious motives on the eve of the *coup* of 1549 or after the triumph of 1550, but rather his purpose during the critical month of November 1549 when he secured the appointment of the first of several councillors of reformed views. If the removal of the catholics can be viewed as a political consequence of the decision to side with the reformers, the decision must have been made by 6 November, the date of Goodrich's appearance. Now, it was widely believed that the catholic Sir Thomas Arundel (of Lanherne), receiver of the Duchy of Cornwall, would be made Comptroller of the King's household early in November in reward for his services against Somerset the month before;[66] as Comptroller (in place of Paget) he should also have been appointed a privy councillor. The Imperial ambassador, who thought he had heard the truth of these matters from one well-acquainted with the intrigues, reported that Warwick tore off his mask of pretended sympathy for the old religion just at the time when it was rumoured that Sir Thomas Arundel was to be made Comptroller. As van der Delft related it, Warwick had suddenly awakened to the fact that a majority of the council were 'Catholics'.[67] It is a little difficult to believe that Warwick discovered only as late as the first week in November that he stood outnumbered by a clique of catholic lords, but clearly, there was something about their catholicism which threatened him personally and politically: his immediate response to the 'discovery' was to create, as van der Delft said, new members of the council from among his followers in order to collect enough votes effectively to usurp control of the government.[68] Theoretically, there was nothing in Sir Thomas Arundel's probable appointment which should have moved Warwick to such precipitous action, but so violently did he respond to Arundel's politics that in 1552, 'at therles sute' especially, Sir Thomas had 'his head with the axe diuided from his shoulders'.[69]

What had Arundel done early in November 1549? We know only that a few days before the date of van der Delft's dispatch of 7 November 1549, Arundel had gone to the Princess Mary asking to be received 'into her service'.[70] Mary put off accepting him, according to the ambassador, because she did not wish to run the risk of being associated with the recent changes in government. Van der Delft understood this to be a reference to the Protector's fall; it is more likely that Mary's current relationship with the men behind Arundel – the catholic privy councillors – prevented her from accepting him then into 'her service', and not the fact of his earlier stand against Somerset. It is highly probable that Warwick secured Goodrich's appointment on 6 November (or a few days earlier) in place of Sir Thomas Arundel's for the reason that the latter was now conducting intrigues on behalf of Mary and the party of Wriothesley and the Earl of Arundel. What sort of intrigues were these and for what purpose?

The author of the 'Notes of the controversy' between Somerset and Northumberland was convinced that 'there was divers catholikes called in to counsell at that instante [that is, early October 1549] for the lady maryes sake she hoping to haue bine Regent'.[71] Since Peckham and Southwell both were catholics and had not

before been privy councillors, they must be the ones here referred
to who were then 'called in to counsell'. But who had summoned
them? It is likely that Wriothesley secured their appointment.
It will be remembered that Wriothesley and Southwell had earlier
co-operated in the destruction of the Earl of Surrey: Southwell
had accused Surrey of treason, Wriothesley had drawn up the
accusations. Ponet speaks of the leading conspirators of 1549 as
including Wriothesley and Southwell on the one hand and Warwick on the other, so it may well be that when Warwick came
to Wriothesley's house in Holborn early in October he found
Southwell already there. As Peckham was perhaps Wriothesley's
kinsman and certainly his close friend (and also later his executor),[72] it seems probable that Wriothesley had brought him into
the conspiracy as well.

The other members of the London council who were executors
appear to have accepted the elevation of Peckham and Southwell
to membership. Were the two added in order to support Mary's
alleged bid to become regent? On 8 October in London van der
Delft heard it rumoured that 'she is to be set up as regent',[73]
and Somerset himself, in an early-morning oration to the assembled guard at Hampton Court on 6 October charged that
Warwick and the London council were 'mynded to make the
lady Mary Regent' after first pulling him down.[74] It has been
assumed that Somerset knew the rumour to be false and so pretended to believe it,[75] but there is no evidence that on the sixth
Somerset was able to determine that the story was true or false.
Writing some twelve or more years later, the author of the 'Notes'
still believed that the London faction (whose members included
'those that was for religion as other wayes') had been moved to
action upon 'a pretence that quene Mary sholde be requent'.[76]
It is a fact that during September the earls of Warwick, Arundel,
and Southampton, and Lord St John had got in touch with Mary,
asking her if she would be willing to lend her favour to their
proposed attack upon the Protector.[77] Had her reply been positive,
and had the plotters actually been contemplating a Marian
regency, they would probably have followed up this initial inquiry
with a suggestion to that effect. But Mary's answer, although not
entirely negative, disallowed such a move; she would not, she
said, interfere in matters of government. Significantly, however,

her letter left open the possibility of a later participation in affairs: she said simply that were she known to favour the conspiracy now, events would move faster; and wasn't it sad to witness the present unhappy state of religion in the realm?[78] Much later (6 April 1551) Mary told the council that she wished only that religion during Edward's minority had remained as it was at the time of her father's death;[79] the catholic conspirators should have found this position politically acceptable in 1549. In any case, they would not themselves have let it be known before 6 October that they intended to put her up as regent: they had not yet moved decisively against Somerset. In one sense, therefore, the Protector's speech of 6 October played into their hands. They could deny his allegation and denounce him as a rumour-monger. And since Mary cannot reasonably have committed herself to the idea of a regency before Somerset's overthrow and the catholics' clear triumph, the London councillors' letter to her of 9 October stands as a perfectly logical attempt to cover themselves either way. Somerset began his oration, they said,

and among many his untrue and idle sayings, declared that . . . we would have removed him from his office, and that we minded to have your Grace to be Regent of the realm . . . which as God knoweth, we never intended . . . neither any of us all at any time, by word or writing, hath opened any such matter to your Grace, as your honour knoweth.[80]

Strictly speaking, some of what they said was probably true: though none of the lords themselves may have written or spoken to Mary, several of them had certainly 'sent' to sound her out on the question of supporting the *coup d'état*.[81] It remains an open question whether, through an agent – Sir Thomas Arundel? – the catholic councillors had also informally raised with her the possibility of a regency. It may be significant that this Arundel, whose beheading Warwick personally sought, was considered by van der Delft to have been 'a prime instrument in uniting the Lords against the Protector'.[82]

It was at some time between about 2 November and 6 November, then, that Sir Thomas Arundel, expecting to be Comptroller, made contact with Mary; that Warwick dropped his catholic pretensions; that the Bishop of Ely became a privy councillor.

The author of the 'Notes' tells us that as the catholics had increased their numbers in order to back Mary's alleged bid for
the regency, Warwick, with Cranmer's help, found the means for
'the lord Marques dorset and Goodrick Busshopp of . . . Eley to
be of the privie counsell to encounter the other syde in nomber',
Dorset and Goodrich 'being protestantes', of course.[83] The author
said that Warwick had earlier 'procured by the meanes of the
Archebusshoppe of Canterbury great frendes abowte the king',[84]
and so he infers that Warwick was able through them to persuade
Edward VI to approve of the addition of Goodrich and Dorset
to the council. The writer does not name these 'great frendes',
but we can reasonably assume that they included several members
of the group appointed in October 1549 to attend upon the King's
person following the Protector's removal – Sir Thomas Wroth,
a gentleman of the privy chamber and one of the few who was
later allowed to remain close to the dying King; Sir Andrew
Dudley, Warwick's brother; Sir Thomas Darcy; and among the
great lords, the Marquess of Northampton.[85] The suggestion that
Cranmer played a decisive role in placing Warwick's friends
about the King is not unlikely. Edward VI said that it was 'by
my consent' that the council had appointed the attendant lords
and knights;[86] Cranmer was certainly one of the few at Hampton
Court in October 1549 from whom the King should unquestionably have accepted advice and to whom the boy should have
been willing to give his consent. It is reported that when Edward
sought an explanation of his uncle's whereabouts at that time, he
sent for Cranmer;[87] it will be remembered that upon the London
council's orders Cranmer had removed Somerset's servants from
about the King.[88] As Warwick himself was one of the six privy
councillors charged with governing the King's person, the claim
that he and Cranmer together were able to obtain the appointment of Goodrich and Dorset doubtless carries much truth.

By 6 November, therefore, it appears that Warwick had successfully thwarted the catholics' attempt to increase their strength
at the board. It is not likely that Mary was really 'hoping' to be
regent, but circumstantial evidence suggests that Warwick had
become alarmed at the intrigues on her behalf, and that his
immediate response was to block Sir Thomas Arundel's appointment to the council by using Cranmer's considerable influence

at court to secure the appointment of the Bishop of Ely instead. Though Warwick's relations with Cranmer were personally cool,[89] the archbishop assisted the earl in what must have appeared to be a good cause. The rumours of early October that Mary was to be made regent had faded, and although they were not strictly true, they reflected a possibility which could not be ignored once the council had triumphed and the catholics, led by Wriothesley, had settled into place at court.

The author of the 'Notes' accepted the canard about Mary because, to one at Hampton Court on 6 October, the rumour helped to explain what was happening in London. The conspirators did not really need Mary nor did she want to be associated with them, but by November the catholics' apparent victory could not be realised in fact without a political anchor at court. Warwick had Cranmer and would eventually get the King, but without Mary and the Imperial alliance which she would bring the conservatives' position was not politically viable. This was made quite clear when (at a time when Warwick was still a 'catholic') Charles V abruptly refused to grant the new government's request for aid against France in the defence of Boulogne.[90] It has been suggested that the Emperor's decision saved the Reformation in England;[91] it would perhaps be closer to the mark historically to say that it effectively destroyed the possibility that the catholic majority of councillors would be able, upon the conclusion of an Anglo-Imperial alliance, to turn back the clock in religion to 1547. Warwick saw this immediately, but that was not really what mattered to him. Charles' rebuff made it possible to forget Boulogne and get on with unfinished domestic business – the removal, or at least the isolation, of Wriothesley. Warwick was probably more interested in ousting Wriothesley than saving Boulogne anyway;[92] the Emperor had given Warwick greater freedom of movement.

But Warwick could take no chances. By November it could be believed that the conservatives did need Mary; a regency should have provided them with both a stable base and a protective cover. Warwick had no more use for catholicism; he must prepare himself for the unexpected – a catholic thrust from within the council which would attempt, with the aid of new appointees, to transform the conspiracy against Somerset into a movement in favour of Mary. In fact, Dudley's actions both in the weeks following the *coup* and after January 1550 – his sudden abandonment of catholicism; his appointment, in quick succession, of men of reformist sympathies; the attempt to rid the council of all catholics; the increasing harassment of Mary; the careful management of Edward's opinion of Mary; the sharp move to the doctrinal left so as to make Mary an outlaw; the attempt to bar her from the succession – become somewhat more explicable if one looks at them in light of the potential threat which Warwick saw in 1549 in an organised group of catholic privy councillors. If it is to be wondered 'exactly what determined Dudley to throw in his lot with the left-wing reformers, rather than with those who aimed at restoring the position as it was in 1547',[93] the answer may very well be here: the advancement of Mary would have meant the end of Dudley's career, the frustration of his ambition for the power which Somerset had held. Reformed religion, during the first week of November 1549, served Dudley's political purposes primarily because it blocked Mary's ascent to a regent's throne. Though a Marian regency appears now to have been an unlikely development, that was not necessarily clear to Warwick late in October.

To contemporaries, in fact, it appeared that Wriothesley's party had actually seized control of the King and the processes of government. Ponet found Wriothesley 'lodged with his wife and sonne next to the king. Every man', said Ponet, 'repaireth to Wriothesley, honoureth Wriothesley, sueth vnto Wriothesley . . . and all thinges be done by his aduise.' Sir Thomas Arundel, he added, was 'promised to be next to the King', and 'Southwell (for his Whisking and double diligence) must be a great Counsaillour in any wise'.[94] To outward appearances, said van der Delft on 7 November, Wriothesley still possessed great authority; 'he is lodged at court' where 'a great number of lords' were calling on him.[95]

What chance was there that the conservatives might really have captured control of the privy council in the period immediately following the *coup d'état*? On the basis of the analysis already made,[96] at least eleven of twenty-four privy councillors could then have been classified as probable Henrician catholics (or sympathisers) – Wriothesley, Arundel, Shrewsbury, Tunstal, Southwell,

Peckham, Dr Wotton, Gage, Cheyne, Baker, and Bromley.[97] On the other side, eight certainly or probably held reformed views – Cranmer, Warwick, Russell, Paget, Herbert, Sir Edward Wotton, Wingfield, and Sadler. Into a third group fall five who might have gone either way – St John, Rich, Petre, North, and Montagu. In the circumstances, however, it was evident that Paget, who favoured the Imperial alliance, had gone over to the conservatives. At one point in September Paget was even urging van der Delft to try to bring Warwick 'round to a better disposition regarding religion'.[98] It is likely that Paget's persuasiveness had swung his old colleague, Petre, into the conservative camp, and van der Delft could observe that St John and Rich were definitely leaning in the same direction.[99] Excluding Bromley, the resulting alignment should have pitted fourteen nominal conservatives against seven councillors of reformed views, with Montagu and North theoretically in the middle. Moreover, Russell was a possible defector to the catholic side.[100]

This apparent majority of conservative voices at the board concealed an all-important fact, however. Upon the dissolution of the Protectorate (13 October), true executive authority fell not to the privy council but to the thirteen privy councillors who were executors of Henry VIII's will. Assuming that Bromley was taking no part in affairs, and that Paget and St John had actually committed themselves to the conservatives, there arose the possibility of a deadlock, with five on either side (Wriothesley, Dr Wotton, Tunstal, Paget, St John versus Cranmer, Warwick, Russell, Herbert, and Sir Edward Wotton) and two (Montagu and North) at the centre. We do not, of course, know whether this sort of split actually developed among the twelve executors who were active between 13 October and about 6 November 1549, but it does appear that the council officially recognised that the executors really held the key votes. In their letter to the King of 9 October, the London faction had twice referred to the duties attached 'to thoffice of a good executour' in 'the performance of your Majestes father's Will,' that is, 'the care of your Majestie and all your most weighty affayrs'.[101] Moreover, at some time shortly after 12 October, one of the groups supporting Warwick or Wriothesley actually tried to secure letters-patent recognising the original executors as the only privy councillors.[102] The attempt

failed, probably on account of the questionable legality of the
provision which would have allowed the King during his minority
to dismiss any of the executors at his pleasure by his further
letters-patent, a clause which, had it taken effect, would have
legitimised the repudiation of Henry's testament, itself the instrument which the conspirators had resurrected as the authority for
their actions as Edward's councillors. What sort of contest for
possession of the King's body and seals might have followed can
only be imagined. The history of this abortive draft commission
lies interred with the many secrets of those months. We know only
that for several weeks the outcome of the struggle at the board
remained an open question. If anything, contemporaries predicted
a return to catholic usages upon the triumph of Wriothesley's
party.[103] On 7 November, Hooper, although still 'greatly appre-
hensive of a change in religion', noted, however, that 'as yet no
alteration has taken place'.[104]

By early November both factions may have decided that only by
creating new members could they hope to overpower the other side.
The rumours that the catholics would select Sir Thomas Arundel
and the fact that Warwick's faction did secure Goodrich's
appointment appear to mark fresh attempts by both sides to
increase their strength. Even so, the real battle continued to be
waged between the leading personalities, the earls of Warwick
and Southampton (Wriothesley). By the end of November it
appears that the catholics had begun tacitly to recognise the
superior position that Warwick enjoyed, the first sign of which
had been the appointment of Goodrich; by 26 November the
council were coming almost every day to Warwick's London residence where, as van der Delft reported, all business was being
transacted.[105] Wriothesley, however, was not attending these
meetings, as he lay ill. On the twenty-sixth, van der Delft warned
Charles V that Imperial hopes might have to be buried with
Southampton.

If he were to fail us now, I should fear matters might never be
righted, for he is still in good hopes of accomplishing this, and a
good part of the council is now disposed, but would go astray and
follow the rest without him, for there is not a man among them of
sound enough judgement to conduct opposition [to Warwick].[106]

In fact, Warwick also lay ill, but his indisposition did not prevent him from meeting with the council at his house, a convenience which had the effect of both demonstrating and enhancing his authority.[107] And his authority was real: it was probably through the influence of his 'great frendes abowt the king' that he was able, before 17 November, to arrange for the making of a 'public edict proclaimed by royal authority, and printed', which announced the further reformation of matters as 'yet untouched ... according to the tenor of the gospel'.[108] And it was certainly through his influence that Dorset was appointed a councillor by 28 November, a development which perhaps explained the very noticeable atmosphere of 'dissention' which van der Delft described at this time (26–28 November).[109] Paget must have seen the move coming, for by 26 November he had switched sides; it was then noticed that he and Warwick had suddenly become 'great friends' and that they were 'constantly' engaged in private discussions.[110] That some sort of bargain was struck between the two is probably documented by the fact of Paget's creation as first Baron Paget of Beaudesert seven days later. Precisely what Paget may have agreed to do is not clear; it is likely that Warwick ordered him to persuade the Lord Chancellor (Rich), the Great Master (St John), and the Lord Privy Seal (Russell) that their best interests lay with a council headed by Warwick.

If St John in particular received this word by 1 December, it would explain his subsequent actions, for he was now to play the chief part in upsetting the conservatives' last bid to reverse the tide which had been running against them. The issue, ironically, which brought about their fall was the question of the fate of the Duke of Somerset, who lay imprisoned in the Tower. Put quite simply, Wriothesley proposed that Somerset be executed for treason, and Warwick, who might otherwise have supported such a motion, rightly interpreted it to presage his own end as well. The circumstances in which Warwick learned that Wriothesley was plotting his death are described by the anonymous author of the 'Notes'. The background to his narrative concerns the council's investigation of the former Protector's conduct of government. Throughout the early part of December small groups of four and five councillors were going almost every day to the Tower[111] to examine Somerset point by point on a series of articles charging him with the mismanagement of the realm. Chief among the examiners were Wriothesley (now out of his sick-bed), the Earl of Arundel, and Lord St John. The narrator states that 'in this the protectors troble' Wriothesley 'was very busye to followe him to death', because as Protector, Somerset had deprived him of the chancellorship. Now, almost three years later, Wriothesley's 'wit and earnestnes' made him the natural prosecutor of Somerset's alleged treasons. But rather than deny the allegations, Somerset 'answered them all directly that thei were done from article to article by the advise, consente, and counsell of the earle of Warwicke'.[112] (This exaggeration is what Somerset's partisans would have liked to believe, of course; the notion that Warwick was an accomplice to Somerset's actions is also reflected in Guaras' statement that Northumberland had 'upheld and counselled Somerset in all things'.)[113] Whatever Somerset actually said, he succeeded apparently in planting doubts in Wriothesley's mind; perhaps the examiner wished to believe the examined. In any case,

after the examination day my lord Wriothesley, being hote to be rewenged of the both for olde groges paste whan he lost his office,[114] said . . . I thoughte ever we sholde fynde them traytors both; and both is worthie to dye for by my advyse. My lord of Arrundell in lyke manner gave his consente that thei were bothe worthie to dye, and concluded there that the day of execution of the lord protector the earl of Warwicke sholde be sent to the toward [*sic*] and have as he had deserved.[115]

St John, who was also present, did not commit himself one way or the other. That same night, however, he went alone to Warwick's place in Holborn and revealed what had passed at the Tower, warning him to 'beware howe he did prosecute the lord protectors death, for he sholde suffer him selfe for the same'. Having heard this, says the author, Warwick 'bente him selfe all he colde to save the protectors lyfe'.[116]

It will be noticed that this account assumes that before St John's revelation, Warwick (as well as Wriothesley) had decided to 'prosecute' Somerset's death; that Somerset would be executed was in fact widely believed after the *coup*.[117] On the 19 December, six days after Somerset had signed the thirty-one articles of submission, van der Delft reported that Warwick, whom he thought a 'very changeable' person, had begun to show Somerset unusual favour; common rumour had it that Somerset's life would now be spared.[118]

In the meantime, Wriothesley had organised his forces,

and all the hole counsell coming to Holburne place wheare the earle of Warwicke laye sicke for the nouste, my lord Wriothesley begaine to declare how worthie the lord protector was to dye and for how many high treasons. The earle of Warwicke hearing his owne condemnation to approche, with a warlyke wisage and a long fachell[119] by his syde, laye his hand thereof and said: my lord you seeke his bloude and he that seekethe his bloude wold haue myne also.[120]

Warwick's 'great earnestnes', says the writer, brought a sudden silence, and the meeting broke up. We do not know when this confrontation occurred; the narrator says simply that 'presently order was taken' for Somerset's release, and Wriothesley and the Earl of Arundel 'were commanded to kepe their howses'.[121]

We may reasonably doubt that the author of the 'Notes', writing some twelve or more years later, was able to quote both Wriothesley's words in the Tower and Warwick's stout hand-on-the-sword speech delivered abed. Nevertheless, the writer seems clearly to have been close to the events described; it is difficult to imagine, for example, that he invented the meeting at Holborn. If he was not himself present on that occasion, he had certainly got his information from one who was.[122] If true, his story explains the events of January–February 1550. We know that Somerset signed the council's thirty-one articles on 13 December 1549;[123] as the bill for his fine and ransom was not introduced into Parliament until 2 January 1550, the confrontation at Warwick's house probably took place at the end of December or perhaps very close to 13 December. The submission of the bill to Parliament, of course, marked the government's decision not to seek Somerset's attainder. Warwick, in delaying his reaction to St John's report of the conversation in the Tower, appears to have gathered his political strength until, at the opportune moment, he was able to strike down Wriothesley and Arundel with the support of a majority of the council. Wriothesley, after all, had made no overt move; there was only St John's word that the catholic earls were seeking Warwick's death. St John had decided to side with Warwick by 2 January; for his efforts he was created

Earl of Wiltshire on 19 January. And with him came Lord
Russell who was made Earl of Bedford on the same day. (Wriothesley charged that St John and Russell had defected out of
envy and ambition.)[124] For Wriothesley, the game was up on 14
January, the day that Parliament ratified Somerset's submission.
Rumour had it that the former Protector would be released in
order to strengthen Warwick's faction against Wriothesley and
Arundel.[125] At any rate, by the fourteenth Warwick had secured
a council order (or perhaps a royal letter) commanding Arundel
and Southampton to vacate their lodgings at court and confine
themselves to their London houses. Wriothesley learned of the
order in advance and left the court in the night. In the meantime,
Rich had also joined Warwick; Sir Thomas Darcy, one of those
who had been appointed to attend upon the King and who was
clearly one of Warwick's 'great frendes' at court, became a privy
councillor on or about 16 January, and on the nineteenth was
made Vice-Chamberlain and Captain of the guard. Warwick
further strengthened his hand at the board by securing the
appointment of Walter Lord Ferrers on the twenty-sixth. (Ferrers
had been in attendance since the sixteenth.) On 30 January,
'by order of the Bord', Sir Thomas Arundel was committed to
the Tower,[126] and Parliament, which had enacted a bill declaring
it treason to conspire the death of a privy councillor, was pro-
rogued on 1 February. On 2 February Warwick assumed the
powers of the office of Lord President, and on the same day the
order went out by which Wriothesley and the Earl of Arundel
were formally 'banished from the Counsell'.[127] Ponet, who
preached at court on 14 March 1550,[128] thought that Wriothesley
feared a 'narowe examination' which could only 'come to some
open shamfull ende', and so 'either poisoned himself' or died of
grief.[129] The author of the 'Notes' confirmed that Southampton
died a broken man. By his own confession to St John he had un-
masked himself,

and so my lord Wriothesley seing all his harte was opened against
him that once before he had submitted him self to and thoughte
now this acte colde never be forgotten and that his ambisions mynde
colde take no place; he killed him self with sorrowe in so much as he
said he wolde not live in such misery if he might.[130]

If the Earl of Arundel had earlier agreed with Wriothesley that

Warwick was 'worthie to dye', we should understand King Edward's famous but heretofore cryptic statement that Arundel had been confined to his house 'for certain crimes of suspicion'.[131] Van der Delft reported that St John, Rich and Russell not only deserted Wriothesley and Arundel in January, but also turned specifically against Arundel; they had done so, he said, 'upon seeing Warwick's determination'.[132] We can suppose that Warwick had determined that he would crush his opponents soon after St John's unexpected visit following the conversation in the Tower. Paget's actions at this time are also more easily explained in light of St John's warning. Van der Delft said that Paget assisted in the moves against Arundel as revenge for Arundel's opposition when Paget lay under suspicion in October for having been too close to the Protector.[133] Armed with St John's testimony, Paget should have found Arundel a welcome target in January. Finally, Ponet's remark that under examination in the Fleet, Southwell 'confessed ynough to be hanged for',[134] now makes sense; doubtless Southwell had earlier agreed with Wriothesley's assessment of Warwick.

On 2 February, then, Warwick stood supreme in the council.[135] The Earl of Wiltshire (St John) had revealed what appeared to be a conservative plot to eliminate both Somerset and Warwick. Warwick countered by saving Somerset's life and thus forcing Wriothesley's hand. When Wriothesley did not strike, Warwick, now with a majority of the executors and council behind him, dismissed all of those who could be identified with the alleged conspiracy. In this Warwick was supported in particular by four new privy councillors of reformed views whose advancements he had secured with the help of the men whom Cranmer had placed about the King. As early as November Warwick had initiated a campaign which would eventually make it impossible for the conservatives to exist politically at court; he had begun to define them out of existence with an ever more radical official religion. The catholic threat against his life in December 1549 may well have convinced him that his political future lay in a realm from which even Mary should one day find herself barred.

8
Conclusion

Throughout the reign of Edward VI we may describe the King's council as the privy council, an established institution composed of a number of identifiable individuals, their high calling defined by the peculiar oath which they swore. Until 12 March 1547 Edward VI's council consisted of the sixteen executors of Henry VIII's last will and one other non-executor; after that time and before 13 October 1549, the King's council consisted of an average of twenty-one members selected personally by the Duke of Somerset, the King's uncle, who, by the terms of the letters-patent authorising him to make these appointments, was constituted Protector of the realm and Governor of the royal person. It is probable that the Protector's ability to choose the King's councillors was written into his commission as a result of the need to expand the council of executors, and also to stifle the actual and potential opposition which Somerset (as Earl of Hertford) faced early in 1547. Hertford had added his brother to the council by February 1547; this move (an act of political compromise in response to Seymour's demand for the governorship of the King) may have required that he admit other royal servants possessing better qualifications than Seymour's. Wriothesley's opposition to Hertford's elevation appears also to have determined that the Protector's patents would confirm none of the executors in their offices as Edward's privy councillors; the threat of exclusion may well have secured a council which initially supported the Protector for the good reason that its members were appointed by his favour.

Although Somerset's appointments violated a dead sovereign's will, the new King's commission nevertheless allowed him to revive the form of the Henrician privy council. Represented at the new board were the great offices of state and household evident in the recent past. Restoring the traditional offices, however, produced a group of office-holders initially divided on one

259

of the great questions of the age – religious reform. Somerset the reformer is usually pictured guiding a like-minded council forward towards the realisation of 'true religion' in England, but this impression fails to recognise that almost one-third (eight) of all who served before the *coup* did not share his progressive views and that four others, including St John and Petre, although they certainly followed his lead, cannot be said to have done so because they were either zealous or genuinely convinced of the need for more radical reform. Even Paget, whose voice was at first counted on Somerset's side, stood closer to the centre than the left, and not primarily for religious reasons, since for him what mattered were the social consequences of a policy. (It was *before* the outbreak of the Western rebellion that he reminded Somerset of the political merits of Henrician catholicism.) In practice, however, this apparent division of sympathies did not put a brake on the pace of reform. Acquiescence earned for every new appointee the perquisites of high office; constitutionally, the Protector could in any case dismiss or ignore dissidents at will.

The council's records bear witness to Somerset's personal style of government. The diplomatic of the council book for the period of the Protectorate reveals that the *Acts of the Privy Council* is not necessarily a record of business transacted in council meetings; it is not a true record of even the occasions of meetings. The register reflects, rather, Somerset's virtual abandonment of the council and his informal dispatch of the King's business in his own household. Paget's unwitting, private testimony suggests that Somerset assumed responsibility for the making of policy in the wake of victory at Pinkie; that he looked to the council for very little advice after January 1548; that in spite of the formality of meetings in 1549 – meetings called in response to Lord Seymour's arrest and the twin crises of war and domestic unrest– he rejected what advice was then offered. Doubtless the Protector understood himself to be able to act without the council; nevertheless, it seems that his colleagues did not expect him to abandon meetings altogether, and when he resumed calling meetings, they wished to do more than merely ratify his already formed decisions.

Somerset's control of the administrative process by which he produced pre-stamped, partially blank signet warrants allowed him to enjoy a constitutional state of being which the council refused to tolerate; effectively Somerset was King: he could order action under the King's signature at his own convenience. Even so, the Protector wished to preserve both a semblance of corporate action as well as a record of the council's complicity in his exercise of the royal prerogative: most of the proclamations made before October 1549 give evidence of collective authorisation; most carry the council's stated consent. In practice, however, the policies proclaimed almost certainly originated with Somerset (a probability which Paget's letters also tend to support). Under an adult King, the council would have performed an advisory function; during Edward's minority, much policy should have originated in council. In fact, the council under Somerset appears to have forfeited both an advisory and a policy-making role.

That the Duke of Somerset alone framed royal policy is not the real issue, however; why his government failed is what matters historically. Certainly his policies weakened his position, and none more so than the Scottish venture, since that one broke him financially, but conceivably he might have averted financial disaster as late as November 1548 had he thrown off the Northern yoke, abandoned Boulogne, and reordered the administration of finance. These things Northumberland finally did, and not merely because Somerset's failure to do so in 1548–9 had made such action necessary by 1550, but because, as so many of Paget's memoranda make clear, neither the cost of waging war against France nor the more calculable charges of peace-time could be carried by the Protector's administrative methods. By mid-summer 1549, Somerset reigned but did not really rule: he held authority but had lost the power to govern because he could no longer finance policies which he had earlier set in motion.

That Somerset's failure was essentially administrative is also explained by his inability to manage the King's men. A sometimes imperious, abrasive, and brittle grandee, he undeniably sparked envy and hurt in those around him; others he maddened with his 'leniency' and lack of resolve. If his arrogance irritated the lords in council, his high-minded sympathies at times ran counter to their sense of the politically necessary. Certainly his refusal to heed their advice touched their pride. Ignoring the expertise at the board, he occasionally looked for assistance to an historically anonymous 'new council' of confidants. Though unwise politically, such tactics need not have doomed his management of affairs, but, as Paget averred, Somerset listened to no man's advice: the duke could not trust men of ability to provide him with the sort of information which the performance of his office required and under pressure – the prospect of financial collapse, the commons' revolt, and so on – he either refused to act when action was imperative or refused in time to delegate power and responsibility to those capable of acting. By temperament he was extremely sensitive to criticism; stubbornness prevented him from abandoning positions inconsistent with the demands of office. If these were traits allowable in some, they became intolerable flaws in the minister possessing a king's authority.

The *coup d'état* which abolished the Protectorate theoretically re-established rule by Henry VIII's executors, and they interpreted their powers as enabling them to appoint new privy councillors. (Many of Somerset's appointees simply stayed on.) But Northumberland (then Earl of Warwick), with the assistance of a group of courtiers whose attendance upon the King had been arranged by the Archbishop of Canterbury, was able in November 1549 not only to begin adding his own adherents, but also, by February 1550, to dismiss those members who opposed him. He was motivated in part by an earlier fear (October 1549) that his attempts to advance his own political position would be blocked by a Marian regency, a possibility which he was not able to ignore when he found the conservatives well entrenched at court and in council after the *coup*. This and an alleged conservative plot against his life in December 1549 determined that he would back the left-wing reformers in religion – and do so with such a doctrinal vengeance that he would be able eventually to make political outlaws of his catholic opponents.

Northumberland's packing produced a larger council by 1553, but not the unwieldy body of forty which many have assumed; in fact, the council then numbered thirty-one, although the effects of Northumberland's control reduced this to about twenty-one truly active members among whom fourteen – those who regularly attended about half or more of all meetings – consistently administered affairs at London. Northumberland dominated the members of this inner ring and so controlled, through them, the

King, the King's household, and the departments of state. Cecil, after Northumberland perhaps the most important figure in this circle, ordered the council's work, translating the duke's will into action at the board. Sir John Gates, the King's Vice-Chamberlain and Northumberland's man in the privy chamber, controlled the flow of information to and from Edward VI and so was able to forward to Cecil council business which carried the King's consent if not occasionally the look of having been proposed by the boy himself. Thomas Lord Darcy, the King's Chamberlain, also spoke with Northumberland's voice to the great peers at the council table; he was another of Dudley's appointees – nine of the fourteen were –and the one most often in attendance at meetings. By rank the most prominent of the fourteen included the Bishop of Ely (Chancellor), the Marquess of Winchester (Treasurer), the Earl of Bedford (Privy Seal), the Marquess of Northampton (Great Chamberlain), Lord Clinton (High Admiral), and Lord Cobham. Of lesser rank but of nearly equal importance in the execution of business were Petre, the senior secretary, Sir John Mason, fluent in French and diplomatic suggestions, and Sir Richard Cotton and Sir John Bowes, men of military and financial affairs.

The fact of usually extensive administrative experience marked the career of nearly every privy councillor before his rise to high office. The significance of the council's composition also lies in the relatively changed nature of the membership after 1549. Thus, whereas two-thirds of Henry VIII's executors and one-half of Somerset's appointees were educated at university, only about two-fifths can be so designated after the *coup*. Among those who first took office under Northumberland the figure is slightly more than one-quarter. There is no evidence that Northumberland specifically sought to exclude university graduates; rather it was his policy to surround himself with aristocratic courtier-soldiers, men such as Dorset, Hereford, Clinton, Cobham, Huntingdon, and Westmorland. Northumberland himself was more the field commander than the court politician or government official; he was essentially security-conscious; his requirements were military; the council under him became substantially martial in character, more so than at any time since 1540. When office or duties required someone with a specialised training, Northumberland turned to him; Goodrich, Mason, Cecil, and Cheke are the obvious examples.

The year 1552 did not witness the inauguration of an alleged 'plan' to reform the council and its work; neither that (non-existent) council of forty nor the actual council of thirty-one was reorganised into the system of committees which historians have thought the King spelled out in his exercises of March 1552. Only a so-called 'council for the state' was created at that time – the other groups were technically unexceptional royal commissions which included non-privy councillors – but the attempt to describe its function leads one to the conclusion that it represented a purely nominal body which simply excluded none of the great officers of state and household, its membership mirroring rather more perfectly Northumberland's political associations than Edward VI's administrative acumen. Privy councillors may have informed Edward VI of their decisions at sessions of the committee 'for the state', those curious and otherwise unrecorded 'meetings' referred to by contemporaries, but there is no hard evidence that the King ordered or concluded business at any sort of meeting. The agendas in Edward's hand prove only that he had copied out his secretaries' notes of business to be concluded in council: well before a rule required them to do so, Cecil and Petre were in the habit of showing such schedules to an obviously precocious lad. The King's state papers thus provide no evidence that the boy really initiated policy, only that he was following its course in council: his agendas document one of his pedantic interests, not his control of affairs. Whether Edward VI understood state business or not is irrelevant. It was in Northumberland's interest to keep the King abreast of his council's activities – hence the importance of the staged sessions of the 'council for the state' – and to convince him that he was being consulted and perhaps even listened to. As for the suggestion that the King occasionally appeared in council proposing business of his own devising: the speeches were real, but we know now that either Gates or Sir Henry Sidney prepared him in advance of such performances, priming him with matters of Northumberland's (or the council's) choosing, leaving it to the duke, in private encounters with the boy, to persuade him that he really was a party to the making of policy. Clever he certainly was, genius of sorts

he may have been, but in his fourteenth year King Edward VI
stood far from the threshold of real power in England. No
organiser of business or governor of men, this bright, pathetic lad
was in fact the manipulated one, more the parrot of Northumberland's plans than the Renaissance prodigy of legend.

It has been thought that the King's and Petre's 'Articles' of
1553 completed the scheme to reorganise the council's work. In
fact, only one of the rules was new in 1553; the others essentially
recognised earlier practice. The true reorganisation of procedure
had occurred in February and March 1550 upon Warwick's
accession to the office of President of the council, and with the
appearance of Paget's 'Advise' for the conduct and administration of privy council business. The President's powers were real
and Warwick exploited them to the full; he called meetings,
presided at meetings, and supervised the secretaries' formulation
of agendas. Paget's rules – the first of their kind – were devised
partly in response to the collapse of rule by council under
Somerset, and partly for the conditions of a royal minority. By
establishing the order for meetings, the dispatch of suits, and the
secretaries' administration of correspondence, the procedures stand
as evidence of the fact that in 1550 the Tudor privy council was
first made subject to a fixed administrative routine.

Nowhere is this more apparent than in the extant council
records: upon the resumption of rule by council it is evident that
the composition and keeping of council documents, as well as the
secretaries' management of such work, was placed upon a rational
basis. Edward's reign marks the appearance of three clerks of the
privy council; in 1550 one of these was assigned the sole responsibility of keeping the book of the council's determinations. The
clerks composed registers of in- and out-letters which for a time
at least the council signed; the clerks also preserved single rough-
and fair-copy minutes of out-correspondence, and these a few
councillors also occasionally signed. Procedures for the clerks'
duplication, dispatch, and filing of the council's papers were at
the same time made systematic, testifying to the relative administrative sophistication of an essentially bureaucratic board.

Functionally, the council after 1549 assumed those powers
which Henry VIII's last will had assigned to the old King's
executors: privy councillors once again formulated state policy,

enforced policy, and exercised a traditional, quasi-judicial competence. In governing the realm, Northumberland's adherents employed to the full their executive and administrative capabilities, but on one occasion, by finding a respondent 'faultie' and imprisoning him, they may have exceeded their usually limited authority to arbitrate disputes between party and party. Similarly, the privy council customarily employed torture only against those (lesser folk) suspected of treason, but councillors may also selectively have put to 'the tortures' a few others whose allegedly great crimes (murder and robbery) attracted the board's attention. The possibly exceptional nature of the council's quasi-judicial activity in Edward's reign is of less significance, however, than the fact of the council's very broad competence as compared with the authority of royal councils generally in the sixteenth century. Among the great princes of Europe, the Valois kings of France called to court councils most closely resembling the Tudor institution, but at no time did any of the indifferently named French bodies – the *conseil du roi, conseil des affaires, conseil d'état, conseil secret, conseil privé, conseil étroit* – exhibit the powers or discharge the responsibilities of the English privy council.[1] Indeed, no European monarch appointed councillors possessed of so comprehensive an ability to act as did the Tudors, and of course Edward VI's privy council is unique in the history of the Tudor council, inasmuch as Edwardian councillors, especially under Northumberland, effectively exercised the full powers of kingship.

The period of Northumberland's rule thus counters the notion that government by council collapsed under the strain of warring court factions. In fact, it was the duke's very deliberate aim, in consequence of his rise to the presidency, to restore the council's recognised competence. The council as an executive and administrative board was not always the responsive organ that he demanded, but it was his achievement to re-establish the privy council as the King's chief instrument of government, the institution born of Cromwell's 'revolutionary' programme of the 1530s. Of course Northumberland was no Cromwell, but like Henry's minister, he understood the requirements of the successful governor. The lesson of Somerset's *débâcle* was that the future lay with a council possessed of full authority, but a council that could be controlled and managed. Avoiding the political liability

of a Protector's discredited title, Northumberland laboured instead
to revive the executive and administrative powers of the Lord
President. Politically, of course, he sought to make the council his
own – by 1553 almost one-half of the members were his appointees; another one-third he had rendered effectively inactive; the
rest he rewarded for their support. Disdaining routine (and frequently ill), he used his position to delegate to privy councillors
more able than he the specialised tasks of government. He demon-
strated how the council could be so organised and managed that
even when frequently absent he could depend upon it to execute
his will. For him to be able to do so it was necessary that the
council adhere to well-defined procedures. That Northumberland
bent administrative procedure to his own purposes there is no
doubt; administratively, the Tudor privy council was already a
mature body by 1553.

Northumberland's achievement has been obscured by his
treasonous last act, and while the scheme to alter the succession
cannot be defended – he and Gates persuaded the King to accept
the plan – his political irresponsibility in the face of Edward's
death does not alter the significance of his attempt to set right the
council's administration of the realm. Northumberland's reputation has also been blackened because of the way he handled
Somerset in 1551–2, but the truth of the matter is that he had
only recently discovered Somerset's true aim – to recover supreme
power at Dudley's expense – and so was left with no alternative
except to destroy him in the politically acceptable manner of the
age – a rigged state trial. By this manoeuvre Northumberland
avoided almost certain anarchy at the top, and so was able to
push forward the council's vital reordering of royal finance.
Somerset may have been more revered by the masses of Englishmen, but one *coup* had already decided that there would be no
return to the Protector's style of government.

The dukes of Somerset and Northumberland both paid the
final price for miscalculation and blunder, but while they were in
power their use of the King's council, their methods of employing
the King's councillors, thus describe two periods of remarkably
contrasting change. On the one hand Somerset's administration
marked the return of something rather like medieval practice –
government by a *de facto* king (the Protector) who called together

only so many councillors as he thought it convenient to consult occasionally, even though these councillors were by this time members of a permanent institution; Northumberland, on the other hand, exercised very much the same power as the Lord President of an organised, continuously working board staffed by his supporters or appointees. Somerset's near-abandonment of the institution brought the King's government close to ruin; that it did not collapse was due chiefly to Northumberland's restoration and unprecedented definition of rule by council.

Appendix 1
Privy councillors in the reign of Edward VI

(Titles given are those held during the reign. Sources for dates: G.E.C., H.P.T., *D.N.B.*)

Baker, Sir John (*c.* 1488/9–1558)
Bowes, Sir Robert (1495?–1554)
Bromley, Sir Thomas (d. 1555?)
Brooke, George (1497–1558), Lord Cobham
Browne, Sir Anthony (d. 1548)
Cecil, Sir William (1520–98)
Cheke, Sir John (1514–57)
Cheyne, Sir Thomas (1487–1558)
Clinton, Edward Fiennes de (1512–85), Lord Clinton and Say
Cotton, Sir Richard (1490–1556)
Cranmer, Thomas (1489–1556), Archbishop of Canterbury
Darcy, Sir Thomas (1506–58), Lord Darcy of Chiche (5 April 1551)
Denny, Sir Anthony (1501–49)
Devereux, Walter (1490–1558), Lord Ferrers, Viscount Hereford (2 February 1550)
Dudley, John (1504–53), Viscount Lisle, Earl of Warwick (16 February 1547), Duke of Northumberland (11 October 1551)
Fitz Alan, Henry (1512–80), Earl of Arundel
Gage, Sir John (1479–1556)
Gates, Sir John (1504?–1553)
Goodrich (*also* Goodricke), Thomas (d. 1554), Bishop of Ely
Grey, Henry (1517–54), Marquess of Dorset, Duke of Suffolk (11 October 1551)
Hastings, Francis (1514?–1561), Earl of Huntingdon
Herbert, Sir William (1506?–1570), Lord Herbert of Cardiff (10 October 1551), Earl of Pembroke (11 October 1551)
Hoby, Sir Philip (1505–58)
Mason, Sir John (1503–66)
Montagu, Sir Edward (1487?–1557)
Neville, Henry (1525–64), Earl of Westmorland
North, Sir Edward (1496?–1564)
Paget, Sir William (1506–63), Lord Paget of Beaudesert (3 December 1549)

Parr, William (1513–71), Earl of Essex, Marquess of Northampton (16 February 1547)

Paulet, William (1483?–1572), Lord St John of Basing, Earl of Wiltshire (19 January 1550), Marquess of Winchester (11 October 1551)

Peckham, Sir Edmund (1495–1564)

Petre, Sir William (1506?–1572)

Rich, Sir Richard (1496?–1567), Lord Rich (16 February 1547)

Russell, John (1485?–1555), Lord Russell, Earl of Bedford (19 January 1550)

Sadler, Sir Ralph (1507–87)

Seymour, Edward (1500–52), Earl of Hertford, Duke of Somerset (16 February 1547)

Seymour, Sir Thomas (1508?–1549), Lord Seymour of Sudeley (16 February 1547)

Smith, Sir Thomas (1513–77)

Southwell, Sir Richard (1504?–1564)

Stanley, Edward (1509–72), Earl of Derby

Talbot, Francis (1500–60), Earl of Shrewsbury

Tunstal, Cuthbert (1474–1559), Bishop of Durham

Wentworth, Thomas (1501–51), Lord Wentworth

Wingfield, Sir Anthony (1485–1552)

Wotton, Sir Edward (1489–1551)

Wotton, Dr Nicholas (1497?–1567)

Wriothesley, Thomas (1505–50), Lord Wriothesley, Earl of Southampton (16 February 1547)

Appendix 2
Clerks of the privy council

At the outset of the reign there were two official clerks, William Honyngs (also Honnynges, Honnyng, Hunnyng), who was serving at £20 yearly, and Thomas Chaloner, at £10. During the summer of 1547, Armagil Waad began serving without fee as the third clerk of the privy council. On 17 April 1548 the council fixed their salaries at £50, £40, and 50 marks, respectively. In letters-patent of 5 and 10 May 1548 the King granted to each of the three men the office of clerk of the privy council for life at the yearly salaries mentioned, payable from midsummer 1547.[1]

An entry of 3 January 1548 makes reference to 'Thomas Smyth' as a 'Clerc of the Counsail'.[2] Mrs Dewar says that 'he was made clerk of the Privy Council' in March 1547.[3] There is no official evidence of Smith's appointment then; as one of Somerset's servants he may have performed some of the duties of the office before Waad began serving without pay at midsummer 1547. The reference of January 1548 is curious; Smith was not an official clerk of the privy council, but whoever was composing the register at that time clearly thought of him as one. As the diplomatic of the register for this period reflects the informality of Somerset's personal government, the reference appears to document Smith's brief career (to 17 April 1548) as an unpaid fourth clerk and thus perhaps one of the Protector's agents on the council's staff.

On or before 1 February 1550 the council committed Honyngs to prison on a charge of stealing certain of the council's papers relating (apparently) to the Bishop of Winchester's case; on 20 April 1550 the Bishop of Ely and Dr Wotton examined him 'that he might be dispatched', but on 28 June the council released him under a recognizance of £200.[4] In the meantime, William Thomas was sworn on 19 April 1550 as the third clerk, Chaloner and Waad advancing to the first and second positions. After 7 April 1551 Chaloner's duties as a commissioner in Scotland precluded his attendance at the board; consequently, the council advanced Waad and Thomas to the first and second clerkships, respectively, and on 24 September 1551 made Bernard Hampton the third clerk.[5] On 12 May 1552 Waad, Thomas, and Hampton each received the King's letters-patent granting them

during the King's pleasure the offices of clerks of the privy council at
£50, £40, and 50 marks, respectively, payable from Michaelmas
1551.[6] Waad and Hampton appear to have held these positions at
the salaries quoted until Edward VI's death (6 July 1553). Thomas
was certainly a clerk as late as 8 October 1552, but on 31 March
1553 he is referred to as 'late clerk' of the privy council.[7] It is not
known whether he resigned his office or was dismissed from it. There
is no evidence that the council filled the resulting vacancy.

Appendix 3
William Lord Paget's
'Advise to the Kinges Counsail'

EGERTON MS. 2603, FOLIOS 33–4

Folio 33a

In the name of god the father the soone, and the holly goost.

Furst, the counsaille to love one another as brethren or deere freendes and one to honor another in theyre degrees whereby will cum to passe that [h *crossed out*] others shall honor them and haue them in great estymacion.

Item: that none of them be contented to here ill spoken of an other and if he do heare any ill, thenne to bring the mattier and reaporter to the counsaill boorde to be harde to the reproche and punishment of the reporter, if his reaporte be fownde woorthie.

Item: that six at the least of the prevey counsaill be [co *crossed out*] contynually attendant in the courte whereof the lorde Chauncelor or lorde Treasorer or lorde great Master or lorde prevey seale or lorde great chambrelayn or lorde Chambrelayn to be two, and one of the Secretaries to be a thirde, and that the sixe in thabsence of the rest maye passe thaffaires occurrent and shall haue theyre procedinges ratefyed by the rest whenne theye cum.

Item: that the counsaill attendant in the courte shall assemble them selfes three dayes in the weeke at the leest for the Kinges affaires, viz. Tewesdaye, Thursdaye, and Satordaye and oftener if the Kinges affaires so require, and shall mete in the counsaill chambre in the morning at viij of the clocke, and sitt till dyner, and aftre noone [till *crossed out*] at two of the clocke, and sitt till foure, and for private sutes theye shall assemble vpon the Sonndaye aftre dyner at two of the clocke, and sitt till foure.

Item: that all lettres shalbe receaved by the Secretarie and brought to the counsaill boorde at the howers of meting onlesse he shall se theye require a very hasty expedicion, in which case he shall reasorte to the highest of the counsaill thenne attendant and he the saide highest, if he shall thinke so nedefull, to assemble the counsaill at what tyme so ever it shallbe.

Folio 33b

Item: that euery man do speake in convenable maner his opinion and conscience frankly in mattiers opened at the counsaill boorde without reproufe, checke, or displeasir for the same of any parson.

Item: that all billes of supplicacion to the Kinges Majeste or the counsaill shalbe delyvered to the Master of the requestes and he to delyver to the lorde presydent all suche that conteign mattier that can not be determyned butt by the King or his prevey counsaill, and the lorde presydent to exhibite them to the counsaill vpon the sonndaye to be ordred as shall appteign, and the partie to receave his answere at the lorde presydentes handes or suche other ministre as the Lorde presydent will appointe on his behaulf.

[*with the following added between the last line above and the next line below in the same but very much compressed hand*]:

saving that all billes of sutes shalbe delyvered to the hed officer of the suter and billes of complaint remitted to the law or courtes of conscience as the case shall requyre.

Item: all offices and benefices of the Kinges gifte to be preferred to the King to be disposed by the more voyces of the counsaill present vpon the Sonndaye at the counsaill boorde, the more voyces to be tryed by two balles, a white and a blacke, to be putt by euery of the counsaill in two seuerall pottes, vpon the one of which pottes the suters name shall be sett, and the counsailor to putt one balle at his pleasour into that pott, and thother ball into thother pott, the sute to take place if theyre shalbe putt more white thenne blacke balles in to the pott with his name. Butt if two sewe for one thinge, thenne either pott to haue a name, and the most white to obteign. If theye be founde equall white balles in either pott, thenne the lorde presydent to preferre the sute and so likewise if more thenne two do sewe for one thing.

Item: that no sute of any the Kinges siruauntes be preferred for them of the prevey chambre butt by one of the six lordes having charge of the Kinges parson, and by the lorde Chambrelayn or vicechambrelayn for them of the outwoorde chambres, closett, and chapell; by the lorde great Master, Treasorer, or Comptroller for them of the householde; By the capitayn for the pensyoners; by the Master of thorses for them of the stable; By the Lorde presydent for the rest.

Folio 34a

Item: that the Clearke having charge of the counsaill booke shall dayle entre all ordres and determynacions by the counsaill, all warrantes for money, the substance of all lettres requiring answere; and the next daye following, at the furst meting, presenting the same by the Secretary (who shall furst consydre wether the entrey be made accordingly) to the boorde, the counsaill shall the furst thing theye do signe the booke of entrees, leaving space for the counsailors absent to entre theyre names whenne theye cum; and the clerke which kepeth the booke shall attende thereunto only, and be burthened with no other charge.

Item: the Secretarie shall see to the keping of all lettres, minutes of lettres to and from the King or the counsaill, Instruccions, and suche other writinges as shalbe treated vpon by the counsaill.

Item: that none of the Kinges prevey counsaill shall in no wise speake or write for his freende in any mattier of iustice betwene party and party, nor in any other mattier aboue one tyme, for that the request of a counsailor is in a maner a commaundement.

[Endorsed]   The remebraunce gyven to my Master by my Lorde
               Paget xxiij Martij 1549
[Addressed] Advise to the Kinges Counsail [in *crossed out*] the xxiijth
               of Marche [155 *crossed out*] 1549

Notes

1 Rymer, *Foedera*, XV, 114.
2 Elton, *Tudor Constitution*, 101.
3 *Ibid.* with reference generally to the whole Tudor period.
4 *Life and Raigne of King Henry the Eighth*, 3.
5 Elton, *Tudor Revolution*, 319; for doubts about this view, see Wernham, *E.H.R.* LXXI (1956), 94.
6 *The Privy Council*, 81.
7 Keir, *Constitutional History of Modern Britain*, 112.
8 Elton, *Journal of British Studies* IV (1965), 23. For the later years, Pulman's *The Elizabethan Privy Council in the Fifteen-seventies* has closed part of the gap.
9 See especially Jordan, *Edward VI: the Threshold of Power*, 452–3, n.6 (where other concurring authorities are cited) and the discussion of this problem above, pp. 38–9 and 132–3.

CHAPTER I : SOURCES

1 This classification is suggested directly by Professor Elton's comments; *Annali della Fondazione italiana per la storia amministrativa*, I (1964), 285.
2 The papers for this period are calendared in H.M.C., *Manuscripts of the Marquess of Salisbury*, vols. I, XIII. Many of these are printed in Haynes, *A Collection of State Papers*.
3 These are calendared in H.M.C., *Manuscripts of the Marquess of Bath*, vol. IV.
4 Transcriptions of some of these are given in the appendix of Sturge, 'The Life and Times of John Dudley'. Numerous single letters of other privy councillors are also on file in the collections of the record offices and repositories listed in the bibliography; references to these and other papers are often found in the various *Reports* of the Historical Manuscripts Commission.
5 B.M., Egerton MS. 2603, fo. 34b, for example; see Appendix 3 and the discussion below, pp. 93–4.
6 *Op. cit.* ed. L. Alston (Cambridge, 1906), 58–9.
7 Elton, *Annali della Fondazione*, I (1964), 286.
8 B.M., Add. MS. 34324, fos. 238–9, dated 31 October 1625.
9 B.M., Add. MS. 48151 (Yelverton MS. 162), printed in Read, *Mr Secretary Walsingham*, I, 423–43.

10 B.M., Add. MS. 48150 (Yelverton MS. 161), now a collection of large unbound unnumbered paper 4to plus 10 other folios which are sewn together. At one time the whole was stitched together as a book with a covering piece of soft vellum and endorsed on the outside cover '1572 Robrt Bele'. The MS. contains the exact forms to be observed in addressing and composing all kinds of council letters, warrants, recognizances, etc.

11 B.M., Harleian MS. 352.

12 PC 2/8, an original register for the period 1 January 1558 to 12 May 1559.

13 The last 3 of 39 unnumbered folios inserted at the end of the first volume (as part of a modern index) bear the water-mark 'J. W. Hatman 1832'.

14 One of King Edward's own travelling coffers may be seen today in the Victoria and Albert Museum. Council's coffers probably were similar, only less ornate. In July 1547 Sir William Cavendish, Treasurer of the chamber, paid 40 shillings to one William Grevie 'for twoo Coffers by him made and delyvered to the Clerkes of the Counsaille'; E 101/426/5, fo. 31.

15 B.M., Stowe MS. 492 is an eighteenth-century copy of PC 2/2 in the P.R.O. Attached (fos. 1–2) is a letter addressed sometime in 1750 by one Charles Gray 'Dear Sir', mentioning the discovery by William Guthrie (1708–70), author of a *History of England* (4 vols., 1744–51).

16 PC 2/2, 2/3, and 2/4, respectively.

17 Cf. *A.P.C.*, III, 143, 3; II, 11; B.M., Egerton MS. 2603, fo. 34a, for typical examples of contemporary styles. Only the third register bears any formal contemporary identification. On the title page is written: 'A Register of King Edward the si [*damaged*] for thiese yeres folowinge: viz. 1550. 1551. 1552. 1553' and under this 'Ar Waad', or Armagil Waad, the senior clerk of the council into whose care the book fell.

18 *Span. Cal.*, XI, 57. The heading on the last folio of the third register reads: 'At Grenewich the xvijth of June 1553', but the rest of the page is blank. Thus ends the official record of the proceedings of Edward's privy council. The matter in question was, of course, the alteration of the succession in favour of Lady Jane Grey.

19 *A.P.C.*, III, 3.

20 PC 2/1, 1–2.

21 For the clerks' tenures, see Appendix 2.

22 *A.P.C.*, III, 4.

23 B.M., Egerton MS. 2603, fo. 34a; cf. Appendix 3.

24 In February 1547 the record refers to the 'Clerkes of the Privey Counseill, *or any one of them* . . .' [italics the author's], *A.P.C.*, II, 11. Cf. *Cal. Pat. Rolls, Edw. VI*, II, 2–4. Of course, one sometimes finds the three clerks called simply 'Clercs of the Counsaile', but this is merely an unintentionally less precise official reference of 17 April 1548: *A.P.C.*, II, 183.

25 *E.H.R.* XXXVII (1922), 345ff.

26 *Ibid.*; Elton, *Tudor Revolution*, 334.

27 Cf. *Cal. Pat. Rolls, Edw. VI* II, 2–4; IV; 285–6; *A.P.C.*, II, 183.

28 *A.P.C.*, IV, 82–3.

29 *Ibid.* II, 354; III, 107; IV, 138.

30 B.M., Add. MS. 34324, fo. 239a.

31 The appearance of notes, texts, and abstracts of council out-letters in the first volume (the register of Somerset's administration to 4 October 1549) is rare.

32 Many of the folios of the first volume (PC 2/2) also bear conical fold lines, i.e. fold lines radiating in from the corners. Changes in temperature and humidity probably caused them to curl (many of these folios were originally loose sheets). If during storage the sheets were then pressed flat under stacks of other papers and/or books – PC 2/2 is the volume which the London cheesemonger had retained for waste paper – we should probably be able to explain the curious fold lines which they now display.

33 *E.H.R.* XXXVIII (1923), 416, n.2.

34 B.M., Egerton MS. 2603, fo. 34a; see Appendix 3.

35 Meetings of 8, 10, 13 June and 8, 10, 11, 13, 15, and 19 July 1550; *A.P.C.*, III, 42–4, 46–9, 64–88.

36 Thus, for the meetings of 8, 10, 11, and 12 July 1550 at Westminster; PC 2/4, 64–77.

37 PC 2/3.

38 Where the strokes of the heading and the attendance list overlap, the ink of the heading appears to lie *over* the ink of the list. If so, the clerk did in fact record the attendances first and added the heading, etc., later. A magnifying glass and strong, ordinary light enable one neither to confirm nor reject this observation (ultra-violet light obscures rather than clarifies the edges of overlapping strokes). Nevertheless, the 'y' of 'Saterday' in the heading appears to this eye to lie over the 'f' of 'of' in 'Archeb. of Cante'; similarly, on p. 47 the ink of the 'f' of 'of' in 'The xjth of December 1549' appears to have been written over the 'C' in 'Archeb. of Canterb.'; PC 2/3.

39 The scene portrayed here probably was very much like the one Sir Julius Caesar drew from his knowledge of late Elizabethan and early Stuart practice. See his description in B.M., Add. MS. 34324, fo. 239a.

40 PC 2/2, 215, 217, 393, 395, 465, 467, and 469, for example. Neither Dasent nor Adair noticed this fact. Adair included this volume among the rough-copy registers which were 'bound books and not merely quires of paper which were to be bound up later'; *E.H.R.* XXXVIII (1923), 417.

41 PC 2/2, 23–34. Pages 23 and 24 are blank. They follow the signed proceedings of 'Sonday vjto februarij at the Towre of Lundon' which fill pp. 17–22. Pages 25–34 constitute a carefully prepared fair copy of Paget's deposition (fair, in contrast to the other rough-copy entries in this volume). Pages 35–9 contain a complete signed day's proceedings headed 'Mondaye the vijth of february at thafforesaid place'. As a group, the six folios which make up Paget's account (pp. 23–34, including the blank folio) are not of precisely the same size as

the other folios of this book, being uniformly shorter: they were inserted at an angle and vary by a quarter of an inch at the spine to half an inch at the outer edge. All six of these sheets retain their original bottom edges, the tops having been trimmed in line with the other pages at the time of binding. Finally, although only one of the folios in this section (pp. 27–8) bears a water-mark, it is a mark not found on any of the other pages of the register.

42 Fitzwilliam (Milton) MS. C.21.

43 In the following phrase from the copy in Paget's letter-book the words in italics were deleted from the copy inserted into the register: 'We therefore depely wayenge, debatinge, and consyderinge all the premisses with our determinacons to serue our soueraigne Lord *duringe his mynorytye and euermore after* duringe our lyefes . . .'; N.R.O., Fitzwilliam (Milton) MS. C.21.

44 The letter-book consists of two parts, a group of three distinct quires and a group of five folios at the end containing Paget's deposition. These five folios consist of two folded sheets (four folios) plus a half sheet (one folio) simply added on. One hand, a small, neat, upright secretary hand, is responsible for the contents of the first three quires. The deposition is in another, freer secretary hand. Both parts were at one time sewn up together within a covering fragment of vellum. The book consists of 31 items, all of them (except the last, Paget's deposition) neat, fair-copy entries of letters and memoranda dating from August 1546 to 10 October 1549. All but the deposition probably were copied out sometime during or after 1551, as the water-mark, a vase initialled 'R D' surmounted by a crown and crescent, suggests that the paper was manufactured in Brussels that year; cf. the watermark which most closely resembles it, figure no. 12808 in Briquet, *Les filigranes*, IV. The last five folios date perhaps from January or early February 1547.

45 N.R.O., Fitzwilliam (Milton) MS. C.21.

46 PC 2/2, 471–95, a section in a hand not otherwise seen in this volume. Taken as a whole, this record – fair-copy material quite distinct from the rough copy record of warrants entered before and after these pages – appears to follow events, but the entire section was clearly written after the fact, for under 'xxv feb.' there is a reference to the Commons' acceptance on 5 March of the bill of treason against Seymour.

47 B.M., Lansdowne MS. 94, fos. 15–16. The first part of the manuscript is a rough draft of the entry for 17 March 1549 in the register; cf. PC 2/2, 495, printed in *A.P.C.*, II, 262–3. The last part, which has been crossed through, mentions that the Bishop of Ely, whom the council had sent to Seymour on the 15th and 17th, returned 'agayn to the Cowrt' informing Paget and Sir Thomas Smith of Seymour's request, that among other things, the day of execution be deferred, but this request the board resolutely refused to honour.

48 *Span. Cal.*, IX, 102.

49 N.R.O., Fitzwilliam (Milton) MS. C.21, Paget to Somerset, 30 August 1547.

50 *A.P.C.*, II, 183–6.

51 *A.P.C.*, II, 8.

52 In fact, Somerset signed proceedings dated 1, 4, 20, 25 September, and 2 October 1547, as well as entries dated 12 and 19 August 1547, unintentional clerical errors for 12 September and probably 29 September, respectively. Somerset was absent from London and the court from 22 August to 8 October; cf. Pollard, *England under Somerset*, 78–9, 155; PC 2/2, 215–34, printed in *A.P.C.*, II, 121–34.

53 B.M., Egerton MS. 2603, fo. 34a.

54 In Somerset's absence, Paget said that the privy councillors in London and at court gathered together for full meetings at court; N.R.O., Fitzwilliam (Milton) MS. C.21, Paget to Somerset, 30 August 1547. Six councillors signed the register after the proceedings recorded under 4 September (not including Somerset, as he was in Scotland): the Archbishop of Canterbury, Lord St John, Marquess of Northampton, Sir Anthony Browne, Sir Anthony Wingfield, and Sir Edward North; PC 2/2, 217–18 (*A.P.C.*, II, 122–3). But eight privy councillors signed a letter to Lord Stafford dated 4 September from Hampton Court: Cranmer, St John, Lord Russell, Thomas Seymour, Paget, Browne, Wingfield, and Sir Anthony Denny; Staffordshire Record Office, D 1720/1/10, p. 427 (a contemporary letter-book of Stafford's).

55 Pollard, *England under Somerset*, 78.

56 Place of meeting is given for 12 of the 74 days' recorded entries, 14 for the 400 days'. From 7 January 1548 to 4 October 1549 at least four meetings are mentioned specifically for which there are no attendances or signatures: one on 15 January 1548 at Hampton Court, 17 April 1548 at Greenwich, 27 August 1548 at Oatlands, and 10 March 1549 at Westminster. Four other days' proceedings are signed, as noted above. No proceedings are listed for at least four of the 400 days given.

57 Letter of 30 September 1547; N.R.O., Fitzwilliam (Milton) MS. C.21.

58 *Span. Cal.*, IX, 299.

59 4, 5, 6, 8, 9, 11, 12, 15, 16, 17, 25, 28, 30 October 1548; *A.P.C.*, II, 224–7.

60 SP 50/2/fo. 24.

61 *Span. Cal.*, IX, 452.

62 *A.P.C.*, II, 155. The register at this time appears to have been composed on or near the dates of the warrants listed; cf. PC 2/2, 262–3, entries covering the week of 1–7 January 1548.

63 *A.P.C.*, II, 183–6.

64 *Ibid.* 190.

65 *Ibid.* 219.

66 *Ibid.* 236.

67 See, for example, the entries for the month of May 1548 which certainly appear to have been written in great haste; PC 2/2, 311–38.

68 All six warrants in *ibid.* 462, for example, are in one clerk's hand, but the first five appear in his neatest, most careful style and the last in his most informal hand.

69 *Ibid.* 171, 182–3, 224, 225.

70 *Ibid.* 315, 224, 225.

71 *Ibid.* 225–8.

72 *Ibid.* 463, 470.

73 *Ibid.*

74 See the records of the warrant bearings dates of 22 and 21 May, respectively; E 101/426/5, fo. 16b and *A.P.C.*, II, 93.

75 Compare the records of the warrant for the clerks' remuneration, dated 3 and 4 April, respectively; E 101/426/5, fo. 12b and *A.P.C.*, II, 81. Another warrant, dated at Greenwich, 9 April 1547, was entered with proceedings dated at Somerset Place on 15 May 1547; E 101/303/4 and *A.P.C.*, II, 92.

76 A warrant dated 21 May 1547 was recorded in the register under 26 May; E 101/426/5, fo. 16b and *A.P.C.*, II, 94–5.

77 Consider two warrants dated at Westminster, 28 February 1547. One requiring Sir Edmund Peckham to pay a Richard Wilbram £100, was entered under 27 February; the other, ordering a payment of £7 1s 0d, was entered under 1 March. There is nothing in the register for 28 February. Cf. E 101/303/4 and *A.P.C.*, II, 44–6.

78 *Thirtieth Report of the Deputy Keeper of the Public Records* (February 1869), Appendix, 212ff.

79 See p. 157 and pp. 329–30, n. 90.

80 An example of a signed file copy of a council letter is 'A minute of the lettres to the speciall men in euery shere v° junij 1548' with the original signatures of eight councillors; SP 10/4/fos. 28–9.

81 SP 10/13/fos. 144–5.

82 Elton, *Annali della Fondazione*, I (1964), 287.

83 See p. 329, n. 88.

84 B.M., Add. MS. 5476, fos. 320–61b, printed in *A.P.C.*, II, 437–509. Ralph Starkey's transcriptions of these letters are in the B.M., Harleian MS, 352, fos. 1–39b. See Dasent's discussion of the Museum volume and Starkey's transcriptions in *A.P.C.*, I, p. xvi; II, pp. ixff.

85 Cf. the entries noting the council's authorisation to Sir William Brabazon, Treasurer in Ireland, to pay Nicholas Bagnall his accustomed fees of office as marshal there. In the letter-book, the very full note is dated 28 March 1547. In the register, the shortened note with a blank space for Bagnall's Christian name, appears with four other warrants as proceedings dated 29 March and is signed by eight councillors. The entries in the two books are in two different clerks' hands. It would appear that Sir Thomas Chaloner, the clerk responsible for the council book, was writing either from memory or from the oral instruction of a superior; B.M., Add. MS. 5476, fo. 333 (*A.P.C.*, II, 462); *A.P.C.*, II, 77. For Dasent's remarks, see *A.P.C.*, II, p. xii.

86 *A.P.C.*, II, p. xvi.

87 *Ibid.* 164.

88 B.M., Harleian MS. 352, fos. 39b–72b, printed in *A.P.C.*, II, 510–57.

89 B.M., Add. MS. 34324, fo. 239a.

90 *Ibid.*

91 B.M., Royal MS. 18 C. xxiv.

92 After a section of blank folios, the heading which first appeared for 19 October 1550 appears again on fo. 14 for 19 October 1551, as if the clerk had begun afresh another book. This practice was not followed afterwards. The paper before and after this date is of the same make and quality, although the author has not been able to identify the water-mark.

93 This letter of 10 October 1551, the draft of which is SP 10/13/fos. 109–10, employs the royal 'we', but doubtless it originated with Warwick and his group; B.M., Royal MS. 18 C. xxiv, fo. 137a. For the other kinds of letters cited here, see, for example, the six entries for 29 November 1552.

94 *A.P.C.*, iii, 411.

95 SP 38/1/fos. 9–17, docquets for 4, 9, 10, 12, and an unknown date in June 1552.

96 SP 38/1/fos. 1–8. The centre-folds of these four sheets bear perforation holes which show that originally the sheets were sewn up together as part of a paper book.

97 Twenty-nine of these papers bear no date, but on the basis of internal evidence they may be dated to this period.

98 See pp. 118–22.

99 See pp. 120–1, 134–5.

100 See points five to seven in Edward's and Petre's rules for the administration of privy council business; Emmison, *B.I.H.R.* xxxi (1958), 203–210.

101 SP 10/13/fo. 22.

102 The twelve are: (1) Hatfield House, Cecil Papers, 151, fo. 32, 1 April 1552, printed in Haynes, 119; (2) *ibid.* fo. 34, May 1552, printed in Haynes, 120; (3) *ibid.* 201, fos. 109–10, 7 March 1553; (4) SP 10/14/ fo. 99, 29 June 1552; (5) *ibid.* fo. 101, about July 1552; (6) SP 10/15/ fo. 33, 4 October 1552; (7) *ibid.* fo. 124, November 1552; (8) SP 10/18/fo. 56, mid-1552; (9) *ibid.* fo. 29, about March 1553; (10) *ibid.* fo. 57, early 1553; (11) *ibid.* fos. 54–5, February–March 1553; (12) SP 46/162/fo. 27, about December 1552.

103 SP 10/15/fo. 124. Suits on these lists also appear with more general affairs of state on council agendas. See, for example, the references to Sir Nicholas Bagnall's suit for Irish lands, SP 10/14/fo. 15, SP 10/13/ fos. 26–7, and SP 10/18/fos. 54–5.

104 They are, respectively: (1) SP 10/14/fos. 147–8, 22 August 1552; (2) SP 10/15/fo. 17, 29 September 1552; (3) *ibid.* fo. 107, 24 November 1552; (4) Hatfield House, Cecil Papers, 151, fo. 98, 29 April 1553; (5) SP 10/18/fos. 45–6, 3 June 1553; (6) *ibid.* fo. 47, 11 June 1553 (cf. Emmison, *Tudor Secretary*, 108–9 and 333–4, n.68); (7) SP 10/15/fo. 57, 20 October 1552.

105 Thus Cecil's agenda for a meeting at 'Hampton Courte. 29. Septembris. 1552' pre-dates the session recorded there on the 30th; SP 10/15/fo. 17; *A.P.C.*, iv, 132.

106 A conditional pardon for one Hussey, for example, which Cecil noted

on his agenda dated 24 November 1552, appears in the register under 26 November, although other business, such as the summoning of several privy councillors to court, is noted among the proceedings in the register for 24 November; SP 10/15/fo. 107 and *A.P.C.*, IV, 177, 178.

107 SP 10/15/fo. 106, the agenda for the meeting at Westminster, 24 November 1552; Cecil noted several nominees for vacant offices. The nominees may have been chosen before the meeting, but the names appear on this list in brackets in the margins in such a way as to suggest that Cecil did not add them at the time of the composition of the agenda.

108 SP 10/13/fo. 17.

109 SP 10/14/fo. 24.

110 SP 10/15/fo. 42.

111 SP 10/14/fo. 84, probably written just before the commencement of the progress of 1552.

112 SP 10/13/fos. 26–7 and SP 10/14/fo. 15, respectively; both lists date to early 1552, sometime before 4 March.

113 (1) SP 10/1/fo. 81, probably dated to 1552 and not 1547 as given in the *Cal. S.P., Dom., 1547–80*, as the reference to Sir Richard Wingfield's mission to Portsmouth also appears on SP 10/14/fo. 70, a memorandum of about May 1552; (2) SP 10/13/fo. 22, 1552; (3) *ibid.* fo. 23, probably 1552; (4) *ibid.* fo. 24, about March 1552; (5) *ibid.* fo. 152, probably 1553; (6) SP 10/14/fo. 13, about April 1552; (7) *ibid.* fo. 14, 1552; (8) *ibid.* fo. 64, about April 1552; (9) *ibid.* fo. 69, about May 1552; (10) *ibid.* fo. 70, May 1552; (11) *ibid.* fo. 148, about December 1552; (12) SP 10/15/fo. 7, about September 1552; (13) *ibid.* fo. 88, about October 1552; (14) Hatfield House, Cecil Papers, 151, fo. 46, 2 October 1552, printed in Haynes, 127–8.

114 SP 10/5/fos. 144–8 and SP 10/14/fos. 115–22.

115 SP 10/13/fo. 98, September 1551, printed in Nichols, *Literary Remains*, II, 487–8; SP 10/5/fos. 149–50, December 1552 to January 1553.

116 All three are in the B.M.: (1) Cotton MS. Vespasian F. xiii, fo. 273, 'Ceirtein pointes of waighty matters to be immediatly concluded on by my counsell', dated 18 January 1552; printed in Nichols, *Literary Remains*, II, 489–90; (2) Lansdowne MS. 94, fos. 17–18, endorsed by Cecil as 'The Kinges majestes memoryall'; approximate date of February 1552; (3) Lansdowne MS. 1236, fos. 19–20, 'A Summary of matters to be concluded', endorsed by Cecil as the King's 'Memoryall' of 3 October 1552; printed in Nichols, *Literary Remains*, II, 543–9.

117 N.R.O., Fitzwilliam (Milton) MS. C.21. W. K. Jordan had not seen the letter-book when he wrote *Edward VI: the Young King*. His references to the letter-book are based on Gammon's unpublished dissertation, 'Master of practices', but such references must be used with caution. For example, when Jordan cites Gammon in referring to what Jordan calls Paget's 'unsolicited . . . statement' of January 1549, it is clear from Jordan's remarks that the 'statement' in question is a

letter of 2 February 1549 in Paget's letter-book and not one of the
letters of 2 or 24 January 1549 or the 'Memoriall' of 25 January 1549;
cf. Jordan, *op. cit.* 300–1 and 301, n.1.

CHAPTER 2: MEMBERSHIP

1 28 Henry VIII, c.7.
2 Rymer, *Foedera*, xv, 114, 115. See Table 1.
3 *Cal. Pat. Rolls, Edw. VI*, i, 97; *A.P.C.*, ii, 67–74.
4 The text of the patent is printed in *Archaeologia* xxx (1844), 478–88.
5 *Ibid.* 489, for the text of this patent.
6 Baldwin, *The King's Council*, 71.
7 Even the Duke of Somerset had to be 'sworne . . . one of the Kinges
  Majesties Pryvey Counsell' upon his readmission to the board on 10
  April 1550; *A.P.C.*, ii, 427.
8 At 'More' Park on 9 October 1540; *Proceedings and Ordinances*, vii,
  58.
9 *A.P.C.*, i, 495.
10 *Ibid.* ii, 6.
11 B.M., Add. MS. 48150 (no foliation), Robert Beale's transcription of
  'The Othe of a Counsellor tempore Edward 6'.
12 In Edward's reign the appointee took the oath orally upon a Bible;
  by 1570, the newly sworn councillor also agreed in writing to observe
  and perform the oath; Prothero, *Statutes and Documents*, 166.
13 B.M., Add. MS. 34324, fo. 238, 'Concerning the Private Counsell of
  the . . . King'.
14 B.M., Add. MS. 48126, fos. 15b–16a, an unpublished section of the
  'eye-witness's account'.
15 Mason and Clinton; *Chronicle*, 25, 29.
16 B.M., Cotton MS. Nero C. x, fo. 84a.
17 Elton, *Tudor Constitution*, 91.
18 *History of the Reformation*, ed. N. Pocock, vol. v, pp. 117–18.
19 Thus, for example, when Professor Elton reprinted in his *Tudor Constitution* the list from N. Pocock's edition (1865) of Burnet's *History of
  the Reformation*, he accepted Burnet's numbering of the nine commissioners, thinking that these were the numbers 'prefixed to them in
  the document', but of course King Edward had not numbered them.
  Burnet had made the nine commissioners the 32nd to 40th privy
  councillors. Cf. Elton, *op. cit.* 96; Burnet, *op. cit.* v, 117–18.
20 Sir Richard Cotton, here designated one of the commissioners, did not
  become a privy councillor until 11 May 1552. As the Bishop of Ely
  was Lord Chancellor at the time of the composition of the list,
  Edward must have written it after 19 January 1552 when Goodrich
  assumed that office. At what time, therefore, when Ely was Chancellor and Cotton was not a privy councillor were all of 'those that be
  now callid into commission' commissioners? It happens that all nine
  of the officials named were members of one or more of three commissions issued during March 1552. Now the council agreed to these

commissions on 3 March and the commissioners received their charge
from Edward's hands on the 15th. The boy therefore composed the
list of his councillors and others 'to be' called into commission at
sometime after 3 March and before 15 March 1552. Cf. B.M., Cotton
MS. Nero C. x, fos. 84–5; *Cal. Pat. Rolls, Edw. VI*, IV, 352–3;
Chronicle, 115.

21 Pollard, *Somerset*, 76. A recent, representative statement is that of
F. G. Emmison, that on 12 March 1547 'all the assistant executors were
added by royal commission to the Privy Council'; *Tudor Secretary*,
66.

22 Professor Jordan (*Edward VI: the Young King*, 72–3, 80) has described two sources (B.M., Lansdowne MS. 160, fo. 273 and *A.P.C.*, II,
63) as original letters-patent dated *1* March and *13* March 1547
appointing, and confirming the appointment of, the same 26 men to
the privy council. That he should have based so much of his recent
account of the authority for Somerset's rule on these two 'patents' is
regrettable, since a casual check shows them to be non-existent. Lansdowne MS. 160, fo. 276 in actually an early seventeenth-century copy
of only that part of the original commission (of 12 March) giving the
names of the 26 nominees; the author has misread and misunderstood
Sir Julius Caesar's endorsement on fo. 277b: 'A note of the names of
Ed: Sixte his Priuie Councell. Aº 1.º Mar: 12º'. But Professor Jordan
also states that on 13 March the privy council asked for a 'fresh commission' confirming the 26 in their offices as privy councillors; he says
that seven councillors signed this 'document'. It is clear that what he
thinks are new letters-patent dated 13 March 1547 is really the council's original 'request' to the King for the patent of 12 March, the
minute of which request was entered into the council book under a
date of 13 March. The seven signatures are those in the register at the
foot of the proceedings for that day.

23 *A.P.C.*, II, 70, 71.

24 Pollard, *Somerset*, 37–8; 80, n.3.

25 In the case of any *one* member's tenure, the resulting lists provide
somewhat less than comprehensive evidence, of course; the available
records give us merely the earliest evidence of his performance in
office and not necessarily the date of his first appearance at the board.

26 Sir Edward Wotton signed a council warrant dated at Somerset Place,
23 February 1548; E 404/229. So far as the author knows, this is the
earliest extant privy council document which Wotton signed and thus
puts him in England at least one month earlier than the date given in
D.N.B.

27 On this and his apparent judicial incompetence, see the article in
D.N.B. There is no evidence that Bromley attended any of the
recorded council meetings held at the Tower, Westminster, and
Somerset Place before 12 March 1547, or at any other meeting thereafter. He signed none of the extant council letters and warrants for
Edward's reign; his name appears on none of the contemporary lists
of privy councillors for the period 12 March 1547 to October 1549.

He signed Somerset's patent of 24 December 1547 not, according to the evident order of precedence, as a non-noble privy councillor, but rather as a judge; cf. *Archaeologia* xxx (1844), 488. The privy council summoned him before them and the King on 12 June 1553 (not a council meeting) as legal counsel to the council; cf. Fuller, *Church History*, iv, 137–44; Nichols, *Literary Remains*, ii, 567.

28 Burnet thought him 'a papist at heart'; cited in *D.N.B.*

29 Rymer, *Foedera*, xv, 116.

30 *Ibid* 115.

31 *A.P.C.*, ii, 4–6.

32 '. . . if any of them [i.e., the executors] fortune to dye the more part of them which shall be for the Tyme Lyving' were empowered to continue to do whatever they thought necessary for the good government of the realm 'during the Minorite aforsayd'; Rymer *Foedera*, xv, 115.

33 The marriage of either Mary or Elizabeth required such agreement; *ibid*. 113.

34 *A.P.C.*, ii, 7.

35 Scarisbrick, *Henry VIII*, 494. Professor Scarisbrick offers an alternative: the will was simply drawn up too quickly. But this also argues that the omission of any provisions for adding to the body of executors represents a 'failure', when in fact the will's repeated references to the possibility of a diminution in the number of councillors and the continuation of government by council during the time of those living (for the duration of the minority) would appear to argue against such a presumed failure.

36 Seymour signed the privy council register at the foot of proceedings of meetings dated 2, 6, and 7 February 1547. On 2 February, for example, he is one of the group identified as the 'Lorde Protectour and others his coexecutors whose names be vunderwritten . . .'; PC 2/2, 12ff. He also signed a privy council letter to the Archbishop of York dated 23 February 1547 at Westminster: SP 46/2/fo. 97.

37 B.M., Add. MS. 48126, fos. 6a–7a. See p. 344, n. 4.

38 See pp. 231–9.

39 *A.P.C.*, ii, 48–57; and note (i) in the article on Southampton in G.E.C.

40 Pollard, *Somerset*, 32; Jordan, *Edward VI: the Young King*, 70. Jordan accepts Pollard's view, which is based on the council's own biased statement in the register; *A.P.C.*, ii, 48–58.

41 B.M., Add. MS. 48126, fo. 15a, a section of the 'eye-witness's account'. This evidence corroborates Burnet's old assertion which Jordan, *op. cit.*, rejected; cf. Burnet, *History of the Reformation* (ed. 1865), ii, 40.

42 *A.P.C.*, ii, 5.

43 That is, they had deprived Wriothesley of his office *as a privy councillor* as well. For the positive evidence of Wriothesley's non-membership, see p. 49.

44 And Wriothesley was not alone; for the political opposition to Somerset from 31 January to 12 March 1547, see pp. 237–8.

45 Hereafter, 'councillor' will always refer merely to one of the King's ordinary councillors and not to a member of the privy council; council and councillor, written thus without quotation marks, will always refer only to the privy council and a privy councillor, respectively.

46 *A.P.C.*, II, 62–3. The fact that Northampton and Cheyne witnessed proceedings dated 12 March does not necessarily mean that they were sworn of the privy council on that day, but the probability that they were so sworn is high, as their signatures do not appear under entries dated earlier than that; the date does show that Somerset admitted them to power much earlier than the Imperial ambassador had thought (by 27 April); *Span. Cal.*, IX, 86.

47 *A.P.C.*, II, 80.

48 B.M., Add. MS. 4801, fo. 217, a later copy of a council letter of 18 March 1547 to Sir Anthony St Leger; the copyist indicated the original signatories, including North, Tunstal, Denny, Herbert, and Petre.

49 *Ibid.* fo. 220, privy council to St Leger *et al.* from Greenwich, 7 April 1547; a later copy with signatories' names provided.

50 *Span. Cal.*, IX, 50.

51 *Cal. S.P. Foreign, 1547–53*, 329.

52 E 101/303/4, council to Sir Edmund Peckham requiring him to deliver £100 to the Lieutenant of the Tower.

53 *Ibid.* council to Peckham ordering him to deliver £30 to one Francis Rovers.

54 Rich continued to rise: on 23 October 1547 he became Lord Chancellor and thus third in precedence after Somerset and Cranmer. He had been seventh among the 'assistants' in the will and ninth among the 26 nominees of 12 March. In the patent of 24 December he was second among the 26. Cf. Rymer, *Foedera*, xv, 116; *A.P.C.*, II, 70; *Archaeologia* xxx (1844), 482.

55 E 404/229.

56 The *D.N.B.* has it that 'his duties at Calais prevented his *frequent* attendance at the council board' (author's italics).

57 See Table 3, which reflects the appointment of the 22nd councillor, Sir Thomas Smith, on 17 April 1548.

58 SP 10/5/fos. 55–67, endorsed 'Touching grete horses etc.', an informal government record described by the editor of the *Cal. S.P., Dom., 1547–80* (no. 17, p. 12) as an 'abstract of the light horses and demilances to be furnished by assessment throughout the realm'.

59 *Ibid.* Van der Delft reported that sometime between 2 and 4 May 1547, Somerset added the Chancellor of the exchequer to the council; this is highly doubtful. Van der Delft thought that North was the other of the 'two new members' added then but, as we have seen, North's membership dates from 18 March 1547 at the latest. Baker's signature does not appear on any extant council record dated earlier than 17 January 1549. This list, dated after Browne's death, shows that Baker was a privy councillor late in 1548.

60 *D.N.B.*, article on Montagu.

61 *A.P.C.*, II, 70; E 101/303/4.

62 He signed a warrant for the great seal as late as 17 May 1548; C 82/884.

63 Wotton and other commissioners to Somerset, 18 July 1548; H.M.C., *Salisbury MSS.*, 1, 54.

64 Sturge, *Tunstal*, 271–80.

65 House of Lords Record Office, 1 Edw. VI, no. 21.

66 *Cal. Pat. Rolls, Edw. VI*, II, 250–1.

67 For Tunstal's opposition to Somerset's policies, see Sturge, *Tunstal*, 274–81.

68 *A.P.C.*, II, 164–5. In a letter to Charles V, van der Delft reported on 23 February 1548 that Northampton 'is only spoken of secretly, and does not show himself at Court'; *Span. Cal.*, IX, 253–4.

69 *A.P.C.*, II, 183; the register records the fact of his taking the oath of office as secretary and not his admission to the privy council.

70 Dewar, *Smith*, 45.

71 SP 10/5/fos. 55–6.

72 SP 61/2/fos. 4–7, to the Lord Deputy and council in Ireland. This letter, it should be noted, is the earliest known evidence of Southampton's readmission, Pollard's unsupported statement to the contrary notwithstanding ('. . . in 1548, if not earlier, he was readmitted to the council board'); article on Southampton, *D.N.B.*

73 N.R.O., Fitzwilliam (Milton) MS. C.21, Paget to Somerset, 24 January 1549. See also, Pollard, *Somerset*, 198–9, and Dewar, *Smith*, 47. On Shrewsbury's efforts at Haddington, see Jordan, *Edward VI: the Young King*, 286–9.

74 *A.P.C.*, II, 236.

75 Montagu, for example, signed a letter dated 23 June 1549 at Richmond; Pocock, *Troubles*, 6–7. Edward Wotton signed a letter from Westminster on 12 September 1549; *ibid.* 73.

76 *Ibid.* 35–6.

77 *A.P.C.*, II, 337. Referring to the *A.P.C.*, Professor Jordan somehow discovered that Wentworth became a privy councillor in February 1550; *Edward VI: the Young King*, 80, n.1.

78 Wentworth signed a privy council letter dated at Westminster, 7 August 1549, to the mayor, etc. of Southampton; the other signatories were Somerset, Rich, and St John; *Letters of the Fifteenth and Sixteenth Centuries*, 72.

79 *Proceedings and Ordinances*, VII, 3–4.

80 An official list of 16 October 1546; *Letters and Papers, Henry VIII*, XXI (pt. 2), no. 332.

81 Elton, *Tudor Constitution*, 91.

82 Pollard, *Somerset*, 79–80.

83 Seven of twenty-two, or 31·9%, to be exact.

84 Source: *A.P.C.* All dates, unless marked with an asterisk (or noted otherwise) indicate date of official swearing-in as well as date of first appearance.

85 The proceedings of 6–10 October 1549 take the form of fair-copy

entries at the beginning of a new council book and so represent the London faction's own record of these events composed *ex post facto*; PC 2/3, 1–13.

86 An original printed proclamation of 8 October 1549 may be seen in the collection of the Library of the Society of Antiquaries, no. 48, 'A Proclamacion set forth by the state and bodie of the Kynges Maiesties Counsayle now assembled at London, conteinyng the very trouth of the Duke of Somerset's evel Government, and false and detestable Procedinges'. Nineteen signatories' names are given; Rich (Chancellor), St John (Great Master and President of the council), Russell (Privy Seal), Northampton, Warwick (Great Chamberlain), Arundel (Chamberlain), Shrewsbury, Southampton, Cheyne (Treasurer of the household), Herbert (Master of the King's horse), Gage (Constable of the Tower), Petre (Secretary), North, Montagu, Sadler, Baker, E. Wotton, Dr Wotton, and Southwell. The text is in Pocock, *Troubles*, 95–101; calendared in Steele, *Tudor and Stuart Proclamations*, I, no. 373. A contemporary MS. copy also exists, Corporation of London Record Office, Journals, 16, fos. 34–5 (and Letter-book R, fos. 37–8); the copyist indicated all of the above names except those of Russell and Herbert. As Russell and Herbert were not in London at the time, they could not in fact have subscribed the proclamation from which the printed version was taken. This MS. copy may, therefore, be the more accurate of the two, the clerk of the court of aldermen having perhaps had before him a document actually signed by seventeen privy councillors.

87 Petre's draft of the proclamation of 10 October, '. . . for strawing abrode of sedicious billes', is SP 10/9/fos. 70–1. Grafton's printed version: Library of the Society of Antiquaries, no. 49. Text in Pocock, *Troubles*, 108–9; calendared in Steele, *op. cit.* I, no. 374. The printed version provides the nineteen names from the proclamation of the 8th plus those of Wentworth, Wingfield, and Peckham. Contemporary MS. copies exist in the Corporation of London Record Office, Journals, 16, fo. 38b and Letter-book R, fo. 43; both copies give these 22 names.

88 Pocock, *Troubles*, 101; the seal referred to must be the great seal of England since the signet was in the possession of the council at Windsor.

89 The proclamation of 8 October was read out at several places in London just after four in the afternoon by the Sheriff of London and Sir Thomas Chaloner, a clerk of the privy council; they were preceded by two trumpets, four heralds, two kings of arms, with the sergeant of the trumpeters and the common cryer riding with their maces before them; Wriothesley, *Chronicle*, II, 26. The making of the proclamation of 10 October 'thorrow alle Ynglond' is described similarly in Nichols, *Chronicle of the Grey Friars*, 64.

90 SP 10/9/fos. 70–1; Pocock, *Troubles*, 108–9.

91 Actually sixteen, but the Earl of Derby was admitted to one meeting only under a special oath; see pp. 66–7.

92 Professor Jordan has wrongly dated the appointments of Devereux (he has Somerset appointing Devereux in January 1549), the Bishop of Ely, and Darcy, as well as Shrewsbury; he has also wrongly attributed membership to Southwell and Peckham before October 1549; cf. *Edward VI: the Young King*, 80, n.1.

93 The article on Goodrich in the *D.N.B.* is in error in stating that he was sworn of the privy council on the accession of Edward VI.

94 The commission, passed under the great seal on 20 November 1549 upon authority of a privy seal warrant dated at Westminster, 14 November, provided for the signing of warrants for payment by at least 6 of the 25 members of the privy council whose names are given; the commission rendered valid all warrants which at least 6 had signed since 6 October 1549, but from the 6 at least 2 among Cranmer, Rich, St John, Russell, Northampton, Warwick, Arundel, Shrewsbury, Southampton, and Wentworth had to be included; *Cal. Pat. Rolls, Edw. VI*, II, 250–1. The privy council as named consisted of the above ten councillors plus Tunstal, Cheyne, Paget, Herbert, Wingfield, Petre, Dr Wotton, Gage, North, Montagu, Sadler, Baker, E. Wotton, Southwell, and Bromley. With his signature Goodrich clearly could not have authorised privy council warrants dated, for example, to October 1549, for this was what the commission empowered the 25 councillors named to be able to have done.

95 B.M., Add. MS. 48126, fos. 15b–16a; see p. 249.

96 See pp. 241–52.

97 Cf. *D.N.B.*, G.E.C.

98 *A.P.C.*, II, 370, 372, 377.

99 See Table 10.

100 B.M., Add MS. 48126, fos. 15b–16a.

101 *A.P.C.*, II, 344–5. The others were Sir Edward Rogers, Sir Thomas Wroth, and Sir Andrew Dudley.

102 Cf. the article on Darcy in G.E.C.

103 *A.P.C.*, II, 330–44.

104 See p. 289, n. 87.

105 Corporation of London Record Office, Journals, 16, fo. 39 and Letter-book R, fo. 43b, MS. copies that the clerk of the court of aldermen transcribed from the originals, which he indicated had been 'Sub-scribed by the lordes, and others of the pryvie counsaill, whose names hereunder do folowe'. There follow 24 names: Cranmer, Rich, St John, Russell, Northampton, Warwick, Arundel, Shrewsbury, Southampton, Wentworth, Cheyne, Paget, Herbert, Wingfield, Gage, Petre, North, Montagu, Sadler, Baker, E. Wotton, Dr Wotton, Southwell, and Peckham. With the exception of Bromley and the Bishop of Durham (whose readmission would shortly be made retro-active to 6 October 1549; see p. 290, n. 94), this list thus stands as an official roster of the full council after the *coup*. For the text of the proclamation, see Hughes & Larkin, I, no. 352.

106 See p. 49.

107 Unpublished article on Peckham, History of Parliament Trust files.

There are references to a Thomas Wriothesley as servant to the cofferer of the household at the time (1529) Peckham held that office, but it is not certain that this Wriothesley was the later Earl of Southampton; Elton, *Tudor Revolution*, 308–9.

108 Dates are 6, 7, 8, 9, 10, 19, 21 October; 28, 29 November; 18, 24, 29 December 1549; *A.P.C.*, II, 330–42; 346–7; 362; 367–8.

109 See p. 289, n. 86 and n. 87; p. 290, n. 105.

110 *Cal. Pat. Rolls, Edw. VI*, II, 250–1.

111 Nichols, *Literary Remains*, II, 246.

112 The most up-to-date account of Southwell's early career is contained in an unpublished article on Southwell in the History of Parliament Trust files.

113 *Span Cal.*, x, 8; Wriothesley, *Chronicle*, II, 33, 41. On the assassination plot, see pp. 254–5. On account of his illness, the council granted Wriothesley licence on 28 June 1550 to leave London for the air of Hampshire, stipulating that he remain within that county and be ready 'to answere and to appeare before the Counsaill' upon pain of forfeiting his recognizance of 5,000 marks. On 8 July Wriothesley requested that he be able to travel to London 'for his healthe' if necessary, adding as a conciliatory gesture that he stood ready to serve the King in Hampshire in the event of any 'commocion' there. The council replied sharply that he was duty-bound so to serve, but granted his request; *A.P.C.*, III, 59, 64, 65.

114 *A.P.C.*, II, 398; *Span. Cal.*, x, 14.

115 *Chronicle*, 19.

116 *Span. Cal.*, x, 14.

117 Cf. *D.N.B.*, article on Arundel.

118 *A.P.C.*, III, 64, 71, 72, 78.

119 See pp. 66–7.

120 'Quelques particularitez d'Angleterre du temps du Roy Edouard et de la Reine Marie', Bibliothèque Nationale, Paris, MS. Ancien Saint-Germain Français 15888, fos. 211–18. This account, written in 1553 by one of the members of the French mission resident in England, confirms Renard's version; cf. Pollard, *History of England*, 62–3.

121 SP 10/13/fo. 128 is the report of Arundel's depositions in the Tower to Northumberland, Northampton, Bedford, Pembroke, and Hoby; it is in the hand of Bernard Hampton, one of the clerks of the council, and is signed by the five councillors indicated. SP 10/13/fo. 130 is another report in a different hand of Arundel's depositions before (1) Northumberland and Northampton, (2) these two plus Pembroke and Bedford, and (3) Bernard Hampton alone; it is signed by the four councillors named.

122 Cf. *D.N.B.*

123 *Span. Cal.*, xi, 13.

124 Council to Hoby, Morison, and the Bishop of Norwich, from Greenwich, 1 July 1553; B.M., Harleian MS. 523, fo. 40b ff (a copy with signatories' names indicated).

125 This is what the author of Arundel's biography in the *D.N.B.* thinks.

126 On 13 October 1549, '. . . for sundry his misdemeanours and indiscreet behaviour heretofore, being thought unmeet to continue any longer of the Privy Council', the lords ordered Sir Thomas Smith 'to be both sequestered from the Council and also deprived from the office of one of his Majesties secretaries'; *A.P.C.*, II, 343–4. The council arrested Somerset on the 11th and abolished the Protectorate and Somerset's membership on the 13th; *ibid.* 342, 343; *Archaeologia* xxx (1844), 489.

127 The Bishop of Durham's name appears on the official membership list of 14–20 November 1549; *Cal. Pat. Rolls, Edw. VI*, II, 250–1. Tunstal took no part in the events of October 1549; although he was in London by 4 November 1549 for the new session of Parliament, he did not attend a privy council meeting until 11 December; see Sturge, *Tunstal*, 283. Gage reappeared at the meeting of 7 October 1549; *A.P.C.*, II, 333. He signed the proclamations of 8 and 10 October; his name is on all later lists of the whole council.

128 Dr Nicholas Wotton signed the two proclamations of 8 and 10 October; his name appears on every later official list. He was appointed one of the King's secretaries on 15 October 1549, replacing Smith; *A.P.C.*, II, 344.

129 See pp. 66–7.

130 So van der Delft reported on 12 April 1550; *Span. Cal.*, x, 62.

131 H.P.T.

132 *A.P.C.*, III, 24.

133 *Chronicle*, 29; *D.N.B.*; G.E.C.

134 *Span. Cal.*, x, 179.

135 B.M., Royal MS. 18 C. xxiv, fo. 375a.

136 G.E.C.

137 *Span. Cal.*, x, 217–19; Jordan, *Edward VI: Threshold of Power*, 122, 132.

138 For example: SP 46/2/fo. 161; B.M., Stowe MS. 595, fo. 44b.

139 B.M., Add. MS. 5751 A, fo. 302: council on progress with the King at Woking (23 August 1550) ordering Wiltshire to melt down the gold plate in the Tower.

140 *A.P.C.*, IV, 15; E 101/546/19.

141 *D.N.B.*; G.E.C.; *A.P.C.*, III, 258–9; IV, 15.

142 Read, *Mr Secretary Cecil*, 37–65; *D.N.B.*, article on Nicholas Wotton.

143 Article on Westmorland in G.E.C., citing *Letters and Papers, Henry VIII*, xxi (pt. 2), nos. 203, 212, 417–21.

144 Sturge, *Tunstal*, 284ff.

145 *Span. Cal.*, x, 263.

146 G.E.C.; *A.P.C.*, IV, 50. One debt of 1,000 marks was for special livery of his lands.

147 Jordan, *Edward VI: Threshold of Power*, 383.

148 See p. 123.

149 *Chronicle*, 58.

150 Jordan, *Edward VI: Threshold of Power*, 52.

151 *D.N.B.*

152 *A.P.C.*, II, 328–9.
153 *Span. Cal.*, x, 9.
154 It was rumoured that the council was deeply concerned about the potential problem of a Derby-Arundel-Shrewsbury challenge; *ibid.* 168, 169.
155 *D.N.B.*
156 *Span. Cal.*, x, 263, 279–80.
157 Scheyfve reported on 17 August 1550 (*ibid.* 166) that it was then 'asserted' that the council had ordered Derby to meet Warwick at Newcastle for the alleged purpose of discussing what role Derby should play in the King's affairs, the council appearing 'to wish to make some change in the government and give him a share in it'. Fearing a trap, Derby declined the meeting saying he was quite content with the government as it was. 'It is rumoured that Lord Warwick's object in going to Newcastle was to seize the person of my Lord Derby by force and take him to London by sea.'
158 Nichols, *Diary of Henry Machyn*, 6; *Span. Cal.*, x, 323.
159 *Span. Cal.*, x, 279–80.
160 *A.P.C.*, III, 329, 333.
161 *Chronicle*, 56.
162 Paget to Somerset, 2 February 1549, N.R.O., Fitzwilliam (Milton) MS. C.21.
163 *Span. Cal.*, x, 282–3.
164 *A.P.C.*, II, 343.
165 Jordan, *Edward VI: Threshold of Power*, 79.
166 *Span. Cal.*, x, 290–1.
167 *Ibid.* 299.
168 *A.P.C.*, III, 359.
169 *Span. Cal.*, IX, 254; *D.N.B.*
170 *Span. Cal.*, IX, 460
171 E 101/546/19.
172 *D.N.B.*
173 *A.P.C.*, III, 6.
174 *Ibid.* 88.
175 *Ibid.* 6; *Chronicle*, 40; Jordan, *Edward VI: Threshold of Power*, 149; Article on Bowes, *D.N.B.*
176 *A.P.C.*, III, 251–2.
177 Almost all of the commissions (13) were concerned with the King's finances – debts, sales of Crown lands, surveys of the courts of revenue, etc.; *Cal. Pat. Rolls, Edw. VI*, IV, 140–2, 144, 278, 352–3, 353–4, 354–355, 355–6, 390–1, 392–3, 393–7, 398; V, 184, 277, 411.
178 Sturge, *Tunstal*, 284–97.
179 Jordan, *Edward VI: Threshold of Power*, 266, 382.
180 See pp. 251, 258.
181 *Span. Cal.*, x, 166.
182 Jordan, *Edward VI: Threshold of Power*, 248.
183 Sturge, *Tunstal*, 284–97.
184 *A.P.C.*, III, 448.

185 Jordan, *Edward VI: Threshold of Power*, 81.
186 Cf. *ibid*. 81–105.
187 Pollard, *History of England*, 62, n.4, citing Froude's transcription of Renard's original report.
188 'Quelques particularitez', Bibliothèque Nationale, MS. Ancien Saint-Germain Français, 15888, fo. 212a.
189 'Relation de laccusation et mort du Duc de Sommerset', *ibid*. fo. 205a.
190 *Ibid*. fo. 205b.
191 *Span. Cal.*, x, 300–1.
192 'Relation', Bibliothèque Nationale, MS. Ancien Saint-Germain Français, 15888, fo. 205. On Richard Whalley's attempts to further this cause, see Jordan, *Edward VI: Threshold of Power*, 75, 79–80.
193 Cf. Pollard, *History of England*, 58.
194 *Span. Cal.*, x, 393.
195 Dorset became Duke of Suffolk, Wiltshire became Marquess of Winchester, and Herbert, who the evening before had been made Baron Herbert of Cardiff, became Earl of Pembroke. Warwick of course became Duke of Northumberland; B.M., Add. MS. 6113, fos. 129–31, a contemporary account of the proceedings at Hampton Court. Cecil received a knighthood at the same time; it was he who had reportedly first heard of the existence of a decisive 'plot' of some sort; *Span. Cal.*, x, 393.
196 Article on Wentworth, G.E.C.
197 PC 2/4, 732. Another contemporary hand added the name of 'Sr Richard Cotton' at the bottom of the list, but Cotton did not become a member of the council until 11 May 1552.
198 Article on Wotton, *D.N.B.*
199 *A.P.C.*, II, 330–59; III, 159, 161; 174–9.
200 Gammon, *Statesman and Schemer*, 179–80 and 274, n.53.
201 *Span. Cal.*, x, 388–90.
202 Gammon, *op. cit.* 179–84.
203 B.M., Royal MS. 18 C. xxiv, fo. 280.
204 In accepting Burnet's date, Professor Elton identified Cotton as the 'controller' of the list; *Tudor Constitution*, 96, n.8. Elsewhere, however, Elton had thought that Cotton was also Comptroller in March 1552; *Tudor Revolution*, 230. Wingfield in fact was Comptroller from 2 February 1550 until his death on 15 August 1552; article on Wingfield, *D.N.B.* A date of March 1552 also explains the identity of the 'Mr Sollicitour' among the nine commissioners: it was Edward Griffyn, Solicitor-General, whom Elton (reasoning from 1553) thought the King must have confused with Gosnald who was also one of the nine commissioners, but the King knew his solicitors, for both Griffyn and Gosnald were members of the commission of 9 March 1552 to execute the penal laws; *Cal. Pat. Rolls, Edw. VI*, IX, 352–3.
205 Nichols, *Diary of Henry Machyn*, 23.
206 For the data of Sir Richard Cotton's career the author wishes here to record his complete and grateful debt to Miss Helen Miller, whose

unpublished biographical essay on Cotton he was granted permission to consult at the History of Parliament Trust.

207 SP 10/14/fo. 11.

208 During the period under discussion, Huntingdon was away from court from the end of November 1551 to mid-May 1552; mid-June to the end of August 1552; 23 September 1552 to 1 March 1553. Thus, before attending the Parliament of March 1553, Huntingdon had been at court for only about two months since November 1551.

209 See the discussion of the committee for the state, pp. 131–6.

210 *Span. Cal.*, XI, 50–1.

211 H.P.T., unpublished article on Cheke which on this point draws upon Strype's *Sir John Cheke*.

212 *A.P.C.*, IV, 285–9.

213 There were 47 official members altogether, but for the purposes of much of this discussion the following will be omitted: Bromley, the absent judge, and the Earl of Derby, whose membership the government considered extraordinary and which in practice was defined merely by his presence at the one unusual meeting. The biographical data upon which the following statistical survey is based was drawn from the following sources: *D.N.B.* (Bowes, Browne, Clinton, Devereux, Dudley, Fitz Alan, Gage, Gates, Goodrich, Grey, Hastings, Herbert, Hoby, Montagu, North, Parr, Paulet, Peckham, Rich, Russell, E. Seymour, Talbot, Wentworth, Wingfield, E. Wotton, N. Wotton, Wriothesley); G.E.C. (Brooke, Clinton, Darcy, Devereux, Dudley, Fitz Alan, Grey, Hastings, Herbert, Montagu, Neville, North, Parr, Paulet, Rich, Russell, E. Seymour, Talbot, Wentworth, Wriothesley); History of Parliament Trust files (Baker, Browne, Cheke, Cheyne, Cotton, Denny, Mason, Peckham, Sadler, T. Seymour, Southwell); Bush, 'The Rise to Power of Edward Seymour'; Cooper, *Athenae Cantabrigienses*; Dewar, *Sir Thomas Smith*; Elton, *Tudor Revolution*; Emmison, *Tudor Secretary*; Gammon, *Statesman and Schemer*; Read, *Mr Secretary Cecil*; Richardson, *History of the Court of Augmentations*; Ridley, *Thomas Cranmer*; Rowse, 'Thomas Wriothesley', *Huntington Library Quarterly* XXVIII (1965), 105–29; Slavin, *Sir Ralph Sadler*; Sturge, 'The Life and Times of John Dudley'; Sturge, *Cuthbert Tunstal*; *Lords' Journals*.

214 Sources: *A.P.C.*; *G.E.C.*; *H.P.T.*; *Chronicle*; *Cal. Pat. Rolls, Edw. VI*; Powicke and Fryde, *Handbook of British Chronology*; unpublished list of chancellors of England, P.R.O.; Gammon, *Statesman and Schemer*.

215 Somerset, Cranmer, Russell, Dudley, Paget, Denny, Herbert, E. Wotton (all executors); T. Seymour, Wentworth, Wingfield, Smith, Sadler (all active before the *coup*); Grey, Goodrich, Darcy, Gates, Cecil, Hoby, Cotton, Cheke (all new after October 1549).

216 Wriothesley, Fitz Alan, Tunstal, N. Wotton, Talbot, Browne, Gage, Baker, Southwell, Peckham, and Cheyne. Stanley (Earl of Derby) and Bromley, who were not included in this analysis, are also reported to have been conservatives in religion.

217 Paulet, Petre, Rich, Brooke, Mason, Montagu, North, Clinton, Neville, Bowes, Devereux.

218 Wriothesley, Fitz Alan, Talbot, Tunstal, Browne, Baker, Gage, Cheyne.

219 In spite of Wotton's background – a brother of the hospital of St Thomas at Rome, a doctor in divinity, civil, and canon law – it taxes one's imagination to describe the man's doctrinal beliefs. The author is accepting here the oblique statement in the article on Wotton in the *D.N.B.* to the effect that his 'opinions were catholic in tendency'.

220 Unpublished article on Mason, H.P.T.

221 Somerset, Cranmer, Wriothesley, Dudley, Tunstal, Paget, N. Wotton, Denny, North, Montagu, Bromley.

222 Bromley and N. Wotton are excluded here.

223 Parr, Fitz Alan, Petre, Rich, and Smith, in addition to the nine active executors noted above.

224 Somerset, Cranmer, Dudley, Fitz Alan, Paget, Petre, Rich, North, Denny, Smith.

225 Cranmer, Dudley, Parr, Goodrich, Petre, Cecil, Rich, Mason, N. Wotton, Montagu, North.

226 Somerset, Wriothesley, Fitz Alan, Paget, Parr, Denny, Smith, Petre, Rich, North, Dudley, Cranmer, Montagu.

227 Dudley, Cranmer, Parr, Goodrich, Petre, Cecil, N. Wotton.

228 Tunstal, N. Wotton, Mason, Smith, Paget.

229 Russell, Cheke, Denny, Cheyne, Sadler, Hoby.

230 Tunstal, N. Wotton, Paget, Wriothesley, Montagu, Bromley; with Bromley, the figure is 15 of the 47 councillors.

231 Wriothesley, Rich, Tunstal, Baker, Petre, Smith, Paget, Montagu.

232 Goodrich, N. Wotton, Cecil, Cotton, Bowes, Montagu, Rich, Petre, Baker.

233 Smith, Cheke, Petre, Cranmer, Goodrich.

234 Paulet, Cranmer, Somerset, Mason, Paget, Wriothesley, Tunstal, N. Wotton, Cheyne, Denny, T. Seymour, Wentworth.

235 Tunstal, N. Wotton, Paget, Cheyne, Mason, T. Seymour, Paulet, Goodrich, Dudley, Cotton, Baker, Russell, E. Wotton, Fitz Alan, Browne, Talbot, Gage, Neville, Clinton, Brooke, Somerset.

236 Somerset, T. Seymour, Tunstal, Dudley, Wriothesley, Petre, Paget, N. Wotton, Russell, Hoby, Mason, Cranmer, Browne.

237 Petre, Paget, Denny, Mason, Hoby.

238 Somerset, Russell, Dudley, Herbert, Denny, Browne.

239 Somerset, Russell, Parr, Dudley, Fitz Alan, T. Seymour, Browne, Cheyne, Gage, Denny, Herbert, Wingfield.

240 Dudley, Parr, Darcy, Russell, Herbert, Hastings, Devereux, Brooke, Clinton, Neville, Talbot, Bowes, Gates, Cotton, Hoby, Sadler, Cheyne, Gage.

241 Neville, Clinton, Brooke, Devereux, Hastings, Darcy, Gates, Cotton, Hoby, Bowes.

242 Somerset, T. Seymour, Russell, Herbert, Cheyne, Denny, Sadler, Darcy, Gates, Clinton, Cheke.

243 Somerset, Russell, Denny, Herbert.

244 Somerset, T. Seymour, Russell, Denny, Herbert, and Cheyne before May 1548 plus Sadler after that date. On the basis of this evidence it is difficult to understand how Professor Jordan can claim that 'almost without exception' the privy councillors under Somerset had risen in the service of the King 'as officers of state rather than as courtiers', *Edward VI: the Young King*, 82. Cf. Elton, *Historical Journal* xii (1969), 702.

245 Russell, Herbert, Cheyne, Sadler, Darcy, Clinton, Gates.

246 Somerset, Denny, Sadler, Russell, Herbert, Cheyne, Fitz Alan, Peckham, Browne, Rich, Paulet, Dudley, Gage, Parr, Wingfield, Neville, Hoby.

247 Somerset, Browne, Denny, Dudley, Paulet, Herbert, Russell.

248 Somerset, Denny, Dudley, Paulet, Herbert, Russell, Rich, Fitz Alan, Wingfield, Parr, Sadler, Cheyne.

249 Dudley, Russell, Herbert, Paulet, Parr, Rich, Cheyne, Sadler, Gage, Neville, Hoby.

250 Somerset, Russell, Dudley, Fitz Alan, T. Seymour, Clinton, Wentworth, Hastings, Grey, Neville, Talbot, Gates, Denny, Wingfield, E. Wotton, Cheyne.

251 Paulet, Dudley, E. Wotton, Russell, Southwell, Cheyne, North, Wingfield, Gates.

252 Baker, Cotton, North.

253 Neville, Parr, Tunstal (who had been President), Talbot (who became President in 1549).

254 Devereux, Herbert.

255 Talbot, Baker, Gates, Cecil, Peckham, North, Southwell, E. Wotton, Dudley, Wingfield, Mason, Montagu, Petre, Paget, Gage, Rich, Somerset, Sadler.

256 Montagu, North, Rich, Wriothesley, Baker, Cotton; if one includes Cecil and Smith as the 'masters' of Somerset's extraordinary court of requests, the number is eight.

257 Sadler, Paget, Petre, Wriothesley, Smith, Cecil, N. Wotton, North, Mason, Gates.

258 Tunstal (a former Lord Keeper), Russell.

259 Tunstal, Wriothesley, Petre, Sadler, Bowes.

260 Gage, Russell, Sadler, Wriothesley, Petre, North, Rich, Cotton, Baker, Southwell, E. Wotton, Denny, Cheke, Cheyne, Paulet, Peckham.

261 T. Seymour, Russell, Paget, Tunstal, Cranmer, Wriothesley, Paulet, Rich, Sadler, Denny, Montagu, Southwell, Mason, Wentworth.

262 Sadler, Cheke, North, Petre, Paget, Montagu, Hoby, T. Seymour.

263 Cranmer, Cheyne, Gage, Tunstal, Goodrich, T. Seymour, Montagu, Paulet, Petre, North, Cheke, Southwell, Baker, Gates, N. Wotton, Cecil, Wingfield.

264 Wriothesley, Smith, T. Seymour, Hoby, Sadler, Denny, Paulet, Wentworth, Talbot, Cecil, Baker, North, Petre, Paget, Montagu, Cheyne.

265 Baker, Bowes, Browne, Cecil, Cheyne, Denny, Dudley, Herbert, North,

Paulet, Petre, Rich, Russell, Sadler, Smith, Gage, Hoby, Paget, Cheke, T. Seymour, Southwell, Wingfield, Wentworth, Wriothesley, Tunstal, Cranmer, Somerset, Parr, Fitz Alan, Stanley, Talbot, Grey, Hastings, Brooke, Goodrich, Clinton, Devereux, and Neville.

266 Somerset, Dudley, Sadler, Wriothesley, Parr, Fitz Alan, Browne, Rich, Russell, Wingfield, N. Wotton, T. Seymour, Tunstal, Gage, Cranmer, Cheyne, Paget, Petre, Paulet, Baker.

267 Penry Williams raised the question in his 'A Revolution in Tudor History?', *Past and Present*, no. 31 (1965), 94–6.

268 Except for the period 31 January to 12 March 1547. Three of Cromwell's men (Cheyne, Rich, Sadler) were members of the council in August 1540; six (all but Southwell) were members in early January 1547.

CHAPTER 3: THE ORDER FOR MEETINGS

1 B.M., Cotton MS. Nero C. x, fos. 86–9, printed in Nichols, *Literary Remains*, II, 552–5; Burnet, *History of the Reformation* (ed. 1865) V, 121–4; *Chronicle*, 181–4; Williams, *English Historical Documents 1485–1558*, 529–31. Folios 86–7, although now separate leaves, originally formed a single sheet; fos. 88–9 have been repaired in such a way that they now form the sheet they once were. The title at the top of fo. 86a is, like the text on fos. 86a–88a, in the King's hand; fos. 88b and 89a are blank, as is fo. 89b, except for the endorsement in Petre's hand: 'For the counsail. 15 Januarij 1552°. R. R. E. 6^1.6°.'

2 SP 10/1/fos. 56–7. R. Lemon, editor of the *Calendar of State Papers, Domestic, 1547–80*, (p. 2) erroneously assigned Petre's memorandum a date of 15 February 1547; cf. Emmison, *B.I.H.R.* XXXI (1958), 203.

3 Emmison, *op. cit.*

4 Emmison admitted that he thought it 'futile' to attempt to assess 'the extent to which Edward's plan was actually "devised" by himself', but thinks that 'one may perhaps suggest' that the King did first write down the rules, that he showed them to Petre, who suggested a few additions (nos. 17–19 in Edward's draft) which the King then added hastily, and that Petre later drew up what Emmison calls 'an official version' of Edward's list, condensing, re-grouping, and re-casting the items into a more logical format; *ibid.* 206. Jordan (*Chronicle*, xxviii–xxxi) accepts Petre's version as deriving from Edward's draft and cites the King's 'Articles' as proof of the boy's 'leadership', his 'firm and orderly administrative sense', indeed, his mature 'concern with administrative reform'.

5 B.M., Egerton MS. 2603, fos. 33–4; given in Appendix 3. The text of the document is in the hand of Paget's unidentified assistant (the same hand, for example, is responsible for Paget's copy of a letter to Somerset of 12 March 1549 preserved among the Paget Papers at Plas Newydd, Angelsey MSS., box II, no. 2). Paget addressed fo. 34b, 'Advise

to the Kinges Counsail [in *crossed out*] the xxiij of Marche [155 *crossed out*] 1549'. The recipient's assistant wrote the endorsement (also on fo. 34b), 'The remembraunce gyven to my Master by my Lorde Paget xxiij martij 1549'. The water-mark, one variation of a gloved hand, fingers closed and extended, pointing to a star, identifies the paper as that commonly used by the secretaries and their clerks for council letters, notes, memoranda, etc.; see Briquet, *Les filigranes*, III, 573–4, figs. 11349–88, especially 11369, 11378, and 11382; Heawood, 'Sources of early-English paper supply', *The Library*, 4th ser., x (1929–1930), 440, figs. 137, 138. The present MS. is bound up in a volume of miscellaneous historical letters and papers (1494–1696) which had formed part of the library of Frederic Ouvry, P.S.A. It was purchased for the British Museum at Sotheby's, 30 March to 5 April 1882; cf. Egerton MS. 2603, *Catalogue of Additions to the Manuscripts in the British Museum, 1882–87*.

6   Emmison published the King's and Petre's 'Articles', *B.I.H.R.* XXXI (1958), 207–10.

7   Paget to Somerset, 30 August 1547; N.R.O., Fitzwilliam (Milton) MS. C.21.

8   *Span. Cal.*, IX, 145–6; cf. Gammon, *Statesman and Schemer*, 139–40.

9   See Paget's letters and memoranda to Somerset from August 1547 to July 1549 in his letter-book, Fitzwilliam (Milton) MS. C.21 at Delapré Abbey, Northampton, and especially the letter of 7 July 1549 of which there are copies in the P.R.O. (SP 10/8/fos. 8–11) and the B.M. (Cotton MS. Titus F. III, fos. 277–9).

10   Cf. Gammon, *op. cit.* 127–32; Jordan, *Edward VI*, 51–61.

11   Gammon, *op. cit.* 172.

12   Plas Newydd, Anglesey MSS., Paget Papers, box II, no. 4.

13   *Ibid.* no. 7, Petre's draft of a safe conduct authorised by the Earl of Bedford, Paget, and Petre (English commissioners for the treaty of peace with France) granting the right to any two French fishing boats to fish 'quietly' in the seas off Boulogne.

14   There is the possibility that Petre asked Paget for 'advice' about council procedure so that he might pass it on to Dr Nicholas Wotton, the second principal secretary of state and a newcomer to that office who would probably have found this detailed 'remembraunce' of a secretary's duties helpful.

15   Gammon does not discuss this. Professor Elton said (*Tudor Revolution*, 353) that 'in 1550 [these] orders were drawn up', but he never mentioned whether they were also passed; later (p. 359) he refers to the MS. as 'the council order of 1550', implying that the rules had been passed, and in the same context goes on to say that this order 'merely put on paper, and made a rule of, what had been the practice of the first great principal secretary', Thomas Cromwell.

16   See p. 10.

17   See pp. 13–14, 18–19.

18   The council adopted the rule and then apparently dropped it; with

one exception, original signatures appear only during June and July 1550 (see p. 278, n. 35). The exception is the meeting of 22 September 1551; see p. 138.

19 Rymer, *Foedera*, xv, 115.

20 *A.P.C.*, II, 5. In their letter of 11 October 1549 which set out, as the clerk's endorsement on the extant draft puts it, 'thole discourse of the duke of Somersetes doinges', the London council once again asserted that they had for reasons of procedure elevated Somerset. The first draft stated that the executors had 'resoloued for the better answering of ambassadors and suche others as shuld be suters vnto the counsell' to make Hertford Protector, but Petre crossed this out and wrote that it had been done 'considering thatt it shuld be expedient to have one, as it wer, a mouth for the rest to whom all suche as had to do with thole body of the counsell might resort'; SP 10/9/fos. 72–81.

21 The 'agreement' of 31 January 1547 laid down 'this special and expresse condicion, that he shall not do any Acte but with thadvise and consent of the reste of the coexecutours in suche maner, ordre, and fourme as in the saide wille … is apoynted and prescribed; which the saide Erle hath promised to perfourme accordingly'. Somerset (then Hertford) and twelve other executors signed this entry in the register; *A.P.C.*, II, 5–6. The provision of the will to which they referred specifically prohibited any one executor from doing anything appointed by the will alone unless a majority of the co-executors agreed in writing to the same; Rymer, *Foedera*, xv, 114.

22 It is interesting to note that the required majority (i.e. nine) of the sixteen executors had not signed the patent of 12 March 1547; only eight had done so. The record of the signing is preserved at Hatfield House among Cecil's papers, vol. 150, fo. 31. The patent itself was not at first enrolled in chancery; after it had passed the great seal Somerset kept it; *A.P.C.*, II, 64. The preservation among Cecil's papers of the clerk's record of the names of the eight signatories (Somerset, Cranmer, Paulet, Russell, Denny, Herbert, Paget, Browne) is explained by the fact that Cecil at the time was a clerk in Somerset's household. The eight councillors who signed the copy of this patent which the council entered in the register under a date of 21 March 1547 were: Somerset, Cranmer, Parr, Russell, Paulet, Paget, Browne, Cheyne; see also p. 285, n. 22. A second point of interest here concerns the formula which the commission of 12 March employed in distinguishing between the authority for government before and after that date. The letters-patent recognised that from 28 January to 11 March, Somerset alone or the privy council with *his* advice, consent, or agreement had been able to accomplish the tasks of government; after 12 March 1547 it would be the Protector with the privy council's advice whenever *he sought it*; *A.P.C.*, II, 71, 72–3. The commission of 24 December 1547 repeated this formula. The ten signatories of the patent of 24 December who were also executors were: Wriothesley, Russell, Paulet, Tunstal, Paget, North, Browne, Herbert, Montagu, Bromley; *Archaeologia* xxx (1844), 478–88.

23 Council in London to English ambassadors, 11 October; SP 10/9/fos. 72–81.

24 *Archaeologia*, xxx (1844), 483.

25 *E.H.R.* xxxvii (1922), 351ff. Cf. Elton, who follows Pollard's view, *Tudor Constitution*, 92–3.

26 B.M., Lansdowne MS. 160, fos. 264–7. There are two sets of notes here: the first sketch is found on fos. 264–5 and is endorsed 'The Lord President of the Kings Privy Counsell. 24 February 1617'; fos. 266–7 contain notes of this material and with a few slight exceptions add nothing to Caesar's first batch of material. In attempting to establish that there had been a Lord President, his place and precedence, his authority, the manner of his appointment, etc., Caesar made little distinction between the late medieval council and the early Tudor privy council, so that one must of necessity place his remarks into their proper context. On the other hand, Caesar's remarks on the operation of the presidency after what we should call the establishment of the privy council (*c.* 1536) appear sound enough. He is quite explicit with regard to sources; in several cases his observations (as he says) are based upon interviews with servants of an old household official, Sir Robert Vernon, who related just before his death what can only have been the functions of the President of the pre-Elizabethan privy council. On Vernon, see Stone, *Historical Journal* x (1967), 280–2.

27 B.M., Lansdowne MS. 160, fo. 264b.

28 Or Lord Steward, as the office is also described in the Act of 1539: 31 Henry VIII, c. 10; cf. Pollard, *E.H.R.* xxxvii (1922), 354. The holder was usually styled Great Master during Edward VI's reign.

29 Except, interestingly, in February 1550 when the Earl of Warwick became Great Master. See p. 301, n. 34.

30 Pollard, *E.H.R.* xxxvii (1922), 354.

31 Article on Paulet in G.E.C.

32 Caesar cites as evidence for this 'a little English booke, of the life, offices, and death of the said Lord Marques, Lord Treasurer of England, in English verse in 8°'. He refers in another place to this same 'little booke written of the life and death of the Lord Paulet, Lord Marquis of Winchester and Lord high Tresorer of England, that he being Lord St. John of Basing and Lord Great Master of the kings howsehold, was made Lord President of the kings Counsell by King Henry the 8 [in 33 *crossed out*] about 34 of his reigne...'; B.M., Lansdowne MS. 160, fos. 266a, 264a.

33 The patent of the treasurership is dated 3 February; *Cal. Pat. Rolls, Edw. VI*, iii, 178.

34 The letters-patent granting him the office of Great Master are dated 20 February 1550; *Cal. Pat. Rolls, Edw. VI*, iii, 189–90. It is almost certain that Edward VI was persuaded to appoint him Grand Master and President on 2 February 1550; indeed, on 1 February 1550 in a letter to an unknown recipient in which he disclosed all of the creations and advances to be made at court the next day, Warwick admitted that 'the Kinges Majeste ... wold I shulde be great Master

of his hignes house' but added, with what surely must have been wry circumspection, that at the moment 'the Presydentship of the councell remayneth sty . . . [*damaged*; *probably*: . . . still in the] kynges handes vndetermyned or disposed'; B.M., Cotton MS. Caligula E. iv, fo. 206. See also Wriothesley, *Chronicle*, II, 32–3; G.E.C., II, App. D, 622; Powicke and Fryde, *Handbook of British Chronology*, 136.

35 B.M., Lansdowne MS. 160, fo. 266b.

36 *Ibid.* Caesar had crossed these phrases through because they did not fit grammatically with what followed, so that he finally wrote the phrase cited in the preceding note.

37 *Ibid.* fo. 264b.

38 There exists an extraordinary star chamber bill of pleading addressed to St John as 'Graunde mastier' of the household and 'president of his Majestes privayt Counsaill'; Sta. Cha. 3: bundle 2, piece 84. For the significance of this and the President's duties with regard to the council's hearing of suits, etc. see pp. 127–8 and Appendix 3.

39 Duke of Northumberland addressing the council at Greenwich, from Oteford, 4 June 1552; SP 10/14/fo. 90.

40 *E.H.R.* XXXVIII (1923), 48.

41 *Ibid.* 51.

42 See p. 138.

43 *E.H.R.* XXXVIII (1923), 51.

44 In the following cases the name in parentheses denotes the location of the court: during 1550: 11 March, Greenwich (Westminster); 28 April, star chamber (Greenwich); 1 May, Baynard's Castle (Greenwich); 7 and 16 May, star chamber (Greenwich). During 1551: 5 February, Paulet's London residence (Greenwich); 29 April, Durham Place (Greenwich); 30 April, 'At London' (Greenwich); 9 August, Richmond (Hampton Court); 22 September, Chelsea (Windsor). During 1552: 1, 2, and 8 July, star chamber (Hampton Court/Oatlands). 20 January 1553, Ely Place (Greenwich). Sources: *A.P.C.*, II, III, IV; Edward VI's *Chronicle*.

45 *A.P.C.*, II, *passim.* The French ambassador also noted the fact that the council assembled for business at the Protector's London lodgings; Lefèvre-Pontalis, *Correspondance Politique*, 239 (a meeting of 21 November 1547).

46 The period considered is 31 January 1547 to 31 January 1548, during which the clerks entered proceedings under 174 dates. It is probable that 68 of these correspond to Somerset Place, although Somerset Place is given or referred to ('in loco predicto', 'apud locum predictum', etc.) only 16 times. That 53 dates (those from 4 May to 28 July, 12 November to 25 December, and 22 January 1548 and after) for which no location is given also correspond to Somerset Place is suggested directly by the fact that the clerks after about 4 May 1547 cited a location only when the place of dispatch had changed, so that the location of proceedings without a place can be taken to be the last-named site in the register. This observation, which is based on the notations for 1547, is supported by the diplomatic of the register

thereafter. The entries for Sunday, 22 January 1548, for example, are dated at Somerset Place. The next reference to a location (Greenwich) falls on 1 April 1548, but in this case, Greenwich appears not only in the heading for that page; 'At Greenwich' also appears in the same but less neat hand in a hastily drawn rectangle at the top left corner. The clerk was clearly very concerned that this second reference should indicate something significant about Greenwich and it was surely that 'At Greenwich', displayed thus so prominently, marked a change from the earlier place of business; interestingly, although no place for them is given, the entries which we assume must relate to Greenwich begin on 2 April, as *nothing* is listed under 'Sundaye the first of Aprilis at Grenewiche'. *A.P.C.*, II, *passim*; PC 2/2, 299.

47 Thus under 15 June 1547 the clerk noted in the register the council's authorisation of a payment of £5 to one John Garsia for riding in post; although no location is given, we assume the authorisation to have been made at Somerset Place, since that was the last-named place given (on 1 June); *A.P.C.*, II, 98. The assumption is correct, for the Treasurer of the chamber's record of payments lists the original warrant as dated 16 June at Somerset Place; E 101/426/5, fo. 20b. Similarly, we assume from the register that most of the entries from 12 November to 25 December date from Somerset Place, although no locations are given; a warrant of 4 December signed by Somerset, Cranmer, Rich, St John, Arundel, Petre, and Herbert is dated 'Somerset [house *crossed out*] place'; E 101/303/4.

48 Thus, for example, the letter to the Sheriff of Northamptonshire, from 'Shene', 21 July 1548, which although from Somerset, nevertheless contains privy council business, B.M. Add. MS. 29549, fo. 9; an original council warrant of 6 December 1548 from Somerset Place signed by Somerset, St John, Russell, T. Seymour, Paget, and Wingfield, SP 15/3/fo. 47; instructions from the council to the Lord Deputy and council in Ireland, 6 January 1549 from Somerset Place, signed by Somerset, St John, Russell, Warwick, Arundel, Shrewsbury, Southampton, T. Seymour, and Cheyne, SP 61/2/fos. 4–7; council to Lord Russell, 10 July 1549, from Syon, Pocock, *Troubles*, 22–4. Odet de Selve frequently reported audiences with the Protector at Somerset's residences in London and at Sheen; see his dispatches of 27 July and 1 December 1547 and 21 January, 9 August, and 15 October 1548, for example; Lefèvre-Pontalis, *Correspondance Politique*, 162, 243, 273, 425, 457.

49 This was the Marquess of Northampton; 28 January 1548; *A.P.C.*, II, 164. See p. 48.

50 Van der Delft reported that with the plague at its worst in London during October 1548 the King retired to Oatlands and Somerset to Syon House; the French ambassador was escorted to Oatlands by some of Somerset's men, but none of the council were 'even at Court at the time'. Council meetings, he said, were held not oftener than once a week at Syon; *Span. Cal.*, IX, 299.

51 Cranmer, St John, Russell, Thomas Seymour, Paget, Petre, Wingfield,

Denny, North; the group must be reconstructed from their signatures to letters during late August and September 1547; Staffordshire Record Office, D 1720/1/10, p. 427; B.M., Add. MS. 4801, fo. 219b; *ibid.* fo. 222. Cf. *Span. Cal.* IX, 141, and Lefèvre-Pontalis, *Correspondance Politique*, 186.

52 Letter of 30 August 1547; N.R.O., Fitzwilliam (Milton) MS. C.21.

53 E 101/426/5. The Treasurer of the chamber paid Manwarynge and his men 49s in December 1547 for such preparations 'by the space of three dayes against the Kingis Highnes repairing thether [to Westminster] from Hamptoncourte'.

54 See the recently discovered eye-witness's account of the reception of the Venetian ambassador attended by the great lords of Church, state, and household; Cairns, *B.I.H.R.* XLII (1969), 109–15.

55 See, for example, Somerset's letter to Russell, 25 September 1549, from Hampton Court; Pocock, *Troubles*, 76.

56 'An Eye-witness's Account,' *E.H.R.* LXX (1955), 605.

57 *Chronicle*, 18.

58 *Ibid.*, Wriothesley, *Chronicle*, II, 32–3; see Appendix 3.

59 *Chronicle*, 29, 124.

60 See pp. 19–20. In three 'items' Paget mentions Sunday as the one day on which all private suits, etc., which could only be determined by the privy council were to be heard; see Appendix 3. When on Thursday 20 October 1547 Somerset wrote to Lord Grey about the council's 'next Assembly apon Sondey coming', it was in the context of the time at which the council would entertain Grey's private suit for lead; SP 50/2/fo. 24. The rules of 1553 scheduled the council's hearing of such suits on Saturdays, reserving for Sundays the 'publique affairs' of the realm; B.M., Cotton MS. Nero C. x., fo. 86a and SP 10/1/fo. 56a.

61 See the discussion of the composition of the council book under Somerset, pp. 15–23.

62 See p. 18.

63 See pp. 21–2.

64 See p. 95.

65 SP 10/9/fos. 72–81; it is interesting that in the letter the council did not once refer to Somerset as Protector.

66 *Ibid.*; the author's italics.

67 They are found in Paget's letter-book, N.R.O., Fitzwilliam (Milton) MS. C.21.

68 *Ibid.* 2 February and 25 December 1548; 24 January, 25 January, and 2 February 1549; Plas Newydd, Anglesey MSS., box II, no. 2, 12 March 1549.

69 N.R.O., Fitzwilliam (Milton) MS. C.21.

70 See p. 178.

71 Van der Delft witnessed the comings and goings at Ely Place; *Span. Cal.*, IX, 476, 489. The council considered substantive matters at Warwick's house and the administrative staff dispatched the paper work at Westminster; witness the signed council and signet-letters from Westminster: council to Lord Cobham (Chaloner's hand), 24 Novem-

ber, with eleven signatures (but not Warwick's), B.M., Harleian MS. 284, fos. 56–7; council to justices of the peace, 20 November, eleven signatures (not Warwick's), SP 10/9/fos. 110–11; King and council to the bishops, 25 December (later copy with signatories' names including Warwick's), SP 10/9/fo. 113. It may be significant that Westminster is given as the place of meeting for only seven of the seventeen recorded meetings during November 1549; no place is given for the other ten. Eleven meetings are recorded for the month of December 1549; a location is given for none when in fact, as van der Delft observed, 'council meetings are being held daily in the house of the Earl of Warwick'. Cf. *A.P.C.*, II, 353–68.

72 This was the inner star chamber in which the privy council met for privy council business; there was also the outer star chamber where, at a table beneath the chair of state, lords of the council also sat to hear star chamber cases. It was this outer star chamber which had come to be called the court of star chamber; Pollard, *E.H.R.* XXXVIII (1923), 49, and XXXVII (1922), 516–17.

73 The location of this particular meeting on 1 February 1550 is surely explained by the fact that this day marked the end of the third session (4 November 1549 to 1 February 1550) of Edward VI's first Parliament.

74 *A.P.C.*, II, 330ff.

75 A clandestine conference on Wednesday, 16 January 1549; from the Marquess of Northampton's deposition regarding Seymour's activities; SP 10/6/fo. 40.

76 SP 10/14/fo. 10; *A.P.C.*, IV, 458; *Chronicle*, 106–7.

77 B.M., Add. MS. 34324, fo. 239b.

78 *A.P.C.*, III, 327.

79 Paget's 'Advise' of March 1550; see Appendix 3.

80 After meetings at Oatlands and Guildford the council moved successively to: a royal residence at Petworth; the late Sir Anthony Browne's place at Cowdray; Halnaker House, about four miles north-east of Chichester, a home of Thomas, Lord de la Warre; Sir Richard Cotton's house at Warblington on the Chichester to Portsmouth road; Bishop's Waltham, a former seat of the bishops of Winchester, at that time in the possession of the Marquess of Winchester; Portsmouth; Thomas Wriothesley's new house at Titchfield; Southampton; Christchurch; Salisbury; Wilton House, the Earl of Pembroke's; 'Motsounde' (i.e. Mottisfont), Thomas Lord Sandys' house in Hampshire; the Marquess of Winchester's ancestral home (a castle) at Basing, about one and three-quarter miles to the east of Basingstoke; Donnington Castle, the Duke of Suffolk's seat just north of Newbury; a monastery at Reading, one of Henry VIII's acquisitions. See *A.P.C.*, IV, 99ff.; Nichols, *Literary Remains*, II, 428ff.

81 No location is given for the six meetings on 7, 9, 10, 12, 13, and 16 September 1551. It is probable that the meetings of the 7th and the 9th occurred at Windsor, as that is where the court lay and where the last few meetings until the 6th were held. But on the 10th the King

removed to Farnham, where he stayed until the 18th. The meetings of the 12th, 13th, and 16th almost certainly took place at Farnham, for there is a copy of a letter in the British Museum to Sir James Croft from 'the court at Ferneham' dated 17 September 1551 and signed by Northampton, Bedford, Darcy, Herbert, and Cecil, all of whom, except Darcy, are recorded in the register as having attended the meetings of the 13th and 16th; Add. MS. 4801, fo. 233; *A.P.C.*, III, 353–60; *Chronicle*, 81–2.

82 B.M., Egerton MS. 2603, fo. 33a.

83 That is, during Edward's reign; the Elizabethan council adopted a Tuesday–Thursday–Saturday schedule on 9 October 1565; *A.P.C.*, VII, 267; see also the similar order of 11 December 1565, *ibid.* 306.

84 During the period 21 February 1550 to 16 June 1553 (1,212 days, or 173 weeks and a day) the clerks recorded 740 meetings or an average of 4·3 meetings per week; there were 73 meetings during the 137 days (19 weeks and four days) from 6 October 1549 to 20 February 1550.

85 Wriothesley, *Chronicle*, II, 26.

86 Points 10 and 11 in Edward's list; 11 and 13 in Petre's. Both lists are printed in Emmison, *B.I.H.R.* XXXI (1958), 203–10.

87 This is the 'year' from 18 April 1552 to 10 April 1553, that is, from the close of the Parliamentary session of 23 January to 15 April 1552 until the beginning of a new cycle in the council's movements, the annual move to Greenwich.

88 From Cotton's appointment in May 1552 until Wingfield's death in August 1552 there were 31 members; the author has not included Bromley in this number.

89 Not including Darcy, Devereux, Peckham, and Bromley, but including Southwell, the Marquess of Dorset, and the earls of Arundel and Southampton.

90 Bromley is not included in any of these totals.

91 Source: *A.P.C.* II–IV. The figures of attendance in this table have been compiled on the basis of the names of members given as present at meetings recorded in the privy council registers.

92 Nine councillors were not members of the committee 'for the state'. Consider their attendance at 218 meetings from 18 April 1552 to the end of the reign (not including 33 meetings on progress): Bromley, none; Gage, none; Montagu, 5 (2·3%); Rich, 6 (2·8%); Sadler, 7 (3·2%); North, 28 (12·8%); Baker, 34 (15·6%); Earl of Huntingdon, 41 (18·3%); George Lord Cobham, 100 (45·9%).

93 By the end of 1551, Cranmer had fallen from Northumberland's favour; see Ridley, *Cranmer*, 335, n.1. Westmorland and Hereford both attended meetings during the Parliamentary session of 1552, but left London immediately thereafter. The King must have been thinking of them when he referred to certain of the council going 'home to their countrees straight after the parliament . . .' but, as he added, when they return to Westminster they 'shal be admitted, of the counsell'. Indeed, all of Westmorland's and Hereford's later appearances fell during February and March 1553, either just before or during the

session of Parliament that year. B.M., Cotton MS. Nero C. x, fo. 85b;
A.P.C., III, 46off.; IV, 212ff.

94 Source: *A.P.C.*, IV. The list ranks privy councillors in descending order
in terms of their attendance at 218 recorded meetings from the close
of the Parliamentary session of 1552 to the end of the reign (not including the 33 meetings during the progress of 1552). The list does
not include Wingfield, who attended 26 of a possible 50 meetings
before the progress (he died August 1552), and Cheke, who attended
eight meetings after 2 June 1553.

CHAPTER 4: THE CONDUCT OF BUSINESS

1 B.M., Add. MS. 34324, fo. 239a.
2 Council to Lord Grey: '. . . where we haue recived certayne lettres owt
of the North in my Lord protectores absence [now for a day or to
added] and opened them as it was his graces pleasure we shuld'; SP
50/4/no. 108
3 *A.P.C.*, III, 188.
4 B.M., Add. MS. 34324 fo. 239a.
5 That is, letters addressed to Protector and council as well as letters
which should have been so addressed but were sent to Somerset alone
or to Paget. Even after his promotion from Secretary to Comptroller,
Paget continued to receive correspondence from English officials
abroad; cf. Gammon, *Statesman and Schemer*, 139–40. Thynne
endorsed much of the news out of Scotland which was sent to the
Protector rather than to the Protector and council; see, for example,
SP 50/3, *passim*.
6 For procedure under Northumberland, see the duke's letter to Cecil
of 9 December 1552 from Chelsea: he forwards several letters to Cecil,
one from the captain of the English garrison at Berwick, one from Dr
Smith in Scotland, and one from the French ambassador, asking Cecil
to give them to Darcy and Gates and 'soche others of my lordes' at
court for consideration; Cecil had apparently not seen the letters; SP
10/15/fo. 141. On 3 September 1552 Northumberland sent to Cecil
(who was with the court on progress between Wilton and Mottisfont)
a packet of letters from Christopher Mount, which packet, he said, he
forgot to deliver to Cecil when he (Northumberland) was last at court;
ibid. fos. 1–3. On 27 July 1552 Northumberland returned to Cecil a
letter from Peter Vannes, which, 'when you haue shewyd the sayd
lettre to the Kinges Majeste, and yf his highnes like the matter you
may therin worke with the rest of my lordes . . .'; SP 10/14/fo. 108.
7 In certain cases, an official might have written essentially duplicate
letters to Somerset and Paget; for example, two letters of John Brende,
Master of Musters in the North Parts, from Berwick, 23 June 1548,
SP 15/2/fos. 179–80. Ordinarily, the letter to Paget should have been
addressed to the council. Similarly, when Peter Vannes, ambassador
at Venice, wrote to the council, he sometimes sent highly important
information to Warwick alone, although the contents of these letters

in fact concerned the King's affairs generally in Italy; see his letter of 15 October 1550 from Venice to Warwick, in which he speaks of the Duke of Urbino's offer to serve English interests in Italy 'vnlest yt wer for maters of the Busshopp of Roome . . .', B.M., Harleian MS. 5008, fos. 181a–182a. At other times Vannes wrote to Warwick and the council in separate letters dated the same day (22 June and 7 September 1550, for example, in Harleian MS. 5008). Some of Sir Thomas Chamberlain's letters from Brussels are addressed to Warwick alone, others to the lords of the privy council, and yet both contain the kinds of intelligence which an ambassador ought consistently to have sent to the council; compare his letter of 1 June 1551 to Warwick with that of 28 July 1552 to the council, for example; B.M. Harleian MS. 353, fos. 108ff.; 120. These practices were not new; compare the similar informal procedures under Thomas Cromwell; Elton, *Tudor Revolution*, 357.

8 SP 10/15/fos. 131–2; SP 10/14/fo. 108.

9 Elton, *Tudor Revolution*, 361–8.

10 The incident was described in detail by Otwell Johnson in a letter to his brother; London, 22 May 1548; SP 46/5/fo. 268.

11 Otwell Johnson noted this fact; *ibid.*

12 *Span. Cal.*, x, 65–6; B.M., Harleian MS. 523, fo. 6b, council to Hoby, 21 April 1550.

13 Examples: Somerset to 'Mr Uvedule', from Sheen, 20 October 1547, in Thomas Chaloner's hand, commanding Uvedale to go to Berwick to assist Lord Grey in paying such sums as Grey should direct; SP 15/1/fos. 82–3. Somerset's instructions of August 1547 to Warwick as Lieutenant-General in the North are in Petre's hand; SP 50/1/fos. 64–7. 'A minute from my Lord Protector to Mr Wilford', 27 September 1548, is a rough draft in Paget's hand; SP 50/4/ no. 109.

14 Somerset to Sir Philip Hoby, for example, from Somerset Place, 23 January 1549, ordering the release of horses belonging to the Emperor's subjects and a request for the release of English merchants arrested at Antwerp; B.M., Harleian MS. 523, fo. 21b (a later copy).

15 A few examples: Petre's rough draft of Somerset's instructions to Lord Clinton of 1 August 1547 is endorsed in Thynne's hand as 'Minute of my lord Clynton instructions, primo Augusti 1547', SP 50/1/fos. 70–71; Paget corrected and made additions to a fair draft copy in Thynne's hand of instructions to Lord Grey for the garrison and castle at Broughty Crag, March 1548, SP 50/3/no. 88.

16 In the letter to Lord Grey referred to above, the Surveyor of the Victuals was to see to the supply of the garrison without troubling the lords of the council further, but Paget crossed through the 's' of 'lordes' and the words 'of the' and added 'protectors grace and' so that the Surveyor was now asked not to trouble 'my lorde protectors grace and Counsaill'. As the letter came from Thynne's hand with Paget's advice, there can be little doubt as to how frequently the other councillors were troubled by such questions; SP 50/3/no. 88.

17 Council to the Dean and chapter of Westminster, 11 April 1549, signed by Cranmer, St John, Wingfield, Petre, Smith; Westminster Abbey, Muniment no. 13242.

18 See, for example, van der Delft's description of the regular procedure, 2 April 1547, *Span. Cal.*, IX, 69–70. Scheduled meetings with ambassadors took place usually after dinner. De Selve arrived for an appointment at Hampton Court on 4 October 1547 only to find the Portuguese ambassador still in conference with the board; 'le chancellyer des augmentations l'ung d'entre eux', kept him official company in the ante-room before leading him into the council chamber; Lefèvre-Pontalis, *Correspondance Politique*, 214.

19 See van der Delft's letters to the Emperor and Queen Dowager, 16 June 1547, *Span. Cal.*, IX, 101–2, 104–6.

20 Van der Delft to the Emperor, 10 July 1547; *ibid.* 122.

21 Examples: he said that on 22 May Somerset notified him of an appointment for 23 May at a stated hour; a long interview followed 'and with this I left'; *ibid.* 267–70. See also similar meetings with Somerset on 21 June 1548 (*ibid.* 273), 21 August 1548 (*ibid.* 283ff.) and 7 September 1548 (*ibid.* 290). It is apparent that the French ambassador was meeting Somerset alone not later than July 1547, although he had earlier talked with at least a few of the council (not councillors also commissioned to negotiate with de Selve in specific matters) at regularly appointed times. De Selve did meet with the councillors remaining with the King while Somerset was in Scotland during September 1547; later he saw only Somerset (with the rare exception of a formal audience with Edward VI); Lefèvre-Pontalis, *Correspondance Politique*, *passim*.

22 Van der Delft to Charles V, London, 16 June 1547; *Span. Cal.*, IX, 102.

23 On 12 December 1547, in response to two questions raised by van der Delft (restitution of the property of Imperial subjects at Boulogne and the renewal of the commercial convention of 1522), Somerset is reported to have replied, 'I will speak to the Council about them, and will send you the answer.' Whether and to what extent Somerset consulted with the council cannot be known; he used the excuse to delay the answer which Petre delivered to van der Delft on 26 December 1547. On 1 June 1549 van der Delft reported that he was 'sent for' by the Protector 'who told me that he had thought over the various [other] points I lately put before him, and had consulted the council upon them', which at the very least was an admission that the ambassador had never seen the council in these matters; *Span. Cal.*, IX, 227, 229, 383.

24 The particular point in question on 8 March 1550 was Somerset's earlier (apparent) plan for Mary's marriage; *Span. Cal.*, X, 39–40.

25 Had de Selve appeared before 'my Lord Protector's grace and the rest of the council', the clerk would probably have recorded it thus, but under simply 'viij° Aug.' in the register, the note quoted here appears last in a list of four entries for that day; as the first three are

warrants for payment in one clerk's hand, they were probably jotted
down that morning, but the last is in a second clerk's hand and so was
surely penned on the spot in immediate response to the conditions of
the ambassador's departure, i.e. from Somerset's presence; PC 2/2,
560. De Selve's dispatches for this period are not available; the
appearance of the ambassador before Somerset alone is supported by
the description in Wriothesley, *Chronicle*, II, 20; cf. Nichols, *Chronicle
of the Grey Friars*, 61. Paget's draft of Somerset's letter of 8 August
from Westminster to Sir Thomas Cheyne refers to the fact that 'this
day the ffrenche [Kyng *crossed out*] Ambassador hath ben with us';
B.M., Add. MS. 27457, fo. 28. See Somerset's similar letter to Russell,
Pocock, *Troubles*, 46.

26 From a discourse entitled 'Against Edward duke of Somersett now
falslie vsurping the name of protector'; possibly a later Elizabethan
copy of the original written during Edward's reign; a seventeenth-
century hand has endorsed it, 'Out of a booke of Sir Tho. Smithe',
B.M., Add. MS. 48126, fos. 2–4.

27 For the articles of October 1549, see Stow, *Annales*, 601–2. William
Seymour thinks the charge discussed here one of a number of 'such
trivialities'; *History Today* xx (August 1970), 584. Professor Jordan
thought all of the articles 'vague and inchoate . . . a thin and tawdry
fabric . . .'; *Edward VI: the Young King*, 523.

28 Petre's draft of the council's letter of 11 October 1549, SP 10/9/fos.
72–81.

29 See the Imperial ambassadors' reports of such meetings at various
times during the period after October 1549. Random examples (references are to *Span. Cal.*): 31 January 1550, x, 17–19; 8 March 1550, x,
39–40; 8 January 1551, x, 198–203. Noted earlier was Dudley's calling
of a council meeting with the French ambassador (René de Mont-
morency-Laval, seigneur de Boisdauphin) on 18 January 1552; SP
10/14/fo. 10. Scheyfve noticed the French envoys with the council on
28 May 1553, *Span. Cal.*, xi, 46.

30 The Emperor's envoys had observed Dudley's meetings with L'Aub-
spine and Boisdauphin (*Span. Cal.*, xi, 62–3) as well as his earlier
frequent interviews (February 1553) with Soranzo, the Venetian
ambassador (*ibid.* 9).

31 SP 10/18/fos. 45–6, an agenda for 3 June 1553; Hatfield House, Cecil
Papers, 151, fo. 98, an agenda for 29 April 1553.

32 Points 6 and 7 on both Edward's and Petre's list, but Petre does not
make reference to the inclusion of unresolved matters; cf. Emmison,
B.I.H.R. xxxi (1958), 208.

33 Hatfield House, Cecil Papers, 151, fo. 98.

34 The secretaries would thus have been requested to present to the
King two different lists of 'things as are to be debated', one on Saturday morning and one again on Sunday evening, the Sunday list
containing new matters as well as the unresolved points of Saturday's
list. Points 5 and 8 on both Petre's and Edward's lists are thus really
identical and therefore repetitious, as both describe the secretaries'

act of presenting to the King on Sunday the business to be appointed for the following week; cf. Emmison, *B.I.H.R.* xxxi (1958), 208.

35   *Chronicle*, xviii–xix.

36   Chapman, *The Last Tudor King*, 186, 236.

37   See Nichols, *Literary Remains*, i, clxii–clxiv; *Chronicle*, xix–xxi. Chapman (*op. cit.* 171–3, 181, 186) bases her account on previous secondary work. See especially William Thomas's political discourses addressed to the King, Strype, *Ecclesiastical Memorials*, ii, pt. 2, 365–389.

38   *Chronicle*, 76.

39   B.M., Cotton MS. Nero C. x, fo. 85a.

40   On 20 November 1552 Scheyfve noted once again that the King 'has begun to be present at the Council'; *Span. Cal.*, x, 493, 592.

41   Petre's version, no. 14, SP 10/1/fos. 56–7.

42   Edward VI's version of the rule, no. 12 in his list, B.M., Cotton MS. Nero C. x., fo. 87a.

43   See p. 133 and p. 316, n. 105.

44   Strype's phrases are apt; he was describing a scene which Cheke must have reconstructed for Foxe upon whose version Strype based his own account. On 20 March 1551 the council sent Cranmer and Ridley to the King to tell him that they had decided for the moment to tolerate Mary's private masses; Pratt, *Acts and Monuments of John Foxe*, v, 700–1; Strype, *Sir John Cheke*, 177–8. Cf. *Chronicle*, 55–6, for Edward VI's brief notes.

45   See p. 283, n. 116.

46   Edward VI dated the memorandum '18°: Januarij. 1551°.' The 18th of January 1552 fell on a Monday, but Cecil's endorsement has the King delivering the agenda to his privy council at the stated place on 'the mondaye being the 19 of Janvary 1551 A°5°. of his Majestes reigne'. As Cecil is more likely to have remembered the day as a Monday rather than as the 18th or 19th, we may assume as correct the date Monday, 18 January 1552. Of the 16 councillors who received the document in the privy chamber that morning, 3 (Duke of Suffolk, Clinton, Gates) are not recorded as having attended the council meeting on the 18th; B.M., Cotton MS. Vespasian F. xiii, fo. 273; *A.P.C.*, iii, 458.

47   This is the famous alteration of the third point, which changed merely the punishment of Somerset's supporters to the execution of both Somerset and his friends. Although in the King's hand, the cancellations and additions clearly reflect Northumberland's hard political decision and the fact that he had persuaded Edward VI of the wisdom of the move by 18 January 1552. Somerset was beheaded on the morning of the 22nd.

48   Edward's fourth head, 'The resolution for the bishops that be nominated', refers to the candidates for the two vacant archbishoprics in Ireland; the King's and Cecil's memorandum on this matter is dated September 1551: SP 10/13/fo. 98. See also Nichols' note in *Literary Remains*, ii, 487–8, n.2. The filling of one of these vacancies was still

a matter of priority in October 1552; see Edward VI's memorandum of 3 October 1552, where it appears as point no. 10 under 'Religion': B.M., Lansdowne MS. 1236, fos. 19–20. Similarly, the 'matter for the exchaung', the 'order with the Londoners', and 'the bishop of Durhams matters' were still being considered on 24 March, 8 June, and 19 June respectively; see the entries under those dates in *Chronicle*, 116, 129–30, 131.

49 B.M., Cotton MS. Nero C. x., fo. 86b.

50 See p. 311, n. 48.

51 'Quelques particularitez', Bibliothèque Nationale, MS. Ancien Saint-Germain Français, 15888, fos. 214b–215b. The translation is the author's who has punctuated the text in such a way as to make the meaning of the original clear. Words in square brackets are the author's, of course.

52 *Ibid.* fo. 215a.

53 *Chronicle*, 25, 75; *D.N.B.*

54 See pp. 143–4.

55 B.M., Add. MS. 34324, fo. 239a. Caesar added: 'But of late time since there hath bene a Lord President of the said Counsell, those propositions are moved by him at the Table to the rest of their lordships . . .'; 'of late time' probably referred to early Stuart practice, as Caesar was writing this in 1625. The secretaries' duties described here should not be confused with the President's superior responsibility of supervising the secretaries' work – the President 'directed the business handled and to be handled' at the board – which Caesar described in his paper of 1617 and which was cited earlier (see p. 97 and p. 301, n. 26).

56 Edward VI's tenth rule set a quorum at four, and his eleventh point allowed four to five to 'reason and debat things . . . and if they agre amongst them selfis then at the next ful assemble of sixe they shal make a parfaite conclusion and ende with them'; B.M., Cotton, MS. Nero C. x., fo. 87a. Petre's rule no. 13 allowed four or five to 'debate thinges against the commyng of more without any resolution'; SP 10/1/fos. 56–7. Paget had said that six of the councillors attendant 'maye passe thaffaires occurrent'; B.M., Egerton MS. 2603, fo. 33a. On the composition of these six, see Appendix 3. For the changing quorum of the medieval council see Baldwin, *The King's Council*, 415. For a discussion of the procedures during Henry VI's minority, see Roskell, *E.H.R.* LXVIII (1953), 223–4.

57 B.M., Egerton MS. 2603, fo. 33a.

58 No. 19 on Edward's list; no. 12 on Petre's; cf. *B.I.H.R.* XXXI (1958), 208–10.

59 No. 15 among the King's rules; no. 18 on Petre's list; *B.I.H.R.* XXXI (1958), 208–10.

60 *A.P.C.*, III, 29.

61 *Chronicle*, 81.

62 SP 10/7/fos. 66–7.

63 The college was to have a president, vice-president, and eleven fellows at yearly fees of £40, £20, and 20 marks respectively; a steward, cook,

and butler at 20 nobles (£6 13s 4d) each; and an under-cook at £5. It was to be required of the fellows that they hold the degree of Doctor of Civil Law; each of them and the vice-president would be rated as masters in chancery with the appropriate yearly fees of that office (20 nobles). The president would enjoy the office of protho-notary of the chancery (worth 40 marks a year). In a second draft of the plan, Smith reduced the proposed number of fellows to eight as well as the fees for the cook, under-cook, and butler. Cf. Dewar, *Smith*, 41 and n.3; Mrs Dewar failed to mention this second draft and was in error in respect of the original number of fellows (eleven, not twelve) and their salary (20 marks, not £20).

64 Smith would have combined Clare Hall and Trinity Hall in order to create King Edward College, but when the enterprising master and fellows of Clare proved stubborn, the royal commissioners sent to visit the colleges turned against the idea. A bill to unite the two colleges was finally rejected by the Commons. See Dewar's account, *op. cit.* 41–2.

65 Elton, *Tudor Revolution*, 352. The Earl of Warwick once violated the rule, to the Duke of Somerset's discomfort; at the time (26 July 1550), Warwick was Lord President and Somerset occupied no office. Scheyfve had asked the council about several admiralty cases involving Imperial subjects and '. . . here my Lord Warwick, speaking before Somerset, who judging by appearances was little pleased about it'; *Span Cal.*, x, 141.

66 'Upon mocion made by the Lord Great Chambrelaine, it was agreed that from hensfoorthe the Gentlemen-at-Armes shulde be placed successively in the pencioners romes at everie avoidaunce, and so give attenduance on his Lordship as their Captaine'; *A.P.C.*, iii, 30.

67 No. 14 among Edward's rules; Petre's version (no. 17) reads: 'When matters bee debated And nott endyd, it shall bee noted how farre the matter is brought, and the argumentes of bothe sides to bee noted'; SP 10/1/fos. 56–7. Cf. *B.I.H.R.* xxxi (1958), 208–10.

68 Pratt, *Acts and Monuments of John Foxe*, v, 701.

69 Cited by Gammon, *Statesman and Schemer*, 125.

70 Paget to Somerset, 8 May 1549; N.R.O., Fitzwilliam (Milton) MS. C.21. Other copies : B.M., Cotton MS., Titus F. iii, fo. 276b; SP 10/7/fo. 8.

71 B.M., Egerton MS. 2603, fos. 33–4.

72 Elton, *Tudor Constitution*, 93.

73 Baldwin quotes Fortescue's observation that no 'lower man durst say anything against the opinion of the great lords'; *King's Council*, 405. See Baldwin's account of the settlement of differences in the medieval council, *op. cit.* 403–4.

74 Technically, the occasion may not have marked a privy council meeting, but van der Delft's description of his interview with 'the Council' on 30 January 1550 illustrates our point: when the ambassador inquired as to the council's position in respect of several detailed questions (Sebastian Cabot's mission, the seizure of Imperial subjects'

sugar and alum, marriage of Princess Mary to the Infante of Portugal), the members present asked him to withdraw to another room. After what the envoy called the particularly loud and 'heated' consultation that he could hear them carrying on, he was recalled. The council lay divided on the substance of these matters; consequently, they declared to him that they wished to discuss them further before giving a reply. *Span. Cal.*, x, 17–19.

75 On Boulogne, see p. 178; in the well-known letter of 7 July 1549, Paget told Somerset, 'I knowe in this matter of the comyns, every man of the counsaill hath mislyked your procedinges and wished yt otherwise'; N.R.O., Fitzwilliam (Milton) MS. C.21. Other copies: SP 10/8/fos. 8–11; B.M., Cotton MS. Titus F. iii, fos. 277–9.

76 Scheyfve reported that on the question of Edward VI's marriage, 'the Council were not agreed, my Lord of Somerset especially refusing his consent'; *Span. Cal.*, x, 226–7.

77 Van der Delft indicated that Somerset had told him this in reply to the ambassador's desire to lay several matters before the council in June 1547; *Span. Cal.*, IX, 102.

78 SP 10/14/fos. 75–6.

79 See the rule in Paget's 'Advise', Appendix 3.

80 Gammon, *Statesman and Schemer*, 172.

81 Malkiewicz, *E.H.R.* LXX (1955), 601–4.

82 One of the council's rules of 1426 stipulated that in the case of a tie in any dispute, that side was to prevail of which the Protector (Humphrey, Duke of Gloucester) was one; Roskell, *E.H.R.* LXVIII (1953), 225. Sir Julius Caesar also discovered this but he seems to have confused the office of Protector during Henry's minority with that of the Lord President; cf. B.M., Lansdowne MS. 160, fos. 267a, 264b.

83 Northumberland to Cecil, from Andover, 30 August 1552: 'ffor asmoche as at my departinge from the Courte, yt was not my chaunce to speke with you, to declare vnto you soche sutes as I made vnto the Kinges majestie, I haue thought good with theis briefly, to signyfye vnto you the same; fyrste, I was A suter to the Kinges majestie, ffor A lease in Reuersion of the syght and demaynes of the late monestary of cisiter, ffor Sir Anthony Kingston as basinge nowe occupieth yt, the which his hignes dyd graunte in the presens of my lord chamberlein, no yeres expressed'; SP 10/14/fos. 161–2.

84 The King noted (in his *Chronicle*, 132), on 25 June 1552 at Greenwich: 'It was agreed that none of my council should move me in any suit of land – for forfeits above £20, for reversions of leases, or any other extraordinary suits, till the state of my revenues was further known.' The author cannot find that the state of the revenues was better known by 30 August, the date of Dudley's letter to Cecil (above, p. 314, n. 83).

85 See, for example, the letter from Northumberland, Pembroke, Huntingdon, and Cecil to the rest of the council, 19 July 1552: '. . . when any order shalbe taken for the delyverye of any landes of the Lord pagett in satisfaction of parte of his fyne, our very good Lords

the Erle of Huntingdon and the Lord Chamberlayne maye not be forgotten'; B.M., Lansdowne MS. 2, fo. 165. See also the other parts of Northumberland's letter to Cecil cited above (p. 314, n. 83), SP 10/14/fos. 161–2.

86 *A.P.C.*, III, 53, 58.

87 On the question of allowing Princess Mary her private mass, the Imperial ambassador demanded of the council a final answer in February 1551; the council replied, according to Scheyfve, that 'their duty obliged them to confer with the King' but, he wrote to the Queen Dowager four days later, 'Paget, as spokesman, exposed to me that the Council without consulting the King's Majesty had conferred together'; *Span. Cal.* x, 234–7. Regarding the King's prohibition against Imperial subjects' shipments of goods to Flanders, Scheyfve wrote to the Queen Dowager on 1 March 1552 that Northumberland had 'told me that the King's Majesty had issued the prohibition for certain reasons of his own without giving any explanation'. Scheyfve must have found this an amusing fabrication, for English customs officials had revealed to Imperial merchants that the orders were the council's; *ibid.* 464. John Johnson, the English merchant, knew that the reason for the prohibition was 'the hindering of the sewtes our nation had at my Lade regent['s] court'; Johnson to Thomas Dison, from Glapthorn, 8 February 1552; SP 46/6/fo. 141.

88 While dining at court once (January 1552), Scheyfve made a point of watching carefully Edward's face and mannerisms; he thought the King remarkably quick of mind for his age, but nevertheless subject completely to Dudley's spell. The King 'kept his eye turned toward the Duke' in order to be able to know to which questions he might with liberty respond. The boy eventually 'withdrew, because of signs the Duke of Northumberland had made to him'; *Span. Cal.*, x, 437–8.

89 For the nine and the evidence of their service, see pp. 303–4, n. 51.

90 Paget to Somerset, 30 August 1547; N.R.O., Fitzwilliam (Milton) MS. C.21.

91 Thomas Lord Seymour to Somerset, from London, 15 September 1547; Plas Newydd, Anglesey MSS., Paget Papers, box II, no. 1.

92 Headed 'for thinterprise of Scotland', the plan assigned to St John the supervision of providing victuals enough for six weeks, the supplies to be collected at Ipswich. He was also to supervise a 'second revictuallement' of the whole army with supplies enough for two months and to take account of the state of the 'carriages' already sent north. Lord Admiral Seymour was to give order for the provision of ships. The whole council was to confer for the levying of men-at-arms (so that Secretary Petre could dispatch letters for that purpose). Warwick was to consider what ordnance and munitions should be necessary and the council was to decide upon the disposition of the remaining naval and land forces; SP 50/1/fos. 72–3.

93 SP 61/2/fo. 134.

94 SP 10/9/fos. 97–8.

95 SP 10/9/fos. 95–6; H.M.C., *Rutland MSS.*, IV, 200.

96 *A.P.C.*, III, 83.

97 The council's instructions to Paget, from Richmond, 12 July 1549. Paget was in Brussels negotiating the arrangements with the Emperor's envoys; B.M., Cotton MS. Titus B. v, fo. 34.

98 Petre and Wotton dealt thus with the Imperial ambassador as late as March 1552; the same two represented the council in that capacity with the French as late as October 1552; *Span. Cal.*, x, 483–5, 578.

99 *Span. Cal.*, xi, 6; *Chronicle*, 117. On 10 July 1552 the council did arrange that two privy councillors should give answer to the Imperial ambassador's presentations during the progress; on 23 July, Hoby and Dr Wotton were dispatched according to the appointment; *Chronicle*, 135, 137.

100 Edward VI's MS., which is the only source for the membership of the committee, lists the following: Archbishop of Canterbury (Cranmer), Chancellor (Goodrich, Bishop of Ely), High Treasurer (Winchester), Northumberland, Suffolk, Privy Seal (Bedford), Northampton, Shrewsbury, Pembroke, Westmorland, High Admiral (Clinton), Hereford, Chamberlain (Darcy), Vice-Chamberlain (Gates), King's Treasurer (Cheyne), Comptroller (Wingfield in March 1552; Cotton after 27 August 1552), Cecil, Petre, Dr Wotton, Hoby, and Bowes. Another name, that of Mason, originally appeared between Cecil's and Petre's, but Edward VI started to write another name through it; the illegible result stands as a cancellation; B.M., Cotton MS. Nero C. x, fo. 85a.

101 Elton, *Tudor Constitution*, 91.

102 *Ibid.*

103 Emmison, *B.I.H.R.* XXXI (1958), 203–10. The basis for this interpretation (which all modern writers have accepted) may be found in Burnet's remark that the 'first thing' accomplished in 1553 was a regulation of the privy council whereby that body was divided into committees, 'and every one of these had its proper work, and days appointed for the receiving and despatching of all affairs', etc.; *History of the Reformation* (ed. 1865), II, 357–8. Burnet's date, 1553, was wrong, but Emmison simply develops Burnet's interpretation as from March 1552.

104 *Cal. Pat. Rolls, Edw. VI*, IV, 355–6. The commissioners were the Earl of Bedford, the bishops of Ely, London, and Norwich, Sir Robert Bowes, Sir William Petre, Sir John Gates, Sir Philip Hoby and Sir Walter Mildmay.

105 B.M., Add. MS. 5498, fos. 58–60, a contemporary copy. The commissioners were the Earl of Bedford, Lord Darcy, Lord Cobham, Sir John Mason, Sir Philip Hoby, the Bishop of London, and the two Masters of the court of requests, John Cox and John Lucas. Cf. *Cal. Pat. Rolls, Edw. VI*, IV, 353.

106 B.M., Egerton MS. 2603, fo. 33b; see Appendix 3.

107 In his paper the King first noted all of his privy councillors' names as well as those of nine other commissioners. Then he wrote: 'The councelours aboue named to be thus deuided into several commissions and charges'. His first draft of the group 'for the state' included the

Chancellor (Goodrich, Bishop of Ely), High Treasurer (Marquess of Winchester), Northumberland, Privy Seal (Earl of Bedford), Northampton, Pembroke, High Admiral (Clinton), Chamberlain (Darcy), Vice-Chamberlain (Gates), Cecil, Petre, Dr Wotton, Hoby, and Bowes, plus Sir Walter Mildmay (a general surveyor in the court of augmentations) and John Gosnald (a solicitor of augmentations). The King crossed off the latter two and inserted the seven additional names into the list according to the places which they should by their various degrees have occupied. This correction necessitated placing the Archbishop of Canterbury first, Suffolk between Northumberland and the Lord Privy Seal, etc; the other five additions included Shrewsbury, Westmorland, Hereford, and the Treasurer (Cheyne) and Comptroller (Wingfield). The King referred twice to the commissions of March 1552 (entries of 3 and 15 March 1552, *Chronicle*, 114, 115), but failed to mention the resulting committee of 21. The corrections referred to represent deletions of the italicised words in the King's statement, 'Theis *only* to attend the matters of the state I wil site with them ons a weke *upon tuesday at afternoon, both to here the certificat of things past and* to here the debating of thinges of most importance'; B.M., Cotton MS. Nero C. x, fo. 85a.

108 See p. 110 and Table 10, p. 111.
109 The committee of September 1547 and the events of October 1549 do not provide examples of the council's dividing. In the former case, Somerset merely appointed a number of councillors to administer the realm from one place (Hampton Court) in his temporary absence; Paget then arranged informally that these councillors should share the burden of attendance at court. October 1549 presents the extraordinary spectacle of two rival factions of the council (one at London, one at Windsor with the King) contesting the government of the realm.
110 A meeting (21 September 1551) at Northumberland's Chelsea residence records an exception; *A.P.C.*, III, 360.
111 Cf. *Chronicle*, 7 July 1552, noting the fact that the Lord Privy Seal, Chamberlain, Vice-Chamberlain, and Petre went with the King.
112 He went with the King over the first half of the progress in 1550, from Guildford to Nonsuch, 14 August to 12 September, but left the court there, attending only one meeting (Oatlands, 2 October) between then and 7 November. He did not go to Farnham in September 1551, holding a meeting instead in his house at Chelsea on 22 September before joining the court at Oatlands for two meetings on the 24th and 25th. After returning from the North Country in 1552, he attended only one meeting at Salisbury on 29 August; *A.P.C.*, III, IV.
113 Sta. Cha. 3, bundle 2, piece 67, a petition endorsed by Cox at Guildford on 21 July. The petition also bears a note from Cox to the commissioners to whom the case was directed; the note is dated 'from the Corte at Waltham the xth of Auguste 1552'. As the supplicant alleged unlawful felling of timber, this was probably a requests case settled by the commissioners.
114 See the London council to the council at court, 13 July 1552, signed

by the Bishop of Ely, Marquess of Winchester, Dr. Wotton, North, Mason, Bowes (and others whose signatures are missing from this badly damaged original), B.M., Cotton MS. Caligula E. iv, fos. 311–314. See also the letters (warrants) to Peter Osborne during July and August 1552 from Oatlands, Guildford, Cowdray, Waltham, Portsmouth, and Southampton; E 101/546/19.

115 SP 10/14/fos. 147–8; *Chronicle*, 141. These must have been the pirates captured by Sir Henry Dudley in March 1552 and taken afterwards to Dover; *Chronicle*, 116.

116 SP 10/14/fos. 153–4. *Cal. S. P., Dom. 1547–80* mistakenly lists this as a letter from William Thomas, rather than from the council on progress with the King at Salisbury, 27 August 1552. For the order, see *A.P.C.*, III, 500 (9 March 1551).

117 See especially the letter of 13 July 1552 from the council at London to the council at court; B.M. Cotton MS. Caligula E. iv, fos. 311–14.

118 SP 15/3/fo. 181, 15 September 1552.

119 *Chronicle*, 81.

120 We know that Wiltshire was with Warwick at Chelsea on the 15th: SP 15/3/fo. 181.

121 The attendances given are recorded as having been those of the 13th; *A.P.C.*, III, 358.

122 *Chronicle*, 82.

123 Wiltshire must have done so, for Cecil, the King recorded, was sent from Windsor to London on the 20th to assist the Lord Treasurer; *ibid.*

124 Bedford, Northampton, Darcy, Herbert, and Cecil signed a letter at the court at Farnham on 17 September (B.M., Add. MS. 4801, fo. 233) and Huntingdon, Gates, and Wingfield probably attended the meeting at Farnham on the 16th (*A.P.C.*, III, 358), but Northampton, Bedford, Darcy, Gates, Huntingdon, and Wingfield were not at the meeting at Chelsea on 22 September (*ibid.* 360).

125 Day, Heath, and Tunstal, all of whom were later deprived of their bishoprics; *Chronicle*, 83.

126 *A.P.C.*, III, 360.

127 Wiltshire, Warwick, Herbert, Cecil, and Mason signed the proceedings for 22 September 1551; PC 2/4, 391.

128 PC 2/4, 388–9.

129 *Chronicle*, 83.

130 *A.P.C.*, III, 362. Bernard Hampton was the clerk thus sworn.

131 *Ibid.* 360.

132 SP 10/13/fo. 98; Nichols, *Literary Remains*, II, 487–8.

133 Wiltshire, Warwick, Northampton, Dorset, Huntingdon, Gates, Herbert, Cecil, Mason, and Bowes; *A.P.C.*, III, 366–9.

134 Until 10 November 1551 at least six of Edward's council countersigned all original bills as warrants for the great seal; *ibid.* 411.

135 *Ibid.* 369. The eight: Wiltshire, Northampton, Dorset, Huntingdon, Herbert, Cecil, Mason, Bowes.

136 The evidence for the fact that Rich and several of the councillors at

London signed the King's bill is contained in the draft of the King's letter to Rich of 1 October 1551; SP 10/13/fos. 109–10.

137 Edward VI recorded that Rich sent back the letter 'because there were but eight hands to it'; *Chronicle*, 84. The note of the King's reply to Rich in the council's docquet-book records: 'A lettre to the Lorde Chauncelor, vpon a lettre wrytten by him to therle of Warwick, wherein was inclosed a lettre of the Counsailes wrytten to him [the letter to the commissioners], whereunto he required more handes, the same lettre having eight handes to it all redy; which thing his majeste misliked, as by the same lettre he signified'; B.M., Royal MS. 18. C. xxiv, fo. 137a.

138 This is the draft of the King's letter to Rich, SP 10/13/fos. 109–10. Read (*Mr Secretary Cecil*, 76 and n.76, p. 475) says that Cecil drafted the letter. The 'my' in Cecil's endorsement of the draft is his contraction for 'mynute' and is not the possessive pronoun: 'j°October 1551. Mynute from the Kynges Majesti to the Lord Ryche, Lord Chauncellor'; SP 10/13/fo. 110b. Read was quoting Nichols' transcription in *Literary Remains*, II, 347, n.2. The text of the King's letter, however, is not in Cecil's hand, but rather that of an unidentified assistant. Of course Cecil may have been the author, but as Rich had written personally to Warwick, it is likely that Warwick dictated much of the reply. The hand may be a clerk's, and the phrasing perhaps even Cecil's, but the message is Dudley's. Interestingly, Edward VI referred to the letter as one 'that I had willed anyone about me to write'; *Chronicle*, 64. Since at this time (1 October 1551) the council was counter-signing signet-letters, many if not all of the ten present at the meeting on the 1st (Cranmer, Wiltshire, Warwick, Northampton, Huntingdon, Clinton, Herbert, Cecil, Mason, Bowes) must have subscribed the royal letter; *A.P.C.*, III, 375. The presence of Cranmer and Clinton is particularly interesting as neither had attended a session since the extraordinary meeting of 22 councillors at Richmond on 9 August 1551. (Cranmer did not attend again until 17 October.) Warwick clearly had summoned them to sign the King's reply to Rich.

139 Rich's letter to Warwick of 29 September has not survived, but we can deduce why the chancellor returned the council's letter to Hampton Court for the signatures of those who had not first signed it. Although it is nowhere expressly stated, Rich and the other councillors at London had probably signed the letter to the commissioners, just as they had signed the bill. The letter, after all, reached them open, not sealed; if, when they received it, it already contained the requisite number of signatures (six) and they wished not to sign it, then they could still have sealed it and sent it to the commissioners. We cannot know really whether fewer than six at Hampton Court had actually signed the letter before dispatching it to Rich; we know only that when Warwick received the letter on the 29th, it displayed eight signatures. However, the King's reply of 1 October clearly distinguished between the 'more handes of our Counsellors' generally which Rich

required above the number of eight and the 'much fewer than viij'
(no matter who they were) of 'the nombre of our Counsell attending
upon our person' at the time the letter was signed. How many were
'much fewer' than eight? One can only suggest that 'much fewer'
probably constituted more than two, in which case fewer than six did
actually sign the letter at the time of its writing. Contrary to what Professor Jordan has implied, therefore (*Chronicle*, 84, n.129), it is
unlikely that the eight recorded as present at the second meeting on the
28th at Hampton Court were the eight who signed the letter. Once
again, we cannot say who were the five or fewer councillors who probably did sign it, but as Warwick and Gates did not attend that
second meeting, it would appear unlikely that the letter to the commissioners carried their signatures.

140 Cf. *A.P.C.*, III, 362.
141 Of the eight at the second meeting on the 28th, five were Dudley's
appointees: Dorset, Huntingdon, Cecil, Mason, Bowes. The other
three, Wiltshire, Northampton, and Herbert, supported Warwick.
142 *A.P.C.*, III, 363.
143 A fact to which the King's letter of 1 October 1551 directly referred;
SP 10/13/fos. 109–10.
144 Cf. *Chronicle*, 135; B.M., Cotton MS. Galba B. xii, fos. 229–31;
Nichols, *Literary Remains*, II, 539–43.
145 To Cecil from Knoll; SP 10/15/fos. 1–3.
146 *Chronicle*, 88.
147 SP 10/15/fo. 30; SP 15/4/fo. 10; SP 10/15/fo. 141.
148 SP 10/18/fo. 9; SP 15/4/fo. 9; SP 10/15/fos. 79–80; SP 10/14/fos.
161–2.
149 SP 10/15/fo. 30.
150 According to the council's records, he attended not one meeting from
25 October 1552 to 29 January 1553; cf. *A.P.C.*, IV, 152–210. He
worried that his long absence from court should be interpreted as
neglect of the King's affairs; in fact he had been ill, as he stated to
Cecil in a letter of 3 January 1553 from Chelsea; SP 10/18/fo. 3.
151 To Cecil, from Ely Place, 7 January 1552; SP 15/4/fo. 1.
152 *Span. Cal.*, x, 610–11.
153 SP 10/15/fos. 149–50.
154 SP 10/18/fo. 11.
155 SP 10/15/fos. 79–80.
156 Hatfield House, Cecil Papers, 151, fos. 7–8.
157 SP 10/15/fo. 141.
158 The Earl of Shrewsbury brought with him to Chelsea on 28 December 1552 an abstract of the council's legislative programme for the
next Parliament; SP 10/15/fos. 149–50. Darcy also served as liaison
between the duke and the board; SP 10/18/fo. 11.
159 *Span. Cal.*, x, 46–7. The clerks recorded 24 meetings for March
1550. All but one of these were convened at Westminster where the
court lay. Warwick attended only four of the 24 meetings, including
the only meeting that month (11 March) which was convened at

Greenwich; *A.P.C.*, II, 403–22. See also van der Delft's report of 31 January and 8 March 1550; *Span. Cal.*, x, 21, 43.

160 From Chelsea, 9 January 1553; SP 10/18/fo. 9.

161 See Dudley's letter to Cecil of 4 September 1552 in which he notes that the merchants' suit for licence to ship cloth to Flanders can be turned to the King's benefit; 'you may yf you think so convenyent breke yt to the kinges majestie, And to soche others as you think wylbe close and secrete in yet.' It was, he said a matter 'which I wolde wishe mought be well conseyved and order taken accordinglie and handeled so that thos persons which I wolde sholde not vnderstand the grounde of the matter . . .'; SP 10/15/fo. 3. On 2 October Cecil noted seven merchants who were to appear before Winchester, Northumberland, and Bedford; Haynes, *State Papers*, 127–8. See also Cecil's text of the agreement made at Syon on 3 October 1552 (*not* 13 October as Jordan would have it; *Chronicle*, 147, n.173) in the presence of seven privy councillors (Northumberland, Suffolk, Darcy, Bedford, Northampton, Cobham, Cecil); SP 10/15/fos. 31–2. Councillors were meeting officially at Hampton Court at this time; there are no meetings recorded for 2 or 3 October; cf. *A.P.C.*, IV, 134–5.

162 SP 10/15/fos. 79–80. The council's letters to Northumberland often really were in answer to his sent to Darcy and Cecil; *A.P.C.*, IV, 66.

163 No one knew this better than Paget who on 23 October 1552 urged Cecil to forward to Darcy his supplication to the lords of the council for a pardon of his alleged offences; Plas Newydd, Anglesey MSS., box II, no. 14.

164 SP 61/4/fo. 219.

165 SP 10/15/fos. 125–6.

166 SP 10/18/fo. 11.

167 SP 10/15/fos. 137–8.

168 SP 10/15/fo. 141.

169 SP 15/4/fo. 14, 4 June 1552, from 'Oteford'.

CHAPTER 5:
THE AUTHORISATION AND ADMINISTRATION OF BUSINESS

1 Some councillors as privy councillors also signed official documents not classified as acts of council. Some of these, especially the bills of certain original Acts of Parliament, are considered in Chapter 6; see pp. 191–2.

2 See p. 14 and pp. 18–20.

3 Adair, *E.H.R.* XXXVIII (1923), 418.

4 Eleven signed the letter of 12 February 1547 to the select gentlemen in Sussex, B.M., Add. MS. 33084, fo. 2.

5 Council to [priests of St Bartholomew's Hospital?], from Westminster, 1 August 1549; Corporation of London Record Office, Journals, 16, fo. 26a (also in Letter-book R, fo. 26).

6 Somerset, St John, Arundel, and Petre to Sir Anthony St Leger, Westminster, 28 November 1547; B.M., Add. MS. 4801, fos. 222b–223a.

Somerset, St John, Russell, Denny to the customs officials at London, from Hampton Court, 5 August 1548; SP 46/1/fo. 173.

7 See Paget's corrected draft of such a letter to Princess Elizabeth, 17 February 1549; Hatfield House, Cecil Papers, 150, fo. 100.

8 Somerset, Cranmer, Rich, St John, Warwick, Arundel, Petre, Denny, North, and Sadler signed the letter to her from Richmond, 7 July 1549, explaining that they had instructed her chaplain to inform her of various matters; Pocock, *Troubles*, 20.

9 Council to the Dean and chapter of Westminster, signed by Cranmer, St John, Wingfield, Petre, and Smith, from Westminster, 11 April 1549; Westminster Abbey, Muniment no. 13242.

10 The author has found only three letters with five or fewer signatures: (1) council to [official in the admiralty court?], from Windsor, 23 September 1552, signed by Winchester, Northumberland, Bedford, Northampton, Cecil; B.M., Add. MS. 36767, fo. 5; (2) council to Sir Thomas Gresham, from Westminster, 24 February 1552 (contemporary copy with five signatures indicated – Northumberland, Bedford, Clinton, Darcy, Cecil), B.M., Add. MS. 5498, fo. 35b; (3) letter signed by Warwick and Herbert to 'Sr Raynolde Scotte' authorising him to sell the royal stores (wood and coal) in his possession and requiring him to turn the money over to the Treasurer of the mints for the King's use ('thes our lettres shalbe your sufficient warrant and discharge in this behalf'), from Greenwich, 27 January 1551; B.M., Add. MS. 33924, fo. 2.

11 Council to Hoby, Bishop of Norwich, and Morison, from Greenwich; B.M., Harleian MS. 523, fo. 40b.

12 The last folios of B.M., Add. MS. 5476; see pp. 24–5.

13 See pp. 25–6.

14 *A.P.C.*, III, 115.

15 Read, *Mr Secretary Walsingham*, I, 425.

16 The clerks endorsed these signed drafts as 'minutes' of the letter sent. Two examples: (a) 'A minute of the lettres to the speciall men in euery shere v° junij 1548', signed by Somerset, St John, Russell, Arundel, Seymour, Cheyne, Wingfield, and Petre, SP 10/4/fos. 28–9; (b) 'Minute of the lettre sent to all the bishops with the booke for thorder of the communion xv° martij 1547 [1548]', with the signatures of Rich, St John, Russell, Arundel, Petre, North, and Edward Wotton; SP 10/4/fos. 3–4.

17 See below, p. 329, n. 89.

18 *Letters and Papers, Henry VIII*, XXI (pt. 2), no. 322.

19 *Cal. Pat. Rolls, Edw. VI*, II, 250–1. The commission was dated 20 November 1549 but was made retroactive to 6 October – i.e. it validated all warrants which six or more of the 25 privy councillors named had issued since that time. It further stipulated that of the six, Cranmer, Rich, St John, Russell, Northampton, Warwick, Arundel, Shrewsbury, Southampton, and Wentworth were to be two.

20 The author has found a fragment of one warrant addressed to Sir

John Williams, Treasurer of augmentations, dated June 1550 and signed by four, Somerset, Goodrich, Wiltshire, and Petre; SP 46/2/fo. 105. There is also an order to Peter Osborne to pay Sir William Cavendish, Treasurer of the chamber, £2,000, dated at Oatlands, 10 July 1552 and signed by Cranmer, Winchester, Gates, Dr Wotton, and Petre; E 101/546/19.

21 *A.P.C.*, III, 4.

22 Council to Peter Osborne to pay Bernard Hampton, clerk of the council, or Nicasius Yetsworth, clerk of the signet, £2,091 13s 4d to be 'delivered over' to the French commissioners, Westminster, 5 December 1552, signed by Winchester, Bedford, Darcy, Dr Wotton, Cecil, and Mason, E 101/546/19.

23 B.M., Cotton MS. Nero C. x, fo. 88a.

24 Examples are three signet warrants for payments in amounts from £200 14s 4d to £500 during April and June 1553: SP 15/4/fos. 111, 116, 121.

25 Warrant of 24 August 1547 from Hampton Court signed by Cranmer, St John, Petre, ordering Peckham to deliver £1,000 to William Johnson for payment of the garrison and labourers at Portsmouth; E 101/303/4.

26 Council to Peckham, to pay £90 to ?, 15 January 1548 at Hampton Court, signed by Somerset, Cranmer, St John, and Northampton; E 101/303/4. Council to Sir Anthony Denny to pay Sir John Lelen, clerk, £34 0s 2d, signed by Somerset, Cranmer, St John, Warwick, and Tunstal; Westminster, 22 March 1547, SP 46/1/fo. 7 (*A.P.C.*, II, 74).

27 Requiring them to pay Richard Bridges £7 10s 0d; William Cecil, then Somerset's secretary, counter-signed the letter; Westminster, 14 May 1548; E 404/105.

28 The stated purpose of the commission of 12 March 1547 and therefore also of 24 December 1547 was to establish 'thundoubted powre and sufficiencie of the saide Lorde Protectour and Counsail to treate and conclude apon any matter wherein they shuld have to do on his Hieghnes behaulf' and also 'for their discharge anempste his Hieghnes in case it shuld please the same hereafter to call them or any of them to accompte for any thing which they shuld do apon foundacion or grounde of their afforesaide charge'; *A.P.C.*, II, 64, 63.

29 Elton, *Tudor Revolution*, 291.

30 The secretary's docquet-book of council warrants for payments made in the King's affairs at Calais, Boulogne, and the North parts in 1549 preserves the record of some of these: for £500 to be sent to the treasurer at Calais, Greenwich, 16 May; £5,000 to pay to [blank] to be conveyed to the treasurer of the wars in the North, Greenwich, 17 May; to Andrew Reignhart, Chancellor to Duke Otto of 'Lunghburghe', £37 10s by way of the King's reward, 21 May; £500 to the treasurer at Calais, 13 June (*A.P.C.*, II 288); £10,000 to be conveyed to the treasurer in the North parts, 3 June; SP 38/1/fos. 1–8. For a list of those issued from 1 April to 29 September 1548, including one

for £2,000 to the Treasurer of the chamber, see the privy seal writ of 23 January 1549, E 404/105.

31 'where our moste dere and welbeloued vncle Edwarde Duke of Somerset...[and] the reste of our pryvie counsaill have directed dyuers warrauntes signed with their handes to you our seid [treasurer and chamberlains]...for paiments by you to be made to dyuers... For all which foresaid warrauntes you our seid Treasourer and Chamberlaynes hathe as yet of vs no pryvie Seale for the dyscharge therof accordinge to the old auncyent course of our seid Courte as we certaynely knowe...'; E 404/105. The council also ordered payment of its diets by privy seal to the exchequer, monies to be paid upon presentation of the council's diet expense books signed by the Lord Chancellor, Lord Treasurer, and Lord Privy Seal or two of them; St James, 16 May 1547, *ibid*. (later copy: B.M., Lansdowne MS. 171, fos. 343b–344a).

32 De Selve had put the question to Paget on 4 March 1547: Lefèvre-Pontalis, *Correspondance Politique*, 111–12.

33 This was Sir John Cheke's declaration at the time he gave evidence against Lord Admiral Seymour, 20 February 1549; SP 10/6/fo. 68.

34 King to council in Ireland; Greenwich, 7 April 1547, signed by Somerset, St John, Russell, Warwick, Cheyne, Arundel, Browne, Petre, Gage, Denny; B.M., Add. MS. 4801, fo. 220. Somerset, Paget, St John, Russell, and Wingfield signed the King's letter to the Deputy and Chancellor of Ireland ('given under our Sign manual and signet at our mannor of otelandyes'), 8 September 1548; *ibid*. fo. 223b. It should be noted, however, that the King's letter to the inhabitants of Kilkenny, Ireland, from Hampton Court, 18 October 1547, may have been counter-signed by Somerset alone; *ibid*. fo. 217b. All of these are later copies with signatories' names indicated.

35 King to council in Ireland, from Hampton Court, 27 August 1547, signed by St John, Russell, T. Seymour, Browne, Wingfield, and North, *ibid*. fo. 222 (also a later copy with signatories' names added). Whereas the usual formula ran '[by] thadvys of our derryst vnkcyll [*sic*] the duke of somersett governor of our person and protector of our Realmes domynyons and subyettes and the rest of our prevy councell...' (King to Sheriff and JPs of Sussex, from Richmond, 12 June 1549, signed only by Somerset: a contemporary copy; B.M., Add. MS. 33084, fo. 4), the formula in this case reads 'by thadvise and consent of our counsell presently attending on our person....'.

36 Elton, *Tudor Revolution*, 276–84.

37 A signet warrant dormant to Sadler, Master of the wardrobe, to deliver bedding and apparel to the Lieutenant of the Tower for the use of the Duke of Norfolk, Westminster, 3 March 1548, signed by Somerset, Rich, Russell, Arundel, T. Seymour, North; SP 46/1/fo. 154. That warrants of this type have not survived is not surprising, as they were addressed to individuals and not to courts of record. Unfortunately, the Treasurer of the chamber's accounts (E 101/426/5) do not indicate whether the council signed the King's letters directed

to his office. Expenditures of the King's treasure outside courts of record should regularly have been authorised by signet warrants, which by this time probably frequently bore the stamp; Elton, *Tudor Revolution*, 281. Cecil retained the record of the delivery of 42,741 ounces of plate from the King's jewel house to the mint on 3 March 1549 on authority of a signet warrant; Hatfield House, Cecil Papers, 151, fo. 40.

38 Paget's draft of one for a pardon dated 4 March 1547 refers to another for the general pardon proclaimed at the coronation: '[we] grawnted our warrant in wryting vndre our signe and subscribed with the handes of our sayd vncle and counsail to the lord chauncelor or keeper of our gret Seale for the makyng out of our sayd pardon vndre our gret seale of England . .'; SP 10/1/fos. 98–9. See also the signed bill of 15 June 1548 by which the King licensed Edward Brokett to exercise the office of Sheriff of Essex and Hertford, signed by Somerset, Rich, St John, Russell, Arundel, Cheyne, Wingfield, and Sadler; C 82/885. (Cf. *Cal. Pat. Rolls, Edw. VI*, III, 51).

39 King to Cranmer, from Hampton Court, ordering him to provide 15 men and horses to serve in Scotland; the formula in all of these is that it is the King's pleasure by the advice of Somerset and 'the rest of our pryvie Counsaill'; B.M., Harleian MS. 6986, fo. 17. A signet-letter dated at Greenwich, 16 April 1547 to the Sheriff and JPs of Wiltshire bears only the stamped signature of Edward VI, but its condition suggests that it never was sent; B.M., Add. MS. 28212, fo. 52.

40 B.M., Add. MS. 28212, fo. 52 and SP 10/2/fo. 4.

41 See the stamped signet warrant to Paget ordering him to raise 500 men; Westminster, 6 August 1549; Staffordshire Record Office, D[W] 1734/4/2/1.

42 *Archaeologia* xxx (1844), 484–5. The patent of 24 December thus replaced a previous commission of 11 August 1547 constituting him lieutenant and captain-general of the wars both by land and sea; Rymer, *Foedera*, xv, 174, where the date is given incorrectly as 1548.

43 Staffordshire Record Office, D[W] 1734/4/2/1.

44 In raising an 'Armye Roiall' to go against Ket, the King's stamped signet warrant to Paget nevertheless also spoke of the need to have 'a mayne force also aboute us', of which Paget's 500 men were to form a part; *ibid.* See also the signet warrant bearing the King's stamp and Somerset's autograph directing the recipients to assemble at court in order to thwart the council's conspiracy; from Hampton Court, 5 October 1549; SP 10/9/fo. 4. The King sent one of these letters to the mayor and aldermen of the City of London ordering them to send 1,000 men to court for the defence of the royal person; the warrant was probably stamped, although the copy of the letter does not of course indicate this; Hampton Court, 6 October 1549; Corporation of London Record Office, Journals, 16, fo. 36a.

45 From London, 8 October 1549; SP 10/9/fo. 42.

46 See, for example, the copy of a typical royal circular letter commanding certain special men in the shires to repair to Windsor Castle with

well-armed horse and foot, there to receive further order; spaces for the number of horse and foot as well as the day of the month on which they were to report were left blank; Richmond, 1 July 1549; SP 10/8/fo. 1. Compare this with an original stamped signet warrant addressed to Paget from Westminster, 6 August 1549: the number of men that Paget was directed to raise ('fyve hundreth') was written in by the same signet clerk later in the space he had left blank; he also added later the closing phrase, 'yeven under our signet at our palace of westminster the vjth of August the third yere of our reign'. A second clerk addressed the letter; Staffordshire Record Office, D[W] 1734/4/2/1.

47 On 10 November 1551 the council noted: 'Where as it hath byn used that to all suche bylls as sholde come to the Kinge's Majesties signature syx, at the least, of his Highnes Counsell sholld set theyr handes as a testemonie that the same came to his Majestie to be signed by theyr counsell and advise, which ordre hath now a long season contynewed...'; *A.P.C.*, III, 411. Example: the King's letter to various JPs, 6 December 1550, from Westminster, bearing the stamped signature at the head and the autographs of ten councillors at the foot; SP 10/11/fo. 26.

48 *A.P.C.*, III, 411.

49 *Ibid.* A few of these docquets remain: SP 38/1/fos. 9–17. For a discussion of these, see pp. 27–8.

50 For the full text, see Hughes & Larkin, nos. 545–9.

51 By the provisions of 1 Edward VI, c. 12; Hughes & Larkin, no. 552.

52 Fourteen constituted a majority, but in 1547 St John held three of the offices named separately in the Act – President, Great Master, and Chancellor (or Keeper of the great seal) – so that Somerset really needed twelve signatures in addition to his own. Cf. Elton, *E.H.R.* LXXV (1960), 214; Elton, *Historical Journal* XII (1969), 705; Elton, *Tudor Constitution*, 23, n.1.

53 Hughes & Larkin, nos. 275–95, but not including no. 285 which, as Professor Elton has pointed out, is not a proclamation; *Historical Journal* VIII (1965), 268.

54 Hughes & Larkin, nos. 296–316.

55 C 82/865. The signatories: Somerset (who, as Somerset and not the Earl of Hertford must therefore have signed this on or after 16 February), Cranmer, St John, Tunstal, Russell, Denny, Herbert, Paget, T. Seymour, North, Wingfield.

56 See the warrant of 17 May 1548 bearing the King's stamped signature and the autographs of Somerset, St John, Russell, Petre, Denny, and Sadler, C 82/884; text: Hughes & Larkin, no. 308. An exact transcription is given in Rose-Troup, *The Western Rebellion of 1549*, App. C, 422–5. Somerset, Cranmer, Rich, Russell, Cheyne, Denny, and North signed the stamped warrant for the proclamation of 17 June 1548, C 82/885; text: Hughes & Larkin, no. 311.

57 SP 10/7/fos. 55–6. The endorsement quoted here appears on another contemporary copy immediately following the draft in the P.R.O.

volume; SP 10/7/fos. 57–8. Hughes & Larkin (no. 333) date the proclamation 23 May; they also cite another copy (B.M., Harleian MS 4943, fo. 227) which bears the note that the council approved the proclamation.

58 Somerset, Cranmer, St John, Tunstal, Russell, Paget, T. Seymour. Of the offices named in the Act, thirteen were represented on Somerset's 'first' privy council (March 1547 to May 1548); taking the names of the offices and supplying the names of the office-holders in 1547 we get, in addition to the seven, Warwick, Arundel, Petre, Cheyne, Gage (until 29 June), Browne, and Montagu.

59 Corporation of London Record Office, Journals, 16, fo. 28b; the clerk of the Common Council copied out the text of the proclamation, entering it directly into the MS. Journal, indicating the signatories' names at the foot. (This is the source of Hughes & Larkin's text, no. 346.) Another clerk also entered a copy similarly into what is now Letterbook R, fo. 28. An early Stuart MS. copy giving these four signatories' names is no. 44 in the collection of the Library of the Society of Antiquaries.

60 That is, it is not to be found in the appropriate file for August 1549, C 82/906.

61 Library of the Society of Antiquaries, no. 45, an early Stuart MS. copy, which indicates that Somerset's name appeared at the foot of the version from which this copy was taken. Grafton did not print this proclamation. Text: Hughes & Larkin, no. 347. Similarly, there is no warrant for this in C 82/906.

62 Hughes & Larkin, no. 346. See the King's orders to Paget to raise these troops, 6 August 1549: Staffordshire Record Office, D[W] 1734/4/2/1.

63 Hughes and Larkin give 77 (nos. 275–351), but nos. 285 and 338 are not proclamations; Cf. Elton, *Historical Journal* VIII (1965), 268. No. 351 is an ordinary signet-letter, not a proclamation, the date of which, furthermore, is 5 October and not the 'furst', but this is the signet clerk's original error and not the editors', a fact borne out by a duplicate dated 5 October which another clerk identified very plainly as the King's letter to all JPs, mayors, sheriffs, etc.: 'This is the verye copye of the kynges Majesties comission sygned with his Majesties seale and hande and with my lorde protectores graces singe'; SP 10/9/fo. 3.

64 Hughes & Larkin, nos. 278, 280–2, 284, 286–7, 291–3, 296–7, 299–304, 306–7, 309–10, 313, 315, 317–37, 339–46, 348–50.

65 *Ibid.* nos. 298, 316, 347.

66 *Ibid.* nos. 289, 290, 295, 305.

67 *Ibid.* nos. 275–7, 279, 283, 288, 294, 308, 311–12, 314.

68 *Ibid.* no. 298.

69 *Ibid.* no. 316.

70 From Petre's draft of the preamble to one of Somerset's military orders; SP 50/5/fos. 34–7.

71 SP 10/10/fo. 70.

72 *Chronicle*, 46–7; Hughes & Larkin, no. 365.

73 See, for example, the stamped warrant of 8 July 1551 with thirteen signatures (Somerset, Wiltshire, Warwick, Bedford, Shrewsbury, Huntingdon, Darcy, Wingfield, Herbert, Gates, Cecil, Paget, Cheyne); C 82/935. Text: Hughes & Larkin, no. 376.

74 Proclamation of 30 October 1549: Corporation of London Record Office, Journals, 16, fo. 39 (also Letter-book R, fo. 43b); after the last line of the text given in Hughes & Larkin, no. 352, this copy continues: 'Subscribed by the lordes and others of the pryvie counsaill whose names hereunder do folowe'; there follow the names of Cranmer, Rich, St John, Russell, Northampton, Warwick, Arundel, Shrewsbury, Southampton, Wentworth, Cheyne, Paget, Herbert, Wingfield, Gage, Petre, North, Montagu, Sadler, Baker, E. Wotton, Dr Wotton, Southwell, and Peckham. See also the proclamation of 11 June 1550 with the names of Somerset, Wiltshire, Bedford, Northampton, Clinton, Ely, Cobham, Paget, and Wingfield; Journals, 16, fo. 64b. An early Stuart MS. copy gives the same nine signatories' names; Library of the Society of Antiquaries, no. 53; text: Hughes & Larkin, no. 360. Proclamation of 20 July 1550: Journals, 16, fo. 66b, with the names of Somerset, Wiltshire, Warwick, Bedford, Northampton, Cobham, Paget, Wingfield, Herbert, Petre, North; text: Hughes & Larkin, no. 363. Once again, the chancery files (C 82/908, 920, and 921, respectively) contain no extant, signed, immediate warrants for these three proclamations.

75 Hughes and Larkin give 36 (nos. 352–87), but they should not have included no. 353; Cf. Elton, *Historical Journal* VIII (1965), 268. The twelve proclamations: nos. 354, 358, 366, 368, 378, 380–3, 385–7.

76 Hughes & Larkin, nos. 378, 382, 385, 387.

77 'For divers good consideracions it was decreed . . .' on 24 August 1550; *A.P.C.*, III, 110–11.

78 B.M., Royal MS. 18. C. xxiv, fo. 165b.

79 *Span. Cal.*, x, 468.

80 B.M., Egerton MS. 2603, fo. 34a.

81 See Wharton's signed original 'Instrucons yevin to my son . . .'; SP 15/1/fos. 1–2.

82 Next to the request for the council's letters of thanks, the councillor (or clerk) wrote 'Lettres to be made without endorcement to be directed by my Lord Wharton'; *ibid*.

83 The abstract is headed 'My Lord Whartons Instruccons [sent by his sonne *written above*] and aunsweres to the same'; next to 'Lettres [of thankes *crossed out*] to the gentlemen on the bordres for their aredynes of sirvice' is 'The same to be sent [and *crossed out*] to be directed by the Lord Wharton'; SP 15/1/fo. 3.

84 Robert Beale recalled in 1592 that 'It hath bine the manner that the Secretarie should abbreviate on the backside of the lettre [received], or otherwise in a bie paper, the substantiall and most materiall pointes which are to be propounded and answered, lest the rest of the Lords will not have them all redd, or shall not have leisure, and let him in a

bie paper make a note breiflie of their resolucions to everie point ...';
Read, *Mr Secretary Walsingham*, I, 425.

85 In other words, what is SP 15/1/fo. 3 was transcribed directly into
B.M., Add. MS. 5476, p. 682.

86 SP 15/1/fos. 4–5; the sheet must have formed part of a group of
drafts of the required documents, as it is endorsed 'answeres to the
Lord Wharton'. At the bottom is the explanatory note (in the same
hand responsible for the notations on fos. 1–3): 'Lettres addressed to
my L. Wharton to be directed at his discreacon vnto such persons as
as he shall think mete and convenient, of the tenor ensuing'.

87 B.M., Add. MS. 5476, p. 683.

88 Mentioned earlier was the note of 30 August 1550 of 'A lettre to Sir
Morice Denys, ... the copy of which lettre appeareth in the booke of
the first entreys'; *A.P.C.*, III, 115. But on 12 October 1551 mention is
made of 'an other lettre to Mr Van, the Kinges Ambassadour towards
the Venesians, of such effect as by the mynute thereof in the Counsell
Chest appeareth'; *ibid.* 411. (In practice, these 'minutes' were not
abstracts or notes, but the original draft or a clerk's fair copy.) It may
be that the registers of out-letters recorded the dispatch of only certain
kinds of letters, distinguished perhaps by their destination, for it is
evident that as early as 5 November 1549 the clerks were retaining
separate copies of some items: the council sent three men to survey the
Channel Islands, 'having with them such Instruccions for that purpose
as by the double therof remayning in the Counsail Chamber may
appere ...'; *ibid.* II, 354.

89 Consider, for example, the council's letter to special persons in every
county, from the court at Oatlands, 3 October 1550. We possess
Petre's first draft (SP 10/10/fo. 87), his second draft (*ibid.* fo. 86)
with cancellations and corrections, and a clerk's fair copy (*ibid.* fo. 85;
there are actually two cancellations of his own mistakes) of the
corrected draft. The fair copy bears the original signatures of Somerset, Northampton, Darcy, Petre, and Cecil. The letter directs the
recipient to enforce the execution of an earlier proclamation for re-
ducing the price of corn and other commodities. Dudley did not sign
it but it cannot have been drawn without his express approval; the
only meeting which he is recorded as having attended from 12 September to 7 November was that of 2 October, the day before the date of
this copy and almost certainly the time at which the decision to compose the letter was taken.

90 Consider the evidence in the case of the production of two letters
drafted, written, signed, and copied at Westminster on 18 December
1551. (1) Petre's rough draft of the council's letter to William Barlow
(Bishop of Bath), Sir Hugh Poulet, Sir John Seyntlow, Sir Thomas
Dyer, and Alex Popham requiring them to supply the Flemish weavers
at Glastonbury with good habitations in Orwell Park and to lend them
certain sums of money for the purchase of wool; endorsed 'Minute of
the counselles lettre to the bisshop of Bathe ... [etc.] xviij decembris
1551'; SP 10/13/fos. 146–7. A clerk copied out this letter in good

style, and another clerk headed this the 'Copie of the counselles lettres to the bisshop of Bathe, Sir Hugh Paulet, Sir Iohn Stloo, Sir Tho. dyer'. Another contemporary hand added facsimiles of the signatures which appeared on the original, those of Cranmer, Winchester, Northumberland, Bedford, Darcy, Ely, Cheyne, Gates, Petre, N. Wotton, and Mason; SP 10/13/fos. 144–5. (2) There exists a second original letter signed by the same 11 councillors to William Crouch, receiver of the Duke of Somerset's revenues in Somersetshire, ordering him to pay to the superintendent of the Glastonbury weavers sums in the total amount of £340 at such times as the Bishop of Bath *et al.* shall order him to; SP 10/13/fo. 148. The council's 'office' copy of this letter (SP 10/13/fo. 149) is in the same hand as the original, but one which is different from that of the copy of the letter to the Bishop of Bath; the clerk who endorsed Petre's draft (SP 10/13/fos. 146–7) also endorsed this copy.

91 Read, *Mr Secretary Walsingham*, i, 427.
92 *Ibid.* 428; no such slips or receipt books exist, however, for this period.
93 Rule of 2 February 1547; *A.P.C.*, ii, 11.
94 Read, *Mr Secretary Walsingham*, i, 426.
95 Because their letter of 20 October 1550 to the Sheriff and JPs of Berkshire concerned the provisioning of the City of London with grain and victual, the council sent a signed copy to the mayor and aldermen; Corporation of London Record Office, Journals, 16, fo. 96b.
96 SP 10/18/fos. 32–44. Folio 32 is Somerset's circular letter to commissioners for the redress of unlawful enclosures, etc., from Richmond, July 1549; fos. 33–6 comprise four copies of this letter, all in the same hand as the original, with the place and date (but no day) given, signed by Somerset; fos. 37–44 include eight copies of the letter in at least three different hands with the place and date omitted, all bearing Somerset's signature.
97 SP 10/8/fos. 73 and 74: two fair copies of the council's letter to ? for the stay of their forces in coming to London, the King's earlier letters notwithstanding; from Westminster, August 1549; both signed by Somerset, Cranmer, Rich, St John, Southampton, Paget, Petre, Smith, North, and Baker. The letters are in two different hands; in both, a space for the day was left blank.
98 SP 15/3/fos. 106–7: the list of 14 gentlemen who were to furnish horse and foot for Warwick's expedition to the North, 30 June 1549; the copyists' instructions at the foot read: 'all thies to be vpon the borders by the xth of August'; endorsed, 'The names of suche as had lettres to furnisshe furthe men with Therle of warrwick with ther nombers etc. xxx° Junij. 1549', SP 10/8/fos. 2–5: a long list of names, with check-marks ('+' or 'o') against most of them, all divided by counties; the clerk's endorsement for the record reads: 'The names of such as had lettres to come or send to Windsour primo Julij 1549'.
99 SP 61/4/fo. 278.
100 B.M., Add. MS. 48150, a late Elizabethan copy of just such a book from Robert Beale's collection.

101 After making out a commission for Russell and others to serve in Devon and Cornwall, Smith wrote Somerset, 'I take this forme to be a verie good forme and to be vsed in all such like hereafter,' from Richmond, 22 June 1549; SP 10/7/fo. 97.

102 See Hatfield House, Cecil Papers, 2, fo. 2, for one of Cecil's lists of such instructions endorsed 'October 155[?] A note of certyne warrauntes for my Lord Threasorer and Sir John yorke'.

103 The secretary ought to command 'the Clerckes of the Councell to approach and give good eare for his better direccion to frame their Lordship's lettre or answer'. Since Beale's other points correctly described Edwardian practice, it is probable that this suggestion as to the employment of the clerks does so as well; Read, *Mr Secretary Walsingham*, 1, 425.

104 Of numerous examples two should suffice: Armagil Waad's and several others' lengthy and detailed draft of the King's letter to the Lord Deputy in Ireland, 17 August 1551, SP 61/3/fos. 136–44; Thomas Chaloner's draft of Somerset's letter to John Uvedale, 20 October 1547, SP 15/1/fos. 82–3.

105 In reply to directions from Somerset, the Bishop of Durham wrote him from Newcastle on 30 September 1547: 'I shuld send you a draught of a Commission to my lorde of Warwyk [and others named in Somerset's letter] made in your name to theim moche like as the Kinges Majestie dyd send to me and the lorde Warden of the Myddle marchies of late to treate with the scottes.' Tunstal suggested, of course, that Somerset was free to add 'the Styles of your grace, the Kinge and all that be in the Commission' as well as any other special instructions; SP 50/1/fo. 130.

106 That Beale's later description – 'Afterwardes, upon sight of the notes thus taken of their Lordships' resolucion, the Clerck of the Councell may drawe a lettre or Minute (if it be a great cause), written with large lines, to be perused by the Secretarie . . . before it be preferred to the other Lords to be signed' – described exactly Edwardian practice is evident from numerous examples. Consider B. Gonson's letter to Petre of 12 May 1549, listing ships ready to sail under Thomas Cotton (SP 10/7/fos. 37–8); on the back (fo. 38b) a clerk drafted one of the passages which appears in the fair-copy instructions of 16 May to Cotton (fos. 43–4), to which Petre added a few lines. See the clerks' wide-spaced drafts of council letters which Petre corrected: instructions for the commissioners to Scotland of April 1551, SP 50/5/fos. 79–83; instructions to Sir Richard Cotton, 21 October 1549, SP 15/3/fos. 117–22; instructions to Russell, 24 June 1549, SP 10/7/fos. 103–8.

107 Mary complied; van der Delft reported the incident, 13 June 1549; *Span. Cal.*, IX, 393–4.

108 Sir Thomas Chaloner to Cecil, from Norham, 14 May 1551; SP 50/5/fo. 86.

109 To Cecil, from Oteford, 30 May 1552; SP 15/4/fo. 10.

110 To Cecil, from Chelsea, 26 December 1552; SP 15/4/fo. 45.

111 On 3 July 1551 the council ordered the clerk, Armagil Waad, to deposit two sums of 800 marks and £50 in the chest until such time as Sir Thomas Moyle should withdraw his inexplicable refusal to collect the capital and interest thus due him; *A.P.C.*, III, 312; 243, 315, 326, 370.

112 B.M., Add. MS. 34324, fo. 239a.

113 This was the recollection of Sir Thomas Wilson (nephew of Dr Thomas Wilson, first Keeper of the state papers) in 1623: '. . . I heard that when papers and writing in King Henry the eight his tyme grew to a great bulk that then this office [Keeper of the council's papers] was created and Secretary pagett . . . had the custody of them before he was a clerk of the consell; and after[wards] my lord burghhley when he came . . . from Cambridg (he [in] the Duke of Somersettes seruice) gatt the keeping of them; and afterward one Borne (he was after secretary of state in Queen Maries tyme) . . .'; SP 45/20/fo. 102b. These comments formed part of a draft of Wilson's letter to an unknown person, but thinking his letter verbose, Wilson deleted the lines from the final version.

114 SP 45/20/fos. 1–17. Cf. *Thirtieth Report of the Deputy Keeper* (1869), Appendix, 212, 224ff.

115 This contemporary evidence (SP 45/20/fo. 1ff.) thus corroborates Beale's statement of 1592: 'Heretofore there was a chambre in Westminster where such thinges, towardes the latter end of King Henry 8, were kept and were not in the Secretarie's private Custodie . . .'; Read, *Mr Secretary Walsingham*, I, 431.

116 SP 45/20/fo. 1ff.

117 *A.P.C.*, I, 135; III, 332.

118 B.M., Lansdowne MS. 160, fo. 266b.

119 SP 10/13/fo. 95.

120 E 101/426/5, fo. 28.

121 *Ibid.* fos. 32, 98.

122 Lefèvre-Pontalis, *Correspondance Politique*, 396.

123 *A.P.C.*, II, 402; III, 82; *Span. Cal.*, x, 110, 342, 375; *D.N.B.*

124 *Span. Cal.*, x, 66.

125 The two books were the first of their kind in English; on Thomas's career and historical importance see Adair's article in *Tudor Studies*, 133–60.

126 *A.P.C.*, III, 269.

127 *Ibid.* 447.

128 B.M., Harleian MS. 523, fo. 26b; *D.N.B.*

129 Thus Chaloner in 1549; E 404/106/bundle 3 Ed. VI.

130 *Ibid.*

131 PC 2/2, 362; *A.P.C.*, I, 210.

132 An attending clerk was entitled to collect 6s 8d from a person wanting an order entered in the register; 10s from those making an appearance upon charge of a misdemeanour; £1 for a copy from the council's records; £2 from a privy councillor on his being sworn in; Dewar, *Smith*, 26–7.

133 In Thomas's case, Adair shows just how lucrative the post could be in terms of the King's cash rewards, outright grants, and offers of easy purchase; *Tudor Studies*, 140–1. With a view to the future, Thomas had dedicated his *Historie of Italy* to the Earl of Warwick in 1549.

134 Honyngs' alleged complicity is based on a damaged late Elizabethan or early Stuart copy of a letter dated 1 February 1550 at Westminster from Cranmer, Rich, Wiltshire, and Dorset to an unknown recipient; 'Syth your Lordships departure hence', they write, 'William Honynges clerke of the counsell, for imbeselm . . . away of an Instrument wherin certayn Iudges and . . . Lawes, declared their opynyons vpon the Bysshop of . . . offences, is Lykewyse comytted' [damaged sections indicated by dots]; B.M., Cotton MS. Caligula E. iv, fo. 207. See Appendix 2.

135 See Otwell Johnson's letter to his brother John, reporting what Waad had told him of the deliberations which for the moment had curtailed a proposed restraint of the export of corn, but warning that a restraint might yet follow (and one did in the terms of a proclamation five days later); London, 19 April 1548; SP 46/5/fo. 254. See also his letter of 12 November 1548, *ibid.* fo. 305, and another of no date, SP 46/6/fo. 173, both of which refer to Waad's special help.

136 Petre's draft bears no heading, date, or contemporary endorsement; it does carry the note, 'Orders and Rules for Councell and dispatch of Business' in a much later hand; SP 10/1/fo. 57b.

CHAPTER 6: GOVERNING THE REALM

1 B.M., Lansdowne MS. 94, fos. 17–18. Northumberland presented this request for a subsidy in the Parliament of 1553.

2 Northumberland to Darcy, from Chelsea, 14 January 1553; SP 10/18/fo. 11.

3 *A.P.C.*, II, 185.

4 'A Discourse' of 28 August 1549, N.R.O., Fitzwilliam (Milton) MS. C.21.

5 'A Remembraunce', *ibid.*

6 *A.P.C.*, II, 184; *Cal. Pat. Rolls, Edw. VI*, I, 93. The commission, also composed of Sir Walter Mildmay and Sir Robert Keilway, bears no date but was probably named about November 1547.

7 *A.P.C.*, II, 185; Lehmberg, *Sir Walter Mildmay*, 21; Dietz, *Finances of Edward VI and Mary*, 83, 86.

8 'A Remembraunce', 2 February 1548, N.R.O., Fitzwilliam (Milton) MS. C.21. Militarily, Paget urged 'in stede of fortifications to waste the countrey before youe to your enemies handes'.

9 The total of all expenses includes naval charges and the cost of suppressing the rebellions of 1549. Cf. Starkey's comprehensive accounts, B.M., Harleian MS. 353, fo. 90ff., made up from the accounts of the treasurers and vice-treasurers of the wars, officers of the ordnance, master victuallers, purveyors, paymasters, treasurers at Boulogne, Calais, etc.

10 N.R.O., Fitzwilliam (Milton) MS. C.21.
11 Dewar, *Smith*, 49–51.
12 N.R.O., Fitzwilliam (Milton) MS. C.21.
13 *Ibid.*
14 'A Memoriall to the Duke of Som[erset]', *ibid.*
15 2 & 3 Edward VI, c. 36; Dietz, *op. cit.* 84–5. The Act also featured a tax on personality and a poll tax on certain aliens.
16 Paget to Somerset, 25 December 1548, N.R.O., Fitzwilliam (Milton) MS. C.21.
17 Paget to Somerset, 2 February 1549; *ibid.*
18 *Ibid.*
19 Cf. Wernham, *Before the Armada*, 152–3.
20 Paget to Somerset, 25 December 1548, N.R.O., Fitzwilliam (Milton) MS. C.21.
21 Jordan, *Edward VI: the Young King*, 292–3.
22 Paget to Somerset, 'ffrom my chambre at court', N.R.O., Fitzwilliam (Milton) MS. C.21.
23 Paget to Somerset, 'ffrom the courte', 2 February 1549; *ibid.*
24 *Ibid.*
25 *Span. Cal.*, x, 262: 9 April 1551.
26 Gammon, *Statesman and Schemer*, 140.
27 Council to Sir Philip Hoby, Greenwich, 21 April 1550; B.M., Harleian MS. 523, fo. 6ff.
28 'Certayne poyntes to be resolved vpon in Counsaill', 17 April 1549; N.R.O., Fitzwilliam (Milton) MS. C.21.
29 Paget to Somerset, 2 February 1549; *ibid.*
30 *Ibid.* The statutes referred to are 1 Edward VI, c. 1 and 2, and 3 Edward VI, c. 1.
31 N.R.O., Fitzwilliam (Milton) MS. C.21.
32 *Ibid.*
33 Paget to Somerset, 'ffrom my chamber in the Courte', 8 May 1549; *ibid.* Other copies: SP 10/7/fo. 8; B.M., Cotton MS., Titus F. iii, fo. 267b.
34 N.R.O., Fitzwilliam (Milton) MS. C.21, 25 December 1548.
35 *Ibid.* 8 May 1549.
36 *Ibid.* 25 December 1548.
37 *Ibid.* 8 May 1549.
38 *Ibid.* 7 July 1549.
39 *Ibid.* 25 December 1548.
40 *Ibid.* 24 January 1549.
41 *Ibid.* 7 July 1549.
42 *Ibid.*
43 *Ibid.*
44 *Span. Cal.*, ix, 197.
45 Pollard, *History of England*, 15–16.
46 Paget to Somerset, 25 December 1548, N.R.O., Fitzwilliam (Milton) MS. C.21.
47 *Ibid.*

48 *Ibid.* 7 July 1549.

49 B.M., Egerton MS. 2623, fos. 9–10, a treatise of 15 articles in a secretary hand, dated October 1550. The water-mark, a gloved hand pointing to a star, probably identifies this as the effort of someone within the government.

50 *Ibid.*

51 'Certayne poyntes', 17 April 1549, N.R.O., Fitzwilliam (Milton) MS. C.21.

52 *Ibid.* 7 July 1549.

53 *Ibid.* 2 February 1549.

54 Council to commissioners at Southampton, from Westminster, 22 March 1549; eight signatures including Paget's; *Letters of the Fifteenth and Sixteenth Centuries* (Southampton Record Society, vol. 22), 62–4.

55 Paget to Somerset, from the court, 12 March 1549; Plas Newydd, Anglesey MSS., Paget Papers, box II, no. 2. The copy in Paget's letter-book, N.R.O., Fitzwilliam (Milton) MS. C.21, is later; the copyist omitted a few words and altered the spelling of others.

56 Pollard, *History of England*, 39.

57 Plas Newydd, Anglesey MSS., Paget Papers, box II, no. 2. Sir William Sharington, Vice-Treasurer of the royal mint at Bristol, had coined testons below the legal weight, keeping the unused bullion as his own. Some of the profits of the mint, perhaps as much as £2,800, he had advanced to the Lord Admiral. Cf. Jordan, *Edward VI: the Young King*, 373, 383–4.

58 Plas Newydd, Anglesey MSS., Paget Papers, box II, no. 2.

59 *A.P.C.*, II, 316–17: 21 August 1549.

60 Smith to Somerset, from Richmond, 22 June 1549; SP 10/7/fos. 96–7.

61 Dewar, *Smith*, 50–1.

62 SP 10/7/fos. 96–7.

63 N.R.O., Fitzwilliam (Milton) MS. C.21.

64 *Ibid.* Another copy: Plas Newydd, Anglesey MSS., Paget Papers, box II, no. 3.

65 'A Discourse' to Somerset and the council, 28 August 1549; N.R.O., Fitzwilliam (Milton) MS. C.21.

66 Paget to Somerset, 25 December 1548; *ibid.*

67 'A Discourse', 28 August 1549; *ibid.*

68 *Ibid.*

69 N.R.O., Fitzwilliam (Milton) MS. C.21.

70 This refers to the Commons' bills which resulted in 'An Acte for Shireffes of Englond to have certen allowances upon their Accomptes', 2 and 3 Edward VI, c. 4; 'An Acte for fynding of Offices before Exchetors', 2 and 3 Edward VI, c. 8.

71 *Chronicle*, 100. There is also the King's list of 'Actes for this parliemente' with Cecil's additions, SP 10/14/fo. 9, printed in Nichols, *Literary Remains*, II, 491–5. Nichols' notes to the various points show that none of the royal proposals (if they really can be considered of the King's conception) was passed. A clerk's list of these bills is SP

10/18/fo. 23, incorrectly dated 1 March 1553 in *Cal. S.P. Dom.*, *1547–80*.

72 R. K. Gilkes states that 'in February 1553, a month before Parliament met, a small Committee of the Council . . . was named "to consyder what lawes shalbe established in this Parliament" '; *Tudor Parliament*, 124. In fact, this is the committee of February 1554 which Mary's privy council appointed two months in advance of her first Parliament. Cf. *A.P.C.*, IV, 398; Neale, *Elizabethan House of Commons*, 378.

73 *A.P.C.*, III, 19–20.

74 5 and 6 Edward VI, c. 8.

75 'An Act for the better and truer making of all manner of Wollen . . . clothes . . .'; SP 15/4/fos. 3–8; 5 and 6 Edward VI, c. 6.

76 On 3 March 1552 'The Bill, signed by the King, exhibited by John Seymour, Esquire, touching the Repeal of an Act of Parliament, made Anno 32° H. VIII. for the late Duke of Somerset's lands intailed' received a first reading in the Commons; *Commons' Journals*, I, 19. The item appears as 'the acte for the repeale of the statute of 32' on an agenda, SP 10/14/fo. 13.

77 Corporation of London Record Office, Journals, 16, fo. 164, a copy indicating that Rich, Wiltshire, Bedford, Wentworth, Goodrich and Dr Wotton assented to the original petition that the King also signed. The original Act bears the sign manual at the head and the signatures of Cranmer, Rich, Wiltshire, Bedford, Wentworth, Goodrich, and Dr Wotton at the foot; House of Lords Record Office, 5 and 6 Edward VI, no. 28.

78 See the Act for the King's general pardon, House of Lords Record Office, 3 and 4 Edward VI, no. 24, signed by Cranmer, Rich, Wiltshire, Bedford, Dorset, Northampton, Tunstal, Goodrich, Wentworth, Paget, Cheyne, Wingfield, Herbert, Darcy, North, Baker, and Montagu. The sign manual appears at the head. An attached proviso in another hand was signed by Cranmer, Rich, Wiltshire, Dorset, Northampton, Tunstal, Goodrich, Devereux, and Wentworth. Cf. *Lords' Journals*, I, 382; *Commons' Journals*, I, 15; Bond, *Archives* III (1958), 208.

79 The Act for the King's general pardon passed in December 1547 was signed at the head (both sheets) by the King and at the foot (of both) by Somerset, Cranmer, Rich, St John, Russell, Arundel, and Tunstal; House of Lords Record Office, 1 Edward VI, no. 21. The Act for the King's general pardon of March 1549 was *not* signed by Edward VI but was signed by Somerset alone (and Mason as Clerk of the Parliaments); *ibid.* 2 and 3 Edward VI, no. 38.

80 House of Lords Record Office, 3 Edward VI, no. 31, signed at the head by the King and at the foot by the following councillors: Cranmer, Rich, St John, Russell, Dorset, Northampton, Warwick, Southampton, Tunstal, Goodrich, Wentworth, Paget, Cheyne, Wingfield, Herbert, Darcy, Petre, Dr Wotton, North, Montagu, E. Wotton, Southwell, and Baker. These provisos are attached; the second, which

originated in the Commons, awards to Sir Thomas Cheyne certain lands held formerly by Somerset and is signed at the head by the King and at the foot by Cranmer, Rich, St John, Russell, Dorset, Northampton, Goodrich, Wentworth, Wingfield, Herbert, Darcy, Baker, and Somerset.

81 See the council's letters of 1547 and 1553 in Elton, *Tudor Constitution*, 293–4. Sturge, in his 'Life and Times of John Dudley', 176–9, discusses the letters of 18 and 19 January 1553 (see the relevant entries in the council's docquet-book, B.M., Royal MS. 18 C. xxiv) in which the council recommended 14 individuals, 11 of whom were actually returned; Sturge, *op. cit.* 179, n.1. Neale referred to the letters of 1553; he thought that twelve of those preferred were returned; *Elizabethan House of Commons*, 273–4. See also Bindoff, *History Today* III (1953), 645; Pollard, *History of England*, 74–6; Pollard, *Somerset*, 275–6.

82 Gammon, *Statesman and Schemer*, 139.

83 *A.P.C.*, III, 400.

84 10 January 1552; *A.P.C.*, III, 457. Cf *ibid.* 459, 470–1. Cf. Pollard, *Somerset*, 275–6.

85 Bindoff, in the *Victoria History of the Counties of England: Wiltshire*, V, 115, 120.

86 Pollard, *B.I.H.R.* XVI (1939), 157, n.4.

87 Gammon, *op. cit.* 139.

88 On 20 November 1549 the Clerk of the House noted: 'It is reperted by Mr. Speker the Kynges plesure to be by [him *crossed out*] his Counsell that the house may treate for the acte of Relief havyng in respect the cause of the grauntyng therof'; House of Lords Record Office, P. 1/fo. 22b.

89 *Commons' Journals*, I, 21, 24. For a brief general account of the role of privy councillors in the House during the Tudor period, see Willson, *Privy Councillors in the House of Commons 1604–1629*, 4–12.

90 In 1548–9 they were Herbert, Denny, Petre, North, Paget, Wingfield, Baker, Smith, and Cheyne. In 1553 they were Cotton, Petre, North, Sadler, Cheyne, Cecil, and Bowes. Cf. *Return of the Name of Every Member of the Lower House*, in *Parliamentary Papers*, pt. I, 375–80; files of H.P.T.

91 *A.P.C.*, II, 193–5; Elton, *Tudor Constitution*, 297–8.

92 Van der Delft to Charles V's council, 27 December 1547; *Span. Cal.*, IX, 238; see also, *ibid.* 345, and X, 17. In the House of Lords the government sought to ensure the attendance of as many members as possible; the fact that most of the 'voices' (proxies) of absentee lords spiritual and temporal were held by privy councillors is not evidence of the council's attempt or potential ability to control the affairs of the upper house. For the debate on the significance of proctorial representation, see Snow, *Journal of British Studies* VIII (May 1969), 1–27 and Graves, *Journal of British Studies* X (May 1971), 17–35.

93 Council to the JPs of Sussex, 12 February 1547, from the Tower; B.M., Add. MS. 33084, fo. 2.

94 B.M., Add. MS. 34324, fo. 239a.
95 Corporation of London Record Office, Journals, 16, fo. 91b.
96 Hughes & Larkin, no. 363.
97 *A.P.C.*, III, 81: 17 July 1550.
98 SP 10/4/fo. 25; this is nominally the King's letter.
99 *A.P.C.*, III, 35: 23 May 1550.
100 *Ibid.* II, 431: 16 April 1550.
101 *Ibid.* II, 407.
102 *Ibid.* II, 312.
103 Hughes & Larkin, no. 371.
104 B.M., Egerton MS. 2623, fos. 9–10.
105 *A.P.C.*, III, 161, 199; IV, 107, 121, 163.
106 Corporation of London Record Office, Letter-book R, fo. 12.
107 *A.P.C.*, III, 256–7.
108 *Letters of the Fifteenth and Sixteenth Centuries* (Southampton Record Society, vol. 22), 66; from Greenwich, signed by Somerset, St John, Russell, and Arundel.
109 *Ibid.* 68–9.
110 *A.P.C.*, III, 31.
111 Somerset and the council to Russell, from Syon, 10 July 1549; Pocock, *Troubles*, 22–4.
112 Hughes & Larkin, nos. 281, 292, 308, 320, 329, 333–4, 339–44, 348 (Somerset's); 352, 356, 358, 363, 371, 374 (Northumberland's).
113 *Ibid.* nos. 298, 314, 317, 318, 323, 325, 330 (Somerset's); 360 and 370 (Northumberland's).
114 *Grafton's Chronicle*, II, 506–7.
115 Skelton, 'The Court of Star Chamber', 20, 199, cited in Elton, *Tudor Constitution*, 163, 170.
116 Corporation of London Record Office, Journals, 16, fo. 118.
117 Council to an unknown lord who had just left the court (Westminster), B.M., Cotton MS. Caligula E. iv, fo. 207, a contemporary copy with signatories' names (Cranmer, Rich, Wiltshire, Dorset).
118 *Chronicle*, 50.
119 *A.P.C.*, III, 225.
120 E 101/546/19, the last warrants for payment of their wages, 30 September 1552.
121 B.M., Wyatt MS. 17, given in Fletcher, *Tudor Rebellions*, 148; cf. Loades, *Two Tudor Conspiracies*, 49.
122 N.R.O., Fitzwilliam (Milton) MS. C.21.
123 *Chronicle*, 50; *A.P.C.*, III, 293.
124 *Chronicle*, 86; B.M., Royal MS. 18 C. xxiv, fo. 138; *A.P.C.*, III, 293, 399.
125 *Span. Cal.*, x, 396.
126 Dietz, *Finances of Edward VI and Mary*, 97.
127 E 101/546/19. Hoby's command had earlier been held by Cheyne; the Earl of Huntingdon was at one time paid for 50 men; *A.P.C.*, IV, 15. As late as 5 June 1551 Paget and Somerset were receiving £500 and £250 quarterly (*ibid.* III, 293) for the posts which they lost in October 1551.

128 *Chronicle*, 100, 123.
129 *A.P.C.*, III, 6–7, 215.
130 The councillors: Bishop of Ely, dukes of Northumberland and Suffolk, marquesses of Winchester and Northampton, earls of Bedford, Huntingdon, Pembroke, Shrewsbury, and Westmorland, Viscount Hereford, Lords Clinton, Darcy, and Rich, Sir Thomas Cheyne, Sir John Gates, and Sir Anthony Wingfield; *ibid.* IV, 49.
131 *Ibid.* IV, 80.
132 *Cal. Pat. Rolls, Edw. VI*, IV, 352–3.
133 B.M., Egerton MS. 2623, fos. 9–10.
134 B.M., Cotton MS. Nero C. x, fo. 84b.
135 SP 10/15/fos. 31–2. The laws (and proclamations) in question, according to the King's identically dated copy of this part of the Syon agenda, touched chiefly riots, forestalling, and regrating; cf. B.M., Lansdowne MS. 1236, fos. 19–20.
136 Cf. Dietz, *Finances of Edward VI and Mary*, 82–102; Feavearyear, *The Pound Sterling*, 64–74; Elton, *Tudor Revolution*, 230–8; Lehmberg, *Mildmay*, 28–39.
137 Feavearyear, *op. cit.* 71; Jordan, *Edward VI: Threshold of Power*, 462.
138 SP 10/13/fo. 24; Haynes, *State Papers*, 119; B.M., Lansdowne MS. 1236, fos. 19–20.
139 Dietz, *op. cit.* 91, n.9.
140 Hatfield House, Cecil Papers, 151, fos. 7–8.
141 *Ibid.*; *A.P.C.*, III, 305.
142 Feavearyear, *op. cit.* 70.
143 Lehmberg, *Mildmay*, 31.
144 *Ibid.*
145 On 19 February 1552 he ordered several gentlemen in Kent and Essex to inquire secretly who among their neighbours were the King's creditors for victuals and provisions; *A.P.C.*, III, 481. Perhaps he really did mean to avoid payment.
146 Feavearyear, *op. cit.* 71.
147 Hatfield House, Cecil Papers, 151, fos. 7–8.
148 *Ibid.*; *A.P.C.*, III, 305; *Chronicle*, 58; B.M., Lansdowne MS. 1236, fos. 19–20.
149 *A.P.C.*, II, 346.
150 SP 10/9/fos. 97–8.
151 *A.P.C.*, III, 29.
152 *Ibid.*
153 Cf., for example, SP 10/15/fo. 17. For one of Cecil's lists of debts, cf. SP 10/15/fo. 92.
154 Hatfield House, Cecil Papers, 151, fos. 7–8.
155 SP 10/5/fos. 149–50.
156 *Cal. Pat. Rolls, Edw. VI*, IV, 144.
157 *Ibid.* IV, 355–6.
158 *Ibid.* IV, 397–8. Privy councillors who were members of both commissions included Goodrich, Cotton, and Gates; Bowes joined the later

commission. Non-councillors on both commissions were Mildmay, John Lucas, and Thomas Mildmay.

159 *Ibid.* IV, 354–5 (13 July 1552); 390–1 (18 November 1552); V, 184 (15 March 1553); 277 (12 December 1552); 411 (23 May 1552).

160 *Ibid.* IV, 391. The members: Northumberland, Bedford, Huntingdon, Darcy, Clinton, Cotton, Sadler, Hoby, Sir Walter Mildmay, Goodrich, and Thomas Mildmay.

161 *Ibid.* IV, 392–3.

162 *Ibid.* V, 413–17. The privy councillors: Cranmer, Northumberland, Suffolk, Winchester, Northampton, Bedford, Huntingdon, Westmorland, Pembroke, Shrewsbury, Hereford, Darcy, Clinton, Hoby, Cecil, Cotton, Mason, Cheyne, and Montagu.

163 *Ibid.* IV, 393–7. Of the nineteen councillors named in the preceding note, only Clinton did not serve. The six additions: Gates, Rich, Sadler, Bowes, Wingfield, and Baker.

164 *Ibid.* V, 417.

165 *Ibid.* IV, 353–4.

166 Elton, *Tudor Revolution*, 231–4.

167 *Cal. Pat. Rolls, Edw. VI,* IV, 391–2. Members: Northumberland, Bedford, Suffolk, Northampton, Shrewsbury, Pembroke, Darcy, Cheyne, Wrothe, and the two Mildmays.

168 Elton, *Tudor Revolution*, 237.

169 Richardson, *Court of Augmentations*, 361–5.

170 *A.P.C.,* IV, 31, 46.

171 *Ibid.* III, 475.

172 Richardson, *op. cit.* 364.

173 *A.P.C.,* IV, 31, 46.

174 E 101/546/19.

175 *A.P.C.,* IV, 58.

176 *Span. Cal.,* XI, 4.

177 E 101/546/19.

178 Elton, *Tudor Revolution*, 109, 255–6.

179 *A.P.C.,* II, 431; III, 133.

180 *Ibid.* III, 26.

181 Council to Wiltshire, from Woking, 23 August 1550; a copy with signatories' names; B.M., Add. MS. 5751A, fo. 302.

182 *A.P.C.,* II, 400; III, 115–16.

183 *Ibid.* II, 431; III, 26; *Chronicle*, 82.

184 Eight such Edwardian commissions carry his name; *Cal. Pat. Rolls, Edw. VI,* I, 93, 261, 368–9; II, 250–1; IV, 393–7; V, 351–65, 413–17.

185 *A.P.C.,* IV, 187; SP 38/1/fo. 3.

186 *Span. Cal.,* IX, 187; X, 259.

187 *A.P.C.,* II, 114–15; Nichols, *Chronicle of the Grey Friars,* 59.

188 Hughes & Larkin, no. 287.

189 *Ibid.* nos. 289, 292, 296–7, 299, 300, 303, 307, 313, 316, 335.

190 *Ibid.* nos. 353, 384, and 385, respectively.

191 B.M., Add. MS. 32091, fo. 142; from Waltham, 30 August 1547.

192 SP 10/8/fo. 107.

193 *Cal. Pat. Rolls, Edw. VI*, III, 165; Jordan, *Edward VI: Threshold of Power*, 244.

194 Plas Newydd, Anglesey MSS., Paget Papers, box II, no. 1.

195 Mercers' Hall, Acts of Court (1527–60), fo. 224.

196 Corporation of London Record Office, Journals, 15, fo. 322; Letter-book Q, fo. 210b.

197 *A.P.C.*, II, 518.

198 *Ibid.* III, 53, 318.

199 *Ibid.* III, 394.

200 *Ibid.* III, 217.

201 Council to the Dean, etc., from Westminster, 11 April 1549; signed by Cranmer, St John, Wingfield, Petre, and Smith; Westminster Abbey, muniment no. 13242.

202 *Cal. Pat. Rolls, Edw. VI*, II, 406.

203 *Ibid.* III, 347; IV, 355.

204 *Ibid.* IV, 114, 354.

205 *Ibid.* I, 78–9.

206 *Ibid.* I, 232; V, 403.

207 *A.P.C.*, II, 545–6.

208 *Ibid.* III, 299.

209 *Ibid.* IV, 18, 59, 166.

210 1 Edward VI, c. 3; Hughes & Larkin, no. 356.

211 Hughes & Larkin, nos. 279, 282–3, 321–2, 324, 326, 332, 364, 367, 372–3, 375–6, 378–9, 381–2, 387.

212 *Ibid.* nos. 278, 280, 295, 301, 304, 306, 310, 315, 319, 331, 345, 349, 355–6, 357, 361.

213 *Ibid.* nos. 284, 286, 311, 347.

214 *Ibid.* no. 290.

215 *Ibid.* nos. 309, 327.

216 *Ibid.* nos. 328, 359.

217 *Ibid.* nos. 336, 366, 380, 383.

218 *Ibid.* nos. 335, 346, 368, 377, 386.

219 *A.P.C.*, III, 272, 334, 427; SP 10/9/fos. 110–11; SP 10/11/fos. 7–11; B.M., Lansdowne MS. 2, fo. 92.

220 *APC*, III, 135, 137, 140.

221 The seven: Shrewsbury, Wiltshire, Goodrich, North, Sadler, Baker, and Bowes; *Cal. Pat. Rolls, Edw. VI*, IV, 140–2.

222 *A.P.C.*, III, 242.

223 Corporation of London Record Office, Journals, 16, fo. 35b and Letter-book R, 39a; *A.P.C.*, IV, 206–7.

224 Mercers' Hall, Acts of Court (1527–60), fo. 256b. Wriothesley, *Chronicle*, (II, 70–1) lists the councillors in attendance.

225 Mercers' Hall, Acts of Court (1527–60), fo. 250.

226 *A.P.C.*, II, 142–3.

227 SP 46/2/fos. 2–3.

228 *Span. Cal.*, x, 528.

229 SP 10/7/fo. 97; *A.P.C.*, III, 106; IV, 220.

230 *A.P.C.*, III, 238.

231 SP 10/4/fos. 75, 77–8.
232 B.M., Royal MS. 18 C. xxiv, fos. 24–5.
233 *A.P.C.*, IV, 236.
234 From the book of orders and decrees of the court, Req. 1/9/fos. 88b, 79a, and 52b, respectively.
235 Elton, *Tudor Constitution*, 103.
236 Paget to Somerset, from Brussels, 30 June 1549; SP 68/3/fos. 158–62.
237 B.M., Harleian MS. 352, fos. 1, 39b.
238 *A.P.C.*, II, 355, 358. The clerk did not enter the decrees in this instance.
239 B.M., Egerton MS. 2603, fo. 33b; see Appendix 3.
240 *Cal. Pat. Rolls, Edw. VI*, IV, 353.
241 B.M., Add. MS. 5498, fos. 58–60, a contemporary copy of the commission is printed in Leadam (ed.), *Select Cases in the Court of Requests*, xci–xciii.
242 *Ibid.*
243 SP 46/2/fo. 124, a parchment bill addressed to the lords of the privy council attendant; no date, but probably before April 1551.
244 SP 10/7/fo. 119, no date, probably June 1549.
245 Plas Newydd, Anglesey MSS., Paget Papers, box II, no. 15; no date, probably November 1552.
246 SP 10/2/fo. 86.
247 E 101/303/9; no date; after October 1551; paper bill addressed to the lords of the privy council.
248 B.M., Add. MS. 36767, fos. 1–4, headed, 'At Somerset place the iijd of Iuly a° R.R.E. vj primo', and endorsed, 'Decree touching thadmiraltie'; familiar contemporary court hand, interlineations, corrections, etc. The account may be an entry from the council's original register of complaints – the book (or collection of papers) which Ralph Starkey saw in 1620.
249 *Ibid.*
250 Corporation of London Record Office, Journals, 15, fos. 365b ff. and Letter-book Q, fos. 239b–241b.
251 *A.P.C.*, II, 386–8.
252 *Ibid.* III, 83–4, 197, 238, 464.
253 Smith, *The Government of Elizabethan England*, 24; Elton, *Tudor Constitution*, 101.
254 Smith, *op. cit.* 24–5.
255 *A.P.C.*, III, 312.
256 *Ibid.* 42.
257 Sta. Cha. 3/8, nos. 45 and 50.
258 Sta. Cha. 3/8, no. 51.
259 Cf. Leadam (ed.), *Star Chamber*, xvii–xviii, on variations in the forms of address.
260 There are 941 cases but only 621 bills of pleading; the total of 621 includes two cases with two bills each, Sta. Cha. 3/4, nos. 43 and 80. Four bills are addressed to Somerset alone; Sta. Cha. 3/1, nos. 14, 54; 4, no. 80; 6, no. 50. Five are addressed to Somerset and the council; Sta. Cha. 3/5, no. 11; 8, nos. 49, 50; 3, nos. 38, 64. Sixteen are

addressed to the council; Sta. Cha. 3/1, nos. 34, 91; 2, no. 63; 3, no. 14; 4, nos. 7, 9, 44; 6, nos. 53–4, 56–7, 69, 71; 8, nos. 51–2; Sta. Cha. 2/22, no. 224. Five are addressed to Lord St John; Sta. Cha. 3/2, no. 84; 3, nos. 3, 67; 5, nos. 20, 50. And one each to Paget (Sta. Cha. 2/6, no. 198) and Rich, Winchester, and the council (Sta. Cha. 3/4, no. 64).

261 Sta. Cha. 3/6, no. 54; see also bundle 1, no. 54, a paper bill addressed to Somerset and endorsed 'To Mr. Eden clerke of the councell in the sterr chamber'. And see Bernard Hampton's list of suits actually considered at the board; the entry of one (the Imperial ambassador's supplication for the release of goods belonging to the Emperor's subjects) bears Cecil's notation ' + remitted f considr y° st ch', i.e. 'remitted for consideration in the star chamber'; Hatfield House, Cecil Papers, 201, fos. 109–10. The nature of the complaint is not indicated; criminal action may have been alleged.

262 Sta. Cha. 3/6, no. 50.

263 The merchant sought the release of confiscated woad and payment for woad which he had delivered; the Fuggers' agent sought restitution of £700 worth of goods in a case similar to that of the Venetian merchant cited above (p. 224); the King's tenants asked that they might be allowed to enjoy the occupancy of their rightful leaseholds; Sta. Cha. 3/8, nos. 49, 50, 51, respectively. None of the plaintiffs asked for a subpoena commanding the defendant's appearance in the court of star chamber.

264 See the proceedings for 7 February and 20 May 1550, for example; *A.P.C.*, II, 385; III, 34.

265 Those recorded 'In the Starre Chamber' on 31 January 1550 did not; *ibid.* II, 336.

266 At Westminster, 21 February 1552; *ibid.* III, 482.

267 *Grafton's Chronicle*, II, 523.

268 The other meeting took place at the house of the Sheriff of London; *A.P.C.*, II, 337.

269 Lodge, *Illustrations of British History*, 170–5. Cf. Edward VI's *Chronicle*, 132. For a full account of Beaumont's case, see Hurstfield, *The Queen's Wards*, 199–204.

270 Cf. *A.P.C.*, III, 41, 171, 216, 316.

271 *Ibid.* 433.

272 Somerset to Sir Thomas Brudenell, from Westminster, 21 June 1548; SP 46/1/fo. 171. See also Somerset to the mayor and citizens of York, from Somerset Place, 16 December 1548, *York Civic Records*, V, 3.

273 *A.P.C.*, III, 41.

274 Wriothesley, *Chronicle*, II, 42; 6 August 1550. Dorothy Gladish collected several other examples of uncomfortable punishments (slitting of the tongue with a hot iron, etc.), *Tudor Privy Council*, 82–3.

275 *A.P.C.*, III, 465.

276 Paget to Somerset, 7 July 1549; N.R.O., Fitzwilliam (Milton) MS. C.21.

277 Elton, *Historical Journal* VIII (1965), 271.

278 B.M., Egerton MS. 2623, fos. 9–10.

279 From St James, 27 October 1552, SP 10/15/fo. 77.

280 Council to Hoby and two others, from Basing, 9 September 1552; B.M., Egerton MS. 3048, fo. 19.

281 *A.P.C.*, III, 407; 5 November 1551.

282 *Ibid.* 230; 5 March 1551.

283 *Ibid.* IV, 201; 7 January 1553.

284 Cf. his letter to Cecil, from Andover, 30 August 1552; SP 10/14/fos. 161–2.

285 Privy council to the Earl of Sussex, from Greenwich, 3 June 1553, requiring him to send Anthony Man and James Gardyner 'unto our custody, to thend we may gyve such ordre for thexaminacion by tortours or otherwyse of the sayd persones, yf they refuse to confesse the trouthe and particularities of theyr lewde doinges . . .' in the matter concerning the theft of three hawks from a lanner's nest in the Lady Mary's park at Windfarthing, Norfolk; signed by Cranmer, Suffolk, Winchester, Bedford, Shrewsbury, Pembroke, Darcy, Cotton, Petre, Cheke; Ellis, *Original Letters*, III, 308–9.

286 Cf. Brooks, *Council of the North*, 17–23, 27; Reid, *King's Council in the North*, 166–80. SP 15/3/fos. 89–103, contemporary instructions to the council in the North; SP 15/2/fo. 106, typical report from the council in the North.

287 Williams, *Council in the Marches of Wales*, 205–12; Skeel, *Council in the Marches of Wales*, 81–3, 218, 272–4.

288 Cf. Holdsworth, *History of English Law*, IV, 83ff.; *A.P.C.*, III, 89, 149, 161, 222. There is also the apparent case of the council's interference in the matter of a complaint introduced into the Commons on 15 February 1552 by Sir Robert Brandlyng, burgess of Newcastle, against Sir John Wytheryngton and others; on 31 March the House resolved that the Duke of Northumberland should 'order the Matter . . . if his Graces Pleasure shall so be'. In fact, as the entry of 5 April reads, 'the Lords of the Council . . . upon their Request' received the bill exhibited by Brandlyng (although, as the clerk noted, the House observed the formula that 'it doth require' the council to receive the complaint). There may have been some real opposition to the council's move, for two days later Brandlyng's bill was 'sent from the Lords of the Privy Council again, to be ordered by this House according to the ancient Customs of this House'. Whereupon, the bill was read in Wytheryngton's presence; he confessed, and by the order of the House, was sent to the Tower. *Commons Journals*, I, 21–2.

289 Cf. Elton, *Tudor Constitution*, 102–4.

CHAPTER 7: POLITICS

1 Smith, *Journal of British Studies* II (Nov. 1962), 17–20.

2 Jordan, *Edward VI: the Young King*, 69–72.

3 *Ibid.* 72.

4 The account is entitled 'Certayne brife notes of the controversy betwene the dukes of Somerset and the duke of Norhumberland . . .';

B.M., Add. MS. 48126, fos. 6a–16a. A. J. A. Malkiewicz discovered the MS. among Robert Beale's papers in the British Museum (originally it was designated Yelverton MS. 141), but Malkiewicz published only the centre section (fos. 7a–15a) of the entire document as 'An Eye-witness's Account of the *Coup d'Etat* of October 1549', *E.H.R.* LXX (1955), 600–9.

5 *A.P.C.*, I, 566.

6 *Ibid.* II, 3–8. For another contemporary account of the proceedings of 1 February, see Alnwick Castle, Syon MSS., no. 467, fos. 106–7, which follows closely the College of Arms MS. printed by Nichols in *Literary Remains*.

7 B.M., Add. MS. 48126, fo. 6b.

8 *Ibid.*

9 Van der Delft to Charles V, 8 February 1549; *Span. Cal.*, IX, 341. Van der Delft's report, which was based upon Warwick's testimony, raises an intriguing question: precisely when was Henry alleged to have uttered his 'no, no', and in response to whose 'election' of Seymour to the council? The date cannot have been 23 January 1547, for Henry himself then appointed Seymour to the King's privy council; the date in question must have been the night of 26 December 1546 when the King called before him his closest advisers (including Hertford and Lisle) in order to read out to them the terms of his will. As this was the occasion of Paget's and the others' suggestions for the inclusion among the assistants' names of those, such as Essex and Arundel, who had been left off the list of executors' names, it is possible that one of the group with the King proposed Seymour as a potential executor. The fact that Seymour was not (on 26 December) a privy councillor could not have disqualified him from consideration, for five of the final appointees (Bromley, Herbert, Montagu, North, E. Wotton) had not served on the council either. It matters little who may have 'elected', i.e. suggested, Seymour; the story remains credible because the man who revealed the information to van der Delft in 1549 was also present on 26 December 1546 – Warwick. True, Warwick was capable of lying, but his revelations of 1549 were all the more powerful for their truth, for the truth equally served his purpose – Seymour's destruction. (For the best reconstruction of what probably occurred on 26 December 1546, see Scarisbrick, *Henry VIII*, 488–91.) Interestingly, Paget is said to have told van der Delft on 24 January 1547 that Edward VI's councillors had been selected by his means, an apparent reference to the council of executors; *Span. Cal.*, IX, 111.

10 The author refers to 'the consultation of making the duke of Somerset lord protector of the realme and of the kinges p[er]son and there vpon secretely agried and not promiced . . .'; B.M., Add. MS. 48126, fo. 6a.

11 The will prohibited any one executor 'to do any thing appointed by our said will alone, onles the most part of the hole Nombre of their Coexecutours do consent and by Writing agree to the same . . .'; Rymer, *Foedera*, xv, 114. The will stated that the governing of the young King was to be one of the council's primary duties.

12 *Grafton's Chronicle*, II, 499–500.

13 *History of England*, IV, 247.

14 *D.N.B.*

15 Van der Delft to Charles V, 29 May 1547; *Span. Cal.*, IX, 91–2.

16 Van der Delft to Charles V, 16 June 1547; *ibid.* 100–1.

17 *Ibid.*

18 *Ibid.* Paget said on behalf of the council that it would never do to let the great seal remain in such 'stout and arrogant hands'; cited in Gammon, *Statesman and Schemer*, 134. Wriothesley's personality seems to have annoyed his colleagues; Grafton spoke of his 'ouermuch repugnyng to the rest in matters of Counsaile'; *Grafton's Chronicle*, II, 499–500. Cf. Holinshed, *Chronicles*, II, 1614.

19 Jordan, *Edward VI: the Young King*, 69–72; cf. *A.P.C.*, II, 48–59.

20 Or so Pollard argued in his article on Somerset, *D.N.B.*

21 The draft is B.M., Harleian MS. 249, fos. 16–17.

22 *Span. Cal.*, IX, 91–2.

23 Wriothesley 'was not onely depriued from hys office of Chauncelor, but also remoued from place and aucthoritie in Consaile'; *Grafton's Chronicle*, II, 499–500.

24 B.M., Add. MS. 48126, fo. 15a.

25 *Ibid.*

26 Article on Somerset, *D.N.B.*

27 *Span. Cal.*, IX, 50.

28 *Ibid.*

29 *Ibid.*, IX, 91–2.

30 *A.P.C.*, II, 64. Italics are the author's.

31 Scarisbrick, *Henry VIII*, 494–5.

32 *Ibid.*

33 Pratt, *Acts and Monuments of John Foxe*, VI, 283.

34 Cited by Pollard, *Somerset*, 198.

35 *Treatise of politike pouuer.*

36 Garnett, *Accession of Queen Mary*, 80.

37 Hayward, *King Edward the Sixth*, 199.

38 The author of the *Chronicle of Henry VIII* alleged that Seymour 'certainly would have been spared if it had not been for the wife of the Protector, who pressed the matter, and said to her husband "My lord, I tell you that if your brother does not die he will be your death"'; Hume, *Chronicle of Henry VIII*, 164.

39 B.M., Add. MS. 48126, fo. 6a.

40 *Ibid.*

41 Garnett, *Accession of Queen Mary*, 81.

42 Bibliothèque Nationale, MS. Ancien Saint-Germain Français, 15888, fo. 213b.

43 *Span. Cal.*, X, 6.

44 'Quelques particularitez', Bibliothèque Nationale, MS. Ancien Saint-Germain Français, 15888, fos. 212b, 213.

45 Pratt, *Acts and Monuments of John Foxe*, VI, 283.

46 For the purposes of the following discussion 'catholic' and 'conserva-

tive' shall denote those who favoured at least a return to Henrician catholicism or who, for political reasons, are known to have favoured such a move. The author recognises that 'catholic' does not adequately describe Wriothesley (cf. Hughes, *The Reformation in England*, II, 81, n.4), just as 'protestant' or 'reformed' does not characterise Paget who opposed him by December 1549; nevertheless, Wriothesley's followers will here be called catholics or conservatives, and Warwick's, reformers.

47 *History of England*, 49.
48 It has been believed that 'Warwick carefully staged the plot to look like a Counter-Reformation'; Smyth, *Cranmer and the Reformation under Edward VI*, 272.
49 Morris, *The Tudors*, 112.
50 Cf. Gardiner to Warwick, 18 October 1549, Muller, *Letters of Stephen Gardiner*, 440–1; Hooper to Bullinger, 7 November 1549, Robinson, *Original Letters*, 70.
51 Hooper to Bullinger, 27 March 1550, Robinson, *Original Letters*, 82.
52 Nichols, *Chronicle of Queen Jane and Queen Mary*, 18–19. It was, said the Italian Rosso, 'una messa publica'; *Historia*, 31–2; cf. the same author's *I successi*, 30–1.
53 To Cecil, from Chelsea, 7 December 1552, SP 10/15/fos. 137–8; cf. Tytler, *England under Edward VI and Mary*, II, 148.
54 Quoted in Smith, *A.H.R.* LXXI (1966), 1241.
55 Cf. Burnet, *History of the Reformation* (ed. 1829), II, pt. I, 144–5.
56 Constant, *Révue Historique* CLXXII (1933), 436–7; Constant, *Reformation in England*, 146.
57 'Quelques particularitez', Bibliothèque Nationale, MS. Ancien Saint-Germain Français, 15888, fo. 212b.
58 *Span. Cal.*, IX, 461–2.
59 *History of His Own Time*, I, 288–9. Van der Delft also spoke of Warwick's 'pretended' sympathies; *Span. Cal.*, X, 7ff.
60 *History of the Reformation* (ed. 1829), II, pt. I, 287.
61 *Calendar of State Papers*, Venetian, V (1534–54), 297–8 (no. 626); *Span. Cal.*, X, 397.
62 Pocock, *E.H.R.* X (1895), 438.
63 Parker, *English Reformation*, 112.
64 Froude, *History of England*, IV, 493; Constant, *Reformation in England*, 146.
65 Wernham, *Before the Armada*, 193.
66 Ponet, *Treatise of politike pouuer; Span. Cal.*, IX, 469–70.
67 *Span. Cal.*, X, 7ff.
68 *Ibid.*
69 Ponet, *Treatise of politike pouuer*. Dixon also quotes Ponet at length on these intrigues; *History of the Church of England*, III, 151–2. On 23 January 1552 the council ordered the King's solicitor to make out a warrant for the beheading of Sir Thomas Arundel; he had been found guilty on a charge of having taken part in Somerset's alleged plot to murder Northumberland; *A.P.C.*, III, 484. Arundel was

executed on 26 February; Nichols, *Diary of Henry Machyn*, 15; Wriothesley, *Chronicle*, II, 66–7.

70 *Span. Cal.*, IX, 467–70.
71 B.M., Add. MS. 48126, fos. 15b–16a.
72 The author is extremely grateful to the History of Parliament Trust for this information (unpublished article on Peckham).
73 *Span. Cal.*, IX, 459.
74 Malkiewicz, *E.H.R.* LXX (1955), 605.
75 *Ibid.* n.4.
76 *Ibid.* 604.
77 *Span. Cal.*, IX, 445. Mary told van der Delft that these four were sounding her out on the question of her support. This evidence contradicts Tytler's belief that St John remained faithful to Somerset until 4 October; cf. *England under Edward I and Mary*, I, 211.
78 *Span. Cal.*, IX, 445–6; cf. Prescott, *Mary Tudor*, 125–6.
79 *Span. Cal.*, X, 259.
80 Tytler, *England under Edward VI and Mary*, I, 249–50; also quoted in White, *Mary Tudor*, 152–3; the draft is SP 10/9/fos. 52–6.
81 *Span. Cal.*, IX, 445.
82 *Ibid.* 467–70.
83 B.M., Add. MS. 48126, fos. 15b–16a; since the author wrote the account sometime after 1561, he was inclined to think of them as protestants. Cf. Malkiewicz, *E.H.R.* LXX (1955), 600.
84 B.M., Add. MS. 48126, fo. 15b.
85 Cf. *Chronicle*, 18; on Wroth's role about the King, see Chapman, *Last Tudor King*, 113, 114, 194, 285.
86 *Chronicle*, 18.
87 Hume, *Chronicle of Henry VIII*, 192.
88 Cf. Pollard, *Cranmer*, 254, and n.1.
89 *Ibid.* 255–6.
90 Cf. Burnet, *History of the Reformation* (ed. 1829), II, pt. 1, 288–9.
91 Ridley, *Cranmer*, 304.
92 *Ibid.*; Ridley is wrong, however, in saying that Wriothesley was expelled from the council before the end of October 1549. Professor Dickens is surely right in saying that before the end of October Warwick had decided to join the reformers; strictly speaking, however, there is no evidence that in October he had in fact decided 'to oust his conservative backers'; *English Reformation*, 315.
93 Parker, *English Reformation*, 112.
94 *Treatise of politike pouuer*.
95 *Span. Cal.*, IX, 467–70.
96 See pp. 83–4.
97 Although Bromley was not active, he should have been able to lend his voice.
98 *Span. Cal.*, IX, 448.
99 *Ibid.* X, 7ff.
100 *Ibid.*
101 *A.P.C.*, II, 338–9.

102 B.M., Cotton MS., Titus B, II, fos. 91–5, endorsed (fo. 95b), 'The forme of a commission by the King to his counsaill'. The text refers to the fact that Edward had 'lately accomplished the age of twelve years'. Strype printed the document; *Ecclesiastical Memorials*, II, pt. 2, 473–476.

103 Pollard, 'The Reformation under Edward VI', *Cambridge Modern History*, II, 497.

104 To Bullinger, from London, Robinson, *Original Letters*, 69.

105 *Span. Cal.*, IX, 476.

106 *Ibid.* 477.

107 Essentially, this was van der Delft's view, *ibid.* 476.

108 Dryander to Bullinger, from Basle, 3 December 1549. This royal proclamation has not survived, but Dryander had certainly seen it before leaving England about the middle of November; it may have been proclaimed as early as 5 November; cf. Robinson, *Original Letters*, 353–4; Ridley, *Cranmer*, 304, and 305, n. 1.

109 *Span. Cal.*, IX, 476–8.

110 It was rumoured that the King had 'demanded of the council' (through Warwick?) that Paget not be sent off to Wales 'where they intended him to reside as President'. Van der Delft thought that the decision to allow Paget to stay had been arranged by Warwick; *ibid.*

111 Cf. *Span. Cal.*, IX, 489.

112 B.M., Add. MS. 48126, fo. 15a.

113 Garnett (ed.), *Accession of Queen Mary*, 80.

114 Warwick had supported Somerset against Wriothesley in March 1547.

115 B.M., Add. MS. 48126, fo. 15b.

116 The Duchess of Somerset was begging him to do this very thing; Hume, *Chronicle of Henry VIII*, 191–2; *Span. Cal.*, IX, 489.

117 'In the meanwhile the Protector was still in the Tower, and every day it was said that either on that, or the next day, he would be led out to have his head cut off'; Hume, *Chronicle of Henry VIII*, 190.

118 *Span. Cal.*, IX, 489.

119 That is, a falchion.

120 B.M., Add. MS. 48126, fo. 16a.

121 *Ibid.*

122 The fact that he could report with so much detail the activities of individual councillors suggests perhaps an association with the minor clerks about the board. Although his former master, Somerset, remained a prisoner at that time, the author may have been informally employed by another councillor or clerk of the council.

123 Burnet, *History of the Reformation* (ed. 1829), II, pt. 1, 292.

124 *Span. Cal.*, X, 7ff.

125 *Ibid.*

126 *A.P.C.*, II, 376.

127 Wriothesley, *Chronicle*, II, 32–3.

128 Cf. Gasquet and Bishop, *Edward VI and the Book of Common Prayer*, 221–3.

129 *Treatise of politike pouuer.*

130 B.M., Add. MS. 48126, fo. 16a.
131 *Chronicle,* 19.
132 *Span. Cal.,* x, 7ff.
133 *Ibid.*
134 *Treatise of politike pouuer.*
135 Cf. *Grafton's Chronicle,* ii, 524, and Holinshed, *Chronicles,* ii, 1702; both record the fact that at the close of the Parliamentary session, the Earl of Warwick had then the 'highest aucthoritie'.

CHAPTER 8: CONCLUSION

1 Cf. Doucet, *Les Institutions de la France au XVIe Siècle,* i, 131–52.

APPENDIX 2: CLERKS OF THE PRIVY COUNCIL

1 *A.P.C.,* ii, 183; *Cal. Pat. Rolls, Edw. VI,* ii, 2–4.
2 *A.P.C.,* ii, 156.
3 *Sir Thomas Smith,* 26.
4 B.M., Cotton MS. Caligula E. iv, fo. 207; *A.P.C.,* iii, 7, 60.
5 *A.P.C.,* iii, 252, 362.
6 *Cal. Pat. Rolls, Edw. VI,* iv, 285–6.
7 Adair, 'William Thomas', in *Tudor Studies,* 147.

Bibliography

I MANUSCRIPT SOURCES

FRANCE

Bibliothèque Nationale
  MSS. Ancien Saint-Germain Français

UNITED KINGDOM

Alnwick Castle
  Syon MSS. [British Museum microfilm no. 323]

British Museum
  Additional MSS.
  Cotton MSS.
  Egerton MSS.
  Harleian MSS.
  Lansdowne MSS.
  Royal MSS.
  Stowe MSS.

Corporation of London Record Office
  Journals of the Common Council
  Letter-books

Hatfield House
  Salisbury MSS., Papers of Sir William Cecil

House of Lords Record Office
  Original Acts
  Original Journals of the House of Commons

Library of the Society of Antiquaries
  Original Proclamations

Mercers' Hall
  Mercers' Company, Acts of Court

Northamptonshire Record Office
  Fitzwilliam (Milton) Correspondence

Plas Newydd, Anglesey
  Anglesey MSS., Papers of William, first Lord Paget

Public Record Office
C 82	Chancery, Warrants for the Great Seal, Series II
E 101	Exchequer, King's Remembrancer, Various Accounts
E 404	Exchequer of Receipt, Writs and Warrants for Issues
PC 2	Privy Council, Registers
Req. 1	Court of Requests, Miscellaneous Books
SP 10	State Papers Domestic, Edward VI
SP 15	State Papers Domestic, Addenda, Edward VI to James I
SP 38	State Papers Domestic, Docquets
SP 45	State Papers Domestic, Various
SP 46	State Papers Domestic, Supplementary
SP 50	State Papers, Scotland, Edward VI
SP 61	State Papers, Ireland, Edward VI
SP 68	State Papers, Foreign, Edward VI
Sta. Cha. 2	Court of Star Chamber, Henry VIII
Sta. Cha. 3	Court of Star Chamber, Edward VI

Staffordshire Record Office and William Salt Library
  Papers of William Lord Paget
  Letter-book of Henry Lord Stafford

Westminster Abbey
  Muniments

II CALENDARS AND PRINTED SOURCES
(Place of publication is London unless otherwise noted.)

Acts of the Privy Council of England. Ed. J. R. Dasent. 32 vols. 1890–1907.

Cairns, C. S. (ed.), 'An unknown Venetian description of King Edward VI'. *B.I.H.R.* XLII (1969), 109–15.

Calendar of Letters, Despatches, and State Papers, relating to the negotiations between England and Spain, preserved in the archives at Vienna, Simancas, and elsewhere. Ed. G. A. Bergenroth *et al.* 1862–1954. 15 vols., in 20 parts. Vol. IX, ed. M. A. S. Hume and R. Tyler; vols. X–XI, ed. R. Tyler. 1912–16.

Calendar of the Patent Rolls preserved in the Public Record Office. Edward VI. 5 vols. 1924–6.

Calendar of State Papers, Domestic Series, of the reigns of Edward VI, Mary, Elizabeth 1547–1580. Ed. R. Lemon. 1856.

Calendar of State Papers, Foreign Series, of the reign of Edward VI, 1547–1553. Ed. W. B. Turnbull. 1861.

Calendar of State Papers and Manuscripts relating to English affairs existing in the archives and collections of Venice, and in other libraries of northern Italy. Ed. R. Brown, G. C. Bentinck and H. F. Brown. 9 vols. 1864–98. Vol. v (1534–54). Ed. R. Brown. 1873.

Catalogue of Additions to the Manuscripts in the British Museum 1882–87.

Ellis, H. (ed.), *Original Letters Illustrative of English History; including numerous royal letters: from autographs in the British Museum, the State Paper Office, and one or two other collections.* 11 vols. in 3 series. 1824–46. (Reprint 1969.)

Elton, G. R. (ed.), *The Tudor Constitution. Documents and Commentary.* Cambridge, 1960.

Garnett, R. (trans. and ed.), *The Accession of Queen Mary: the contemporary narrative of Antonio de Guaras, a Spanish merchant resident in London.* 1892.

[Grafton, R.] *Grafton's Chronicle; or History of England. To which is added his table of the bailiffs, sheriffs, and mayors of the City of London. From the year 1189, to 1558, inclusive.* 2 vols. 1809.

Haynes, S. *A Collection of State Papers Relating to Affairs in the Reigns of King Henry VIII, King Edward VI, Queen Mary, and Queen Elizabeth, from the year 1542 to 1570.* 1740.

Historical Manuscripts Commission. *Calendar of the Manuscripts of the Most Hon. the Marquess of Salisbury preserved at Hatfield House, Hertfordshire.* 20 vols. 1883–1968.

The Manuscripts of His Grace the Duke of Rutland, K.G., preserved at Belvoir Castle. Vol. iv. 1905.

Report on the Manuscripts of the Most Honourable the Marquess of Bath preserved at Longleat. Vol. iv, Seymour Papers 1532–1686. Ed. Marjorie Blatcher. 1968.

Holinshed, R. *Chronicles of England, Scotlande, and Irelande.* 1577.

Hughes, P. L., and Larkin, J. F. (eds.), *Tudor Royal Proclamations.* Vol. 1 (1485–1553). New Haven, Conn., 1964.

Hume, M. A. S. (trans. and ed.), *Chronicle of King Henry VIII of England. Being a contemporary record of some of the principal events of the reigns of Henry VIII and Edward VI.* 1889.

Jordan, W. K. (ed.), *The Chronicle and Political Papers of King Edward VI.* 1966.

Journals of the House of Commons. Vol. 1. S.a.; s.l.

Journals of the House of Lords. Vol. 1. S.a.; s.l.

Leadam, I. S. (ed.), *Select Cases in the Court of Requests.* A.D. *1497–1569.* [Selden Society] 1898.

Select Cases before the King's Council in the Star Chamber commonly called the Court of Star Chamber. Vol. II. A.D. *1509–1544.* [Selden Society] 1911.

Lefèvre-Pontalis, G. (ed.), *Correspondance Politique de Odet de Selve, Ambassadeur de France en Angleterre, 1546–1549.* Paris, 1888.

Letters of the Fifteenth and Sixteenth Centuries from the Archives of Southampton. Ed. R. C. Anderson. Publications of the Southampton Record Society, vol. 22. Southampton, 1921.

Letters and Papers, foreign and domestic, of the reign of Henry VIII. Ed. J. S. Brewer, J. Gairdner, R. H. Brodie. 21 vols. in 33 parts. 1862–1910. Vol. 1 revised in 3 pts.; 2 pt. addenda by Brodie, 1920–32.

Lodge, E. (ed.), *Illustrations of British History, Biography, and Manners, in the reigns of Henry VIII, Edward VI, Mary, Elizabeth & James I, exhibited in a series of original papers selected from the MSS. of the noble families of Howard, Talbot, and Cecil.* 2nd ed. 3 vols. 1838.

Malkiewicz, A. J. A. (ed.), 'An Eye-witness's Account of the *Coup d'Etat* of October 1549'. *E.H.R.* LXX (1955), 600–9.

Muller, J. A. (ed.), *The Letters of Stephen Gardiner.* Cambridge, 1933.

Nichols, J. G. (ed.), *Chronicle of the Grey Friars of London.* [Camden Society, old series, no. LIII] 1852.

The Chronicle of Queen Jane, and of two years of Queen Mary, especially of the rebellion of Sir Thomas Wyat. [Camden Society: old series, no. XLVIII] 1850.

The Diary of Henry Machyn, citizen and merchant-taylor of London from A.D. 1550 to A.D. 1563. [Camden Society, old series, no. XLII] 1848.

Literary Remains of King Edward the Sixth. 2 vols. Roxburghe Club, 1857.

'The Second Patent appointing Edward duke of Somerset Protector, *temp.* King Edward the Sixth; introduced by an historical review of the various measures connected therewith'. *Archaeologia* XXX (1844), 463–89.

Pocock, N. (ed.), *Troubles Connected with the Prayer-Book of 1549.* [Camden Society, new series, vol. 38] 1884.

Ponet, John. *A Shorte Treatise of politike pouuer, and of the true Obedience which subiectes owe to kynges and other ciuile*

Gouernours, with an Exhortacion to all true naturall Englishe men. [Strasbourg] 1556.

Pratt, J. (ed.), *The Acts and Monuments of John Foxe.* 8 vols. 1877.

Proceedings and Ordinances of the Privy Council of England. Ed. H. Nicolas. 7 vols. 1837.

Prothero, G. W. (ed.), *Select Statutes and other Constitutional Documents illustrative of the reigns of Elizabeth and James I.* Oxford, 1894.

Return of the Name and Every Member of the Lower House of the Parliaments of England, Scotland, Ireland . . . 1213–1874 in *Parliamentary Papers* LXII (1878), pts. I–III.

Robinson, H. (trans. and ed.), *Original Letters relative to the English Reformation, written during the reigns of King Henry VIII, King Edward VI, and Queen Mary: chiefly from the archives of Zurich.* Cambridge, 1846.

Rosso, G. R. *Historia della cose occorse nel regno d'Inghilterra, in materia del Duca di Notomberlan dopo la morte di Odoardo VI.* Venice, 1558.

I svccessi d'Inghilterra dopo la morte di Odoardo-Sesto fino alla givnta in qvel regno de sereniss. don Filippo d'Austria, principe di Spagna. Ferrara, 1560.

Rymer, T. (ed), *Foedera, Conventiones, Litterae, et cujuscunque generis acta publica inter reges Angliae et alois quosvis imperatores, reges, pontifices, principes, vel communitates.* 20 vols. 1704–35.

Smith, Thomas. *De Republica Anglorum.* Ed. L. Alston. Cambridge, 1906.

The Statutes of the Realm. 11 vols. 1963.

Stow, J. *Annales, or A Generall Chronicle of England.* 1631.

Townsend, G. and Cattley S. R. (eds.), *The Acts and Monuments of John Foxe.* 8 vols. 1837–41.

Tudor and Stuart Proclamations 1485–1714. Calendared by Robert Steele under the direction of the Earl of Crawford. Vol. 1: England and Wales. Oxford, 1910.

Tytler, P. F. (e.d.), *England under the reigns of Edward VI and Mary, with the contemporary history of Europe, illustrated in a series of original letters never before printed.* 2 vols. 1839.

Williams, C. H. (ed.), *English Historical Documents 1485–1558.* 1967.

Wriothesley, Charles. *A Chronicle of England during the Reigns of the Tudors from* A.D. *1485 to 1559.* [Camden Society] vol. I, new series, no. 11, 1885; vol. II, new series, no. 20, 1887.

York Civic Record. Vols. 4 and 5. Ed. A. Raine. Yorkshire Archaeological Society (Record Series, vols. 108, 110), 1945, 1946.

III SECONDARY WORKS

Adair, E. R. 'The Rough Copies of the Privy Council Register' *E.H.R.* xxxviii (1923), 410–22.
'William Thomas: a forgotten clerk of the Privy Council' in R. W. Seton-Watson (ed.), *Tudor Studies presented by the Board of Studies in History in the University of London to Albert Frederick Pollard* (1924), 133–60.
Baldwin, J. F. *The King's Council in England during the Middle Ages.* Oxford, 1913.
Bindoff, S. T. 'A Kingdom at Stake, 1553'. *History Today* iii (1953), 642–8.
'Parliamentary History, 1529–1688' in *The Victoria History of the Counties of England: a History of Wiltshire.* Vol. v. 1957, 111–70.
Bond, M. F. 'Acts of Parliament: some notes on the original acts preserved at the House of Lords, their use and interpretation'. *Archives* iii (1958), 208.
Briquet, C. M. *Les filigranes.* 4 vols. Paris, 1907.
Brooks, F. W. *The Council of the North.* Historical Association pamphlet. Rev. ed., 1966.
Burnet, G. *The History of the Reformation of the Church of England.* 3 vols. Oxford, 1829.
History of the Reformation of the Church of England. Ed. N. Pocock. 7 vols. Oxford, 1865.
Chapman, H. W. *The Last Tudor King: a Study of Edward VI.* 1961.
Cokayne, G. E. *The Complete Peerage of England, Scotland, Ireland, Great Britain, and the United Kingdom.* New ed., rev., enlarged by V. Gibbs. 12 vols. 1910–19.
Constant, G. 'La Chute de Somerset et l'Elévation de Warwick: leurs conséquences pour la réforme en Angleterre (octobre 1549–juillet 1553), *Révue historique* clxxii (1933), 422–54.
The Reformation in England. Introduction of the Reformation into England, Edward VI (1547–1553). Trans. E. I. Watkin. 1941.
Cooper, C. H., and Cooper, T. *Athenae Cantabrigienses.* Vol. i, 1500–1585. Cambridge, 1858.
Dewar, M. *Sir Thomas Smith: a Tudor Intellectual in Office.* 1964.
Dicey, A. V. *The Privy Council.* 1887.
Dickens, A. G. *The English Reformation.* Rev. ed., 1967.

Dictionary of National Biography. Ed. L. Stephen and S. Lee. 22 vols. 1908–9.

Dietz, F. C. *Finances of Edward VI and Mary*. Smith College Studies in History. Vol. III, no. 2. Northampton, Mass., 1918.

Dixon, R. W. *History of the Church of England from the Abolition of the Roman Jurisdiction*. 6 vols. 1878–1902.

Doucet, R. *Les Institutions de la France au XVIe Siècle*. 2 vols. Paris, 1948.

Elton, G. R. 'The Good Duke', *Historical Journal* XII (1969), 702–6.

'Government by Edict?', *Historical Journal* VIII (1965), 266–71.

'Henry VIII's Act of Proclamations', *E.H.R.* LXXV (1960), 208–22.

'The Problems and Significance of Administrative History in the Tudor Period', *Journal of British Studies* IV (1965), 18–28.

The Tudor Revolution in Government. Administrative Changes in the Reign of Henry VIII. Cambridge, 1953.

'Why the history of the Early-Tudor Council remains unwritten', *Annali della Fondazione italiana per la storia amministrativa* I (1964), 268–96.

Emmison, F. G. 'A Plan of Edward VI and Secretary Petre for Reorganizing the Privy Council's Work, 1552–3', *B.I.H.R.* XXXI (1958), 203–10.

Tudor Secretary: Sir William Petre at court and home. 1961.

Feavearyear, A. *The Pound Sterling. A History of English Money*. 2nd ed., rev. by E. V. Morgan. Oxford, 1963.

Fletcher, A. *Tudor Rebellions*. 1968.

Froude, J. A. *History of England from the fall of Wolsey to the defeat of the Spanish Armada*. 12 vols. 1893.

Fuller, T. *Church History of Britain from the birth of Jesus Christ until the year 1648*. Ed. J. S. Brewer. 6 vols. Oxford, 1845.

Gammon, S. R. *Statesman and Schemer. William, First Lord Paget – Tudor Minister*. Newton Abbot, 1973.

Gasquet, F. A., and Bishop, E. *Edward VI and the Book of Common Prayer*. Rev. ed., 1928.

Gilkes, R. K. *The Tudor Parliament*. 1969.

Gladish, D. M. *The Tudor Privy Council*. Retford, 1915.

Graves, M. A. R. 'Proctorial Representation in the House of Lords during Edward VI's Reign: a Reassessment', *Journal of British Studies* X (May 1971), 17–35.

Hayward, J. *The Life and Reign of King Edward the Sixth, with the beginning of the Reigne of Queene Elizabeth*. 2nd ed. 1636.

Heawood, E. 'Sources of the early-English paper supply', *The Library*, fourth series, X, no. 4 (1930), 427–54.

Herbert of Cherbury, Edward Lord. *The Life and Raigne of King Henry the Eighth.* 1649.

Holdsworth, W. S. *A History of English Law.* Vols I–III, 3rd ed., 1922–3; vols. IV–V, 1924.

Hughes, Philip. *The Reformation in England.* 3 vols. 1953.

Hurstfield, J. *The Queen's Wards. Wardship and Marriage under Elizabeth I.* 1958.

Review of G. R. Elton (ed.), *The Tudor Constitution. E.H.R.* LXXVII (1962), 727–31.

Jordan, W. K. *Edward VI: the Young King. The Protectorship of the Duke of Somerset.* 1968.

Edward VI: the Threshold of Power. The Dominance of the Duke of Northumberland. 1970.

Keir, D. L. *The Constitutional History of Modern Britain 1485–1911.* [5th ed.] 1955.

Lehmberg, S. E. *Sir Walter Mildmay and Tudor Government.* Austin, Texas, 1964.

Loades, D. M. *Two Tudor Conspiracies.* Cambridge, 1965.

Morris, C. *The Tudors.* 1967.

Neale, J. E. *The Elizabethan House of Commons.* 1949.

Parker, T. M. *The English Reformation to 1558.* 2nd ed., 1966.

Pocock, Nicholas. 'The Condition of Morals and Religious Belief in the Reign of Edward VI', *E.H.R.* x (1895), 417–44.

Pollard, A. F. 'Council, Star Chamber, and Privy Council under the Tudors', *E.H.R.* XXXVII (1922), 337–60, 516–39; XXXVIII (1923), 42–60.

England under Protector Somerset. 1900.

The History of England from the Accession of Edward VI to the death of Elizabeth. 1910.

'The Reformation under Edward VI' in *The Cambridge Modern History*, vol. II, ed. A. W. Ward, G. W. Prothero, S. Leathes. Cambridge, 1907.

Thomas Cranmer and the English Reformation 1489–1556. 1965.

'The Under-Clerks and the Commons' Journals (1509–1558)', *B.I.H.R.* XVI (1939), 144–67.

Powicke, F. M., and Fryde, E. B. (eds.), *Handbook of British Chronology.* 2nd ed., 1961.

Prescott, H. F. M. *Mary Tudor.* 1962.

Pulman, M. B. *The Elizabethan Privy Council in the Fifteen-seventies.* 1971.

Read, C. *Mr Secretary Cecil and Queen Elizabeth.* 1965.

Mr Secretary Walsingham and the Policy of Queen Elizabeth. Oxford, 1925.

Reid, R. R. *The King's Council in the North.* 1921.

Richardson, W. C. *History of the Court of Augmentations 1536–54.* Baton Rouge, La., 1961.

Ridley, J. *Thomas Cranmer.* Oxford, 1966.

Rose-Troup, F. *The Western Rebellion of 1549. An account of the insurrection in Devonshire and Cornwall against religious innovations in the reign of Edward VI.* 1913.

Roskell, J. S., 'The Office and Dignity of Protector of England, with special reference to its origins', *E.H.R.* LXVIII (1953), 193–233.

Rowse, A. L. 'Thomas Wriothesley, first Earl of Southampton', *Huntington Library Quarterly* XXVIII (1965), 105–29.

Scarisbrick, J. J. *Henry VIII.* Berkeley and Los Angeles, 1968.

Seymour, W. 'Protector of the Realm', *History Today* XX (1970), 577–84.

Skeel, C. A. J. *The Council in the Marches of Wales. A Study in Local Government during the Sixteenth and Seventeenth Centuries.* 1904.

Slavin, A. J. *Politics and Profit: a Study of Sir Ralph Sadler, 1507–47.* Cambridge, 1966.

Smith, A. G. R. *The Government of Elizabethan England.* 1967.

Smith, L. B. 'Henry VIII and the Protestant Triumph', *A.H.R.* LXXI (1966), 1237–64.

'The Last Will and Testament of Henry VIII: a question of perspective', *Journal of British Studies* II (Nov. 1962), 14–27.

Smyth, C. H. *Cranmer and the Reformation under Edward VI.* Cambridge, 1926.

Snow, V. F. 'Proctorial Representation in the House of Lords during the Reign of Edward VI', *Journal of British Studies* VIII (May 1969), 1–27.

Stone, L. 'Office under Queen Elizabeth: the Case of Lord Hunsdon and the Lord Chamberlainship in 1585', *Historical Journal* X (1967), 279–85.

Strype, John. *Ecclesiastical Memorials, relating chiefly to Religion, and the Reformation of it, and the emergencies of the Church of England, under King Henry VIII, King Edward VI and Queen Mary I.* 3 vols., 6 parts. Oxford, 1822.

The Life of the Learned Sir John Cheke, Knight. Oxford, 1821.

Sturge, C. *Cuthbert Tunstal: Churchman, Scholar, Statesman, Administrator.* 1938.

Thirtieth Report of the Deputy Keeper of the Public Records. 1869.

Thou, Jacques August de. *History of His Own Time.* Trans. [from the Geneva ed. of 1620] B. Wilson. 2 vols. 1729.

Wernham, R. B. *Before the Armada: the Growth of English Foreign Policy 1485–1588.* 1966.

Review of G. R. Elton, *The Tudor Revolution in Government*. *E.H.R.* LXXI (1956), 92–5.

White, B. *Mary Tudor*. 1935.

Williams, P. *The Council in the Marches of Wales under Elizabeth I*. Cardiff, 1958.

'A Revolution in Tudor History?', *Past and Present*, no. 31 (1965), 94–6.

Willson, D. H. *The Privy Councillors in the House of Commons 1604–1629*. Minneapolis, Minn., 1940.

IV THESES AND UNPUBLISHED ARTICLES

Bush, M. L. 'The rise to power of Edward Seymour, Protector Somerset, 1500–47'. University of Cambridge, 1965.

Gammon, S. R. 'Master of practices: a life of William, Lord Paget of Beaudesert 1506–63'. Princeton University, 1953.

History of Parliament Trust. Unpublished biographical sketches of Members of Parliament. Tavistock Square, London.

Skelton, E. 'The Court of Star Chamber in the Reign of Elizabeth'. University of London, 1930.

Sturge, C. 'The Life and Times of John Dudley, Earl of Warwick and Duke of Northumberland 1504–1553'. University of London, 1927.

Index